AMERICAN ETHNICITY

American Ethnicity

By JOSEPH HRABA
Iowa State University

F. E. Peacock Publishers, Inc.
Itasca, Illinois 60143

Copyright © 1979

F.E. Peacock Publishers, Inc.
All rights reserved
Library of Congress
Catalog Card No. 78-61877
ISBN 0-87581-236-8
Printed in U.S.A.
Second Printing, 1980

In memory of Josef Hraba,
my grandfather and an immigrant.

Contents

Preface

Ethnicity is a personal as well as a professional concern to me. It has been a component of my life since childhood, and I see it as a vital part of American history. Since childhood I have looked across three generations, from that of immigrant grandparents to my own. The transformation of labor needs about which I write—from the agrarian, to the industrial blue-collar and now to the white-collar economy—is manifest in these three generations of my family. My grandparents made the transition from European peasants to American industrial workers, on the railroad and in the packinghouses, and my parents made the transition to clerical work. I now do another kind of white-collar work. The ethnic diversity of America has also been a first-hand experience for me, since I was raised in a city of immigrant labor, both foreign and American born.

Many people have helped me with this book in one way or another. My gratitude starts with my family, my wife and son, who did all the things while I was writing this book that I should have and did not. The comments of anonymous readers chosen by the publisher have contributed significantly to this work, and to them I am grateful. I wish to thank many people at F. E. Peacock Publishers for their assistance with and faith in this project; this especially applies to Ted Peacock. I am most grateful to my friend and colleague, Eric Hoiberg, for his unselfish help with reading earlier drafts of several chapters. I also thank other colleagues at Iowa State University for their encouragement and support over the past two years. Two graduate students and two typists, Jan Fiechtner, Barbara Larson, Marcie Wassom, and Von Woods, have contributed much to the preparation of this manuscript, and I thank all four of them. My appreciation is finally extended to the social scientists whose works are represented in this book—which is dedicated to a very special people—ethnic Americans of all races and nationalities.

PART I

Introduction

CHAPTER 1

The Social
Sciences and
Ethnic Relations

INTRODUCTION

The history of America is inseparable from that of its racial and ethnic groups, and thus interest in American ethnicity is tantamount to interest in America itself. Reflecting the magnitude of ethnic and racial heterogeneity in this country, we have always had diverse opinions about race and ethnic relations. This is as true for social scientists as it is for the American public at large. One major purpose of this book is to present the variety of perspectives on race and ethnicity offered in the social sciences.

Over the past 70 years or so, the social sciences have made notable contributions to the study of American ethnic and race relations. One of these earlier in this century was the recognition that there are no pure races, which turned the study of race and ethnicity away from biological differences and toward group relations (Reuter, 1945:456). The sociological study of race and ethnicity began around the end of the 19th century, when "social thought was almost completely dominated by biological concepts and points of view" (Reuter, 1945:454). This idea, labeled Social Darwinism, was more of an ideology than a science, a point of view that paid almost exclusive attention to biological differences between races which supposedly rendered some groups more fit than others to rule and prosper. Social Darwinism was part of the larger

3

Darwinian view of evolution, which saw evolution as a process of universal competition, lethal selection, and the survival of the fittest. This metaphor of a natural struggle for subsistence and the survival of the fittest was applied directly to the study of race relations in human society by the Social Darwinists.

Social science evolved, however, as social thinkers moved beyond biological analogies and began to analyze race, ethnicity, and society itself as social phenomena. Human society is part of the natural order, to be sure, but it is also above that order and incapable of being fully explained by analogies to the natural world. This is equally true for race and ethnic relations. In the 20th century, social scientists increasingly turned to the evocative metaphors of earlier 19th-century social evolutionism, leaving behind those of Social Darwinism.

Social Evolutionism is a tradition of studying human society as a social entity apart from the natural order, on the assumption that culture distinguishes humans and society from nature. More specifically, it is a tradition of analyzing the modernization of human society in this manner. Nearly all social thinkers of the 19th century were concerned with changes in Western society, changes which have come to be called the modernization process. Societal modernization has been identified with industrialization, the spread of education and literacy, urbanization, the growth of bureaucracy, the increasing impersonality of human organization, and, most importantly, the diversification of the occupational structure. In the course of modernization, the occupational structure of a society grows broader with the addition of industrial blue-collar jobs and white-collar positions.

ETHNIC EVOLUTION AND SOCIETAL MODERNIZATION

The social evolutionists predicted the demise of the folk community as a result of modernization. The changing occupational structure of society, they thought, would bring the eclipse of community. The old homogeneity and organic harmony of the folk group would become increasingly improbable with the occupational diversification of society. People did too many diverse things in the modern era to feel the old consciousness of kind and solidarity. Nor could peasant life be truly transplanted to the growing industrial cities, as the social fabric of the village and the peasants' communion with nature were fractured by their migration to the industrial city. Finally, bureaucracy in modern society would more and more serve the functions once served by the family in traditional society. Education, work, and welfare would all be done outside the home, in large-scale bureaucracies and away from the folk bonds of family, village, and neighborhood. The entire process would bring a growing impersonality to life, a loss of community.

This theme was made popular in the middle of the 20th century by the mass society theorists in sociology. This type of analysis was particularly applied to certain folk groups caught in the modernization process, that is, ethnic and racial groups, and this constituted the beginnings of sociological analysis of race and ethnicity in modern society.

Since the sociological analysis of race and ethnicity has its roots in 19th-century social evolutionism, its thematic concern has been the evolution of racial and ethnic groups in the course of societal modernization. As this theme applies to racial and ethnic groups in American society, this is also the theme of this book. A notable lore has accumulated in sociology and psychology which concerns changes in ethnic and race relations in the modernization process. This lore will be surveyed in the chapters to follow and used to interpret the histories of major ethnic groups in America.

The relations among racial and ethnic groups that have evolved with a changing American society are called ethnic evolution in this book. The insight of 19th-century social evolutionism is that the basic nature of a society changes in the process of its modernization. Specific factors in this process are the diversification of the occupational structure and the spread of public education. When this insight is applied to an analysis of ethnic groups in such a society, the issue becomes the impact of occupational diversification and mass education on these groups and their relationships. The modern academic lore on race and ethnicity is organized around this issue, which constitutes the focus of this book.

The modernization process and ethnic evolution are both implicated in and inseparable from the changing labor needs of a society. As the originally agrarian American society has undergone two major changes in its labor needs, its modernization has formed three distinct phases: agrarian, industrial, and postindustrial. These phases represent the larger process of the modernization of American society and are the context for ethnic evolution in this country (see Table 1).

Table 1 Ethnic Evolution and the Modernization of American Society

Agrarian Society	Industrial Society	Postindustrial Society
1600-1865	1865-1945	1945-Present
	Societal Change and Ethnic Evolution ⟶	

Note: Dates are approximations only.

America was first an agrarian society, with the bulk of its labor force in farming. This era coincided with the expansion of the Western frontier.

Later, following the Civil War and the settlement of the frontier, the country became an industrial nation, and the stream of immigration from other lands began to flow into the cities. During the late 19th and early 20th centuries these immigrants built the industrial base of the nation. After World War II, there was a second change in the nation's labor needs as the need grew for white-collar workers. This represents the postindustrial phase of American society. Ethnic and racial groups have evolved with these changes in America, either keeping pace with them or falling behind. Our task is to explain these different courses of ethnic evolution, and we begin by turning to the sociological lore on race and ethnic relations in American society.

THE SCHOOLS OF THOUGHT ON AMERICAN ETHNICITY

Assimilationism, ethnic pluralism and ethnic conflict theory constitute the three principal schools of thought on race and ethnic relations. As perspectives, they are organized around the issue of the impact of societal modernization on America's ethnic and racial groups.

Assimilationists contend that modern society assimilates its racial and ethnic groups (Chapter 2). This theory "views ethnicity as a survival of primary, quasi-tribal loyalties, which can have only a dysfunctional place in the achievement-oriented, rationalized, and impersonal social relationships of the modern, industrial-bureaucratic order" (Metzger, 1971:635). Modernization results in the absorption of folk groups into a mass society. Racial and ethnic groups move off the land and into large, ethnically diverse industrial cities, send their children to a unitary school system, and eventually disperse throughout a broad range of occupations characteristic of the modern era. The assimilation of these folk groups results. This position on ethnic evolution is closely connected with the early Chicago School of sociology, particularly with the works of Robert Park and Louis Wirth. Gunnar Myrdal, another proponent of assimilationism, takes this point of view in his epochal work *American Dilemma* (1944). The contact hypothesis is a current expression of this perspective, having in common with both 19th-century social evolutionism and early 20th-century assimilationism the postulation that ethnicity as a folk form and sentiment is eclipsed by the forces of modernity.

The pluralists argue, on the other hand, that folk groups survive the process of societal modernization (Chapter 3). Ethnic and racial groups change, to be sure, but they also remain constant in a modernizing society as a source of social identity, a sense of community, and the basis for resource competition. Pluralists point to evidence of ethnicity in modern societies the world over and claim that ethnicity is as much a part of modern society as it is of traditional society. Pluralism arose originally as a counterpoint to assimilationism, a position taken by Will Herberg (1955) and more recently by Milton Gordon (1964) and by Nathan Glazer and Daniel Moynihan (1970, 1975). In the 1970s an addition to sociological pluralism has emerged out of anthropology, in a set of works known collectively as the New Ethnicity School.

Conflict theory expands on the theme of intergroup competition for resources in modern society (Chapter 4). According to assimilationists, modernization brings increased opportunity for the absorption of all folk groups into a unitary society. The process works through the occupational diversification of society and the corresponding expansion of public education. The conflict alternative to assimilationism has its origins in a countervailing view of the modernization process, one that is also prefigured in 19th-century social evolutionism. According to conflict theorists, modernization exacerbates competition and conflict among folk groups vying for the expanded opportunities in modern society. Chapter 4 examines the exact nature of this competition and conflict, the parties involved, and the resources in modern society for which they vie.

The level of analysis shifts in Chapter 5 from intergroup exchange in a changing American society to the prejudice of individual Americans—that is, from sociology to psychology. Three major traditions in the psychology of prejudice are examined in this chapter, with the understanding that analysis of ethnic relations at the societal level must be complemented by analysis of individual prejudice and discrimination. The evolution of American society and the psychology of the peoples who have lived in it are in reality inseparable. The social forces of intergroup exchange are interwoven into the thoughts and feelings of the individuals involved. This chapter reiterates this fundamental fact.

The three theories of race and ethnic relations, plus the psychology of prejudice and discrimination, are commonly regarded by sociologists as competing perspectives on American ethnicity. To the exclusion of the others, one theory or another is seen as an essentially correct depiction and explanation of ethnic evolution and societal modernization. In Chapter 6, however, it is argued that these theories are actually complementary. Each theory is only a partial explanation of societal modernization and ethnic evolution, but each makes up for some of what the other theories lack, and together they offer a fuller understanding of ethnic evolution in the modernization process. Modernization does bring more opportunity for assimilation, through the mechanisms of white-collar work and mass public education, but it also results in increased intergroup competition and conflict over these mobility routes. The result is both alteration and persistence in America's racial and ethnicity diversity. Considerations of race and ethnicity in school admissions and in hiring and promotion today attest to the endurance of ethnicity, while its changes are also obvious. The evolution of folk groups is indeed implicated in the modernization process, a process which has meant, paradoxically, both the assimilation of these groups and their endurance.

This broader view recognizes the possibility that some groups are assimilated into the modern order, while others are excluded from it. Thus, some groups converge with the modernization process, while others diverge. It is generally the powerful who are included in the modern society, while the weaker are excluded from it. Powerful groups keep pace with the modernization of a society, particularly with a nation's changing labor needs, while weaker groups lag behind, largely because of prejudice and discrimination. The powerful assimilate; the weaker do not. The products of these dual phenomena of inclusion and exclusion, evolutionary convergence and divergence, are both change in and persistence of racial and ethnic variation in a society. All of these social processes have been correlated with the prejudices (or lack of them) of individual Americans. So, in Chapter 6, it is argued that the nature of the exchange between ethnic groups is reflected in the thoughts and feelings that members of these groups have had toward one another.

Groups exchange land, labor, and capital in the course of societal change and their own evolution. The impact of societal modernization on the evolution of any ethnic group involves its exchange with other groups. Ethnic evolution and societal modernization began in this country with the conflict over land between immigrant groups and indigenous people. The more powerful immigrants took land from the indigenous groups, who have since been excluded from American society and have been on an evolutionary course divergent from it. The stereotypes of indigenous people held by early immigrant settlers reflected this historical fact and reinforced their economic self-interest in expropriating Indian land.

The growing need for agrarian labor on the frontier brought more immigrants to the country, and the fate of these groups has been implicated in the country's changing labor needs. As these needs have evolved from agrarian to industrial blue-collar jobs and finally to white-collar work, some groups have kept abreast of these changes while others have not. Some groups, while themselves converging with the modernization process, have excluded others from the modern mechanisms for assimilation, white-collar work and education, creating the dual phenomena of evolutionary convergence and divergence. The convergence and divergence of immigrant groups have been reflected in ethnic stereotypes and prejudice directed at them, not unlike the historical ethnocentrism exhibited toward American Indians.

The role of capital in ethnic evolution is also analyzed. The focus is on the accumulation of capital by a minority group, one that is excluded from the larger society, to enable it to provide its members with some internal alternative to the prejudice and discrimination in the external society.

IMMIGRATION

The story of ethnic evolution in America begins with the immigration of diverse groups into the United States. Since 1820 the federal government has kept records of this immigration which show that from 1820 to 1961 over 42 million people immigrated into the country (Bennett, 1963). At its peak, late in the 19th and early in the 20th centuries, immigration into the United States represented 60 percent of the world's total migration. Table 2 shows the volume of this human movement into the United States from 1820 to 1930, its peak period.

Table 2   Immigration to the United States, 1820-1930, by Decades

1820–1830	151,824
1831–1840	599,125
1841–1850	1,713,251
1851–1860	2,598,214
1861–1870	2,314,824
1871–1880	2,812,191
1881–1890	5,246,613
1891–1900	3,687,564
1901–1910	8,795,386
1911–1920	5,735,811
1921–1930	4,107,209

Source: U.S. Immigration and Naturalization Service, Annual Report (1946).

These figures include immigrants from Africa, Asia, Europe, and Mexico, who together comprise the bulk of the immigration into the United States.

Africans

From 1502 to 1860, 9.5 million Africans were, without their consent, transported to the New World, and 6 percent of this total slave trade came specifically to the United States (Fogel & Engerman, 1974). The majority of slaves, over 6 million, were brought to the Americas in the 18th century, and the peak years of slave importation into this country were 1730–1770 and 1780–1810. Between 1780 and 1810 about as many slaves were brought into the United States as had been introduced in the previous 160 years. The United States, along with Great Britain, passed legislation prohibiting slave trade in 1807. By the time of Emancipation, almost 60 years later, only 1 percent of the black population in this country was foreign-born.

Europeans

Between 1820 and 1960, over 34.5 million Europeans immigrated into the United States. This represents 82 percent of the total immigration into the country in this period, making Europeans the largest immigrant group in America. Table 3 shows this immigration by decade and the percentage coming from either northern and western Europe or southern and eastern Europe.

Table 3   European Sources of Immigration to the United States, Distribution by Percentages and Decades, 1820–1920

Decade	Total European Immigration	Northern and Western European (Percent)*	Southern and Eastern European (Percent)
1821–1830.............................	98,817	68%	2%
1831–1840.............................	495,688	82	1
1841–1850.............................	1,597,501	93	.3
1851–1860.............................	2,452,660	94	.8
1861–1870.............................	2,065,270	88	2
1871–1880.............................	2,272,262	74	7
1881–1890.............................	4,737,046	72	18
1891–1900.............................	3,558,978	45	52
1901–1910.............................	8,136,016	22	71
1911–1920.............................	4,376,564	17	59

*Percentages may not total to 100 because of rounding and European immigration from other countries.

Source: Based on data in Marian T. Bennett, *American Immigration Policies* (Washington, D.C.: Public Affairs Press, 1963).

Immigrants from northern and western Europe are the so-called old immigrants, having generally come to the United States before those from southern and eastern Europe. There was a large influx of Irish immigrants into the country from 1830 to 1860, due to the dire poverty of Irish peasants and more specifically, the potato famine. The percentage of immigrants coming from Ireland peaked in these years, although significant immigration from Ireland continued later. Largely because of political turmoil in Germany at midcentury, many Germans joined the Irish in coming to the United States. The German percentage of total immigration peaked between 1840 and 1860. Later, after the Civil War, many Scandinavians immigrated into the country, settling primarily in the Midwest.

In the 1880s there was, for the first time, a significant immigration into the United States from southern and eastern Europe. Between 1890 and 1920 this so-called new immigration exceeded that from northern and western Europe. Most of the immigrants from southern Europe were from Italy, and over 3.8 million Italians came to the United States between 1891 and 1920. Immigrants from eastern Europe were principally from the old Austro-Hungarian Empire, Poland, and Russia. Many of these immigrants were Jewish people, especially those from Russia, who were fleeing from religious persecution there. Mass immigration into the

Irish peasants in the 1880s. These conditions were shared by peasants throughout Europe. Library of Congress.

United States from Eastern Europe ushered in an era of immigration restrictions, culminating in the passage and implementation of the quota acts of the 1920s.

Asians

From 1820 to 1960, over 1 million Asians immigrated into the United States, most having come from China (409,439) and Japan (329,886). The Chinese and Japanese are the two largest Asian immigrant groups in the country. Table 4 shows the total Asian immigration in its peak years and the percentage that was either Chinese or Japanese.

Table 4   Asian Sources of Immigration to the United States, Distribution by Percentages and Decades, 1850–1920

Decade	Total Asian Immigration	From China (Percent)	From Japan (Percent)
1851–1860.............................	41,455	100%	0%
1861–1870.............................	64,630	99	0
1871–1880.............................	123,823	99	0
1881–1890.............................	68,382	90	3
1891–1900.............................	71,236	21	36
1901-1910.............................	243,567	8	53
1911–1920.............................	192,559	11	44

Note: Percentages may not total to 100 because of rounding and Asian immigration from other countries: India and Turkey.

Immigrants from China came to the United States before those from Japan, in connection with the Gold Rush in California in the 1850s, the building of the transcontinental railroad in the 1860s, and the construction of an agrarian empire in California in the 1870s and 1880s. After 1880, Chinese immigration fell off due to the Chinese exclusion acts. Japanese immigration picked up where Chinese immigration left off, however, the mass of it occurring between 1890 and 1920. Many of these Japanese immigrants had earlier migrated to Hawaii, and from Hawaii they came here, replacing at first the Chinese in the fields of California. Substantial Japanese immigration stopped with the Quota Act of 1924 and picked up again only after World War II as Japanese war brides entered the country.

Mexicans

Mexican Americans are considered in Chapter 7 as both an indigenous people and an immigrant group. Approximately 200,000 Hispanos were living in the Southwest in the middle of the 19th century, when the United States assumed control of that region with the treaties of Guadalupe Hidalgo and the Gadsden Purchase. Hispanos are indigenous people relative to the rest of us (except for the American Indian). After the turn of the century there was an influx of Mexican immigrants into the country, in connection with the Mexican Revolution as well as the growing agrarian empire in our Southwest. Mexicans literally took the places of the Chinese and Japanese in the fields of California. Mexican immigration reached its peak in the decades of 1911–1920, 1921–1930, and 1951–1960. World War I and the Korean War stimulated immigration from Mexico, and the Great Depression was a factor in reducing it. The number of Mexican immigrants by decades is shown in Table 5.

Table 5 Mexican Immigration to the United States, Distribution by Decades 1910–1960

Decade	Number of Mexican Immigrants
1901–1910	49,642
1911–1920	219,004
1921–1930	459,287
1931–1940	22,319
1941–1950	60,589
1951–1960	299,811

Immigration as a Response to Labor Needs

Immigrants came to America for numerous reasons, many of which were noneconomic and had little to do with land, labor, or capital. Many fled from religious persecution or political turmoil, or to evade military draft. Most immigrants, however, came here for land on the frontier, for jobs in the nation's emerging industrial order, or for other economic reasons. That is, the growing labor needs of the nation brought the immigrants here. The close connection between the business cycle and the cyclical fluctuations in immigration after the Civil War reflects the larger economic reasons why people came to this country (Jerome, 1926/1973). The immigrant—the free one, at least—was a seller of labor and migrated toward its demand. Thus began ethnic evolution in America, an evolution that is still very much tied to the nation's changing labor needs.

Immigrant laborers as a class usually found at first nothing better than unskilled work. This does not mean that the immigrants lacked skills and were capable of only crude physical work. On the contrary, many were skilled artisans or small farmers who, because of the occupational structure of industrial America, became members of a class of blue-collar workers or domestic servants. The bulk of the immigration into this country occurred in its industrial phase, 1865–1945, and those were the jobs available at the time. There were exceptions, of course; many Scandinavian and German immigrants settled as agriculturalists in the Midwest, and some of America's present minority groups spent many years as agrarian wageworkers. This is especially true of Asians, blacks, and Mexican Americans.

As the nation's labor needs have changed, so have the immigrant groups. The expansion of white-collar work and public education has meant better integration of many immigrants and their native-born offspring into the larger American society (see Chapter 6). At the same time, however, this expansion has meant a decreasing need for immigrant labor and its subsequent exclusion from the United States. Now that so many jobs require an education and cultural skills, in both blue-collar and white-collar work, there is no longer a great need for foreigners. Moreover, many of the unskilled jobs which once comprised the bulk of the nation's labor needs have been exported overseas since World War II, to take advantage of cheaper labor. Recently the Zenith Corporation decided to adopt the practice of maintaining runaway shops, in an effort to catch up with its competitors' prices. While changes in the nation's labor needs have been a significant force in the assimilation of earlier immigrant groups, they also currently exclude foreign labor from this country. In this case, as in others, inclusion and exclusion occur one with the other in ethnic evolution and societal change.

IMMIGRATION RESTRICTIONS

The modernization of American society has facilitated the inclusion of some ethnic groups in the larger society, but it has at the same time resulted in the exclusion of others. The larger process of intergroup inclusion began with immigration, while exclusion began with the restriction of immigration. Immigration and its restriction symbolize a larger truth about ethnic evolution and societal change; they embrace the dual and paradoxical phenomena of intergroup inclusion and exclusion, and evolutionary convergence and divergence.

Initially, from 1820 to 1880, the United States had no policy restricting immigration. This was the free period of immigration, which ran parallel to the agrarian phase of American society and the expansion of the western frontier. While some states had immigration restrictions at this time, "there were no federal immigration laws other than those passed with the intent of assisting immigration" (Bennett, 1963:15). These acts were meant to improve conditions during trans-Atlantic crossings for immigrants and otherwise to prevent their exploitation.

Immigration policy changed, however, and the federal government, from 1875 to 1924, passed and implemented several acts meant to selectively restrict immigration. This is the selective period of immigration. From the start, the element of racism was very much a part of efforts to limit immigration. In the middle of the 19th century there was great agitation on the West Coast against Chinese labor; as a result, in 1879 the

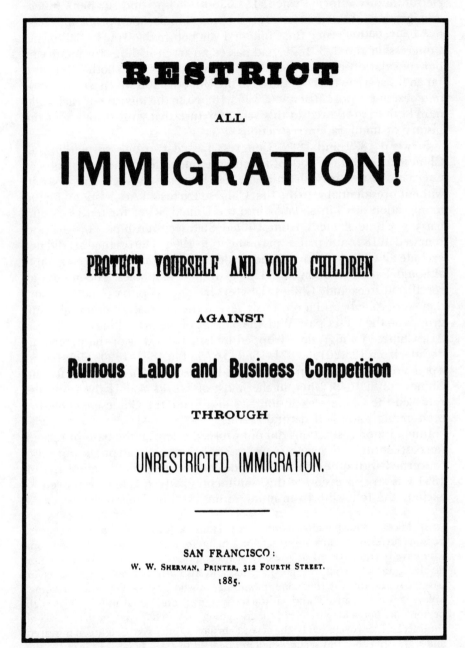

Figure 1 *An anti-immigration pamphlet, 1885.*
Smithsonian Collection of Business Americana.

electorate of California voted, 154,638 to 833, to end further Chinese immigration into that state. Thus the first "immigration problem" faced by Congress concerned the Chinese. Even before that vote in California, Congress on March 3, 1875, had passed an act providing "for inquiry by our consular officers into contracts of immigrants from both China and Japan for services to be rendered in the United States which were lewd or immoral in purpose" (Bennett, 1963:16). Note the mixture of racial and moral criteria reflected in this act, a mixture that runs throughout the history of immigration restrictions.

Between 1879 and 1882, Congress passed two bills suspending all Chinese immigration, both of which were vetoed for being in violation of international treaties with China. In May 1882, however, Congress passed without presidential veto the first Chinese Exclusion Act, suspending the immigration of Chinese labor into the United States for ten years and barring Chinese aliens from United States citizenship. This act was renewed in 1892 and made "permanent" in 1904. The original act did not exclude all Chinese; tourists and students, among others, were exempt, although later legislation closed many of these loopholes. The intent was specifically to exclude Chinese laborers from the country ("coolie" labor, they were called), and it obviously served the interests of other laboring groups on the West Coast. With the passage of the first Chinese Exclusion Act, Chinese immigration dropped by half from that of the preceding decade, from 123,201 in 1871–1880 to 67,711 in 1881–1890. Thus began a policy of racial exclusion in the United States, one that continued for the Chinese until 1943, when in the midst of World War II the Congress repealed the Chinese exclusion acts and made the Chinese eligible for both immigration and naturalization.

Immigration restrictions did not proceed solely on the basis of race in the past century, however, as Congress and the American public were also concerned with other classes of undesirables. The Immigration Act of 1891 was an expression of this sentiment, in which Congress moved to exclude the following from immigrating into the United States:

. . . all idiots, insane persons, paupers or persons likely to become a public charge, persons suffering from a loathsome or a dangerous contagious disease, persons who have been convicted of a felony or other infamous crime or misdemeanor involving moral turpitude, polygamists, and also any person whose ticket or passage is paid for with the money of another or who is assisted by others to come, unless it is affirmatively and satisfactorily shown on special inquiry that such person does not belong to one of the foregoing excluded classes, or to the class of contract laborers excluded by the act of February twenty-sixth, eighteen hundred and eighty-five, but this section shall not be held to exclude persons living in the United States from sending for a relative or a friend who is not of the excluded classes under such regulations as the Secretary of the Treasury may prescribe:

Provided, That nothing in this act shall be construed to apply to or exclude persons convicted of a political offense, notwithstanding said political offense. . . . (Bennett 1963:21-22)

Early in the 20th century, with the passage of immigration acts in 1903 and 1904, more classes of aliens, such as anarchists and children unaccompanied by their parents, were excluded.

The immigration restrictions based on racial grounds which began late in the 1800s with the Chinese exclusion acts inspired early in the 1900s widespread public sentiment and political pressures for excluding Japanese immigrants as well. Accordingly the United States negotiated with Japan a gentlemen's agreement in 1907–1908 which limited immigration from Japan to former resident aliens or relatives of resident aliens. The aim of the agreement was to virtually arrest further Japanese immigration, confining it to these small classes of aliens or relatives of aliens. However, the practice of resident aliens taking Japanese picture and excursion brides circumvented the intent of this act (see Chapter 9). The Japanese population on the West Coast continued to grow as a consequence, creating even more pressure for restriction of the Japanese. In 1920 picture brides were made illegal, and in 1922 Japanese aliens in the United States were declared ineligible for citizenship. Finally, in 1924, Japanese immigration was almost completely stopped, since Japan was given no quota in the quota act of that year. Japanese immigration from 1931 to 1950 amounted to only 3,503 people.

The Quota Act of 1924 was meant to stop immigration from southern and eastern Europe as much as from Asia. Along with Asians, southern and eastern European immigrants were excluded from the United States on racial grounds. Two important pieces of immigration legislation were passed just prior to 1924, and in both sentiments are expressed against immigrants from southern and eastern Europe which would be repeated in the Quota Act of 1924. In 1917 Congress passed, over the veto of President Woodrow Wilson, an immigration act that included a literacy test: "Thereafter every newcomer would have to earn admission into the New World by demonstrating his ability to read" (Handlin, 1973:259). The purpose of this test was to restrict severely immigration from Italy and the Slavic East, where education and literacy were not widespread, without also restricting immigration from nothern and western Europe. The peasants from southern and eastern Europe still came, after learning to read and write. All prior immigration legislation inconsistent with the principles of the Immigration Act of 1917 was repealed by this act, and classes of excluded aliens on grounds other than nationality and race were extended.

The Johnson Act enacted in 1921 is actually the first quota act passed by

Congress: "Its solution also was to limit the number of any nationality entering the United States to 3 percent of foreign-born persons of that nationality who lived here in 1910, as determined by the census" (Bennett, 1963:41). Since there were fewer immigrants from southern and eastern Europe in the country in 1910 than in 1920, the census of 1910 was used to determine national quotas. This act did reduce immigration from southern and eastern Europe, the intent of Congress all along. Countries in the Western Hemisphere were not assigned quotas, and at this time large-scale immigration from Mexico began. We may suspect, however, that stimulating Mexican immigration was not what members of Congress had in mind.

Racism was very much a factor in the literacy test of 1917 and the Johnson Act of 1921, and it had been officially expressed in the earlier reports of the Immigration Commission in 1911. The administration of the immigration service had been reorganized in the Immigration Act of 1907, thus creating the Immigration Commission. This commission in 1911 issued its 42-volume report on the new immigrants, "proving" that the immigrants from southern and eastern Europe were incapable of assimilation and were even biologically inferior to the Nordic stock out of western and northern Europe. The search for a scientific rationale in the exclusion of southern and eastern European immigrants continued, however, in subsequent years.

Dr. Harry Laughlin, a geneticist in the Eugenics Records Office, was asked by the House Immigration Committee to prepare a report on the new immigrants. In November of 1922 he expressed to the committee these "scientific" views:

We in this country have been so imbued with the idea of democracy, or the equality of all men, that we have left out of consideration the matter of blood or natural inborn hereditary mental and moral differences. No man who breeds pedigreed plants and animals can afford to neglect this thing. (Handlin, 1957:132)

To "prove" the genetic inferiority of the new immigrants, Laughlin used the record of committals of old and new immigrants to public institutions, ignoring the fact that because of their poverty the new immigrants were forced to seek help only in such facilities. The older immigrants were better off and could afford the alternative of private care. Besides, there was no consistent pattern differentiating new from old immigrants across such indicators as feeblemindedness, insanity, crime, or epilepsy. (Handlin, 1957). The supposed difference between old and new immigrants was little more than a fiction that existed in the minds of some people.

Another of these people was Arthur Sweeney, a psychologist, who

Slavic miner in Pittsburgh District, 1910. Lewis W. Hine Collection. Local History and Genealogy Division. The New York Public Library. Astor, Lenox and Tilden Foundations.

reported in 1923 to the House Committee on Immigration and Naturalization that:

We cannot be seriously opposed to immigrants from Great Britain, Holland, Canada, Germany, Denmark, and Scandinavia . . . . We can, however, strenuously object to immigration from Italy . . . Russia . . . Poland . . . Greece . . . Turkey . . . . The Slavic and Latin countries show a marked contrast in intelligence with the Western and northern European group . . . . *They think with the spinal cord rather than the brain* . . . . We shall degenerate to the level of the Slav and Latin races . . . pauperism, crime, sex offenses, and dependency . . . guided by a mind scarcely superior to the ox. (Pavalko, 1977:19; italics added)

Bennett (1963:32-33) summarized much of the sentiment against the new immigrant in this era:

Immigrants from southern and eastern Europe generally are not only ignorant but their low standards of living tend to depress the American wage standard and to create slums, unemployment and crime.

By reason of their adherence to cultures of their origin, the new immigration is hostile to the Protestant religion and other free institutions of America and foments views which will undermine the American way of life.

This immigration has the effect of replacing native with foreign stock by depressing the birthrate of natives. This is because the native is reluctant to bring children into the world to compete with the low kind of labor competition afforded by the new immigrant.

If a lower race mixes with a higher race in sufficient numbers, history teaches us that the lower race will prevail. The lower race will absorb the higher when the two strains approach equality in numbers. The lowering of a great race means not only its own decline, but that of human civilization.

These preposterous pronouncements on the new immigrant culminated in the Quota Act of 1924, the most restrictive of all immigration legislation, which was essentially in force until 1965. The principal features of this act include:

1. Quota restrictions were based on national origin.
2. The quota base was changed from the census of 1910 to that of 1890, to further restrict immigration from southern and eastern Europe.
3. The quota admissible in any one year was reduced from 3 to 2 percent based on the 1890 census, thus lowering the total quota.
4. The classes of aliens exempted from exclusion were reduced.
5. After 1929 the national-origins formula was based on the 1920 census.

The last provision represents a compromise struck in Congress between the friends of southern and eastern Europeans and their restrictionist foes. The 1890 census was used as a base for national quotas up to 1929, and then the 1920 census was adopted. With the passage of this act and the Great Depression which soon followed, immigration into the United States was greatly reduced. There were nearly 2.5 million European immigrants into the United States in 1921–1930, while in the following decade, 1931–1940, there were less than 350,000 immigrants from Europe.

In 1952 the Walter-McCarran Immigration and Naturalization Act was passed by Congress. With this act the quota system was sustained, although Asiatic countries were granted token quotas. While the elimination of race as a barrier to immigration and naturalization was a professed aim of this act, the racial quota system with respect to immigration from southern and eastern Europe was only slightly altered. Other classes of aliens—the insane, the diseased, criminals, and paupers—continued to be excluded.

The immigration laws of the United States were more thoroughly revised in 1965. National quotas were replaced by international ones. The Eastern Hemisphere was given a quota of 170,000 per year, with a maximum of 20,000 from any one country. The Western Hemisphere was granted a quota of 120,000 per year, without any specific national limitation. Preferences were extended to relatives of U.S. citizens, resident aliens, and persons with desirable occupational skills. This act was in full operation by 1969, when 359,000 immigrants came to the United States compared to a yearly average between 1951 and 1960 of just over 250,000.

This short history of immigration and its restriction is only a part of a larger history of ethnic evolution in American society. That evolution has brought both the inclusion and exclusion of racial and ethnic groups, as symbolized here by immigration and immigration restriction. Both sets of factors—inclusion and exclusion, and evolutionary convergence and divergence—will be analyzed in this book. This analysis reflects not only our ethnic roots but also the roots of contemporary sociology in 19th-century social evolutionism.

THE PLAN OF THE BOOK

This book consists of ten chapters which constitute three parts. The first chapter introduces the theme of the book and alone comprises the first part of the book. Sociological and psychological perspectives on race and ethnic relations in American society are surveyed in Part II, Chapters 2 through 6. Chapters 2, 3, and 4 examine the sociological lore on ethnic evolution and societal change, which includes the theories of assimilation, ethnic pluralism, and ethnic conflict. The psychology of prejudice and discrimination is analyzed in Chapter 5, and the complementarity of these theories is stressed in Chapter 6.

This perspective of theoretical complementarity is then applied to the evolutions of American Indians and Mexican Americans in Chapter 7, black Americans in Chapter 8, and Asian Americans in Chapter 9. The theme is that these groups have exchanged land, labor, and capital in the course of their own evolutions and the development of American society. The evolutions of America's indigenous groups have been closely tied to the exchange of land, while those of its immigrant groups have been more fully implicated in the nation's changing labor needs. Capital is also important in ethnic evolution; the role of capital and the ethnic subeconomy for a minority group is analyzed in Chapter 9, on Asian Americans.

Chapter 10 is a summarization of the perspectives in the social sciences on the minorities, namely, social pathology and ethnic communalism. From the first of these perspectives, the minority group is said to disintegrate under the pressures of prejudice and discrimination, while from the second perspective it is preserved. Chapter 10 is organized around the expression of and evidence for these points of view. Pathology and communalism in our framework also represent two perspectives on the evolutionary divergence of minority groups. When excluded from modern society, do these groups lose or conserve their folk solidarity and identity? We argue that the ethnic subeconomy and the political mobilization of a minority group greatly affect which of these courses of evolutionary divergence the group takes.

REFERENCES

Bennett, Marian T.
   1963 American Immigration Policies. Washington, D.C.: Public Affairs Press.
Fogel, Robert W., and Stanley L. Engerman
   1974 Time On the Cross: Evidence and Methods—A Supplement. Boston: Little, Brown and Company.
Glazer, Nathan, and Daniel P. Moynihan
   1970 Beyond the Melting Pot: Jews, Italians, and Irish of New York City. Cambridge, Massachusetts: Harvard University Press.
Glazer, Nathan, and Daniel P. Moynihan (eds.)
   1975 Ethnicity: Theory and Experience. Cambridge, Massachusetts: Harvard University Press.
Gordon, Milton
   1964 Assimilation in American Life. New York: Oxford University Press.
Handlin, Oscar
   1957 Race and Nationality in American Life. Boston: Little, Brown and Company.
   1973 The Uprooted. Second Edition. Boston: Little, Brown and Company.
Herberg, Will
   1955 Protestant-Catholic-Jew. Garden City, New York: Doubleday and Company Inc.
Jerome, Harry
   1926
   1973 Migration and the Business Cycle. New York: National Bureau of Economic Research, Inc.

Metzger, L. Paul
  1971 "American Sociology and Black Assimilation: Conflicting Perspectives." American Journal of Sociology 76(January):627-648.
Myrdal, Gunnar
  1944 American Dilemma: The Negro Problem and Modern Democracy. New York: Harper and Row, Publishers
Pavalko, Ronald M.
  1977 "Racism and the New Immigration: Toward a Re-interpretation of the Experiences of White Ethnics in American Society." Paper read at the annual meeting of the American Sociological Association, Chicago.
Reuter, E. B.
  1945 "Racial Theory." American Journal of Sociology 50(May):452–461.

PART II

Perspectives on American Ethnicity

CHAPTER 2

Assimilationism

INTRODUCTION

Assimilationists posit that America's ethnic and racial groups evolve toward assimilation into modern society, a theory which has been prevalent in 20th-century sociology and which was prefigured in 19th-century social evolutionism. Societal modernization was equated with the eventual eclipse of the folk community by the social evolutionists, and assimilationists subsequently applied these same evolutionary concepts to ethnicity in America, arguing for its eventual eclipse in modern society. Key terms and basic assumptions of this school are presented. After a discussion of 19th-century social evolutionism, early masterpieces and current expressions of assimilationism are surveyed. The chapter ends with an assessment of this perspective on American ethnicity.

KEY TERMS

Ethnic Group

Ethnic groups are self-conscious collectivities of people who, on the basis of a common origin or a separate subculture, maintain a distinction between themselves and outsiders. The maintenance of ethnic boundaries may be manifested in the territorial segregation of a group, in the circumscribed social participation of its members, in ethnically distinct patterns of thought and sentiment, or simply in a consciousness of ethnic kind and historical continuity. An ethnic group may be either cultural or racial, as long as the above criteria are met.

There has been disagreement in the social sciences over the usage of the term *ethnic group.* The convention in early assimilationism was to define an ethnic group as both a cultural group and an ecological entity. An ethnic group, therefore, was considered both a cultural group and one that was concentrated in an urban ghetto. The implication was that ethnic groups exist only in cultural and physical isolation. This confusion of ethnicity in general with its more specific manifestation in isolation and segregation is certainly characteristic of assimilationism, and some say it is an important limitation of the school.

One convention among sociologists today is to distill ethnic group diversity in America into the dichotomy of majority of minority groups (e.g. Kitano, 1974; Simpson and Yinger, 1972; Vander Zanden, 1972; Yetman and Steele, 1975). Minority groups in this country typically include American Indians, Asian Americans, black Americans, and Mexican Americans, who share the common experience of being the objects of majority group prejudice and discrimination. The majority group is usually considered to be all white Americans, regardless of their ethnic and religious origins. While this convention has merit, it will not be followed in this book for the reasons that it oversimplifies ethnic diversity in America and tends to be ahistorical. That is, ethnicity has always meant more than a simple dichotomy, and most ethnic groups, even today's majority groups, have been minorities at one time or another in American history. Thus, we define an ethnic group more inclusively, as a self-conscious collectivity of people who move through time, and consider how the ways in which they manifest their ethnicity may change as they do.

Another convention of sociologists is to make a distinction between racial and ethnic groups. Racial groups today are considered the nation's nonwhite groups, indigenous and immigrant alike, while the term *ethnic group* is reserved for whites. This is another convention that will not be followed in this book. The term *race* has come to have such ambiguous and often contradictory meanings that it is no longer useful in the study of ethnic evolution in American society. For instance, while only nonwhite groups are now seen as races distinct from that of white Americans, earlier in the century Jews, Italians, and Slavs were so considered. Racial labels shift from one historical period to another. Furthermore, the distinction between racial and ethnic groups implies that racial groups are not also ethnic groups, which is obviously false. Thus we define all groups in America, regardless of their race, as ethnic groups, so long as they meet the criteria set forth above.

Ethnic Evolution

Ethnicity is an evolving or emergent phenomenon, and groups and their relations with one another and with the larger society change in the course of ethnic evolution.

Assimilation is one aspect of ethnic evolution—the one emphasized in this chapter.

Assimilation

According to common usage in the social sciences, *assimilation is the process by which diverse ethnic and racial groups come to share a common culture and have equal access to the opportunity structure of a society.* Vander Zanden (1972:258) defines assimilation as "a process whereby groups with diverse ways of thinking, feeling, and acting become fused together in a social unity and a common culture." There are two components of assimilation, integration and acculturation. The phrase "fused together in a social unity" refers to integration, or "the fusion of groups in the sense that social interaction is no longer predicated upon one's racial or ethnic identity" (Vander Zanden, 1972:261). Because of *integration,* members of racial and ethnic groups are no longer segregated with respect to their residence and social participation, and they experience equal access to education, jobs, and other opportunities in the wider society. *Acculturation,* the second component of assimilation, refers to the fusion of groups into a common culture. Different racial and ethnic groups acculturate by becoming similar in their thinking, feeling, and acting.

ASSUMPTIONS OF ASSIMILATIONISM

1. *Ethnic evolution in America results in the assimilation of the nation's ethnic groups.*
2. *Assimilation is assumed to result from some sort of natural history or to be a product of societal modernization, an outcome of industrialization, occupational diversification, urbanization, and the spread of mass education and literacy.*

SOCIAL EVOLUTIONISM

Evolution was the great theme of 19th-century science. After Darwin published his theory of organic evolution in 1859, interest in evolution grew in all the sciences, including the social sciences. In the emerging science of society—sociology—the concern was with social evolution, or the process of societal modernization. Initially, the Darwinian principles of organic evolution were applied directly to the study of social evolution, but sociological principles replaced those borrowed earlier from biology, and the study of societal modernization eventually became a social science. In the same manner, the study of ethnic evolution by the assimilationists became a social science.

Assimilationists hold that the ethnic community is eclipsed by the modernization of American society, an idea that was clearly on the horizon in 19th-century social evolutionism. The social evolutionists had

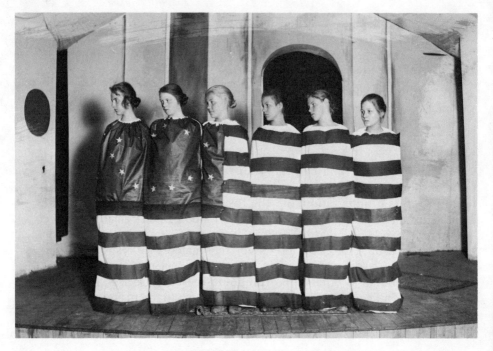

School girls taking assimilation to the extreme. Reproduced through courtesy of New York Historical Association, Cooperstown, New York.

predicted the collapse of the folk community in the course of societal modernization; it was said to disappear with the rise of new occupations and economic classes, in the evolution toward an industrial, urbanized, and politically centralized modern society. With the occupational diversification of folk groups, their economic class stratification and their spatial dispersion in industrial cities, the very basis of folk life was said to disappear. This message from 19th-century Europe was later translated by American sociologists to mean the eventual end of the ethnic community in modern American society. At the turn of the century, at the very beginning of American sociology, pioneer American sociologists adopted 19th-century intellectual traditions from Europe in their analysis of the then contemporary American society. Assimilationism was simply part of this larger trend.

Profound changes had been taking place in 19th-century Europe. Many countries there were being transformed from agrarian societies, with simple divisions of labor and largely rural populations, into industrial societies, with complex divisions of labor and growing urban populations. Social evolutionists attempted to forecast the future of Western society on the basis of these 19th-century trends. While several aspects of this change were obvious, such as the mass migration of agrarian laborers into urban industrial centers, the social evolutionists also detected some not-so-obvious changes in the human condition, changes associated with the shift from agrarian to industrial society. A fundamental alteration in human relations was discerned. Social evolutionists envisioned a transformation of the medieval bonds of blood and place, the basis of peasant life, into individual anonymity and rationally calculated human exchange in modern society. Modern people would relate to each other as commodities in marketplaces, each trying to maximize individual profit. Impersonal bureaucracy, as a symbol of this change, would replace the communal organization of life. Assimilationists read this legacy as reason for the eventual demise of ethnicity in modern American society.

Assimilationists were indebted to both basic variants of social evolutionism, the one that predicted conflict in the course of societal modernization, and the other that forecast cooperation and harmony in the modernization process. The first tradition is the conflict branch of social evolutionism, represented by Karl Marx, and the second tradition is the functional branch of social evolutionism, represented by Émile Durkheim.

Conflict Branch

Karl Marx characterized all history as a class struggle. By the 19th century, the capitalist class had displaced feudal nobility as the dominant class in industrial society. According to Marx, however, social evolution would continue, and industrial capitalism would inevitably evolve toward a class conflict between capital and labor, the bourgeoisie and the proletariat. The proletariat would eventually reverse the domination of the bourgeoisie and organize a classless utopia. With the realization of this utopian state, the evolutionary process would end.

In Marx, assimilationists found a precedent for their prediction that social evolution would bring ethnic assimilation in 20th-century America. Marx had argued that capitalism would elevate the class consciousness of industrial workers. By becoming class conscious, workers would become correspondingly less concerned with traditional loyalties, such as those associated with family, land, locality, and nationality, which might otherwise divide them. All of these, of course, are particular expressions of ethnicity. Ethnicity would be erased, first as the proletariat mobilized for the class struggle, and finally as the universal fraternity of workers was established in the utopian state. Class consciousness is the modern mentality, Marx argued, and folk sentiments would become obsolete and fade in the modern era.

Functional Branch

Émile Durkheim, in *Division of Labor in Society,* originally published in 1893, ascribed the social evolution of the West to the changing mode of production, specifically the increasingly complex division of labor in industrial society. Like Marx, Durkheim argued that this evolution had brought the demise of the European feudal order, but, unlike Marx, he argued that the functional interdependence inherent in a complex division of labor, along with other evolutionary forces, would provide for a gradual transition, without class conflict, from folk to modern society.

Durkheim wrote that "social life comes from a double source, the likeness of consciousness and the division of labor. The individual is socialized in the first case, because, not having any real individuality, he becomes, with those he resembles, part of the same collective type . . . " (1893/1947:226). Likeness of consciousness comes from people doing the same thing, day in and day out, when there is a simple division of labor. This condition characterized the folk society of the past, and it was called *mechanical solidarity* by Durkheim.

According to Durkheim, the division of labor becomes more complex in the course of societal modernization, moving Western society away from a state of mechanical solidarity. The like-mindedness of the past is no longer possible when workers are divided into a myriad of occupations characteristic of modern society. Mechanical solidarity is impossible across workers in diverse jobs, although it can be maintained within certain occupational groups. The chance for individuality and, by implication, the pursuit of self-interest increase in the industrial city. Does this mean Marxian class war, or worse yet, the Hobbesian war of all against all? Not according to Durkheim, who saw a new social order arising out of the fact that participants in a complex division of labor are interdependent, each requiring the goods and services of others. This product of specialization is the basis for a new moral order in modern society which is called *organic solidarity*.

Durkheim believed that occupational specialists would realize their interdependence, appreciate the larger whole of which they are part, and cooperate. A complex division of labor from the start represented a cooperative effort to avoid occupational competition. The larger point was that modernization was to bring a new type of social solidarity, providing conditions that would integrate diverse specialists into a complex society, which, according to Durkheim, could be buttressed by state regulation and moral education. By the same token, the diversity of modern society spelled the end of mechanical solidarity for folk groups. Folk solidarity could be transplanted to industrial cities only for a time, while migrant groups themselves lived in isolated ghettos and worked at the bottom of the new occupational hierarchy. These groups eventually would diffuse into the modern city's complex division of labor, however, and become diversified into what are now called *ethclasses*. They would disperse in urban space, lose their folk solidarity, and ultimately disintegrate. Occupational interdependence and other secondary forms of social control would then supplant the lost solidarity of the folk past. This is what many contemporary sociologists would read from Durkheim in their analysis of 20th-century American society.

While Durkheim argued with Marx over the role of class struggle in societal modernization, he agreed with Marx that ethnicity would be eclipsed by the formation of modern occupational classes. The idea that the interests of occupation and economic class would replace folk consciousness of kind in the mentality of modern man is shared by both men and is the theme of social evolutionism in general. It is also the theme of 20th-century assimilationists: The folk community will disintegrate with the occupational diversification of its members, and occupational and class interests will replace folk sentiments in the process. Early assimilationists even suggested that all this is inevitable. Lyman (1972) observed that this belief in an inevitable and unilinear evolution of the human condition, which is evident in both social evolutionism and assimilationism, ultimately returns to basic notions of Aristotelian natural history. A set course for historical change is advanced in natural history, and any deviation from this course is judged as accidental. Some assimilationists do assume a set course for ethnic evolution, toward eventual assimilation, and some dismiss alternatives to assimilation as accidents or as transitional and merely passing phenomena.

With motifs such as these, assimilationists looked at the obvious ethnicity in early 20th-century America and saw concealed there the forces for its cessation.

ASSIMILATIONISM

Robert Ezra Park

In the relations of races there is a cycle of events which tends everywhere to repeat itself . . . . The race relations cycle which takes the form, to state it abstractly, of contact, competition, accommodation and eventual assimilation, is apparently progressive and irreversible. Customs regulations, immigration restrictions and racial barriers may slacken the tempo of the movement; may perhaps halt it altogether for a time; but cannot change its direction; cannot at any rate reverse it . . . . (Park, 1926/1950:150)

This is Robert Park's famous race relations cycle, which reveals his belief in an unilinear evolution of race relations. As folk groups move off the land and into modern, industrial cities, they come into contact with one another, compete with one another for a time, eventually reach an accommodation, and ultimately assimilate. All of this is inevitable, according to Park, reflecting the determinism of 19th-century social evolutionism.

After contact, racial groups challenge one another's prerogatives in the modern city, resulting in intergroup competition, a phase of the race relations cycle that recapitulates Darwin's struggle for survival and the concept that evolution is propelled by blind, impersonal forces of competition (cf. Theodorson, 1961). This concept was an axiom not only of Darwinian biology but also of economic liberalism—the idea that human exchange in the modern world is propelled solely by the competitive forces of the laissez-faire marketplace, in accord with the laws of demand and supply. Folk groups compete for many things in the city, some of which involve subsistence, such as jobs and housing, while others involve only symbolic value, such as the competition for status and the conflict between different cultures. At this stage of the race relations cycle, race consciousness, solidarity, and prejudice are all evident.

Park believed the physical and social distance between folk groups in the modern city would be reinforced by their initial competition, and the city would resemble at first an interdependent collection of *natural areas,* each with its distinct ethnic population or economic activity. "As the city increases in population, the subtler influences of sympathy, rivalry, and economic necessity tend to control the distribution of population" (Park, 1915:579). Moreover, "each separate part of the city is inevitably stained with the peculiar sentiments of its population. The effect of this is to convert what was at first a mere geographical expression into a neighborhood, that is to say, a locality with sentiments, traditions, and history of its own" (p. 579). That is, ethnic ghettos become moral enclaves, or ethnic communities with distinct ethnic subcultures within which future generations are socialized, continuing the pattern of ethnic pluralism into the modern order.

According to Park, race relations in the modern city evolve past competition, however, and toward accommodation and eventual assimilation. The natural tendency for strife and struggle is supplanted by the equally deterministic trend toward human communication and intimacy, resulting in accommodation and assimilation. Competition is settled in the form of some moral order, as folk groups reach a mutual understanding about their exchange in the city and erect rules around that exchange, enforced by moral authority. This is the stage of accommodation. Natural areas are subject to change, too; as ties of ethnicity weaken, successful individuals move out and find places in business and the professions among other groups, and this is registered in change of residential location. With accommodation, groups no longer struggle for survival, and while competition might still occur, groups now compete for status and prestige only, not for subsistence.

Race relations evolve past accommodation, too, Park maintained, and the cycle proceeds to and ends with assimilation. Park believed that intimacy inevitably ensues from the secondary relations among members of different ethnic groups, established as they diffuse into a modern city's complex division of labor:

In our estimates of race relations we have not reckoned with the effects of personal intercourse and the friendships that inevitably grow up out of them. These friendships, particularly in a democratic society like our own, cut across and eventually undermine all the barriers of racial segregation and caste by which races seek to maintain their integrity. (Park, 1926/1950:150)

Park observed elsewhere that employers of one race ultimately realize that their exploited employes of another race are human beings just like themselves. Frazier (1947:268, 269) noted that "the sociological theories of Park in regard to race relations were developed originally in close association with W. I. Thomas," who as early as 1904 argued that "race prejudice could be dissipated through human association." Personal intimacy between the races apparently replaces impersonal competition as an evolutionary force and thus moves race relations inevitably toward assimilation. This point of view is now called the *contact hypothesis* in contemporary research.

Park turned to the old German adage that the city makes men free, allowing them to pursue their own individual self-interests as they see fit, unencumbered by the authority of the folk group. Members of folk groups diffuse throughout a complex division of labor characteristic of the modern city, break away from the primary controls of the folk past transplanted for a time in urban ghettos, and relocate in other areas of the city. There, in the suburbs, members of different ethnic groups, who now share common vocational interests and status, will eventually be assimilated. That is, the occupational diversification of folk groups ultimately leads to their disintegration. Frazier (1947:270) remarked that Park "regarded race relations in the United States as part of a world process in which culture and occupation was coming to play a more important role than inheritance and race." In Park's own words:

Every device which facilitates trade and industry prepares the way for a further division of labor and so tends further to specialize the tasks in which men find their vocations. . . . The outcome of this process is to break down or modify the older organization of society, which was based on family ties, local associations, on culture, caste, and status, and to substitute for it an organization based on vocational interests. (1915:586)

The new order of Park is that of Durkheim. As individuals in industrial cities are freed from the bonds of the folk past and are diffused throughout a complex division of labor, vocational interests and the economic interdependence of diverse vocational groups replace folk identity as the expression of solidarity in modern society, and secondary forms of social control replace ethnic loyalties in the governance of the modern city. Lyman (1972) finds also in Park's writings the expectancy that once racial strife is resolved in accommodation and assimilation, the decks would be cleared in America for class struggle. This shows the influence of another 19th-century thinker on Park, Karl Marx. Park (1939:45) stated: "race conflicts in the modern world, which is already or presently will be a single great society, will be more and more in the future confused with, and eventually superseded by, the conflicts of the classes."

Park's race relations cycle is a paradigm of the general case of ethnic evolution in modern society. The cycle goes through four stages, terminating in the assimilation of racial and ethnic groups into the modern society. The evolutionary forces behind the cycle return to the basic ideas of 19th-century social science: the increasingly complex division of labor, the expansion of individual freedom due to the weakening of folk bonds in industrial cities, the impersonal competition of individuals in the laissez-faire marketplace, and the eventual eclipse of bonds of blood and place by vocational or class interests. To this Park added that human cooperation and interracial intimacy would ultimately succeed competition, even accommodation, and bring assimilation. At a higher level of abstraction, the race relations cycle represents the effort of modern society to achieve a new equilibrium and social order.

Park dichotomized the dynamics of social life into natural and social forces. While the natural force of impersonal competition organized life at the biotic level, or that of the territorial community, human communication, cooperation, and intimacy organized life by a different principle at the societal level. Hollingshead (1961:109) summarized this habit of Park by writing "Man as animal is organized competitively in the scheme of nature, but man as social being is organized cooperatively into groups through communication."

Does the race relations cycle exist at the biotic or societal level, in the scheme of nature or in human society? Park answers that race relations exist on many levels, including the ecological, economic, political, cultural, and personal (Park, 1950). Of course, race relations can span all these spheres of life, but if race relations exist at the biotic level, how do we explain the inevitable evolution toward assimilation? We know Park believed that as members of different groups disperse in space, they come into contact, cooperate and grow intimate with one another, and ultimately assimilate. Cooperation and intimacy are sociological principles, of course, and if Park meant to locate the race relations solely in the scheme of nature, it is hard to understand how the cycle could evolve beyond the point of blind, impersonal competition. The fact is that the sociological principles of cooperation and intimacy are explicitly included in the race relations cycle and are given the upper hand, and it is these principles, not natural forces, that bring assimilation.

In practice Park alternated between natural and sociological principles in explaining the dynamics of human life. However, it is clear that with the race relations cycle social principles supersede natural ones, moral forces succeed biotic ones, and human communication, cooperation, and interpersonal intimacy supplant impersonal competition and inevitably bring assimilation. The larger point is that evolutionary forces, both the biotic and social, are deterministic, and they propel the race relations cycle on an inevitable course. This was at least the case before Park's experiences in Hawaii (cf. Lyman, 1972; Park, 1950). Because of what he saw there, Park changed his mind late in life about the inevitability of assimilation, arguing instead that race relations can terminate in a caste system, a majority-minority arrangement, as well as assimilation. Moreover, he believed the terminus of the cycle would be fully contingent on the culture in which the cycle takes place. In this manner, the concept of natural history was finally replaced in Park's writings on ethnicity by the image of an open-ended and culturally contingent ethnic evolution. There is no question now that the race relations cycle evolves in accord with sociological rather than biological principles.

Park took seriously the message of Darwin that organic life is organized through impersonal competition. He also agreed with certain social thinkers who argued that human life, by contrast, is organized through a moral order and symbolic communication. He tried to reconcile these opposing ideas with a dichotomy, assuming that while impersonal competition organizes human life at the biotic level, communication, mutual understanding, and morality organize human life at another level, that of human society. The dichotomy was permeable in practice, however, and his race relations cycle, for instance, includes both the forces of impersonal competition and those of human communication, cooperation, and intimacy.

While Park applied certain Darwinian principles in his analysis of race relations, and while he persisted for some time in thinking the race relations cycle is as much a natural history as is the idea of organic evolution, he always superimposed humanity, or human cooperation and intimacy, on the tendency for competition and domination in nature. Furthermore, he never drew from Darwin the analogy of fixed racial traits as did the Social Darwinists (Reuter, 1945). This is very much to his credit, for it helped place the study of American race relations in the social sciences rather than in biology, an event that has had great implications for national policy with respect to race relations.

Louis Wirth

Not only does the ghetto tend to disappear, but the race tends to disappear with it (Wirth, 1928/1956:125).

This short passage from *The Ghetto*, originally published in 1928 and republished in 1956, suggests more than one habit that Louis Wirth shared with Robert Park. Louis Wirth was first a student of Robert Park and later a colleague of his at the University of Chicago. In his dissertation, published as *The Ghetto* (1928), Wirth applied Park's race relations cycle to the special case of Jews in Chicago. Park's race relations cycle is a natural history of race relations in the abstract, while Wirth's *The Ghetto* represents the more specific natural history of Jewish assimilation in Chicago. The history passes through the stages of contact, competition, and accommodation, ending with assimilation. Wirth shares with Park the conviction that societal modernization brings the demise of the folk group, in this case Jews. Jewish assimilation is due to occupational diversification, residential dispersion, and the growing intimacy between Jews and others in a modern society.

Wirth followed Park in another way. The dualism of natural and social forces is as evident in Wirth's natural history of Jewish assimilation as it is in Park's race relations cycle. The Jewish ghetto on Maxwell Street was originally organized around economic competition among Chicago's

Jewish ghetto on Hester Street, New York, where life was like that on Maxwell Street, Chicago. National Archives.

ethnic groups; it was an economic niche for Jews, although the ghetto subsequently evolved into a moral enclave as well. Eventually, the principles of contact and intimacy between Jew and Gentile would supplant intergroup competition altogether, and Jews would ultimately assimilate. This is the same progression of explanatory principles found in Park's more general race relations cycle.

Wirth measured Jewish assimilation with ecological markers; as Jews moved from one settlement to another in Chicago, they also moved closer toward their assimilation. Thus, "not only does the ghetto tend to disappear, but the race tends to disappear with it." The premise is that the folk group survives in modern society only with its residential segregation and isolation from others. Once groups disperse in modern cities and come into contact, however, they grow intimate with each other and eventually assimilate.

FIRST SETTLEMENT The first settlement in Chicago for Jewish immigrants was a ghetto in an area not far from the Loop and near the marketplace on Maxwell Street:

Maxwell Street, the ghetto's great outdoor market, is full of color, action, shouts, odors, and dirt. It resembles a medieval European fair more than the market of a great city of today. Its origins are to be sought in the traditions of the Jews, whose occupations in the Old World differed little from what they are here. . . .

It has been said that the Poles and Galicians seldom patronize a modern department store, but that they prefer the thrill which comes with shopping on Maxwell Street. Buying is an adventure in which one matches his wits against those of an opponent, a Jew. The Jews are versatile; they speak Yiddish among themselves, and Polish, Russian, Lithuanian, Hungarian, Bohemian, and what not, to their customers. They know their tastes and their prejudices. They have on hand ginghams in loud, gay colors for one group, and for one occasion; and drab and black mourning wear for others.

The noises of crowing roosters and geese, the cooing of pigeons, the barking of dogs, the twittering of canary birds, the smell of garlic and of cheeses, the aroma of onions, apples, and oranges, and the shouts and curses of sellers and buyers fill the air. Anything can be bought and sold on Maxwell Street. . . . Everything has value on Maxwell Street, but the price is not fixed. It is the fixing of the price around which turns the whole plot of the drama enacted daily at the perpetual bazaar of Maxwell Street (Wirth, 1956: 232-233).

It has been the custom for Jews throughout Europe to reside near marketplaces, e.g., in Frankfurt and Prague, and Jewish immigrants quickly became the dominant group on Maxwell Street by transplanting their Old World traits. Moreover, "the immigrants drifted to the slum because here rents were lowest—a primary consideration" (Wirth, 1956:198).

The ghetto was a natural area, representing an ecological niche for

Jewish immigrants at first and later becoming a cultural enclave as well. Life on Maxwell Street quickly elaborated on the theme of economic adaptation, and by 1900 the Jewish community of Chicago contained 50 congregations, 39 charities, 60 lodges, 13 loan associations, 11 social clubs, and 4 Zionist organizations. Wirth (1956:193) found that "In its initial stages the Jewish community is scarcely distinguishable from the rest of the city. As the numbers increase, however, the typical communal organization of the European ghetto gradually emerges."

Moreover, these organizations were not the full measure of Jewish communal life in the ghetto; only by adding the theaters, restaurants, cafes and second-story bookstores, the informal associations among friends and family, the philosophical discussions over chess or pinochle, and the gambling dens and cigar stores on Maxwell Street does the full picture of ghetto life begin to emerge. The hub of ghetto life was the synagogues. There were 50 of them by 1900, indicative of the religious diversity among these immigrants.

Old World class distinctions and tribal prejudices were also transplanted to Chicago. As the ghetto elaborated, it simultaneously differentiated into *Landsmannschaft*, religious groups, and economic classes. *Landsmannschaft* were more or less autonomous networks which segregated Jew from Jew, based on their geographical origins in the Old World:

A *Landsmannschaft* has its own patriarchal leaders, its lodges and mutual aid associations, and its celebrations and festivities. It has its burial plot in the cemetery. . . . hand in hand with the ties of sympathy between the members of a *Landsmannschaft* go also the antagonisms and prejudices between these groups which have been brought over from the Old World. (Wirth, 1956:223-224)

Religious differences among the Orthodox, Conservative and Reform Jews crystallized into separate congregations which were often conterminous with nationality differences. The Russian and other eastern European Jews tended to be more Orthodox or Conservative than the German Jews. The economic class hierarchy of the ghetto also separated Jew from Jew; on the average, the Russians were lower on this hierarchy than the Germans. By the turn of the century, Wirth observed, these divisions were rigidly fixed.

SECOND SETTLEMENT Over time ghetto residents became more diverse, particularly more occupationally diverse, and it was the German Jews who first achieved higher status occupations. This diversification is identified by Wirth as the start of the disintegration of the ghetto and thus the disappearance of the Jewish people in America as a group. Once the immigrants were able to afford higher land prices, they looked for more desirable locations elsewhere in the city. Many families moved to Lawndale, or Deutschland as it was known among the Jews. This was the area of second settlement. Not only was this an ecological movement in Wirth's scheme, it represented the larger process of Jewish assimilation as well:

His whole world collapsed one evening when his oldest son, after the Friday evening meal, said to him that now, since he was going to law school and the family was pretty well fixed, and as he had acquired some friends whom he would like to invite to his house, they ought to move out of the ghetto. "The ghetto!" said the father, "Are you dreaming? What do other people have that we haven't got? Don't you like this flat? Isn't the furniture good enough? Isn't this home swell enough for you?"

That night the old man could not sleep, and the next morning in Shul he was a little bewildered by the services. His mind was wandering. A month later they moved to Central Park Avenue, in Lawndale. The son felt happier, but the father didn't go down to his store on Roosevelt Road and Jefferson Street on the street car with quite the same zest mornings as he used to when they lived upstairs over the business. Nor did he feel the same way when he went to the synagogue. His *Landsleute*, he noticed, looked at him with a rather quizzical air; they didn't shake hands with the warmth of days gone by, and they weren't quite as familiar as they used to be.

Two years later, when the son had opened a law office, the father sold his store and began to dabble in real estate, using his son's office as his headquarters. He had found that the synagogue on the near West Side was too far away, and had joined a congregation on Douglas Boulevard, three miles farther west. He had trimmed his beard a little, too. He still played chess with his son, but instead of discussing the Talmud they discussed the real estate boom on Crawford Avenue. Once in a while he soliloquized, "And I thought I was rich; why, I have made more money in the last year or two than I made during the twenty years before. Yes, I lived in the ghetto and didn't know it." (Wirth, 1956:241-242)

Residence in Lawndale was identified with the Americanization of Jews, including the secularization of Judaism and the desire among the residents to fit into the larger society.

Correlated with Jewish residential mobility was occupational diversification, and both meant the inevitable end of the Jewish folk group in modern America. This notion comes straight from 19th-century social evolutionism. The modal occupational type in the ghetto had been the merchant and peddler, but in Deutschland it was the real estate salesman. The consumption patterns of Lawndale residents became conspicuously American as well as plainly conspicuous. The latter is a particular instance of accommodation. Jews no longer competed with others for subsistence, only for status through consumption. At the same time, residents of Lawndale became disinterested in the sacred affairs of Judaism, and accordingly, the prestige of the religious scholar declined, as did rabbinical influence over Jewish communal life. Many Jews now turned toward Christian Science, ethical culture, and rationalism, according to

Wirth. Glazer (1957) termed these changes a transition from Judaism to Jewishness, and one in which the secular aspects of Jewish life survive while the sacred dimensions of Judaism wane.

THIRD SETTLEMENT It takes a second move to a third settlement in the suburbs, however, for Jews to assimilate completely. Movement to the suburbs was identified with the full assimilation of Jews. As the Gentiles fled the area, Lawndale eventually became a Jewish enclave, and there the residents continued to be Jewish without much effort. In the suburbs, on the other hand, as contact with other Americans became a daily occurrence, and as intimacy with Gentile neighbors and friends grew, Jews would ultimately assimilate, although in the process they would be reminded of the positive aspects of Jewish life. Assimilation would take the forms of religious conversion, intermarriage, and greater Jewish participation in the associations of the larger society. Jewish customs, communal associations, and even identity would be lost, or modified beyond recognition. "In the ghetto the synagogue . . . is predominately orthodox; in the area of second settlement it becomes 'conservative'; and on the frontier it is 'reformed' " (Wirth, 1956:256). Intimacy between Jew and Gentile would grow in the suburbs, on the frontier, bringing to an end the natural history of Jewish assimilation. Only historical accidents would interrupt this race relations cycle, such as an increase in anti-Semitism.

Wirth's analysis of the specific case of Jewish assimilation mirrors Park's more general race relations cycle. Recourse to biotic and social forces to explain ethnic evolution is seen in one work as it is in the other. Initial settlement of Jewish immigrants, in the specific case, is a function of impersonal economic factors and is seen as part of the intergroup competition for subsistence. Human cooperation and intimacy, however, supersede intergroup competition and eventually result in Jewish assimilation. Both Wirth and Park made reference to the principles of organic evolution, or the struggle for survival, and those of 19th-century social evolutionism, or the eclipse of the folk community in modern society.

Gunnar Myrdal

The main trend in history is the gradual realization of the American Creed, which is carried by high institutional structure, particularly education, which puts a constant pressure on race prejudice, counteracting the natural tendency for it to spread and become more intense (Myrdal, 1944:80).

Equating America's historical destiny with the realization of the American Creed, Gunnar Myrdal anticipated the eventual assimilation of black Americans in *An American Dilemma: The Negro Problem and Modern Society* (1944). White Americans will finally embrace and put into practice the racial egalitarianism of the American Creed and resolve their long-standing moral dilemma over the historical discrimination against black Americans, and blacks will finally assimilate, Myrdal believes.

Gunnar Myrdal was brought to the United States by the Carnegie Foundation to collaborate with American social scientists in a monumental study of American race relations. Myrdal, a Swedish social scientist and politician, was chosen by the foundation to head this study on the premise that race relations was such an emotional issue among Americans that a fresh mind was needed. He was also chosen because Sweden had not been an imperial power over people of color.

The publication of *An American Dilemma* represents a significant development in the assimilationist thesis. While Myrdal continues with a natural history of race relations, he discontinues the Chicago School custom of making recourse to both natural and social forces to explain the evolution of race relations. Thus his work represents a turn away from Darwin and toward social evolutionism, or the exclusive reliance on sociological and psychological principles to explain ethnic evolution. Myrdal was critical of Park's use of a natural explanation of race relations and was particularly critical of its laissez-faire policy implications. If the race relations cycle is inevitable and thus beyond human intervention, what is there to do? Myrdal sought, by contrast, an entry in the "vicious cycle" of race relations in this country, and that entry was the resolution of the American dilemma. The irony is that commentators would later judge Myrdal's work to be as much a natural history of race relations as Park's was, with no more specific policy directive (cf. Cox, 1948; Ellison, 1964; Lyman, 1972; Metzger, 1971).

Myrdal's explanation of the evolution of American race relations is a cultural one, making recourse exclusively to social and psychological phenomena, and specifically to American ideals. Myrdal writes: "Not since Reconstruction has there been more reason to anticipate fundamental changes in American race relations, changes which will involve a development toward American ideals" (1944:xix). This fundamental change is identified as a change in the racial attitudes of whites.

American ideals have always implied racial equality and have historically been supported by high institutional structures in America, such as Christianity, English law, and the enlightened doctrine of human rights evident in our founding documents such as the Declaration of Independence. These Myrdal calls the "general valuations" of the American people. On the other hand, white Americans have been over time prejudicial and discriminatory toward black Americans, due to their "specific valuations." Nevertheless, whites have tried to adhere to American ideals, and as a result they have historically experienced a moral dilemma between their more general American ideals and their specific valuations with respect to race. However, Myrdal said, this dilemma will be resolved ultimately, the American Creed will win out, and black Americans will at last assimilate. Myrdal was as certain as Park and Wirth in this prediction of assimilation: "The main trend in history is the gradual realization of the American Creed" (Myrdal, 1944:80).

Despite the natural tendency for racial prejudice to grow and spread, the racial equality implicit in the American creed counters it, according to Myrdal. Since Americans are rational, they will eventually believe in either racism or the American Creed, but not in both. Rationality causes a strain toward consistency between general and specific valuations. Because of the moral authority of and institutional support for the American Creed, specific valuations will be brought into line with the general valuations of American ideals. This spells an end to white racism.

The ultimate success of the American Creed lies in the fact that it is carried by high American institutions, whose influence will increase with further industrialization, urbanization, and the spread of mass education and literacy. That is, the success of the American Creed comes with the further modernization of American society. The resolution of the American dilemma is made certain, in the fashion of a natural history, by Myrdal's coupling of the social forces of modernity with American rationality. Thus whatever racism remains in modern America is merely vestigial and is sure to wane as the nation proceeds along the course on which it is already set—toward modernity. Black assimilation in America is destiny, and its pace is impeded only by unequal modernization of the regions of the country and, by implication, the unequal eradication of a murky, irrational folk mentality.

While *An American Dilemma* is rich in its description of Negro conditions of the era, black desire for assimilation is unquestionably assumed. Modes of Negro thought about black pluralism and racial struggle are discounted. It was Myrdal's frank assumption that the future of black Americans would be determined by the attitudes and actions of white Americans. Thus, the race consciousness of blacks, or any attitudes inconsistent with assimilation they might have, hardly mattered in their evolving relationship with the larger society. The vicious cycle between white prejudice and Negro living conditions would be broken with the resolution of the American dilemma, a resolution made inevitable by the evolutionary forces of modernity, and one which would result in the improvement of Negro living conditions.

Cruse (1967) and Ellison (1964) are critical of Myrdal's depiction of the black community, seeing in it the assumption of unequivocal black support for assimilation and the contention that black life-styles are exaggerated, pathological distortions of life-styles in the white community. They counter with the observation that all blacks have not desired assimilation, and all blacks have not distorted themselves in the image of white society. Ellison (1964:316) writes: "It does not occur to Myrdal that many Negro cultural manifestations which he considers merely reflective might also embody a *rejection* of what he considers 'higher values.' "

Myrdal looked forward to a fundamental change of heart by white Americans toward putting American ideals into practice. Since these ideals are supported in the higher institutions of the larger society and are spread with modernization, Myrdal was certain that the American dilemma would be ultimately resolved in favor of the American Creed. This version of ethnic evolution sounds every bit as inevitable as do the natural histories of Park and Wirth, for, like the other two, Myrdal followed the precepts of social evolutionism, predicting the assimilation of folk groups in modern society. Unlike the others, however, he made no reference to the principles of organic evolution or the struggle for subsistence, basing his prediction of assimilation solely on the evolution of certain cultural principles.

W. Lloyd Warner and Associates

W. Lloyd Warner was an anthropologist who carried out much of his research on American ethnicity at the University of Chicago. Warner and his associates carried on certain Chicago School traditions, such as measuring assimilation as social class mobility, a methodology that was implicit in the works of Park and Wirth. Warner and his followers discontinued reference to a natural history of assimilation, however, making it not only problematical in modern society but also expressly contingent on the cultural and biological differences between a group and the larger society. Warner and his associates have made a voluminous contribution (Davis, Gardner, and Gardner, 1941; Warner, 1959; Warner and Associates, 1949; Warner and Low, 1947; Warner and Lunt, 1941, 1942; Warner and Srole, 1945).

Warner's primary interest was the study of small American communities, particularly the social stratification of such communities, and his work on ethnicity took place in the context of these larger studies. He proposed that the stratification of American communities of 5 to 10 thousand people typifies the social stratification of this country as a whole. In their field studies Warner and his colleagues used a methodology common among anthropologists which is called *participant observation*. In participant observation the social scientist is both a scientific observer of and a participant in what is studied, in this case small American communities. It is argued that with this technique the social scientist can supplement objective assessment of the subject matter with subjective impressions of it.

Warner and his colleagues would select from among townsfolk of the community being studied a panel of judges who would rank their friends and neighbors into socially inferior and superior positions. In their evaluations of a fellow resident, judges considered the person's occupation, source of income, house type, neighborhood of residence, and participation in community organizations. This is called the *reputational approach*, for obvious reasons. In this manner the social stratification of a community was assessed. From the judges' rankings, Warner and his associates typically found that residents of small cities fall into one of six classes: upper-upper, lower-upper, upper-middle, lower-middle, upper-lower, and lower-lower. These classes constitute a hierarchy of socially superior and inferior positions within a community.

Ethnic groups as well as individual residents of a community could be ranked on the class hierarchy. The mobility of an ethnic group upward in this hierarchy was the measure of its assimilation. In this fashion blacks and whites in Old City (Natchez, Mississippi), the Norwegians of Jonesville (Morris, Illinois), and a multitude of ethnic groups in Yankee City (Newburyport, Massachusetts) were studied.

In Yankee City both the occupational and residential changes of several ethnic groups over many decades were charted. Table 1 shows the occupational changes of ethnic groups in Yankee City. The higher the score, the higher is the occupational status of a group.

Table 1   Occupational Status Indexes of Yankee City Ethnic Groups, 1850–1933

Group	1850	1864	1873	1883	1893	1903	1913	1923	1933
Irish	1.62	1.76	1.74	1.76	1.84	1.94	2.14	2.31	2.52
French Canadian					1.95	2.10	2.14	2.23	2.24
Jews							3.10	3.22	3.32
Italians							2.32	2.29	2.28
Armenians							2.46	2.51	2.56
Greeks								2.53	2.34
Poles								1.88	1.97
Russians									1.95
Total ethnics									2.42
Total natives									2.56

Source: W. Lloyd Warner and Leo Srole, *The Social Systems of American Ethnic Groups* (New Haven, Conn.: Yale University Press, 1945).

Note the unilinear trend among these groups toward improving their occupational status; it proceeds in only one direction, toward progressive assimilation, except for Italians. The occupational status index consists of IA (unskilled), IB (skilled factory), IC (skilled craft), IIA and B (managerial), and III (professional), and these statuses are assigned scores from 1 through 6.

Changes in residence typically follow occupational mobility, and improvement in residential status was another correlated measure of assimilation in Warner and Srole's (1945) study. Like Park and Burgess (1921), they partitioned a city into zones and assigned a number to each zone representative of its residential status. The mobility of ethnic groups as they moved from lower to higher status zones was thereby charted. Table 2 shows this mobility for selected groups.

Without exception, ethnic groups moved to higher status locations in Yankee City with passing decades. Advancement in residence and occupation were identified with the assimilation of Yankee City's ethnic groups, and assimilation was judged to be reached when a group's residential and occupational status corresponded to that of the community as a whole.

Table 2   Residential Status Indices of Eight Ethnic Groups, 1850–1933

Group	1850	1864	1873	1883	1893	1903	1913	1923	1933
Irish..........................	1.70	1.95	2.11	2.11	2.12	2.22	2.37	2.57	2.85
French Canadian......					1.67	1.78	1.77	2.13	2.43
Jewish.......................							1.93	2.14	2.77
Italian.......................								2.21	2.38
Armenian..................								2.39	2.57
Greek........................								2.40	2.54
Polish........................								1.25	1.40
Russian.....................									1.32

Source: W. Lloyd Warner and Leo Srole, *The Social Systems of American Ethnic Groups* (New Haven, Conn.: Yale University Press, 1945).

While Warner and Srole (1945) continued and made more explicit the custom of equating assimilation with residential movement and occupational mobility, they discontinued the convention of positing a natural, inevitable, and completely deterministic course—except for accidents— toward assimilation. Instead, they made ethnic evolution fully contingent, more open, and indeterminate. No longer was it considered inevitable; instead, assimilation was said to depend on factors both external and internal to an ethnic group.

Park and Wirth made recourse to both biotic and social principles in explaining the course of ethnic evolution toward assimilation. Myrdal made no reference to biotic principles, while he maintained the idea of an inevitable evolution toward assimilation in the modern era. Warner and his associates proceeded one step further, making assimilation an empirical question rather than a presumed fact in modern society. They felt that the assimilation of racial minorities is especially problematical in this country.

External factors in the assimilation of a group include its subordination by others, largely on the basis of its cultural or biological dissimilarity to the host society. Cultural dissimilarities between an immigrant group and the larger society involve language and religious differences, for instance, while biological differences refer to physical traits such as skin color. Generally, the greater the differences between immigrant and host, the slower is the rate of immigrant assimilation. Assimilation is also contingent on the order of succession of immigrant groups, for early-arriving groups assimilate faster than later arrivals, holding constant cultural and biological differences.

The rate of assimilation also depends on certain conditions internal to an immigrant group, according to Warner and his associates. These were collapsed under the rubric of the strength of the ethnic subsystem (ethnic community or communalism). A strong ethnic subsystem was thought to retard assimilation. The strength of an ethnic subsystem itself was a function of the size of the ethnic group, its intentions for immigrating to the United States, its proximity to the homeland, and its power to control the lives of its members through a communal network of ethnic associations, schools, church, and family. A large immigrant group with many members intent on returning to a nearby homeland would have a strong ethnic subsystem and would assimilate only slowly.

Considering the external and internal contingencies of assimilation simultaneously, Warner and Srole (1945:285-286) made three summary propositions:

1. The greater the difference between the host and the immigrant cultures, the greater will be the subordination, the greater the strength of the ethnic social systems, and the longer the period necessary for the assimilation of the ethnic group.
2. The greater the racial difference between the populations of the immigrant and host societies, the greater the subordination of the immigrant group, the greater the strength of the social subsystem, and the longer the period necessary for assimilation.
3. When the combined *cultural* and *biological* traits are highly divergent from those of the host society, the subordination of the group will be very great, their subsystem strong, the period of assimilation long, and the processes slow and usually painful.

The third proposition applies particularly to black Americans. "There is a system of white and of Negro castes, and also a system of social classes within each caste, further stratifying groups and defining privileges" (Davis and Dollard, 1940:12-13). This is the summary conclusion drawn by Warner's associates upon studying race relations in the South, in Old City (Davis and Dollard, 1940: Davis et al., 1941). Race relations in Old City were considered typical of those throughout the South.

Ethnic groups in Yankee City, with few exceptions, moved up the social class ladder with each succeeding generation. This pattern was taken to be indicative of white ethnic assimilation in the entire North. In the South, however, blacks were enclosed in a racial caste, and generation after generation blacks did not advance beyond the color barrier. Racial castes were endogamous, marriage was restricted to members of the same caste, and social mobility was confined by caste boundaries. Blacks in Old City could rise to the upper class only with their own caste, and the black upper class was roughly equivalent to the white middle class. This color barrier to marriage and mobility threw into doubt the assimilation of blacks. The racial caste system of Old City is shown in Figure 1.

RACIAL ASSIMILATION

Racial assimilation was always a matter of some uncertainty among assimilationists, even though some were quite certain that modernization brought assimilation in the abstract. As an indication, Park wrote about

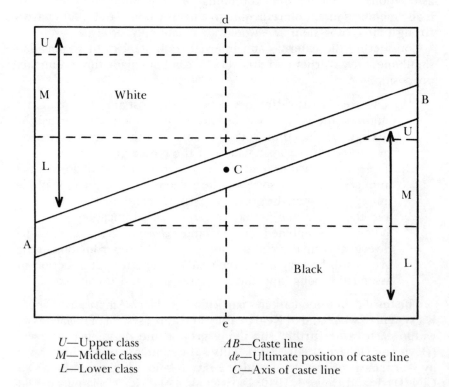

U—Upper class	AB—Caste line
M—Middle class	de—Ultimate position of caste line
L—Lower class	C—Axis of caste line

Figure 1 *Warner's diagram of the caste system in the Deep South.*
Source: Allison Davis, Burleigh B. Gardner, and Mary R. Gardner, *Deep South* (Chicago: University of Chicago Press, 1941). © 1941 by The University of Chicago.

the role of racial visibility in reinforcing the social distance between people, how it heightened racial consciousness, and how it impeded the pace of the race relations cycle (cf. Lyman, 1972; Park, 1950). Park had in mind both blacks in the South and Asians on the West Coast. But, "racial barriers may slacken the tempo of the movement [of the race relations cycle]; may perhaps halt it altogether for a time; but cannot change its direction; cannot at any rate reverse it . . ." (Park, 1950:150). Racial visibility, stereotypes, and prejudices were mere accidents on the metaphysical course to ultimate assimilation; at least this was Park's position until his experiences in Hawaii. Myrdal, too, predicted ultimate racial assimilation with the resolution of the American dilemma. It was Warner and his associates who later voiced serious misgivings about the eventual assimilation of black Americans, likening race relations in the South to the seemingly everlasting caste system of India. The assimilation of white immigrant groups was simply a matter of time, by contrast, and the data from Yankee City gave every indication that white ethnic assimilation in terms of social class mobility was virtually inevitable.

In the current debate over the issue of racial assimilation, it is argued by some that the evolution of blacks is unique in American history, and in no manner is it analogous to those of white immigrant groups. This assumed uniqueness of blacks is dramatized by drawing an analogy between the history of blacks in America and the caste system of India, in line with the convention of the Warner school, or by drawing the analogy between black Americans and the people who had been subjected to 19th-century colonialism.[1] It is argued by others, however, that the experiences of blacks are different only in degree from those of white immigrant groups in this country.

Black Evolution Is Unique

The caste hypothesis argues that the history of blacks in the South is similar to that of lower castes in India, and the colonial model draws the analogy between black Americans and colonized people elsewhere in the world. Both suggest that the evolution of black Americans cannot be compared to that of any other group in this country.

CASTE MODEL   The caste hypothesis was proposed in the works of Davis and Dollard (1940), and Davis et al. (1941), and the notion of a racial caste is continued in the writings of Dollard (1957). Berreman (1960) has incorporated both prior formulations and criticisms of the analogy in a more recent statement of the caste hypothesis.

Berreman argued that the caste system of India and race relations in the southern United States were analogous: In both instances, inequality was

---

[1]Cox (1948) argued that Warner and his associates did not originate the caste hypothesis.

institutionalized, hereditary, and permanent, and it was maintained by the higher castes to allow them to continue their exploitation of the lower castes. Dollard (1957) added that the gains to whites in the South from the racial caste system included economic, sexual, and status advantages. Economic gains to whites centered around the perpetuation of cheap black labor, and sexual gains accrued from the fact that white men had access to partners of both races, a condition others did not share. Since all blacks were considered to be below all whites, deference toward whites was expected from all blacks as a matter of practice, and this instance of inequality had been institutionalized into a racial etiquette. Religion in India and racism in the South justified the respective caste systems.

Irritated with critics of the caste hypothesis who contend that while blacks in the South were dissatisfied with their circumstances, the lower castes of India were content with their lot, Berreman (1960:121) contested this criticism as invalid and based on a false premise:

The point here is that ideal intercaste behavior and attitudes in India are much like those in America, while the actual interaction and attitudes are also similar. Commonly, ideal behavior and attitudes in India have been contrasted with real behavior and attitudes in America—a fact which has led to a false impression of difference.

Berreman pointed to other similarities between the caste system of India and the historical racial situation in the South. While members of the advantaged groups were paternalistic toward members of disadvantaged groups, disadvantaged group members resentfully played their stereotyped subordinate role for favors. Moreover, there were rigid rules of avoidance between castes in both instances, and class hierarchies existed within castes in both India and the South. Berreman admitted to one dissimilarity: Abolition of the caste system in India was anticipated with ambivalence, since it meant, for most castes, mingling with inferiors as well as equals and superiors. Since blacks had no inferior in the South, they viewed the demise of the racial caste system with no ambivalence at all.

COLONIAL MODEL   The colonial model draws an analogy between the experiences of people subjected to 19th-century colonialism and those of black Americans. While the colonial analogy has been popular among several students of American race relations, Blauner (1969) has most explicitly argued for the use of it. Blauner made the distinction between colonialism as a social, economic, and political system and colonization as a process. It is the latter that Afro-Americans share with the colonized peoples of the 19th century. The values and culture of the colonized groups were destroyed in both historical instances. Furthermore, the colonized groups were administered to by representatives of the majority—the police, in the case of Afro-Americans. Finally, racism justified both colonial policies. However, there is one difference:

Colonization outside of a traditional colonial structure has its own special conditions. The group culture and social structure of the colonized in America is less developed; it is also less autonomous. In addition, the colonized are a numerical minority, and furthermore they are ghettoized more totally . . . . (Blauner, 1969:398)

Moore (1970:471) argued that the colonial model describes the experiences of Mexican Americans without need of an analogy. The experience of Hispanos in New Mexico is a case of classic colonialism:

Not only was the relationship between the Mexican and the Anglo-American "involuntary" involving "racism" and the "transformation . . . of indigenous values," but the culture of the Spanish American was well developed, autonomous, a majority numerically, and contained a full social system . . . .

Moore contended that by Blauner's own criteria for colonialism, the contact between Anglos and Hispanos in New Mexico better fits the colonial model than do the experiences of blacks in this country. On the other hand, Moore wrote that the experiences of Mexican Americans in Texas and California progressively deviate from the classic colonial experience, although these, too, may fall under the colonial rubric.

Black Evolution Is Different Only in Degree

It is the contention of other sociologists that the evolution of black Americans is not unique, although it is different in degree from the evolutions of other immigrant groups. Nathan Glazer (1971) argued that the points made by Blauner do not truly distinguish between the experiences of blacks and those of other ethnic groups in America. Glazer first summarized what he considers to be Blauner's key points:

First, the ethnic ghettoes arose more from voluntary choice, both in sense of the choice to immigrate to America and the decision to live among one's fellow ethnics. Second, the immigrant ghettoes tended to be a one and two generation phenomenon; they were actually way stations in the process of acculturation and assimilation. . . . The Black Ghetto on the other hand has been a more permanent phenomenon. . . . Afro-Americans are distinct in the extent to which their segregated communities have remained controlled economically, politically and administratively from the outside . . . . (1971:450–51)

Glazer contended that while blacks were brought involuntarily to the South as slaves, their later migration to urban ghettos in the North and West was as voluntary as the earlier European immigration into the country. Blauner argued that white ethnics dispersed from their ghettos into the suburbs in a generation or two, while blacks have remained concentrated in racial ghettos for longer because of racial discrimination.

Blauner underestimated the persistence of white ethnic segregation and overestimated black segregation, Glazer argued, observing that Kantrowitz's (1969) index of segregation between Swedes and Russians in New York City is 70.7, and that of blacks is 80. This is a difference in degree rather than one of kind.

Glazer believed Blauner's main point is that white immigrant groups quickly assumed political and economic control over their own ghettos, while blacks have not achieved this measure of self-determination in their ghettos at a comparable rate. The rate at which an ethnic group attains control over its own affairs is a complex issue. Glazer asks: Is it accurate to compare such rates for blacks with those for all white ethnic groups, for we find that while blacks are behind the Irish they are very much ahead of the Poles in assuming a role in politics? Another complexity in making comparisons on rates of assimilation is in the calculation of those rates. Obviously, the numerators must consist of indicators of assimilation; however, what time span is to be the denominator? If it is the entire history of blacks in the United States, then their comparative rate of assimilation is so slow as to be truly unique. However, if the denominator is a shorter historical period, the time blacks have lived in those of the nation's cities that have presumably assimilated other immigrant groups, then their rate of assimilation is close enough to those of others that racial assimilation appears to be only a difference in degree.

. . . there are almost none [of the elements of continuity] between the experience of the Negro slave in the South and the free immigrant worker in the North. But there are elements of continuity—and important ones—between the experiences of immigrant workers in the North and black migrants in the North. (Glazer, 1971:458)

And it should be remembered that "It was only by 1940 that blacks formed as large a part of New York City as the Italians and their children formed in 1900" (Glazer, 1971:453).

O'Kane (1969) observed that white immigrants in the nation's cities took three routes toward their assimilation: labor, politics, and crime. Important structural changes have occurred in the urban labor market, however, since blacks have migrated to urban areas. A decreasing demand for unskilled labor, due to automation, and the more general shift from blue to white-collar work now limit blacks' mobility chances up the labor hierarchy, in O'Kane's estimation. On the other hand, blacks can use urban politics and crime as mobility routes, as have other groups, and they will have the same experiences as others have had at dislodging those ahead of them. These observations suggest that we should always put the issue of assimilation, racial or otherwise, in the context of a changing society. We plan to do this in subsequent chapters.

CONTACT HYPOTHESIS

Intimacy between members of different ethnic and racial groups has always been considered by assimilationists to be the link between accommodation and assimilation. Intergroup intimacy began with the disintegration of ethnic ghettos, or the elimination of physical distance between groups, a process that would culminate in the suburbs. People from diverse backgrounds would become cordial neighbors, members of the same business associations and social clubs, close friends, and their children would eventually intermarry. Intimacy of this sort was crucial for assimilation in modern society.

But could the nation realistically expect interracial intimacy and thus racial assimilation? The assimilationists were always somewhat uncertain in their answer. Park wrote that racial visibility and stereotypes impeded the pace of the race relations cycle, and, of course, Warner and his associates observed that intimacy stopped at the color line in the deep South. Early interest in the prospect of interracial intimacy has continued and has come to be called the *contact hypothesis*. Zeul and Humphrey (1971:464) explain: "According to this proposition, increased interaction between whites and any minority group, such as Negroes, makes for favorable attitudes on the part of whites, greater acceptance of the blacks, and integration [assimilation] of the racial groups."

Support for the contact hypothesis comes from research on interracial contact in a variety of settings, including the armed forces, public housing projects, residential neighborhoods, school settings, summer camps, and workplaces, as well as laboratory experiments (cf. Cohen and Roper, 1972; Pettigrew, 1969; Zeul and Humphrey, 1971). However, other research suggests that interracial contact does not always conform to the contact hypothesis (e.g. Molotch, 1969). Contact can make matters worse, as attested to by the contact between white police and black citizens in recent urban violence. Allport (1954) concluded that four conditions must be present in interracial contact for it to produce any measure of intimacy: (1) The black and white participants must be of roughly equal status, (2) pursuing common goals, (3) in a cooperative manner, and (4) the contact must be sanctioned in law and by political authorities.

Pettigrew (1969:56) observed that "All four of his [Allport's] conditions maximize the likelihood of shared values and beliefs." Pettigrew makes an important point: From the perspective of the philosophy behind both assimilationism and the contact hypothesis, the point is that blacks and whites must be equally modernized. They must share alike in the modern mentality of educational and occupational achievement, middle-class respectability, and racial egalitarianism; they must share in the entire roster of modern traits for there to be any intimacy in their contact. Indeed, Zeul and Humphrey (1971) concluded that it is not that interracial contact brings acceptance of blacks, rather it is the degree to which whites were cosmopolitan before contact. It is how modern they are in their tastes, highbrow in their leisure pursuits, educated, and nonparochial in their self-identifications that makes whites accepting of close contact with blacks. In a word, it is modern man who will assimilate. All of this overlooks the fact that it is the white-collar and educated white who has been until recently most removed from job competition with blacks, due to the historical discrimination against the latter. Thus we are brought back to social evolutionism and the concept that modernity brings the assimilation of folk groups into a unitary society.

CONCLUSION

Assimilationism has made significant contributions to our understanding of American ethnicity, but there are limitations to this perspective. As long as the assimilationists held to a natural history of ethnic evolution, the prediction of assimilation could be neither proven nor disproven. The prediction was not put in a time frame; rather it was stated that assimilation would take place eventually. But exactly what does eventually mean? Does it mean that assimilation will occur within a decade, a generation, two or three generations, or in some distant future? Moreover, when assimilation did not occur as expected, it was explained that certain accidents or obstacles had interfered with the natural course of race relations, and such cases never were taken as evidence contrary to the tenets of the race relations cycle. Park never found a single case in support of his prediction of inevitable assimilation, but he held to the validity of the cycle into old age (Lyman, 1972). A natural history is not capable of empirical test, for it transcends time and every imaginable societal condition that might alter its course.

Ethnic evolution in a natural history is likened to a mechanical process; once set in motion, it moves like some great machine inevitably and without purpose toward a final state. This mechanical metaphor of human life was the mainstay image of social evolutionism. Gumplowicz wrote in 1899: "The individual simply plays a part of the prism which receives the rays, dissolves them according to fixed laws and lets them pass out again in a predetermined direction and with a predetermined color" (p. 157). The mechanical metaphor found in social evolutionism and assimilationism was fused with science in Newton's concept of the universe as a great machine (Matson, 1966). This imagery came to be shared in biology, psychology, and the social sciences in the 19th century (Polanyi, 1944). Whether the phenomenon under study was physical, biological, psychological, economic, or social, the image was the same: Evolution is mindlessly propelled by mechanical forces. Many commentators have noted this laissez-faire, mechanical quality of assimilationism (cf. Cox, 1948; Ellison, 1964; Lyman, 1972; Myrdal, 1944).

In physics, faith in the mechanical motif was seriously shaken early in the 20th century by the works of Einstein, Heisenberg, and Planck, among others (Matson, 1966). However, assimilationists were analyzing ethnicity at the same time with the mechanical metaphors of 19th–century science, apparently unaware of the challenge to mechanism in physics. Moreover, much of the general sociology of the time buttressed the tenets of assimilationism. The theme of modern society as a mass society, one consisting of isolated individuals in large cities bereft of social bonds, and the stress of contemporary functionalism on impersonal utility, not personal loyalty or human sympathy, as society's flywheel, suggest that assimilationism was but a part of general sociology.

Nevertheless, human purpose and sentiment always had an important role in Park's natural history of ethnic evolution. Human communication, cooperation, and intimacy were all necessary for the completion of the race relations cycle. Neither Park nor Wirth nor any other assimilationist ever expunged humanity from race relations, nor did they reduce intergroup relations to the level of the impersonal struggle for survival. The student can readily imagine what the race relations cycle would have been without reference to communication, mutual understanding, and intimacy. The irony is that as an explanation of ethnic evolution, these human variables were every bit as mechanical as was impersonal competition.

With Myrdal's *American Dilemma* ethnic evolution was put exclusively in the context of human culture, and reference to biotic and impersonal forces in race relations was discontinued. Myrdal analyzed American race relations as a moral dilemma, the American dilemma it was called, and he predicted that it would finally be resolved in favor of racial equality. While setting ethnic evolution in the context of human culture represents an advance for this school, Myrdal's analysis is still not totally adequate. Cox (1948) observed that race relations are mystified by Myrdal and made part of an American morality play between good (American Creed) and evil (racism), one that takes place in the metaphysical setting of the American soul.

Another limitation of assimilationism is its tendency to identify ethnicity in general with ethnic segregation in particular. Ethnicity cannot exist in this scheme outside the ghetto. Not only is this an unnecessarily narrow definition of ethnicity, it has the effect of seriously questioning only the assimilation of Americans of color, especially that of black Americans. Many blacks are poor, living in ghettos, and phenotypically distinct. Racial visibility was considered a possible impediment to assimilation even by Park, and Warner and his associates elaborated on this theme in their caste hypothesis. It was felt that when both biological and cultural traits of a group are divergent from those of the larger society, then assimilation of such groups is a slow and painful process.

Questioning only racial assimilation protects the assimilationist thesis to a degree. The implication is that except for the unique cases of certain racial groups, the assimilation thesis works. Because white immigrant groups no longer live only in ghettos and have risen from the bottom of the nation's social ladder, they have assimilated. With the occupational diversification and ecological dispersion of Jewish Americans, for instance, there was assimilation, in Wirth's scheme. He did not see the possibility "that members of the third (and later) generations of an ethnic minority may maintain a particular subculture, not lose their identity, although they are neither isolated nor concentrated in specific ecological areas" (Etzioni, 1959:257).

The hypothesis of the uniqueness of color prejudice and evolutions of people of color possibly errs in two directions. First, the evolutions of various people of color in America, including those of American Indians, Asian Americans, black Americans, and Mexican Americans, are hardly identical. They diverge from one another as much as they diverge from the evolutions of white immigrant groups. For instance, Chinese and Japanese Americans have assimilated to a far greater degree than have blacks, even more than many white immigrant groups, if we measure assimilation in terms of social class mobility. Is it too obvious to note that these Asians are as physically distinct from whites as are blacks? By the same token, American Indians are far less assimilated than blacks, even though both share the common experience of color prejudice. The emphasis of color prejudice in ethnic evolution appears unable to make such distinctions among the evolutions of the different peoples of color in America.

The proposition that color is virtually the only impediment to assimilation in modern society unfortunately never forced sociologists "to abandon the idea that ethnicity is a dysfunctional survival from a prior stage of social development" (Metzger, 1971:644). This is the second error, by implication, of the hypothesis on the uniqueness of racial assimilation (or the lack of it). Ethnicity might be as important in modern society as it was traditionally; at least, we should be open to this possibility.

REFERENCES

Allport, Gordon W.
    1954 The Nature of Prejudice. Reading, Massachusetts: Addison-Wesley Publishing
        Company.
Berreman, Gerald D.
    1960 "Caste in India and the United States." The American Journal of Sociology
        66(September):120-127.

Blauner, Robert
1969 "Internal Colonialism and Ghetto Revolt." Social Problems 16(Spring):393-409.
Cohen, Elizabeth G., and Susan S. Roper
1972 "Modification of Interracial Interaction Disability: An Application of Status Characteristic Theory." American Sociological Review 37(December):643-657.
Cox, Oliver Cromwell
1948 Caste, Class and Race. New York: Doubleday and Company, Inc.
Cruse, Harold
1967 The Crisis of the Negro Intellectual. New York: William Morrow and Company, Inc.
Davis, Allison, Burleigh B. Gardner, and Mary R. Gardner
1941 Deep South. Chicago: University of Chicago Press.
Davis, Allison, and John Dollard
1940 Children of Bondage. Washington, D.C.: American Council on Education.
Dollard, John
1957 Caste and Class in a Southern Town. Third Edition. New York: Doubleday and Company, Inc.
Durkheim, Émile
[1893] The Division of Labor in Society. (Translated by George Simpson.) Glencoe,
1947 Illinois: Free Press.
Ellison, Ralph
[1953] Shadow and Act. New York: Random House.
1964
Etzioni, Amitai
1959 "The Ghetto—A Re-Evaluation." Social Forces 37(March):255–262.
Frazier, E. Franklin
1947 "Sociological Theory and Race Relations." American Sociological Review 12(June):265–271.
Glazer, Nathan
1957 American Judaism. Chicago: University of Chicago Press.
1971 "Blacks and Ethnic Groups: The Difference and the Political Difference It Makes." Social Problems 18(Spring):444–461.
Gumplowicz, Ludwig
1899 The Outlines of Sociology. (Translated by Frederick W. Moore.) Philadelphia: American Academy of Political and Social Science.
Hollingshead, A. B.
1961 "A Re-examination of Ecological theory." In George A. Theodorson (ed.), Studies in Human Ecology. New York: Harper and Row, Publishers.
Kantrowitz, Nathan
1969 "Segregation in New York City, 1960." American Journal of Sociology 74 (May):685–695.
Kitano, Harry
1974 Race Relations. Englewood Cliffs, New Jersey: Prentice-Hall, Inc.
Lyman, Stanford M.
1972 The Black American in Sociological Thought: A Failure of Perspective. New York: Capricorn Books.
Matson, Floyd W.
1966 The Broken Image. New York: Anchor Books.
Metzger, L. Paul
1971 "American Sociology and Black Assimilation: Conflicting Perspectives." American Journal of Sociology 76(January):627–647.
Molotch, Harvey
1969 "Racial Integration in a Transition Community." American Sociological Review 34(December):878–893.
Moore, Joan W.
1970 "Colonialism: The Case of the Mexican Americans." Social Problems 17 (Spring):463–472.

Myrdal, Gunnar
1944 An American Dilemma: The Negro Problem and Modern Democracy. New York: Harper and Brothers, Publishers.
Oberschall, Anthony (ed.)
1972 The Establishment of Empirical Sociology: Studies in Continuity, Discontinuity, and Institutionalization. New York: Harper and Row, Publishers.
O'Kane, James M.
1969 "Ethnic Mobility and the Lower-Income Negro: A Socio-Historical Perspective." Social Problems 16(Winter):302–311.
Park, Robert Ezra
1915 "The City: Suggestions for the Investigation of Human Behavior in the City Environment." American Journal of Sciology 20(March):577–612.
1939 "The Nature of Race Relations." Pp. 3–45 in Edgar T. Thompson (ed.), Race Relations and the Race Problem: A Definition and Analysis. Durham, Duke University Press.
1950 Race and Culture. New York: Free Press.
Park, Robert E., and E. W. Burgess
1921 Introduction to the Science of Sociology. Chicago: University of Chicago Press.
Pettigrew, Thomas F.
1969 "Racially Separate or Together?" Journal of Social Issues 25(1):43–69.
Polanyi, Karl
1944 The Great Transformation. New York: Farrar and Rinehart, Inc.
Reuter, E. B.
1945 "Racial Theory." American Journal of Sociology 50(May):452–461.
Rose, Peter I., Stanley Rothman, and William J. Wilson
1973 Through Different Eyes: Black and White Perspectives on American Race Relations. London: Oxford University Press.
Simpson, George Eaton, and J. Milton Yinger
1972 Racial and Cultural Minorities: An Analysis of Prejudice and Discrimination. Fourth Edition. New York: Harper and Row, Publishers.
Theodorson, George A.
1961 Studies in Human Ecology. New York: Harper and Row, Publishers.
Vander Zanden, James W.
1972 American Minority Relations. Third Edition. New York: Ronald Press Company.
Warner, W. Lloyd
1959 The Living and the Dead. New Haven, Connecticut: Yale University Press.
Warner, W. Lloyd, and J. O. Low
1947 The Social System of Modern Factory. New Haven, Connecticut: Yale University Press.
Warner, W. Lloyd, and Paul S. Lunt
1941 The Social Life of a Modern Community. New Haven, Connecticut: Yale University Press.
1942 The Status System of a Modern Community. New Haven, Connecticut: Yale University Press.
Warner, W. Lloyd, and Leo Srole
1945 The Social Systems of American Ethnic Groups. New Haven, Connecticut: Yale University Press.
Warner, W. Lloyd, and associates
1949 Democracy in Jonesville. New York: Harper & Row.
Wirth, Louis
[1928] The Ghetto. Chicago: University of Chicago Press, pp. 232–33, 241–42. © 1956 by
1956 The University of Chicago.
Yetman, Norman R., and C. Roy Steele
1975 Majority and Minority: The Dynamics of Racial and Ethnic Relations. Second Edition. Boston, Massachusetts: Allyn and Bacon, Inc.
Zeul, Carolyn, and Craig R. Humphrey
1971 "The Integration of Blacks in Suburban Neighborhoods: A Reexamination of the Contact Hypothesis." Social Problems 18(Spring):462–474.

CHAPTER 3

ETHNIC PLURALISM

INTRODUCTION

A famous historian of American ethnicity, Oscar Handlin, once confessed that not until he sat down to write a history of America's immigrants did he realize that their history is the history of the country. This confirms the suspicion that the significance of ethnic pluralism in the United States is neither widely known nor truly appreciated. Assimilationism has been the unofficial national doctrine, and little lasting significance has been granted to ethnic pluralism in a modern society like our own, which has hardly encouraged appreciation for ethnic diversity. However, there have always been those who have maintained that ethnic diversity endures in a modern society, though their opinions have been in a minority. Among them are the pluralists, who believe that ethnicity has social, economic, political, and psychological functions in modern society.

In assimilationism American society is likened to a melting pot, suggesting the absorption of diverse groups into the modern mass society. Only the assimilation of certain racial groups was ever seriously questioned. Pluralists contend, however, that the single melting pot is the wrong metaphor and suggest instead the idea of many melting pots to depict ethnic evolution in American society more exactly. Rather than fusing into one mass society, ethnic groups fuse together in several melting pots, each distinct from the others. Rather than disappearing, ethnicity evolves into new forms and expressions in the course of societal modernization.

This is a chapter on ethnic pluralism as a sociological perspective on American ethnicity. Following the format of the preceding chapter, the key terms of pluralism are presented and assumptions of pluralism are identified. Then the works of contemporary pluralists are surveyed and an assessment of pluralism brings the chapter to a close.

KEY TERMS

Ethnic Group

Ethnic groups were defined in Chapter 2 as self-conscious collectivities of people who, on the basis of a common origin or a separate subculture, maintain a distinction between themselves and outsiders. Such boundary maintenance may be manifest in circumscribed social participation, or in distinctive patterns of thought, sentiment, or action. This definition is generic, allowing evidence for ethnicity to take many forms.

Assimilationists have tended to restrict their usage of ethnicity, or, more specifically, of ethnic boundaries, to evidence of the territorial isolation and occupational concentration of ethnic groups. They consider that ethnic groups exist only in ghettos and when members are concentrated in a narrow range of jobs, so that they are isolated from others. In research on assimilation the occupational diversification and residential dispersion of a group was identified with its assimilation, a convention that Warner and Srole (1945) made explicit in their Yankee City study. This methodology both reflected the tradition of urban ecology in assimilationsism and was an extension of social evolutionism. The central concept of assimilation is that folk groups inevitably disappear in the modernization process.

Pluralists contend that this usage of ethnicity is too exclusive. DeVos (1975:12) recently commented that "The degree to which some territorial concept is necessary to the maintenance of ethnic identity, symbolically or actually, must be considered in relation to the use of nonterritorial definitions of ethnic uniqueness . . . . " DeVos thinks that ethnic "boundaries are basically psychological in nature, not territorial" (p. 6), in line with Barth's (1969) work. Thus, DeVos offers a more inclusive definition of an ethnic group as a "self-perceived group of people who hold in common a set of traditions not shared by others with whom they are in contact." Ethnic identity is not necessarily manifest in either territorial isolation or distinctive economic activity, for it is more generally the "subjective symbolic or emblematic use of any aspect of culture, in order to differentiate themselves [ethnic group members] from other groups" (p. 16). By implication, any nationality group, whatever its occupational composition and residential dispersion, can be an ethnic group so long as it somehow maintains its boundaries.

Bennett (1975) contends that the old definitions of ethnicity, those which located ethnicity in distinct things such as segregated neighborhoods, do not apply in the modern world of intercommunication and movement. Ethnicity is a cognitive category and always has been, he argues. The new ethnicity is a badge phenomenon, which can be voluntarily displayed in the presentation of self and can be used in both personal and group strategies to achieve certain objectives in a modern society. Therefore, an ethnic group is defined broadly in this book as *a self-conscious collectivity of people who maintain a distinction between themselves and outsiders, based on origin or a separate subculture, and such boundary maintenance may be manifest in circumscribed social participation or in distinctive patterns of thought, sentiment, or action.*

Pluralism

There are two dimensions of pluralism: cultural and structural. *Cultural pluralism refers to the existence of distinct ethnic subcultures in a society which affect and make variable the way people think, feel, and act. Structural pluralism means that ethnic identity is evident in social interaction in a society, manifest in either restrictions on social interaction or in the use of ethnic identity in open and free exchange.*

As for ethnic pluralism in the United States, Gordon (1964) observed that modern American society is composed of several ethnic subsocieties, the boundaries of which limit the social interaction of Americans, and that these subsocieties have distinct subcultures which interpret the national ethos for their members. Moreover, these ethnic subsocieties are not limited to racial groups.

Ethnic Evolution

Ethnicity is an evolving or emergent phenomenon, and groups and their relations with one another and the larger society change in the course of ethnic evolution. The continuation of ethnic pluralism in modern society is one dimension of ethnic evolution and is the one emphasized in this chapter. Groups may fuse together in larger entities in the course of ethnic evolution, but this means the continuation of ethnic pluralism, not assimilation, so long as these larger groups remain distinct from each other in the larger society.

ASSUMPTIONS OF ETHNIC PLURALISM

1. *While relations among ethnic and racial groups in America evolve, this evolution does not necessarily bring the assimilation of these groups into a single, monolithic entity.*

2. *As relations among ethnic groups evolve, the expression of ethnicity changes. In America, ethnic boundaries have generally grown more inclusive and less*

restrictive, and ethnic identity and its cultural expression have become more domestic and less foreign.

3. *Reasons for the persistence of ethnicity in modern American society include the nation's tolerance for ethnic pluralism, the sociopolitical role of ethnic groups in modern society, and the psychological functions served by ethnicity.*

REEVALUATION OF PARK AND WIRTH

The discussion of ethnic pluralism begins with critiques of two early works of assimilationism: Park's race relations cycle and Wirth's natural history of Jewish assimilation. This is followed by a survey of several contemporary pluralists. The pluralist concept of ethnicity becomes broader and more comprehensive as we go, so that toward the end of the chapter it is seen as a pervasive and persistent state of consciousness in modern society, and one that is indeterminately manifest in a variety of ways.

Park's Natural History of Assimilation

THE RACE RELATIONS CYCLE[1] In Robert Park's natural history, the cycle of race relations inevitably ends with assimilation. Emory Bogardus, too, believed that race relations formed a cycle, but he did not believe that it inevitably evolved toward assimilation. Studying the reception of Asian and Mexican immigrants on the West Coast, Bogardus (1930:621) observed:

There is first curiosity and sympathy, followed by economic welcome which brings an increase of numbers. The third stage is industrial and social antagonism as competition develops. Next comes legislative antagonism, succeeded by fair-play tendencies, after which a sixth stage of quiescence is reached. The last phase is found in the second-generation difficulties, the assimilated children being only partially accepted by natives.

Bogardus's cycle begins with native curiosity and sympathy toward Asian and Mexican immigrants. The "strangeness coupled with his original fewness of numbers make him appear helpless" (Bogardus, 1930:613). Apparently, the strangeness of these immigrants invoked curiosity, while their perceived helplessness stimulated the sympathy of natives. Asian and Mexican immigrants also received an economic welcome, especially from employers. This welcome followed from the fact that these immigrants were willing to work for less pay than native labor.

Since immigrant labor undercut the wage rates of native labor, it is understandable that the third stage of the cycle is industrial and social

---

[1] Additional revisions of Park's race relations cycle can be found in Banton (1967), Brown (1934), and Kitano (1969). These revisions share with Bogardus (1930) the idea that a natural history of assimilation should be retired.

antagonism. Bogardus (1930:614) notes that first "sporadic outbursts of prejudice against them [immigrants] have occurred, and the organized movements have gained a tremendous momentum . . . . Organized labor has usually been the leader in protesting against the . . . immigrants, on grounds of protecting labor against unfair competition and pulling down of standards built up at great sacrifice by American workers."

The fact that these immigrants were economic threats was not the only issue around which opposition to immigration was mobilized. Fear about the volume of immigration grew—"There has seemed to be uncounted millions on the way"—and this fear was intensified by the perceived high birthrates of Asian and Mexican immigrants. Moreover, as some of the immigrants attempted to move out of their ghettos and into the residential areas of natives, opposition toward them enlarged and grew more heated. Bogardus remarked in a snide manner that at this stage of the cycle, "Natives do not appreciate how they may bring about the assimilation and acculturation of both the first- and second-generation immigrants . . . " (p. 615). This stage of Bogardus's cycle is similar to Park's stage of competition. Bogardus believed that intergroup antagonism continued into legislative action against the immigrants, the fourth stage of his cycle.

Invariably a "fair-play" movement developed, and during this fifth stage of the cycle intergroup antagonism was prevented from going to extremes. The fair-play movement, however, did not prevent the passage of legislation restricting Asian immigration. After passage of such legislation, accommodation was achieved. "Assured that the impending danger is safely thwarted, the antagonistic organizations modify their attitudes" (p. 616).

While Park proposed that ethnic evolution ended with assimilation, based largely on the workings of intergroup communication and intimacy, Bogardus's cycle ended on the note of *second-generation difficulties*. He observed that while second-generation immigrants, particularly Asian, were losing contact with the home country, they were being accepted only partially in the United States, the land of their birth and citizenship (p. 617). While Park and Wirth admitted that prejudice and discrimination might impede the pace of evolution toward assimilation, it was their conviction that such difficulties are passing phenomena and that assimilation is inevitable. Bogardus did not share in the conviction that mutual understanding and intimacy inevitably result and that they bring assimilation.

THE SOCIAL DISTANCE SCALE Distance between ethnic groups was an important concept in the works of Park and Wirth, for the process of assimilation was said to be the reduction of such distance. To Park and Wirth, intergroup distance meant primarily the spatial distance between ethnic groups, or their residential segregation. The residential movement and spatial dispersion of an ethnic group were identified with its assimilation.

Bogardus defined the distance between ethnic groups more abstractly, as an attitude or a mental phenomenon that may or may not be manifest in physical segregation. He (1928) constructed a social distance scale by first asking people if they would admit members of 40 different ethnic groups to:

1. Close kinship by marriage.
2. My club as personal chums.
3. My street as neighbors.
4. Employment in my occupation.
5. Citizenship in my country.
6. My country as visitors.
7. Or would exclude from my country.

Bogardus proposed that the above items formed a rank order of social distance, with the least amount of distance expressed in item 1 and the greatest amount of distance expressed in item 7. The social distance scale became a popular research instrument, and results from using it over many years show that Americans have consistently wished to maintain distance between themselves and certain ethnic groups. A review of these findings and criticisms of the social distance scale is found in Simpson and Yinger (1972). The point is that Bogardus made the notion of intergroup distance more general and abstract. It is not only or specifically the spatial distance between groups, or their ecological segregation; it is instead a more abstract predisposition or preference to maintain social distance in either a spatial or a symbolic way. Thus ethnic boundaries can persist as social distance in the absence of spatial segregation, outside ghettos.

Wirth's Natural History of Jewish Assimilation

On the occasion of the republication of Wirth's *The Ghetto* in 1956, Amitai Etzioni (1959:257) wrote that Wirth viewed Jewish ethnicity as both "a place and a state of mind." These two expressions of ethnicity were so fused in Wirth's scheme that the ecological movement of Jews out of the ghetto was necessarily equated with the extinction of the group. But in Etzioni's words: "Obviously Jews return to Judaism without returning to the physical ghetto . . . . They return to a group without an ecological base, a phenomenon which Wirth's conceptual scheme does not cover" (p. 258). This habit of seeing in ethnicity nothing so much as its demise in modern society follows from the legacy of 19th-century social evolutionism. Etzioni said that "Park and Wirth, following the mass society theories, assume that eventually every *Gemeinschaft* will become a *Gesellschaft*" (p.

259). In other words, every folk society becomes a modern society, and this means the eventual disintegration of the folk group.

Ethnicity can exist in modern society and outside a ghetto, however, and Etzioni finds in Wirth's own work evidence of how this might occur:

There is common identity, tradition, values and consciousness. Often there are common sentiments and interests based on past experience, education, and communication. The common bond is reinforced through ethnic newspapers, organizations, clubs, and synagogues, where members meet, even though they do not live next to each other and are not concentrated in one ecological area. (Etzioni, 1959:258)

Another implication of Wirth's own analysis is that settlement outside the ghetto may even activate certain aspects of Jewishness: "contact with others and others' cultures makes the Jew conscious of the positive values of his own tradition" (Etzioni 1959:257).

Herbert Gans (1951) found that the movement of Jews to the suburbs did indeed make them conscious of their own traditions, and, he noted, a Jewish community was soon formed in one suburb of Chicago to conserve these traditions. According to Wirth, Jews would most likely assimilate through religious conversion and intermarriage in the suburbs, but when Gans studied Jewish residents of Park Forest, Illinois, he found there little evidence of such assimilation.

In 1949 2,000 families resided in Park Forest, of which 141 were Jewish. Jewish families in Park Forest were like their Gentile neighbors in many ways:

The Jews of Park Forest dress as do other Park Foresters, enjoy similar leisure time activities, read the same newspapers, look at the same movies, hear the same radio programs . . . . They observe few traditional Jewish religious practices; the village's isolation from synagogues and Kosher food shops has probably discouraged observant Jews from becoming tenants, and brought problems to those few who did (Gans, 1951:333).

Nonetheless, Gans found that 100 of the Jewish families had formed a fledgling Jewish community: in just one year a Jewish lodge, a National Council of Jewish Women's chapter, a B'nai B'rith school, and even a Board of Jewish education had emerged (p. 333). From the beginning, it was important for these suburbanite Jews to "recognize" whether or not any of their neighbors were Jewish (p. 333). Gans attributed the emergence of a Jewish community in Park Forest to this sense of Jewish identity, or, more specifically, to the desire of parents there for socializing their offspring into Jewish traditions, and to their feeling that they could be more relaxed around their own kind. A Jewish subculture did emerge in Park Forest, although it was different from traditions in the ghetto. In the suburbs, "the Jews are distinguished by a feeling of 'social consciousness,' by concern over political and social problems, by a tendency toward humanistic agnosticism" (p. 337).

Gans noted that the transplantation of ethnicity in this suburb was not confined to that done by Jews: "Both the large Catholic group . . . and the smaller Lutheran one also consist of a religious body, men's and women's social organizations, and a more or less extensive informal community . . . . Both communities developed more quickly than the Jewish one . . . " (p. 337).

Novak (1971) suggested to America's ethnic whites—the Poles, Italians, Greeks, and Slavs—that they, too, remain unmeltable ethnic groups outside their immigrant ghettos, notwithstanding his own experiences with the Anglo-American establishment:

I am born of . . . those Poles, Italians, Greeks, and Slavs, those non-English-speaking immigrants numbered so heavily among the working-men of this nation . . . . Nowhere in my schooling do I recall any attempt to put me in touch with my own history. The strategy was clearly to make an American of me. English literature, American literature, and even the history books, as I recall them, were peopled by Anglo-Saxons from Boston . . . . Not even my native Pennsylvania, let alone my Slovak forebears, counted for very many paragraphs . . . . I don't remember feeling envy or regret: a feeling, perhaps, of unimportance, of remoteness, of not having heft enough to count. (pp. 63–65)

Another criticism of Wirth is that he underestimated the durability of the ethnic neighborhood. The fact is that not only racial segregation but ethnic segregation as well has persisted in American cities. Glazer (1971) cited findings that many ethnic groups in New York City have tended to move en masse to new residential locations, and Rosenthal (1960) documented such movement of Jews in Chicago over three and four generations. Driedger and Church (1974) identified at least two patterns by which ethnic segregation has persisted in Winnipeg, Canada. Jews there tended to move over time to new locations en masse, while the French tended to remain in their old neighborhoods. Guest and Weed (1976) recently analyzed patterns of ethnic segregation in Cleveland, Boston, and Seattle and concluded:

The continued existence of ethnic segregation in American cities is clear from these results. There is no evidence that it will disappear in the near future. In particular, its constancy in the 1960s, with slight increases among some groups, supports the idea of continued ethnic ties in American cities. Given the alleged rise of ethnic and racial consciousness in the past few years . . . , this finding is hardly a surprise. (p. 1109)

More specifically, "For Cleveland the data indicate some clear declines in residential segregation since 1930 for 'new' southern and eastern

European ethnic groups; 'old' groups, however, actually increased in segregation" (p. 1088).

This pattern emerged not only in central cities but also in suburbs. Thus, the "old" immigrant groups, those from northern and western Europe and Canada, who have been in America for some time and presumably are the most assimilated, have actually become slightly more segregated from one another in all three cities and, in Cleveland, from southern and eastern Europeans as well. Guest and Weed believed that ethnic residential segregation is highly related to differences among these groups in social status, in partial support of Park's and Wirth's thesis. The recent rise in ethnic consciousness, the fact that "ethnic groups may serve as political-interest groups in the metropolis," and the possibility that "residential ties on the basis of ethnicity may counterbalance some of the less agreeable aspects of urban life" (Guest and Weed, 1976: 1109) were given as reasons for the persistence of ethnic residential segregation in modern America.

The persistence of ethnic segregation in the United States is illustrated above by the movement of groups en masse to new neighborhoods, and in some instances it has grown greater in recent years. Furthermore, even as members of different ethnic groups dispersed into the suburbs and came into contact with one another, ethnic consciousness of kind and nonterritorial forms of ethnicity have endured. Ethnicity has also survived in the old neighborhoods, the old immigrant ghettos.

Gerald Suttles (1968) studied such a neighborhood in Chicago and found that while several ethnic groups now live there together, they symbolically and temporally maintain a social distance among themselves. Since this neighborhood is on the near west side of Chicago, Suttles called it the Addams area in reference to Jane Addams, whose Hull House had been located nearby. About the residents, Suttles reported that at the time of his study, "approximately one-third are Italian, a quarter are Mexican, 17% are Negro, and 8% or less are Puerto Rican" (p. 22). Earlier, the neighborhood had been an Italian one. In this neighborhood in the inner city, the Italians had not been fully succeeded by other ethnic groups in 1965, and they still comprised one-third of the residents and were the numerically dominant group.

Ethnic boundaries were clearly evident in the daily routines of the area residents. While Italians, Mexicans, blacks, and Puerto Ricans were in constant physical contact and were tolerant of one another, their daily life was still demarcated by ethnic boundaries. Ethnicity circumscribed social interaction in the churches, clubs, business establishments, taverns, and recreational areas of the neighborhood. People tended to limit their interaction to their own kind, particularly in the case of their primary relationships. Ethnicity was a basis for personal trust, and the personal bonds prompted by ethnic consciousness of kind were vital to social intercourse in the area, for otherwise the residents had little reason for trusting one another.

Communication habits and clothing styles also helped maintain ethnic boundaries in the neighborhood. Italian was the daily language of the older Italians, and their English was badly broken. Likewise, Spanish was the daily language among the older Mexicans and Puerto Ricans. The area youth used "jive," a special idiom of English at which the black youths were particularly expert. Young Mexican and Puerto Rican males also engaged in jive talk, but "the Italians seldom use any of this vocabulary even to the point of not understanding it" (Suttles, 1968: 65). Ethnic boundaries were also buttressed by patterns of nonverbal communication. The reluctance of blacks "to look them in the eye" bothered Italians, while blacks complained that Italians "stare you down." Clothing styles also communicated ethnic identity. While wearing leather jackets and black pants was common among young Italian, Mexican, and Puerto Rican males, it was rare among black males. Only blacks wore bandanas around their foreheads, an article of attire locally known as the "rag."

Even in the commercial exchange between store owners and customers, ethnicity was evident. There were establishments that catered to only one ethnic group and sold ethnically specific products. If an outsider entered such a store, he was greeted with "Whatta you want?" and it was assumed that he had lost his way. There were 92 such businesses in the Addams area, and all were quite small. In other stores, outsiders were treated as guests. A guest had to pay deference to his host, the owner, and display an appreciation for the ethnic flavor of the establishment. At businesses open to all ethnic groups, such as the area's short-order cafes, members of different ethnic groups would take turns:

Thus the typical practice is for one group to enter only when they notice that the cafe is empty. Occasionally, then, one will see a group pass by, look in, and pass on because it is already occupied. However, the group may wait some distance from the cafe and later, after the first group leaves, the second will enter. (Suttles, 1968:51)

So it was in this neighborhood in a modern city that daily life, including commercial transactions, was ordered in time and segmented in space by ethnicity.

CONTEMPORARY PLURALISTS

Milton Gordon

Milton Gordon made an influential statement of ethnic pluralism in *Assimilation in American Life* (1964). Gordon proposed in this work that America continues to be a pluralistic society, composed of ethnic subsocieties, as well as those of region, rural/urban residence, and social class. Each of these subsocieties has a distinct subculture which translates more or less the national ethos to the members of the subsociety. An ethnic subsociety is "a network of organizations and informal social relationships which permits and encourages the members of an ethnic group to remain in the confines of the group for all of their primary relations and some of their secondary relationships at all stages of the life cycle" (p. 34). The primary relations within any subsociety are the principal sources of self-identification for group members, and they act as crucibles in which the members' interpretations of the larger national ethos are formed. Thus subsocieties have subcultures, or shared styles of thinking, feeling, and acting.

Gordon identified four ethnic subsocieties in this country—blacks, Catholics, Jews, and white Protestants—and there was a residual category for intellectuals. The contemporary ethnic mosaic of America is demarcated by race, religion, and to a declining extent by nationality, as people from diverse national origins have assimilated into the larger religious subsocieties. These ethnic subsocieties are, of course, connected to one another, mainly through the secondary relations of their members. None of these subsocieties is a truly homogenous entity, however, for each is stratified by region, rural/urban residence, and the social classes of its members, or by the other subsocieties of America. This matrix of subsocieties forms the basis of the larger American society.

It is the intersection of ethnic subsocieties and social classes which Gordon stresses. Such an intersection results in ethclasses, and there are generally three ethclasses within each ethnic subsociety. That is, there are three socioeconomic classes of blacks, Catholics, Jews, and white Protestants. Gordon believes that ethclasses are the most fundamental subsocietal units in America. More than any other subsocietal unit, ethclasses confine primary relationships, since friendships, family ties, club memberships, and so on are normally formed within a single ethclass. Thus it is principally within ethclasses that Americans are socialized into subcultural values, marry, and then socialize their own children.

While assimilation has occurred in American history, it has been through means of a complex and uneven process. The components of assimilation according to Gordon are shown in Table 1.

Certain aspects of assimilation have occurred earlier and more rapidly than others. For instance, acculturation usually begins earlier than structural assimilation in a group's evolution and proceeds more rapidly; currently most ethnic groups in the country now conform to Anglo-American standards of style. Structural assimilation in most instances comes later, particularly as regards the integration of others into the primary relations of Anglo-Americans. These barriers to structural

Dutch girls sweep street for annual tulip festival in Holland, Michigan.
United Press International Photo. Acme 5/19/49.

Table 1 Variables in the Assimilation Process

Subprocess or Condition	Type or Stage of Assimilation
Change of cultural patterns to those of host society	Cultural or behavioral assimilation (Acculturation)
Large-scale entrance into cliques, clubs, and institutions of host society, on primary group level	Structural assimilation
Large-scale intermarriage	Marital assimilation (Amalgamation)
Development of sense of peoplehood based exclusively on host society	Identificational assimilation
Absence of prejudice	Attitude receptional assimilation
Absence of discrimination	Behavior receptional assimilation
Absence of value and power conflict	Civic assimilation

Source: From *Assimilation in American Life* by Milton M. Gordon. Copyright © in 1964 by Oxford University Press, Inc. Reprinted by permission.

assimilation mean that intimacy remains largely confined by ethclasses within the separate ethnic subsocieties of modern America.

In Gordon's view, assimilation has occurred in several melting pots, and race and religion now mark the boundaries within the modern ethnic mosaic. Groups have grown simultaneously larger, from nationality to religious groups, and more diverse, and they are now large, stratified subsocieties. Nevertheless, America has remained a pluralistic society. This is the essential point of ethnic pluralism. Pluralists reject the notion that assimilation is inevitable in modern society, that occupational diversification and residential dispersion of folk groups necessarily mean their disintegration. Bogardus, Etzioni, and Gordon all find cause and evidence for the folk community in modern society. The folk community has changed, however, and, according to Gordon, nationality groups have evolved into larger religious subsocieties. This thesis was stated earlier by Herberg in his critique of mass society theory.

Will Herberg

Will Herberg shares with Milton Gordon the belief that ethnic pluralism for white Americans has evolved from a network of separate nationality groups into a system of religious subsocieties and subcultures. People from diverse national origins have assimilated into one or another of the nation's major religious groups: Protestants, Catholics, and Jews. The reasons this evolution has stopped short of full assimilation include certain individual needs and a societal tolerance for religious but not national diversity:

. . . not only was the immigrant expected to retain his old religion, as he was not expected to retain his old language or nationality, but such was the shape of America that it was largely in and through his religion that he—or rather his children and grandchildren—found an identifiable place in American life. (Herberg, 1955:40)

Americans have had an enduring need to have a particular niche in their society, to be a member of a specific group within the larger American society. Since the larger society has tolerated religious diversity but not variance in nationality and language, the identity needs of millions of Americans have been displaced from nationality to religious groups. America has not become a mass society, Herberg argued, but instead has evolved into a state of religious pluralism.

The American identity crisis began for European immigrants with their uprooting in the Old World and transplantation in the New World. This is largely true for African, Asian, and Latin immigrants as well. Handlin (1973:97) described the feelings of European immigrants this way: "Loneliness, separation from the community of the village, and despair at the insignificance of their own human abilities, these were the elements that, in America, colored the peasants' view of their world." These immigrants felt as if they were cogs in a great machine over which they had little control; they were alienated from American society.

So the immigrants turned to each other for help: "the newcomers took pains early to seek out those whom experience made their brothers; and to organize each others' support, they created a variety of formal and informal institutions" (Handlin, 1973:152). Whenever possible, the immigrants organized with others from the same village or region of the old country. Vecoli (1970) writes that there once were 20 Little Italies in Chicago alone. Wirth (1928) reported that the Jewish ghetto in Chicago was nothing so much as several European villages and religious communities. These immigrant enclaves represented impersonal adaptation to a new environment, to be sure, but they were also expressions of peoples' need to relax and celebrate with their own kind.

Language and national culture shaped the immigrant groups' evolution into its next stage. Immigrants from different regions of a single country in Europe found in America that they shared a common language and a national identity associated with that language. Other Americans cared little about the regional distinctions among Italians, for instance, and regarded them all simply as Italians. Did they not all speak Italian? The same was true for many other immigrant groups. The general trend of evolution was that immigrants from distinct districts, prefectures, or regions became larger nationality groups in America.

This transformation was more or less completed by the second generation: "The sons of immigrants had no memory of Old Country places, no recollection of the village solidarity" (Handlin, 1973:173). What the second generation remembered were their experiences in America: "By actual membership in the group and by participation in its activities, they knew they were Irish or German or Italian or Polish" (Handlin, 1973:173). They also knew they were Protestant, Catholic, or Jew. Religion had survived the transfer from the Old World, and religion was passed by the first generation to the second, and later it would be passed by the second generation to the third.

Many of the second generation were hyphenated Americans, still a particular kind of American. This generation had a double consciousness, not unlike that observed of black Americans. Some members of the second generation identified with the ethnic nationalism of their immigrant fathers, while others thought of themselves as strictly American. But most were in the middle, both ethnic and American. They had been reared in two worlds, one foreign and one American, and for many this experience resulted in what social commentators of the day called the second-generation phenomenon. At the same time, Herberg (1964) notes, "The various activities of the ethnic group began to shrivel and disappear; the ethnic group itself, in its older form at least, became less and less intelligible and relevant to American reality. It was the end of an era" (p. 100).

Herberg goes on to say, "If it was the end, it was also a beginning." By now the third generation had come of age. As to the spirit of this generation, Herberg refers to Hansen's famous dictum, "What the son [second generation] wishes to forget, the grandson [third generation] wishes to remember" (Herberg, 1955:43). Those of the third generation "have no reason to feel any inferiority when they look aound them. They are American born. Their speech is the same as those with whom they associate. Their material wealth is the average possession of the typical citizen" (Herberg, 1964:100).

Both the foreignness of their grandparents and the embarrassment it had caused their second-generation parents were largely irrelevant to the third generation. But this brought an identity crisis: What kind of Americans were the third generation to be?

The oldline ethnic group, with its foreign language and culture, was not for them; they were Americans. But the old family religion, the old ethnic religion, could serve where language and culture could not; the religion of the immigrants . . . was accorded a place in the American scheme of things that made it at once both genuinely American and a familiar principle of group identification. (Herberg, 1964:100–101)

Herberg cited Kennedy's studies of intermarriage in support of his thesis that by the third generation ethnic pluralism was transformed into religious pluralism. Kennedy (1952:56) summarized her studies in New Haven, Connecticut, as follows:

This report . . . shows that the "triple-melting-pot" type of assimilation is occurring through intermarriage, with Catholicism, Protestantism, and Judaism serving as the three fundamental bulwarks. Protestant British-Americans, Germans, and Scandinavians intermarry; Catholic Irish, Italians, and Poles form a separate intermarrying group; while Jews remain almost completely endogamous.

To the extent that intermarriage reflects structural pluralism in general, this evidence supports Herberg's contention that the pluralism of nationality groups has been transformed into that of religious groups.

Based on data also gathered in New Haven, Hollingshead (1950) drew conclusions on intermarriage consistent with those of Kennedy. These conclusions, in summary form, are:

They [racial mores] divided the community into two pools of marriage mates . . . . Religion divided the white race into three smaller pools. Persons in the Jewish pool in 97.1 per cent of the cases married within their own group; the percentage was 93.8 for Catholics and 74.4 for Protestants . . . . The ethnic origin of a person's family placed further restrictions on his marital choice. In addition, class position and education stratified the three religious pools into areas where an individual was most likely to find a mate. (p. 627)

However, Thomas (1951) contended that the findings of Kennedy and Hollingshead on intermarriage in New Haven are not necessarily indicative of marriage trends throughout the country. Examining mate selection among Catholics in various areas across the country, Thomas found that in the decade of 1940–50, one-third of the nuptials sanctioned by the Church were mixed marriages, unions between Catholics and non-Catholics. With respect to marriages which were not sanctioned by the Church but which involved Catholics, Thomas observed that nearly 40 percent of these marriages in the East and Midwest were mixed. On the basis of such evidence, Thomas argued that the triple-melting-pot hypothesis is untenable as it applies to Catholics.

Kennedy (1944:332) had projected that *"while strict endogamy is loosening, religious endogamy is persisting and the future cleavages will be along religious lines rather than nationality lines as in the past."* Contrary to this prediction, Thomas argued that intermarriages by Catholics will increase in the future. With the halt of European immigration, nationality groups are becoming less of a factor in reinforcing religious endogamy, and as the Church and family lose their control over mate selection, attitudes toward religious exogamy are becoming more tolerant. Moreover, mixed marriages have a cumulative effect, for offspring of mixed marriages are themselves more likely to intermarry.

The significance of rates of intermarriage for the issue of ethnic and religious pluralism in this country is not clear. Gordon (1964) noted that the conversion of one partner to the religion of the other is extensive in mixed marriages, and after such conversions couples might participate together in one of America's religious subsocieties. He questioned whether:

. . . interfaith marriage in American society today serves as an effective bridge between major religious groups or simply as a preliminary step to the entrance of the intermarried couple into the subsociety of one or the other faiths of the spouses. Current research on intermarriage in the United States tells us little or nothing about the answer to this query. (p. 216)

In response to Gordon's query, Greeley (1970) found in two recent surveys that in over 80 percent of the cases—Protestants—including Baptists, Lutherans, Methodists, and Presbyterians—were married to other persons of the same denomination. This religious homogeneity in marriage among Protestants was a product of their practice of marrying within their own denominations, as well as a significant amount of conversion after marriage. Similarly, at least 86 percent of the Catholics in the surveys were married to Catholics, and 94 percent of the Jews were married to Jews. On the part of Catholics and Jews, however, this homogeneity was largely the product only of people marrying within their own religion, in contrast to the more variable pattern among Protestants.

Gerhard Lenski, in *The Religious Factor* (1963), tested some additional hypotheses of Herberg's on ethnic and religious pluralism in the United States. Lenski read Herberg's thesis in this manner:

Herberg suggests . . . that the very impersonality of so much of modern life creates in individuals a need for communal relationships, broader than the family, but narrower than the total society. Earlier in American history ethnic groups served such a function . . . . Today such groups are rapidly disintegrating, but many of the needs they served continue to be felt. In this situation, Herberg argues, Americans are turning increasingly to their religious groups, especially the three major faiths, for the satisfaction of their need for communal identification and belongingness (Lenski, 1963:11).

Herberg objected to the mass society theory of modern urban life, which posited that religion in modernity would become exclusively association-al, a highly compartmentalized aspect of life, and limited to church or synagogue attendance. Herberg countered that religion continues to be communal, "a nucleus around which a variety of social relationships is organized, as in the typical agrarian community" (Lenski, 1963:11).

Lenski (1963) tested this hypothesis from data collected in the Detroit area, examining the strength of both communal and associational bonds within four socioreligious groups there: Jews, white Catholics, white Protestants, and Negro Protestants. Respondents were asked the religion of their spouses, that of other close relatives, and that of their close friends to ascertain the strength of communal bonds within socioreligious groups. It was reasoned that the stronger such bonds were, the more people's relationships would center around the nucleus of their socioreligious groups. All of the Jewish respondents reported being married to Jews, 96 percent reported that their close relatives were Jewish, and 77 percent reported that their close friends were all Jews. Jewish communal bonds were quite strong.

Among the Catholic resondents, 70 percent stated that they were married to Catholics and 79 percent said that their close relatives were Catholic, but only 44 percent reported that their close friends were exclusively Catholic. Of the white Protestants responding, 73 percent were married to Protestants and 76 percent had close relatives who were Protestants, but only 38 percent reported that all or nearly all of their close friends were Protestants. As for Negro Protestants, 98 percent reported being married to blacks and said that all their close relatives were black, and 90–95 percent reported that all their close friends were black. Thus, communal bonds within all four socioreligious groups were strong to moderate, with the exceptions of the friendship patterns of white Protestants and Catholics. Moreover, nearly two-thirds of the respondents reported that if they tried to join another faith, their relatives would be disturbed.

Associational bonds within all four socioreligious groups were generally weaker than were communal bonds. Only 12 percent of the Jewish respondents reported weekly attendance at synagogue or temple, while 30 percent of the white Protestants and 40 percent of the Negro Protestants reported weekly church attendance. However, 70 percent of the Catholic respondents reported weekly attendance at Mass. Except for Catholics, the associational bonds of these respondents were weak to moderate, while the communal bonds within the socioreligious groups were by comparison quite strong. While these findings are evidence for the continued existence of religious subsocieties, particularly in a communal sense, they have little bearing on the hypothesis that nationality has been transformed into religious identity.

Lenski reasoned that if people turn away from nationality and toward religion for identity satisfaction in the process of their Americanization, then church attendance should increase with each succeeding generation born in this country. Actually, this hypothesis is a modification of Herberg's original formulation, which posited a decline in church attendance with the second generation and a return to church by the third generation. However, Lenski found little support for this original hypothesis. An index of Americanization was constructed which included educational and occupational mobility, the tendency for wives to work, and the number of generations that a family had lived in the urban North. Americanization measured in this manner was associated with the strengthening of the associational and communal bonds of both Catholics and white Protestants. The associational bonds of Negro Protestants and white Jews were weakened in the process of Americanization, however, while their communal bonds were unaffected. Thus, Lenski concluded that, with some modifications, "our findings confirm Herberg's thesis that the Americanization process is linked with the recent strengthening of religious associations" (1963:44).

Abramson (1973) questioned the whole notion that nationality is necessarily transformed into religious pluralism. He noted important and persistent nationality differences in religious involvement over the generations. Both German and Polish Catholics became more involved in the Church in America over the decades, while Irish and French-Canadian Catholics became disengaged from the Church over time. Italian Catholics continued to be as indifferent as ever toward the Church. Thus, only the Germans and Poles conformed to the generational hypothesis. The Italians persisted in their historical indifference toward the Church, and as memories among the Irish and French-Canadians of their historical struggles with Anglo Protestants in their homelands faded, so did their religious involvement in America.

While Herberg believed that religion was replacing nationality as the crucible for identity and communal participation among white Americans, he granted that nationality may continue to be important in politics. Glazer and Moynihan studied intergroup politics in New York City, and indeed found the persistence of nationality in the city's politics.

Nathan Glazer and Daniel Moynihan

In the first edition (1963) of *Beyond the Melting Pot,* a classic study of the Italians, Irish, Jews, Blacks, and Puerto Ricans in New York City, Nathan Glazer and Daniel Patrick Moynihan wrote that "Religon and race define the next stage in the evolution of the American Peoples" (p. 315). This prediction is similar to those of Gordon and Herberg, although Glazer and Moynihan did hedge their bet, writing that the American nationality was still evolving and no final form was in sight. Nevertheless, from the evidence amassed in the early sixties, they concluded that the nation was evolving toward pluralism of race and religion.

In the second edition of the study, however, they wrote "Thus, religion as a major line of division in the city is for the moment in eclipse. Ethnicity and race dominate the city, more than ever seemed possible in 1963"

(1970:ix). They offered three hypotheses for the apparent resurgence of ethnicity during the 1960s.

First they proposed that occupational identity has lost "status and respect" and is currently being replaced by ethnicity in the service of self-identification. It is better to be known as Irish, for example, than as an assembly-line worker. To us all, being an ethnic is perhaps preferable to being a proletariat or bourgeoisie, a working stiff or a pencil pusher. Among blue- and white-collar workers alike, ethnicity may be replacing the job as a source of social identification. Is it not more pleasant to answer the question, "Who are you?" than "What is your career?"

Glazer and Moynihan proposed in a second hypothesis that "for the first time a wave of ethnic feeling in this country has been evoked not primarily by foreign affairs but by domestic developments" (1970: xxvi). Many of these "domestic developments" stem from the recent Civil Rights movement and have strengthened feelings of nationality while they have weakened religious identity, so that, for example, "the identity of Catholic is no longer self-evident, to those holding it or to those outside the church" (p. xxxvii). While the Catholic Church once helped implement the conservatism of the Italians and Irish in New York City, in its stands on Communism, parochial schools, and sex, for instance, many Italians and Irish late in the sixties felt deserted by the Catholic clergy over the issue of race relations. The eclipse of religion in this manner led Glazer and Moynihan to concede that "just as religion in the 1950s covered for ethnicity, ethnicity in the 1960s covers for racism" (1970: xxxviii).

The migration of Puerto Ricans and southern Blacks into New York City and the racial strife of the 1960s increased the saliency of race for city politics. Specifically, the liberal elite of Manhattan took political power from working-class Catholics and Jews in New York City and gave expression to Puerto Rican and black interests at the expense of those of the white ethnics:

The Protestants and better-off Jews determined that Negroes and Puerto Ricans were deserving and in need and, on those grounds, further determined that these needs would be met by concessions of various kinds from the Italians and the Irish . . . and the worse-off Jews. The Catholics resisted, and were promptly further judged to be opposed to helping the deserving and needy. On these grounds their traditional rights to govern in New York City *because they were so representative of just such groups* were taken from them and conferred on the two other players, who had commenced the game and had in the course of it demonstrated that those at the top of the social hierarchy are better able to empathize with those at the bottom. (Glazer and Moynihan, 1970:xiii)

With each election politics revived nationality in new York. Of course appeals to the ethnic vote were at times disguised expressions of the concerns of certain economic classes in the city, and paradoxically, ethnic

A company of Evzones, the elite of the Greek army, march down Fifth Avenue, New York City, in the Greek Independence Day parade. United Press International Photo.

appeals often allowed politicians to skirt fundamental, controversial issues.

It is not only in New York City that ethnicity plays a role in politics, for ethnicity has important political functions in many modern societies. In a more recent work, Glazer and Moynihan (1975:9) wrote:

The welfare state and the socialist state appear to be especially responsive to ethnic claims. This is everywhere to be encountered: an Indian minister assuring his parliament that "Muslims, Christians and other minorities" will receive their "due and proper share" of railroad jobs; a Czech government choosing a Slovak leader; a Chinese prime minister in Singapore choosing an Indian foreign minister, and so on.

However, the raison d'etre of ethnicity is not to be found merely in political appeals or in the decline of religious and occupational identity, for ethnic identity is far more basic:

Beyond the accidents of history, one suspects, is the reality that human groups endure, that they provide some satisfaction to their members and that the adoption of a totally new ethnic identity, by dropping whatever one is to become simply American, is inhibited by strong elements in the social structure of the United States. It is inhibited by a subtle system of identifying, which ranges from brutal discrimination and prejudice to merely naming. It is inhibited by the unavailability of a simply "American" identity. (Glazer and Moynihan, 1970: xxxiii)

The pluralist version of ethnic evolution in America is that, due to the occupational diversification of folk groups and the variety of experiences and opportunity modernization brings, ethnic groups have become more diverse, stratified into ethclasses, for example, and simultaneously have grown larger, into ethnoreligious groups, for example. The process stops short of full assimilation, however, as the folk group continues to play a role in the modern order, in politics and as a source of psychological identity and orientation. Novak (1977:8) wrote:

The new ethnicity does not entail: (a) speaking a foreign language; (b) living in a subculture; (c) living in a "tight-knit" ethnic neighborhood; (d) belonging to fraternal organizations; (e) responding to "ethnic" appeals; (f) exalting one's own nationality or culture, narrowly construed . . . . Rather, the new ethnicity entails: first, a growing sense of discomfort with the sense of identity one is supposed to have—universalist, "melted," "like everyone else"; then a growing appreciation for the potential wisdom of one's own gut reactions (especially on moral matters) and their historical roots; a growing self-confidence and social power; a sense of being discriminated against, condescended to, or carelessly misapprehended; a growing disaffection regarding those to whom one had always been taught to defer; and a sense of injustice regarding the response of liberal spokesmen to conflicts between various ethnic groups, especially between "legitimate" minorities and "illegitimate" ones.

RECENT DEVELOPMENTS IN PLURALISM: THE NEW ETHNICITY

In recent works on American pluralism, ethnicity is considered to be ultimately a psychological phenomenon which can be expressed in any identity display. Ethnic identity is commonly asked for and given in the course of social interaction, for it is helpful and sometimes critical that we know the ethnicity of another person in order to anticipate how that person will respond to us. It would be good to know if someone is a Polish American before starting into a series of Polish jokes. Barth (1969) suggested that when it facilitates interaction, ethnicity of the participants will be made evident, and it will be left latent when it hinders interaction. The implication is that ethnicity is a general state of consciousness, an identity which is not necessarily obvious but which can be voluntarily displayed in overt behavior in a variety of settings.

This conception of ethnicity, sometimes called the *new ethnicity,* has become popular among several anthropologists. In Bennett's (1975:3) words, this new ethnicity refers to "the proclivity of people to seize on traditional cultural symbols as a definition of their own identity—either to assert the Self over and above the impersonal State, or to obtain the resources one needs to survive and to consume." In the words of DeVos (1975:16), "ethnic identity of a group of people consists of their subjective symbolic or emblematic use of any aspect of culture, in order to differentiate themselves from other groups." Despres (1975:190-191) phrased it this way: "ethnic groups are formed to the extent that actors use ethnic identities to categorize themselves and others for purposes of interaction." The view that all these authors share is that ethnicity is an internal attitude which only predisposes, but does not make necessary, the display of ethnic identity in interaction.

Bennett (1975:4) wrote that the new ethnicity includes both an identity badge in "the search for the self and the definition of group boundaries" and a behavioral strategy "for acquiring the resources one needs to survive and to consume at the desired level." That is, ethnicity is revealed for both expressive and instrumental purposes. On the one hand, it is the assertion of self in an otherwise impersonal world. This usage of ethnicity is akin to its role in resolving the American identity crisis, one referred to by both Herberg and Glazer and Moynihan. The larger proposition is that a folk identity is needed in a modern society. Ethnic identity can also be utilized in strategies to obtain scarce resources, as Glazer and Moynihan saw ethnicity being used in New York City politics. The ethnic quota system in employment and education is possibly the best contemporary example of ethnicity used in this manner. For whatever purpose it is used, ethnicity and ethnic boundaries in the present world of interethnic communication and contact are emergent in human interaction and can be displayed in a myriad of ways. Thus the expression of ethnicity is by no means limited to intergroup isolation and segregation, as the assimilationists have implied.

Some sociologists agree that ethnicity is more than segregation and that the latter is as much an ecological adaptation as it is an expression of ethnicity. Summarizing this position, Yancey, Ericksen, and Juliani (1976) observed that as much as ethnicity itself, it was the concentration of immigrant workers around huge, centralized factories, in the absence of rapid local transportation, that had formed the ghettos of southern and eastern Europeans in the nation's cities. With the decentralization of work and with the availability of the automobile, such residential concentration is no longer necessary. Today, poverty and racism keep more blacks in ghettos than black consciousness of kind does. Of course, ghettos help preserve ethnicity in its traditional forms, but ethnicity can certainly persist outside ghettos and evolve into new forms and expressions.

These formulations of the new ethnicity owe a debt to the earlier work of Barth (1969). Barth observed that in the social sciences ethnicity usage made reference to both biological and cultural criteria. But cultural patterns and breeding pools are as much a product of ecological adaptation as they are indications of ethnicity, Barth argued. Moreover, reliance on such measures of ethnicity loses sight of intergroup relations; all over the world today ethnic groups are in sustained and systematic contact. However, ethnic boundaries persist even in a world of intergroup contact and communication, as the dichotomization of outsiders and insiders continues in the course of sustained intergroup contact. Thus the proper study of ethnicity is the study of ethnic boundaries, how they emerge and are maintained and manipulated in daily encounters. This is the methodological focus of the new ethnicity school.

In no manner do these authors imply that ethnic boundaries are evident in all daily encounters. Many types of social intercourse have little, if any, bearing on ethnic identity. In other types of encounters, however, ethnicity is used in either an expressive or an instrumental way. Vander Zanden wrote in 1973 that this situational variance in the expression of ethnicity could be an exciting new direction in the study of American ethnicity. As an indication of that promise, he cited research on African workers who kept their tribal identities latent while at work, but whose personal lives were still organized around tribal affiliations. Minard (1952) studied black and white coal miners in America some years ago and found the same pattern of intergroup cooperation at work and racial separation at home.

As to the reasons for the persistence of ethnicity in the modern world, those beyond self-expression and resource acquisition, DeVos (1975:17) speculates that ethnic identity is "a feeling of continuity with the past, a feeling that is maintained as an essential part of one's self-definition." In addition, "ethnicity in its deepest psychological level is a sense of survival." It is "a sense of personal survival in the historical continuity of the group." In a word, ethnic identity can impart both history and future.

CONCLUSION

The pluralists and assimilationists have both analyzed ethnic evolution in America but have come to different conclusions about it. Assimilationists predicted that modernization would eventually bring the eclipse of ethnicity and the establishment of a unitary society. Given their tendency to equate ethnicity in general with segregation and occupational concentration of ethnic groups in particular, the assimilationists' predictions seemed to be supported by the residential dispersion and occupational diversification of America's white ethnic groups in the 20th century. Only Americans of color remained segregated and were denied full access to the evolving opportunity structure of American society, according to the assimilationists, and only racial assimilation is still seen by them as being problematical.

Pluralists agree that the distinctiveness of ethnic subcultures has diminished with the geographical dispersion and occupational diversification of America's white ethnic groups, and that there has been a gravitation toward Anglo conformity. They insist, however, that structural pluralism persists to this day, for some white ethnic groups and racial minorities alike. In terms of Park's race relations cycle, pluralists contend that ethnic evolution has proceeded to accommodation for many groups, but not beyond it.

Some ethnic groups have been integrated into the institutions of the larger American society, in politics, education, and the economy. However, this structural assimilation is largely confined to people's public lives, or secondary relationships, while their private lives and primary relationships are still infused with ethnicity. Ethnic pluralism for some groups has evolved from residential and occupational separation to ethnically unrestricted participation in public life. However, in their private affairs, at the emotional center of life, people still maintain their ethnicity. This is part of the pluralist version of ethnic evolution in America.

Ethnicity is and always has been ultimately a psychological phenomenon, an attitude and part of a person's subjective consciousness of kind. It is not necessarily manifest in any restriction on social interaction, what one can do with whom. This position represents the new ethnicity school, one that was pioneered in the work of Barth. In the modern world of extensive intergroup contact and communication, ethnic boundaries are often psychological and voluntarily implemented, either as expressions of self or as behavioral strategies. Nevertheless, ethnicity is as real in the modern world as it ever was in the past. Ethnicity has not been muted in modern America as much as its expressions have become more and more diverse and less and less exclusive. The evolution of ethnicity is not necessarily linear, moreover; in the future, it might evolve backward toward forms which do exclude outsiders. Ethnic evolution is indeterminate, contingent on human consciousness, dependent on people's needs as they perceive them, and fully subordinate to human purpose.

While social scientists agree that the pluralist position is an improvement on the early assimilationist view that ethnic evolution is unilinear and inevitable, not all are happy with where the pluralists have brought us. Some object to equating ethnicity with a subjective consciousness of kind (cf. Despres, 1975). Even though these critics have no better alternative, as Despres observes, they still have a sound point. The validity of their criticism does not rest, however, on the common observation that ethnic boundaries as psychological phenomena are so fluid as to be meaningless. LeVine and Campbell (1972) observed that ethnic boundaries of all sorts have been fluid throughout human history and are no more permeable today than they ever were in the past. Nor is the validity of their criticism found in the objection of these critics to ethnicity being made an internal attitude. The study of attitudes, including the reduction to attitudes of complex social phenomena, has been common in American social sciences, ever since the demise of instinct theory (cf. Allport, 1968). Rather, the validity of their criticism lies in the observation that when pluralists argue that ethnicity persists because of an American identity crisis, a crisis which seems to continue indefinitely with no end in sight, they appear to grant an inevitable, perpetual existence to ethnicity in the manner that assimilationists have made its demise inevitable.

In their attempts to explain the persistence of ethnicity in America, pluralists have made repeated recourse to an American identity crisis. However, this concept has never been defined and measured with any precision and remains a vague and even mystical notion. Even if we agree with the pluralists and assume that Americans do face an identity crisis, we could argue that the resolution of such a crisis can come in forms other than ethnic identity. There are functional alternatives to ethnicity in resolving the American quest for a sense of home, as the recent adoption by thousands of Americans of religions rooted in the East suggests. In any case, recourse to notions such as an American identity crisis, sense of continuity with a historical peoplehood, and a sense of history provides only vague and weak explanations for the endurance of ethnicity.

In our view, ethnicity is both objective and subjective, sociocentric and egocentric, and its expression is contingent on the nature of society in which ethnic relations are implicated. According to Yancey et al.

(1976:392), ethnicity is contingent in significant ways on a set of interrelated societal conditions:

... ethnicity, defined in terms of frequent patterns of association and identification with common origins ... is crystallized under conditions which reinforce the maintenance of kinship and friendship networks. These are common occupational positions, residential stability and concentration, and dependence on common institutions and services. These conditions are directly dependent on the ecological structure of cities, which is in turn affected by the processes of industrialization.

Yancey et al. are correct that, as an objective and sociocentric phenomenon, ethnicity is reinforced through systematic isolation of ethnic groups and historically occurred in the United States in residential segregation and occupational stratification. Isolation allows for the emergence and persistence of distinct subcultures. In the course of the modernization of American society, conditions have changed, however, and the isolation of ethnic groups from each other and from the larger society has certainly declined. Nevertheless, ethnicity as a psychological phenomenon can exist and be expressed in the course of frequent intergroup contact and communication in the modern era.

As long as ethnicity either facilitates self-expression or can be used in the competition for scarce resources, it will endure. Thus, Glazer and Moynihan (1970) believe that ethnicity was revived in the 1960s due to the ethnic realities of American politics at the time. Subjective ethnic identities were rekindled and evolved in many instances into the objective forms of political interest groups. Here in the United States and elsewhere in the world, ethnicity has become a legitimate and effacious way to make resource claims in the modern state. So long as it plays a role in resource competition in American society, ethnicity as a subjective consciousness of kind will endure here. And it is always possible that ethnicity will again take more objective and social forms, particularly that of the political interest group.

REFERENCES

Abramson, Harold J.
1973 Ethnic Diversity in Catholic America. New York: John Wiley and Sons, Inc.
Allport, Gordon W.
1968 "The Historical Background of Modern Social Psychology." Pp. 1–80 in Gardner Lindzey and Elliot Aranson (eds.), The Handbook of Social Psychology. Reading, Massachusetts: Addison-Wesley Publishing Company, Inc.
Banton, Michael
1967 Race Relations. New York: Basic Books, Inc., Publishers.
Barth, Fredrik (ed.)
1969 Ethnic Groups and Boundaries: The Social Organization of Culture Difference. London: George Allen & Unwin.

Bennett, John W. (ed.)
  1975 The New Ethnicity: Perspectives from Ethnology. St. Paul, Minnesota: West Publishing Company.
Bogardus, Emory S.
  1928 Immigration and Race Attitudes. Boston, Massachusetts: D.C. Heath and Company.
  1930 "A Race-Relations Cycle." American Journal of Sociology 35 (January):612–617.
Brown, W.O.
  1934 "Culture Contact and Race Conflict." Pp. 34–47 in Edward B. Reuter (ed.), Race and Culture Contacts. New York: McGraw-Hill Publishing Company.
Despres, Leo A.
  1975 "Toward a Theory of Ethnic Phenomena." Pp. 187–207 in Leo A. Despres (ed.), Ethnicity and Resource Competition in Plural Societies. The Hague: Mouton Publishers.
DeVos, George
  1975 "Ethnic Pluralism: Conflict and Accommodation." Pp. 5–41 in George DeVos and Lola Romanucci-Ross (eds.), Ethnic Identity: Cultural Continuities and Change. Palo Alto, California: Mayfield Publishing Company.
Driedger, Leo, and Glenn Church
  1974 "Residential Segregation and Institutional Completeness: A Comparison of Ethnic Minorities." Canadian Review of Sociology and Anthropology 2 (February):30–52.
Etzioni, Amitai
  1959 "The Ghetto—A Re-Evaluation." Social Forces 37(March):255–262.
Gans, Herbert J.
  1951 "Park Forest: Birth of a Jewish Community." Commentary 21(April):330–339.
Glazer, Nathan
  1971 "Blacks and Ethnic Groups: The Difference and the Political Difference It Makes." Social Problems 18 (Spring): 444–461
Glazer, Nathan, and Daniel P. Moynihan
  [1963] Beyond the Melting Pot: The Negroes, Puerto Ricans, Jews, Italians, and Irish of
  1970 New York City. Cambridge, Massachusetts: The M.I.T. Press.
  1975 "Introduction." Pp. 1–26 in Nathan Glazer and Daniel P. Moynihan (eds.), Ethnicity: Theory and Experience, Cambridge, Massachusetts: Harvard University Press.
Gordon, Milton
  1964 Assimilation in American Life. New York: Oxford University Press.
Greeley, Andrew
  1970 "Religious Intermarriage in a Denominational Society." American Journal of Sociology 75(May):949–952.
Guest, Avery M., and James A. Weed
  1976 "Ethnic Residential Segregation: Patterns of Change." American Journal of Sociology 81(March):1088-1111.
Handlin, Oscar
  1973 The Uprooted. Second Edition. Boston: Little, Brown, and Company.
Herberg, Will
  1955 Protestant-Catholic-Jew. Garden City, New York: Doubleday and Company, Inc.
  1964 "The Triple Melting Pot in the Third Generation: From Ethnic to Religious Diversity." Pp. 99–104 in Richard L. Simpson and Ida Harper Simpson (eds.), Social Organization and Behavior. New York: John Wiley & Sons, Inc.
Hollingshead, August B.
  1950 "Cultural Factors in the Selection of Marriage Mates." American Sociological Review 15(October):619–677.
Kennedy, Ruby Jo Reeves
  1944 "Single or Triple Melting Pot? Intermarriage Trends in New Haven, 1870–1940." American Journal of Sociology 49(January):331–339.
  1952 "Single or Triple Melting Pot? Intermarriage in New Haven, 1870–1950." American Journal of Sociology 58(July):56-59.

Kitano, Harry H. L.
  1969 Japanese American: The Evolution of a Subculture. Englewood Cliffs, New Jersey: Prentice-Hall, Inc.
Lenski, Gerhard
  1963 The Religious Factor: A Sociologist's Inquiry. Garden City, New York: Doubleday and Company, Inc.
LeVine, Robert A., and Donald T. Campbell
  1972 Ethnocentrism: Theories of Conflict, Ethnic Attitudes and Group Behavior. New York: John Wiley and Sons, Inc.
Minard, Ralph D.
  1952 "Race Relationships in the Pocahontas Coal Fields." Journal of Social Issues 8(1):29–44.
Novak, Michael
  1971 The Rise of the Unmeltable Ethnics (copyright © 1971, 1972 by Michael Novak. Originally appeared in Harper's Magazine.) Reprinted by permission of the publisher, Macmillan Publishing Co., Inc.
  1977 Further Reflections on Ethnicity. Middletown, Pennsylvania: Jednota Press.
Rosenthal, Erich
  1960 "Acculturation without Assimilation? The Jewish Community of Chicago, Illinois." American Journal of Sociology 66(November):275–288.
Simpson, George Eaton, and J. Milton Yinger
  1972 Racial and Cultural Minorities: An Analysis of Prejudice and Discrimination. Fourth Edition. New York: Harper and Row, Publishers.
Suttles, Gerald S.
  1968 The Social Order of the Slum: Ethnicity and Territory in the Inner City. Chicago: University of Chicago Press.
Thomas, John L.
  1951 "The Factor of Religion in the Selection of Marriage Mates." American Sociological Review 16(August):487–491.
Vander Zanden, James W.
  1972 American Minority Relations. Third Edition. New York: Ronald Press Company.
  1973 "Sociological Studies of Black Americans." Sociological Quarterly 14(Winter):32-52.
Vecoli, Rudolph J.
  1970 "Contadini in Chicago: A Critique of the Uprooted." Pp. 216–228 in Leonard Dinnerstein and Frederic Cople Jaher (eds.), The Aliens: A History of Ethnic Minorities in America. New York: Appleton-Century-Crofts.
Warner, W. Lloyd, and Leo Srole
  1945 The Social Systems of American Ethnic Groups. New Haven, Connecticut: Yale University Press.
Wirth, Louis
  [1928] The Ghetto. Chicago: University of Chicago Press.
  1956
Yancey, William L., Eugene P. Ericksen, and Richard N. Juliani
  1976 "Emergent Ethnicity: A Review and Reformulation." American Sociological Review 41(June): 391–402.

CHAPTER 4

Ethnic Conflict Theory

INTRODUCTION

Ethnic conflict theory, assimilationism, and pluralism constitute the three major themes in the sociological lore on American ethnicity. Through eduction and orientation, this lore provides a perspective on the folk group in modern society and the evolution of ethnic and racial groups in the course of societal modernization.

According to assimilationists, the forces of modernity inevitably lead to the demise of folk groups and their assimilation into a mass society. Only the assimilation of certain racial minorities was ever considered to be a possible exception to this principle. Pluralists argue, however, that while the folk group changes in the course of societal modernization, it nonetheless endures. One reason for the endurance of ethnic groups is intergroup competition in modern society. This observation introduces the theme of conflict theory. From the perspective of ethnic conflict theory, competition and conflict among ethnic groups increase in the process of societal modernization, thus creating the conditions for ethnic struggle and exploitation rather than assimilation. The issues of competition, power, and inequality are brought into the analysis of American ethnicity with the addition of conflict theory.

The format of this chapter is similar to that of the others. Key terms and major assumptions of ethnic conflict theory are first presented, followed by a discussion of historical and current expressions of this theory. The chapter concludes with an assessment of this perspective on American ethnicity.

KEY TERMS

Ethnic Competition

Ethnic competition refers to the mutually opposed efforts of ethnic (or racial) groups to secure the same scarce objectives. This concept of intergroup competition is consistent with uses of the term by other sociologists. For instance, Newman (1973:112) stated, "The term 'competition' refers to any situation in which social groups evidence mutually opposed attempts to acquire the same social resources or reach the same goals." Groups can compete for both material and symbolic resources, for jobs, property, and wealth as well as for honor and status. Broom and Selznick (1963:33) observed that competition is not necessarily recognized by the parties involved: "When groups become aware that they are in competition they are called rivals." Intergroup competition and rivalry are basic to intergroup conflict.

Ethnic Conflict

"Social conflict may be defined as a form of group relationship (or interaction) involving a struggle over the rewards or resources of a society or over social values, in which the conflicting parties attempt to neutralize or injure each other" (Newman, 1973:110). In other words, *ethnic conflict is a form of intergroup rivalry during which groups try to injure each other in some way.* Intergroup conflict between white settlers and American Indians, between native whites and Asian immigrants, and between blacks and whites are some instances in American history.

Ethnic Stratification

Ethnic stratification refers to a form of intergroup relations in which powerful ethnic groups limit the access of subordinate groups to societal resources, including wealth, power, and prestige. Stratification is a particular instance of intergroup accommodation in which some racial groups dominate others. Intergroup conflict often brings ethnic stratification, as conflicting parties attempt to undermine each other's competitive positions. Examples of ethnic stratification in American history include the isolation of American Indians on reservations and the racial caste system of the agrarian South.

Ethnic Evolution

Ethnicity is an evolving or emergent phenomenon, and groups, their relations with one another and with the larger society, change in the course of ethnic evolution. Intergroup competition and conflict comprise one dimension of ethnic evolution—the one emphasized in this chapter.

ASSUMPTIONS OF ETHNIC CONFLICT THEORY

1. *Intergroup competiton and conflict are basic to the modernization of American society.*

2. *In the course of conflict, groups try to impair their rivals, and this often results in systems of stratification.*

3. *Systems of ethnic stratification also are subject to change in the course of ongoing intergroup competition for societal resources.*

The assumptions of ethnic conflict theory follow from those of a larger conflict analysis of modern industrial society, a theory which characterizes modern society as an arena for the struggle among its subgroups (Dahrendorf, 1959; Horton, 1966; Lenski, 1966). Strife and struggle are inevitable in the evolution toward industrial modernity, in this version of social evolution, which maintains that as the occupational structure grows broader, as opportunity expands, folk groups will compete with each other for wealth, power, and privilege. Indeed, from the perspective of conflict theory, all history is a process of struggle, oppression, and more struggle.

HISTORICAL CONFLICT THEORY

Some current sociologists have complained that American sociology has been preoccupied with assimilationist themes in its study of ethnicity (Metzger, 1971; Wilson, 1973). L. Paul Metzger comments that while conflict and pluralist alternatives to the assimilationist perspective can be found in the social sciences, assimilationism "continues to hold sway as a kind of official orthodoxy within the sociological establishment" (1971:638). He faults this orthodoxy and cites as an indication of its inadequacy the fact that social scientists were as much surprised by the racial unrest of the 1960s as was everyone else. Specifically, Metzger maintains that implicit liberal ideological assumptions involved in the study of American race relations had left social scientists shortsighted and unable to foresee the recent racial conflict. The liberal tenet making for this myopia, Metzger says, is the belief that America has been undergoing orderly change toward racial assimilation, and the resolution of the racial problem simply followed from the course on which American society was already set.

By this reading of the history and future of race relations, all stages of the race relations cycle prior to assimilation are to be seen as only transitional, and assimilation is seen as sure to come with the increasing emphasis upon rational, impersonal, universalistic (and therefore, by leap of faith, humane) relationships between the races which is engendered in an increasingly modern society. Thus, whatever racism remained in the urban North and West of America was seen in the liberal vision as merely vestigial and sure to wane with further modernization.

Metzger (1971:638) believes that this myopia might be corrected by an analysis "in the Marxian tradition" which cites the determinants of racism "in the economic institutions and the struggle for power and privilege in society." Unlike the liberal tradition in sociology, the Marxian perspective is capable of predicting the continuation of racism, mounting black discontent, and racial conflict in modern America, according to Metzger.

Marxism

Is it entirely true, however, that an analysis of ethnicity in the Marxian tradition would remedy the myopia Metzger observed in assimilationism? In our view, Marxism prefigures assimilationism as much as it does ethnic conflict theory. Did not Marx predict the eclipse of ethnicity in the evolution of capitalism? People, it was said, would become increasingly class conscious and would assimilate into one of two economic classes in preparation for the ultimate class struggle. Any remnant of ethnic consciousness in modernity was dismissed by Marx as an instance of false consciousness, and out of keeping with the realities of his scientific socialism.

Other conflict theorists of the past century shared with Marx the conviction of the inevitable disintegration of ethnicity in the modern industrial state. For instance, Gumplowicz (1899:119) observed that while industrial classes in the modern state have their origins in the historical contact between primitive hordes, and "no state has arisen without original ethnical heterogeneity," ethnic conflict is transformed into economic class conflict in the modern state. Powerful racial and ethnic groups force weaker ones into compulsory labor, thus changing the character of the conflict to a struggle between economic classes. The powerful class, to regulate class conflict in its own favor, establishes state sovereignty and thus attempts to perpetuate through political authority the economic inequality it has forced on others. Through their control of the state, the powerful protect their property and enforce their exploitation of others' labor. In the larger sense, property rights and all forms of contractual relationships replace the folk bonds of blood and place in the evolving nature of group conflict in the industrial West.

On the other hand, the tradition of conflict theory certainly does alert the contemporary sociologist to the possibility of intergroup conflict in modern society. Does not this tradition locate the dynamics of social evolution in the struggle for wealth, power, and privilege? If we do not confine our anticipation of conflict to that between economic classes—between the bourgeoisie and the proletariat, in particular—should we not expect that in modernity racial and ethnic groups, too, will struggle for wealth, power, and privilege?

An expansion of the term *folk* is required in the translation of orthodox Marxism into ethnic conflict theory. This means we must entertain the possibility that ethnic groups, not only economic classes, will struggle for wealth, power, and privilege in modern American society. However, we find little evidence in Marxist circles for this expansion. For instance, Cruse (1967) lamented the apparent inability of black Marxists in 20th-century America to incorporate black nationalism into their reading of the role of blacks in modern America:

> Negro Communists had the elements within their reach for creating an independent black radical program for the true benefit of the black masses, but were led astray because their eyes were on what Moscow was saying and their minds, subordinate to white Marxist leadership and thinking, were not attuned to what Negroes needed in America. (p. 137)

About this same time, Robert Park was writing that when the race relations cycle was completed, the social arena would be cleared of racial impediments to the inevitable class struggle (cf. Lyman, 1972).

Social Darwinism

Charles Darwin wrote in 1859 that the natural force behind organic evolution is the lethal struggle among the species for survival, and the naturally fittest survive in this struggle. This epochal work was entitled *On the Origin of Species by Means of Natural Selection; or, The Preservation of Favored Races in the Struggle for Life.* The Social Darwinists argued by analogy that social evolution is located in the struggle for survival between racial and nationality groups, and in the course of this struggle the more powerful groups naturally come to dominate the weaker races (racial stratification). Racial conflict and domination were simply seen as part of the larger natural order, impervious to human intervention. Racial and ethnic traits were also considered to be naturally determined and fixed, which rendered some races more fit than others to rule. This ideology helped justify some racial realities in America, including Jim Crow treatment in the South, the conquest of American Indians, the nation's experiment with imperialism in the late 1800s, and the restriction of immigration from Asia and southern and eastern Europe in the 20th century (cf. Banton, 1967; Handlin, 1957; Hofstadter, 1944). The representatives of Social Darwinism include Walter Bagehot's *Physics and Politics* (1869/1948), Benjamin Kidd's *Social Evolution* (1894/1921), G. V. de Lapouge's *Les Sélections Sociales* (1896), H. S. Chamberlain's *Foundations of the Nineteenth Century* (1911), Madison Grant's *The Passing of a Great Race*

(1916), and Lothrop Stoddard's *The Revolt Against Civilization* (1922), among others.

However, as Hofstadter (1944) observed, it is easy to exaggerate the significance for race theory of Darwin's work. Arthur de Gobineau published *The Inequality of Human Races* (1915) originally in 1854, five years prior to the publication of Darwin's theory on natural selection. Still, the authority of Darwin's work did stimulate the tendency to explain racial inequality as an inevitable product of natural selection. In the end, however, Social Darwinism and other variants of this position faded from the American scene. Social Darwinism lost its popularity among the American public after World War I, according to Hofstadter (1944), for in the public mind it had been associated with German militarism. According to Oberschall (1972), public opinion also turned against the business trusts and monopolies, arrangements that the Social Darwinists had supported. In the social sciences, arguments for hereditarily fixed racial traits were supplanted by notions that human nature was environmentally conditioned and always alterable. The emerging social psychology of 20th-century America preferred to see mankind as a bundle of propensities, triggered by the social environment, rather than a fixed product of biology.

These changes in theory were part of a larger process in the social sciences. From 1890 to 1920 American sociology was undergoing professionalization, searching for its proper role in the American university. Sociologists had to convince others that theirs was an independent academic discipline, with its own content, assumptions, and methods, and not a mere derivation of the more established discipline of biology. This required sociologists to relinquish the naturalism of biology, and it necessitated an end to the organic analogy in the science of society:

After 1906, as the seventeen sociologists [fathers of sociology] discussed the boundaries of their new discipline, there were the unmistakable signs that some of them were beginning to recognize the contradiction between insisting that sociology was an autonomous science with its own order of phenomena to account for and their continued reliance upon natualistic analogies. . . . (Cravens, 1971:13)

At the same time sociology allied with the Progressive movement, and particularly with the social reformers of the era (Oberschall, 1972). The naturalism of Social Darwinism and its laissez-faire approach to social problems were obviously not in the game plan of the social reformers.

By the time Park formulated his now-famous race relations cycle, only remnants of Social Darwinism are left in the sociological study of race. In Park's work, for instance, one finds the concepts of competition and conflict, reflecting the influence of Darwin on Park. There is also the undercurrent of naturalism and inevitability in his cycle, a laissez–faire approach, by implication, to racial problems. The race relations cycle proceeds to assimilation due to human sympathy and intimacy, however, which are strictly non-Darwinian notions. Moreover, scholars who followed Park moved even further away from Darwinism.

Social Darwinism was not to be a vehicle for bringing ethnic conflict theory into 20th-century American sociology. It was inconsistent with the temper of the era, which favored a conception of mankind conditioned by the social environment and not a man as a fixed and inevitable product of natural causes. So Metzger's (1971) survey of the social scientific literature on American race relations found little in the way of a conflict alternative to assimilation.[1]

ETHNIC CONFLICT THEORY

Social Evolution and Ethnic Conflict

The social envolutionists contended that all forms of ethnicity would fade away with industrialization, urbanization, and the spread of education and literacy—specifically, with the rationalization of the human condition. Rationality would replace sentimentality in the modern order, in which ethnicity as a form of folk sentimentality has no function. This was the thesis of assimilationism. Metzger (1971:635) noted that

. . . the belief that racism is incompatible with the major features of modern social organization has roots which go far deeper than Myrdal's liberal optimism. . . . It is, in fact, rooted in what is perhaps the major theme of modern sociological theory—the shift, in Cooley's terms, from "primary" to "secondary" relations as the basis of social order.

Pluralists disagreed with assimilationists on the basic point and argued that folk sentimentality is not fully displaced by rationality in modern society. Conflict theorists also disagree with assimilationists on this point, contending that modernization brings increased intergroup struggle and strife, continually reviving ethnic boundaries and consciousness and making them current.

Ethnic competition and conflict replace the paternalistic relations of traditional society in the course of societal modernization, according to Van den Berghe (1967). Traditional society was pastoral, had little manufacturing, was based on a simple division of labor, and was characterized by extreme ethnic stratification and rigid racial caste systems. Social mobility for subordinate groups was virtually impossible in

---

[1]While assimilationism was orthodoxy in the sociological establishment, there were some conflict alternatives to assimilationism, a point Metzger readily conceded. These theories will be presented in this chapter.

traditional society. With industrial capitalism, a complex division of labor, and the greater opportunity for social mobility for all groups, ethnic relations become competitive. This brings a response of greater ethnic prejudice and aggression. As people from different racial and ethnic groups compete openly in modern society, intergroup hostility is exacerbated, while segregation averts constant conflict.

William Newman (1973:115) has hypothesized that "The degree to which different social groups view each other as competitive threats, and therefore the frequency of social conflict between them, is directly proportional to the degree to which competition and achievement are prescribed norms in society." To the extent that achievement and competition characterize modern society more than traditional society, Newman's hypothesis is consistent with Van den Berghe's (1967) proposition that social evolution brings competitive race relations, not assimilation. Newman amplifies this with the idea that normative emphasis on success and social mobility predisposes members of different groups to view one another as competitive threats, and this increases the chances for intergroup conflict. Intergroup conflict may be expressed through conventional channels for grievances, or it may transcend these channels. The former is called *consensus-bound conflict,* and the latter is termed *consensus-projecting conflict.* Legal tactics exemplify consensus-bound conflict, while attacks on property and people illustrate the latter.

The greater the disparity in wealth between two groups, the more likely is the deprived group to engage in consensus-projecting conflict, according to Newman. A deprived group usually does not have ready access to societal channels for the legitimate expression of grievances, and even if such access were available, because of its historical deprivation it is likely to reject societal norms, including those over the channeling of grievances. By the same token, material parity among a nation's racial and ethnic groups will shape intergroup conflict into consensus-bound expressions of conflict, and conflict will validate the basic norms and institutions of that nation. Moreover, groups are less likely to go to extremes in such cases, for they are unwilling to destroy the society in which they all benefit to some degree.

In summary, Newman's argument is that societies with "a competitive ethos, regardless of the source of that ethos, will exhibit more frequent social conflicts than societies that exhibit a paternalistic ethos" (1973:138). The implication is that intergroup conflict characterizes modern society more than traditional society. Originating in societal values of competition and achievement, conflict in modern society is structured by the comparative wealth among groups. The greater is the disparity of wealth, the more likely is it that conflict will be an all-or-nothing affair.

Oppression often results from strife and struggle, in the view of conflict theory. Competition for wealth, power, and privilege results in oppression when a powerful group comes to dominate a weaker one. This is ethnic stratification, a form of intergroup accommodation in which powerful groups limit the access of weaker groups to societal resources. However, ethnic evolution continues, and systems of ethnic stratification too can change as wealth, power, and privilege are won and lost.

Emergence of Ethnic Stratification

Social stratification begins with competition for wealth and privilege, and it results directly from the power of one party to dominate others in the course of their competition. Ethnic stratification is a particular instance of social stratification, one that specifically involves the domination of one ethnic group by another. Along with their competition for wealth and the comparative power of ethnic groups, a third element in the formation of ethnical stratification, called *ethnocentrism,* is thought to be important by some sociologists (e.g., Barth and Noel, 1972; Blalock, 1967; Kinlock, 1974; Noel, 1968; Vander Zanden, 1972; Wilson, 1973). In the words of Barth and Noel (1972: 345), "we suggest that ethnocentrism, competition, and relative power of the groups involved constitute a set of variables which are necessary and sufficient to explain the emergences of ethnic stratification."

Social stratification is a system for the distribution of goods and services, or wealth, according to Lenski (1966). People will share wealth in accordance with human needs at the subsistence level, but once a surplus of wealth is produced (that beyond the subsistence level), there will be competition for the control of this surplus. To the extent that surplus wealth is far greater in modern than in traditional society, this implies intergroup competition is greater in modern society. Power rather than human need will determine the distribution of wealth in modern society. The expansion of opportunity that comes with societal modernization means more competition among ethnic groups, and the power of some groups over others, as applied through discrimination, means that they will diverge. Powerful groups modernize while the weaker ones do not, at least not to the same extent and at the same rate.

While power originates with and is ultimately based on force, the control of subordinates through coercion is so costly to a dominant group that it attempts to transform force into political authority, or legitimate rule. Gumplowicz (1899:121) found that the transformation of power gained by force into political and legal rights is the foundation of the modern nation-state: "The hostile contact of different social elements of unlike strength is the first condition for the creation of rights; the conditions established by force and accepted in weakness, if continued peacefully, become rightful."

When successful at legitimizing its power into political authority, a dominant group enjoys not only power and the privileges associated with power; it also has the pleasure of prestige, or the deference of those deprived of power and privilege. Nevertheless, authority may be lost for one reason or another, and as its authority wanes a dominant group will typically turn to force again in order to maintain its position. This further erodes its authority. Thus power evolves and forms political cycles: force, its legitimization and institutionalization into political authority, and the return to force (Lenski, 1966).

The power of a group is based on its numbers, its control of other power resources, and its capacity to mobilize these resources (Blalock, 1967). The size of a group relative to that of other groups is the best measure of its numerical strength. The larger the comparative size of an ethnic group, the greater is its comparative power, if all other things are equal. The issue of additional power resources is complex (cf. Blalock, 1967). At the risk of oversimplifying, it can be said that a group can exercise power through force or through political authority. It follows that power is based on control of the military, of violence in general, or of the channels of legitimate political rule. There is a common denominator to which both force and political authority reduce, however, and that is control over the means of production, or a group's possession of surplus wealth. If all other things are equal, the greater the surplus wealth of a group, the greater is that group's power. This principle has been demonstrated again and again in the course of American history. The conquest of the American Indians and the subordination of black labor by white landowners in the South are two illustrations which come immediately to mind.

The power resources of a group must be mobilized for it to dominate others effectively in a system of racial stratification. Mobilization of power depends on the generality and liquidity of a group's power resources. Wilson (1973:17) argued that "the greater the generality of the resources a group controls, the greater is the scope of the group's power ability; the larger the number of resources a group has at its disposal, the more alternative means it has to reach its goal." In other words, the greater is the generality of a group's power, the greater is the range of power application and the stronger is the group's dominance.

The liquidity of power resources is "the extent to which they can be deployed or mobilized to exert influence. Some resources can be deployed easily and quickly because the mechanisms that facilitate their mobilization or application exist" (Wilson, 1973:17). A good illustration of the principles of generality and liquidity of a group's power resources is found in frontier contact between settlers and American Indians. White settlers possessed surplus wealth, a monetary economy that made the

Plantation owner, near Clarksdale, Mississippi, 1936. A good illustration of ethnic stratification. Lange; Library of Congress.

surplus a general and liquid power resource, and a centralized political authority in the federal government, all of which facilitated the mobilization and deployment of their power in the conquest of American Indians.

Nearly all conflict theorists hold to the conviction that intergroup competition and comparative power are elements in the rise of racial stratification, but the role of ethnocentrism in racial stratification is a matter of some disagreement. Ethnocentrism refers to the tendency of members of a racial or ethnic group to consider their own physical appearance and way of life as superior and most honorable, while their respect for the styles of others is a function of how closely those styles approximate their own. Ethnocentrism ultimately involves the issue of honor. Some theorists feel that honor is as important in ethnic stratification as are intergroup competition and comparative power. Often one group will subordinate another because of its abhorrence for the culture or race of that group, and not merely for its economic advantage. Those in the Marxian tradition oppose this view and consider ethnocentrism merely incidental to the economic determinants of ethnic stratification. They feel that ethnocentrism or racism is nothing more than a ruse for the more fundamental reality of the exploitation of labor by capital.

THE MARXIST TRADITION Oliver Cromwell Cox is one exponent of the Marxian tradition. In his classic study of race relations in the South *(Caste, Class and Race,* 1948), he wrote that "The fact of crucial significance is that racial exploitation is merely one aspect of the problem of the proletarianization of labor, regardless of the color of the laborer" (1948:333). Marx had observed that there are those who labor, and there are those who live off the labor of others. Cox saw the essence of southern race relations as white capital living off black labor. Of course, Cox was critical of the assimilationist school, and particularly the caste hypothesis of Warner and his associates (see Chapter 2). He read in this school the tendency to locate racial exploitation in the folk customs of the South, while, in his mind, racial exploitation was rooted in economic incentives:

Sometimes, probably because of its very obviousness, it is not realized that the slave trade was simply a way of recruiting labor for the purpose of exploiting the great natural resources of America. This trade did not develop because Indians and Negroes were red and black, or because their cranial capacity averaged a certain number of cubic centimeters; but simply because they were the best workers to be found for the heavy labor in the mines and plantations. . . . (Cox, 1948:332)

Not custom but coercion, particularly the threat of violence, has historically kept blacks in their place in the South. The shootings, whippings, and lynchings of blacks made evident the extralegal status of black people, and because they were outside the protection of the law, blacks had to turn to their white bosses for personal protection. This further guaranteed for white capital the dependability and tractability of cheap black labor. White capital did use political authority, too, in its domination of black labor, as Key (1949) noted, but violence or force was used to buttress the legal subordination of blacks.

Cox conceded that there is one slight difference between race relations and the history of class struggle: "Although both race relations and the struggle of the white proletariat with the bourgeoisie are parts of a single social phenomenon . . . . in race relations the tendency of the bourgeoisie is to proletarianize a whole people" (1948:344). Nevertheless, he says that racism is merely a "socio-attitudinal facilitation" of the capitalist exploitation of black labor. Racism was first made possible when the capitalist class defeated the moral authority of the Roman Catholic Church and was later reinforced by the rise of Social Darwinism, or scientific racism.

In suggesting correctives for race relations in the South, Cox again demonstrated his belief that racial exploitation is essentially the capitalist exploitation of labor: "As a matter of fact, the struggle has never been between all black and all white people—it is a political class struggle" (1948:573). As to the leadership in this struggle, Cox comments: "these leaders [blacks] cannot give Negroes a 'fighting' cause. None can be a Moses, George Washington, or Toussaint L'Ouverture; he cannot even be a Mohandas Gandi—*a Lenin will to be a white man*" (p. 572; italics added).

V. O. Key (1949) shared many of the same assumptions about race relations in his impressive study of southern politics. Key, too, cast race relations into an elite-mass conflict formula, one that specifically included an elite of white landowners and the mass of black and white labor in the South. Key set the study of race relations in southern politics and thereby turned attention to the control of black labor through the manipulation of political authority. He argued that the disfranchisement of blacks followed from the need of elite whites (capital) to undermine a two-party political system in the South, and particularly the Populist alliance between black and white labor. This is a historical instance of capital playing off one group of labor against another.

White capital from the South's black-belt counties had thwarted a two-party system in the South by the 1890s, according to Key. They established a single-party system instead, one that they dominated. A two-party system would have been fatal to the interests of white landowners in the black-belt counties, for it might have led to their losing political and economic control of those counties. If there had been a two-party system in the South, the Populist alliance between black and white labor might have assumed political leadership over much of the region and thus over its black-belt counties. Of course, this would have meant the end of the exploitation of cheap black labor by landowners in those counties. But that did not happen, and as blacks were disfranchised, the yeoman whites of the South were politically manipulated. They were bribed when necessary, but the political instrument of racism often kept this class of propertyless whites in line with the class interests of the elite and aligned against their own class interests. Thus capital dominated the proletariat of both races by playing workers of one race off against those of another. Ethnocentrism (racism) was a tool of capital to perpetuate its exploitation of labor. Other writers also attest to the role of racism in uniting different classes of whites in the post-Reconstruction South (Woodward, 1955/1974).

However, it was not only the planters from the black-belt counties who used this formula. Key observed that once the Populists had gained control of the Democratic party in both Georgia and South Carolina, they too disfranchised the black vote. They needed to prevent any alliance between blacks and their white political opponents. Indeed, "The progressives had special reason for disfranchising Negroes; The Bourbon element usually had the longer purse to meet the cost of the purchasable vote" (Key, 1949:550).

In *Black Awakening in Capitalist America* (1970), Robert Allen wrote that economic incentives have always been at the root of racial colonialism (ethnic stratification) in America. First there was the exploitation of black labor in agriculture and domestic service, and with the diminishing need for unskilled black labor, exploitation has evolved into abuse of the black consumer. Allen called this more recent instance of black exploitation neocolonialism. To appeal to and exploit the black consumer, white corporate power has a need for the cooperation of the black middle class; they need black faces in advertising and in finance offices, for instance. White capital had always needed the cooperation of black intermediaries to exploit black labor fully, but the softer sell required in the milking of the black consumer necessitates more than ever the cooperation of the black middle class.

White corporate power must pension off the black masses through income maintenance programs, as it simultaneously co-opts the black middle class. The former can be accomplished with little cost to white corporate power, since most of the financial support for such programs comes from the taxpayers. As Allen read it, the ultimate result of this strategy is the enlargement and intensification of the class divisions within the black community. Black solidarity will disintegrate in the process, and any black challenge to white corporate power will be arrested by dividing blacks in this manner. William Wilson (1978) notes that the government, through affirmative action programs, has also played a role, one equal to the private sector, in creating a gap between privileged and poor blacks.

THE WEBERIAN TRADITION Other theorists argue that ethnic group competition and the rise of ethnic stratification cannot be reduced to class conflict and economic exploitation. These writers share the view of Max Weber that social stratification is multidimensional and not reducible to the single dimension of economic class. Weber observed that all social institutions are not economically determined, even in a capitalist society. Weber distinguished three separate dimensions of social stratification: class, status, and power. Economic classes are located in the distribution of wealth in a society, status groups are identified with the distribution of honor, and political parties are situated in the distribution of power.

Members of different economic classes have different life chances, including unequal amounts of wealth, and encounter disparities in material living conditions and life experiences. Political parties, on the other hand, are rationally organized efforts toward the attainment and maintenance of social power. They are implicated in political decision making, whatever the issue. While political parties may advance the interests of an economic class or of a status group, this is not necessarily the case, and a party may operate with the intention of simply expanding or maintaining its power. Status groups are theoretically distinct from both political parties and economic classes and are situated in the distribution of honor. Honor ultimately follows from the monopolization of fashion and rests on the preservation of social distance between the honorable and those who are disreputable, pedestrian, and lacking in proper taste.

Intergroup conflict and racial stratification involve all three of these dimensions, some theorists argue. Ethnic groups struggle over the control of surplus wealth, and comparative power determines the outcome of this struggle, to be sure. But it is equally certain that ethnic struggle and stratification also involve the issue of honor. For instance, Noel's (1968) theory of ethnic stratification holds that "competition [for surplus wealth, we have argued] provides the motivation for stratification, ethnocentrism channels the competition along ethnic group lines, and relative power determines whether either group will be able to subordinate the other" (Barth and Noel, 1972:337).

In these expanded formulations, ethnocentrism is seen to play a role in the formation of racial stratification equal to those of intergroup competition and comparative power. For one thing, ethnocentrism facilitates the identification of rivals in intergroup competition for wealth. Those groups who stand in sharp contrast to one racial group in physical appearance and cultural style will be most likely identified as rivals by that group. Skin color and cultural style can become emblematic of intergroup rivalry. Moreover, systems of racial stratification not only serve in the protection of wealth and power, they also help a wealthy and powerful group in the conservation of its honor. In a system of ethnic stratification, subordinate groups are limited not only in their access to wealth and power but also in their access to the symbols of prestige and privilege. Intergroup conflict and racial stratification involve the issue of honor as much as they do the distribution of wealth and power.

The personal experiences of Malcolm X attest to the saliency of racial honor in America:

> Shorty soon decided that my hair was finally long enough to be conked . . . . "so you know it's going to burn . . . . it burns bad. But the longer you can stand it, the straighter the hair."
>
> He made me sit down, and he tied the string of my new rubber apron tightly around my neck, and combed up my bush of hair . . . . He also thickly vaselined my neck, ears and forehead. . . .
>
> My eyes watered, my nose was running. I couldn't stand it any longer; I bolted to the washbasin. I was cursing Shorty with every name I could think of. . . .
>
> My first view in the mirror blotted out the hurting. I'd seen some pretty good conks, but when it's the first time, on your own head, the transformation . . . . is staggering.
>
> The mirror reflected Shorty behind me. We both were grinning and sweating. And on top of my head was this thick, smooth sheen of shining red hair—real red—as straight as any white man's. (Malcolm X, 1966:52-54)

Later in his life Malcolm looks back at this experience:

> This was my first really big step toward self-degradation: when I endured all of that pain, literally burning my flesh to have it look like a white man's hair. I had joined that multitude of Negro men and women in America who are brainwashed into believing that the black people are "inferior"—and white people are "superior"—that they will violate and multilate their God-created bodies to try to look "pretty" by white standards. (p. 54)

Frantz Fanon wrote, in *The Wretched of the Earth* (1963), that racial violence is necessary for Africans in their revolt against white colonialism. Violence will cleanse their sense of racial inferiority, which was instilled in the minds of African natives by their colonial masters. The revolt against colonialism will be a racial struggle between black natives and white settlers, and one that will surge in accord with a racial rhythm, conducted by native leaders and not by a "white Lenin." Racial conflict is not some disguised form of class struggle, in Fanon's view.

In his book *Who Needs the Negro?* (1971), Sidney Wilhelm observed that racism existed before the rise of capitalism, exists today in noncapitalist society, and historically has brought racial subordination in whatever economic system it has occurred. As capital displaces labor in the

American economy, through the mechanization and automation of the production process, it is specifically the black worker who is displaced. White corporate power will promote the dismissal of blacks from any meaningful and secure place in American society, according to Wilhelm, and this process has already begun with the simultaneous mechanization of southern agriculture and northern industry. Much of black labor is obsolescent; now that the unskilled black worker is no longer needed, he will be dismissed from both American agriculture and industry. Wilhelm felt that white workers did not share in this plight, for it is racism that shapes the displacement of American workers, and the process might ultimately result in black extermination.

It is obvious that ethnocentrism has a role in intergroup conflict and stratification, and to argue otherwise is to overlook an important dimension of American ethnic and race relations. However, to argue that ethnocentrism will result in the extermination of black Americans is taking this thesis to its extreme. For instance, Edna Bonacich (1976) took exception with Wilhelm's thesis on the displacement of black workers. She argued that black unemployment since World War II can be explained without reference to racism. The high unemployment rates of blacks, especially young males, began around 1940, after the equalization of the wage rates of black and white workers in major industries. Without a reserve of cheap black labor, capital turned to other alternatives, including cheaper labor overseas and the automation of production here at home. Blacks in urban ghettos can still find work in sweatshops, but because of their political-class sophistication and the welfare alternative to such undesirable jobs, they do not take up such work:

The "displacement" phase was one in which blacks were desirable employees relative to whites but threatened the gains of the latter. Protective legislation equalized the two groups in terms of labor price but also drove up the price of labor, leading capital to seek cheaper alternatives. As a result, black labor has been bypassed for machines and other cheap labor groups, here and abroad, creating a class of hard-core unemployed in the ghettos. This reality took a while to emerge after the New Deal and only became full-blown in the mid-1950s when black unemployment reached its current two-to-one ratio. (Bonacich, 1976:49)

Displaced in this manner from mainline industrial jobs, unskilled blacks are unwilling today to work in marginal sweatshops, and in significant numbers they have turned to the alternative of welfare.

THE LABOR VS. LABOR CONFLICT FORMULA Several writers share the conviction that intergroup strife, struggle, and oppression involve the elite of one racial group and the masses of another. Even those who disagree on the role of ethnocentrism in ethnic conflict and stratification agree on this. It is the struggle between capital and labor that gives rise to ethnic stratification, reflecting the Marxian legacy in conflict theory. There are some conflict theorists, however, who locate the emergence of ethnic stratification in the struggle between *workers* from different racial groups, thus departing from the elite vs. the masses conflict formula.

In *The Economics of Discrimination* (1957/1971), Gary Becker argued that white capital in America realizes no economic gain from racial discrimination in workers' wage rates and is actually disadvantaged by such discrimination. When capital pays higher wage rates to white workers because of discrimination against the employment of blacks, it loses twice. First, it experiences artificially high labor costs and, consequently, decreased profits and a reduction in its investment capital. Thus, in theory, white capital has less opportunity to exploit black consumers, a second loss. Black labor is also obviously disadvantaged by discrimination in wage rates. The interests of white labor are, on the other hand, met by this sort of discrimination, and the interests of black capital are inadvertently served. Their competition with white capital is decreased in direct proportion to white capital's labor costs and inability to invest in the black community.

White capital might have a taste for ethnic discrimination, even though it is to its economic disadvantage. However, Becker believes that it has been the white trade unions which have discriminated against black workers, not capital, and for economic reasons. This has been particularly so in cases where black workers were direct substitutes for white labor and could displace them.

Bonacich recently argued that the dynamics of ethnic antagonism lie in the competition between workers of different ethnic groups. Ethnic antagonism "is intended to encompass all levels of intergroup conflict, including ideologies and beliefs . . . behaviors . . . and institutions . . . " (Bonacich, 1972:549). One institution of particular interest to Bonacich is the split-labor market, a special instance of ethnic stratification in the labor market.

There are three classes of people involved in the formation of a split-labor market: capital and labor from a powerful ethnic group, and labor from weaker ethnic groups. Not capital, but labor, from the dominant group has the incentive to exclude workers of weaker groups from the better jobs in the labor market. This can result in a labor caste system, or split-labor market, as was once found in the South (cf. Cox, 1948). It is assumed that the motive of capital is to employ the cheapest and most tractable labor group possible, regardless of race or ethnicity, and, as a rule, minority labor is the cheaper and more tractable alternative. Cheaper labor groups can be used by capital to break strikes organized by higher paid labor, for instance, and can otherwise be used to displace majority group labor, if capital is free to implement its interests.

If such displacement is not possible, capital can turn to automation as a strategy for replacing high-paid labor. Thus, capital cannot be held directly responsible for the formation of the split-labor market, for its class interests lie in the inclusion of the cheaper minority labor in the labor market. "This interpretation of caste contrasts with the Marxist argument that the capitalist class purposefully plays off one segment of the working class against the other . . . " (Bonacich, 1972:557).

It is because of its powerlessness that minority labor is often a cheaper and more docile alternative to labor from the majority group. Because of their poverty, their lack of both political and informational resources, and their sojourning motives in some cases, minority labor is frequently willing to work for less. Minority labor also wishes to avoid strikes, other sorts of labor disputes, and efforts at unionization, as was true for many immigrant groups into this country. Under these circumstances labor from majority and minority groups do not ally. Instead, there appears to be an alliance between minority labor and capital against labor from the dominant group, and the latter will attempt to meet the perceived threat of minority labor. If minority labor must be imported, domestic labor will attempt to restrict the entry of immigrant labor into the country; such immigration restrictions have been common in American history. If cheaper labor is indigenous or had immigrated prior to restrictive legislation, dominant labor will attempt to undermine it through a form of stratification called a split-labor market, whereby "The higher paid group controls certain jobs exclusively and gets paid at one scale of wages, while the cheaper group is restricted to another set of jobs and is paid at a lower scale" (Bonacich, 1972:555). Bonacich continues: "caste systems tend to become rigid . . . developing an elaborate battery of laws, customs and beliefs aimed to prevent undercutting." Cheaper labor groups are not only excluded from job apprenticeships, they are denied "access to general education, thereby making their training as quick replacements more difficult" (p. 556), and they are politically weakened as well. Thus, "the solution to the devastating potential of weak, cheap labor is, paradoxically, to weaken them further, until it is no longer in business' immediate interest to use them as replacements."

Racial and ethnic stratification in the labor market has been a recurrent phenomenon in American history, and many immigrant groups have shared in these experiences. Blacks were excluded from the textile mills in the post-Reconstructionist South and remained in agrarian labor pools under the white planters. In the past century, Chinese were forced out of mining and all sorts of desirable jobs on the West Coast, and later, in the 20th century, Japanese immigrants had some of the same experiences there. Mexican farm labor duplicated in the Southwest some of the dimensions of the black experience in the South. In the Northeast, Poles worked in factories under Irish foremen, who in turn worked under Anglo managers. It was the Irish who had been the common laborers in the 19th century, and so concentrated were they in unskilled labor that a joke of the era asked why the wheelbarrow was man's greatest invention, to which Americans answered, because it had taught the Irish to walk on their hind legs. Such has been the character of the ethnic and racial stratification of labor in this nation.

CHANGE IN ETHNIC STRATIFICATION

In conflict theory, modern society is characterized as undergoing constant change, and modern systems of ethnic stratification are no exception to this rule. So it is not the case that minority workers have had no recourse but to remain at the bottom of the nation's labor hierarchy, held there in perpetuity by either more powerful labor groups or capital. Mobility has always been possible. This experience has been shared by all immigrant groups. One means of escape was for a group to become a *middleman minority,* as the process (described below) is termed by sociologists. The experiences of Asian Americans on the West Coast demonstrate this instance of ethnic mobility. Another means of escape was for members of a minority group, as individuals, to find opportunity in very special areas of American society. The black athlete is an example.

Chinese and Japanese immigrants were once relegated to the bottom of the labor hierarchy on the West Coast, at the same time that further Asian immigration into the country was restricted. In the face of this exclusion, both groups evolved more or less into middleman minorities. Bonacich (1973) feels that this evolution of Asian immigrants was as much rooted in their motives for immigrating as it was in the fact that they faced discrimination in America. Asian immigrants were sojourners who were willing to work hard and suffer short-term deprivation in the United States, with the hope of accumulating savings here and then returning with these savings to their homelands. This resulted in antagonism toward them. Chinese and Japanese immigrants subsequently took up work in particular industries, retail sales and import-export businesses, for instance, and still put a premium on hard work and thrift. They concentrated on enterprises open to them which provided a portable livelihood or easily liquidated investments so that skills and savings acquired here could be transported home. Industrial concentration enhances in-group solidarity among the members of a middleman minority, since they are in similar trades and have little incentive for making more than superficial contact with outsiders. In a word, they do not assimilate. Their solidarity gives them a competitive edge over others in the host society by providing access to cheap and docile labor from within their own ranks, by facilitating the internal generation of capital, and by vertically integrating an entire industry, as occurred in the case of Japanese growers, wholesalers, and retailers of fruits and vegetables in Southern California before World War II (Bonacich, 1973:587).

A middleman minority may face hostility from several sectors of the larger society. This is the other side of the coin. Japanese shopkeepers on the West Coast were in conflict with certain interests of white customers, with white businessmen, and with organized labor. Their ability to use cheaper Japanese labor undercut both white business competitors and labor unions. As a consequence, all three groups—customers, capital, and labor—could unite against Japanese Americans during World War II on the issues of their clannishness and presumed disloyalty to the country. Mobility out of a caste-labor system and into a middleman minority enlarged the scope of the racial antagonism against Japaneses Americans.

The black athlete illustrates another method of escape from caste barriers. Only a small number of individuals rise from the bottom of the socioeconomic hierarchy in this manner. Of course, the black athlete is by no means a unique case; we still hear of one ethnic group or another dominating a certain sport.

Blalock (1967) analyzed the entry of blacks into professional and big-league baseball, as personified by Jackie Robinson's experience with the old Brooklyn Dodgers: "Once the racial barrier was broken when Jackie Robinson joined the Brooklyn Dodgers, there was an almost immediate rush to tap this reservoir of skilled manpower" (p. 94). Blalock argued that blacks entered professional sports and found equal opportunity there long before such a situation could even be imagined to exist in the general labor market.

There are several reasons minority members find opportunities first in sports. Dodger management had the power to prevent white athletes from maintaining racial barriers in professional baseball, once it decided to bring blacks into the sport. It could have discharged recalcitrant white players, replacing them from a large pool of talent, black and white. The size of this pool was partly due to the skills involved in baseball. While racial barriers prevented blacks from cultivating skills needed in other areas of the economy, the development of athletic skills was virtually unaffected by caste barriers. Black baseball talent had actually been husbanded in the Negro leagues. Moreover, families of aspiring athletes are not required to make large investments—money black families as a class did not have—in the sports training of their young, for much of these costs is covered in public services like recreational centers and sports programs in the schools, and there are also athletic scholarships. All of these factors make the training of an athlete different than that of a doctor or lawyer. Thus, sports has been a niche in the labor market which has been relatively open to talent from all backgrounds, and one in which ethnic and racial barriers have been difficult to maintain.

Asian businessmen and black athletes are just two instances of how caste barriers may be circumvented. In the abstract, too, a system of ethnic stratification itself may change, for reasons which follow from the formation of ethnic stratification. That is, as competition, comparative power, and ethnocentrism change, so does the larger system of ethnic stratification.

This does not imply that intergroup competition, comparative power, and ethnocentrism are necessarily the ultimate causes for the formation and change of ethnic stratification. While these factors do cause stratification, they are also parts of a much larger system, the total society in which both they and ethnic stratification exist. Social forces in the larger society can alter intergroup competition, comparative power, and ethnocentrism and thereby change a system of ethnic stratification. Some of these forces are technological innovations, demographic shifts, catastrophes, and value transformations (Shibutani and Kwan, 1965). To illustrate, American Indians experienced phenomenal rates of natural decrease after their contact with European settlers. This drastic demographic change helped alter the comparative power of American Indians and white settlers, which finally resulted in white dominance and the exclusion of Indians from their own land. It must be emphasized in this case and others that for technological developments, demographic shifts, catastrophes, value transformations, or any other factor in the larger society to alter a system of ethnic stratification, the changes must somehow affect intergroup competition, comparative power, and ethnocentrism.

Lenski (1966) argued that people are motivated to seek privilege ceaselessly as long as there is a surplus of wealth, and as a rule the powerful find it while the weaker do not. The struggle for privilege may be endless in the abstract, but a particular case of intergroup competition for surplus wealth can nevertheless terminate as long as two conditions are met. Intergroup competition can end with either assimilation or exclusion. Once a dominant group fully absorbs another, formerly subordinate group, stratification between these two groups is no longer possible. The struggle for privilege and stratification might well continue past assimilation, but the process can no longer involve these two as distinctive ethnic groups.

Intergroup competition can also terminate with exclusion. A subordinate group might break off contact with a dominant group by migrating elsewhere, as exemplified in America by the movement of indigenous peoples further into the interior in the hope of escaping European encroachment. Intergroup rivalry was only temporarily halted in this case, for it occurred again and again on the frontier as European settlement expanded. This is an example of voluntary exclusion, but exclusion can also be involuntary or forced. Involuntary exclusion can come in the form of forced migration or extermination. The latter took on horrendous proportions during World War II; the Nazis went so far as to engage in genocide and then plan a museum in Prague, Czechoslovakia, dedicated to an exterminated people, European Jews.

Furthermore, there have been occasions when ethnic groups have simply ceased to regard one another as competitors, at least for a time. Because of a catastrophe, for instance, competitive groups may fuse their efforts into a joint, cooperative endeavor for their mutual survival. Such cooperation often accompanies war, when groups forget their differences and unite in a larger national effort against an external enemy. Once the external threat disappears, however, there is often a return to intergroup competition.

Power allows one group to dominate another in a system of racial stratification, but power can be lost as well as won. For one thing, rulers of one group can lose their authority to govern other groups; even as I write, the authority of whites to rule over blacks is declining throughout southern Africa. This is an instance of what Shibutani and Kwan (1965) called a transformation of values. If a dominant group is to maintain control as it loses its authority, it must resort to the use of force. However, with the application of force the dominant group further erodes its claim to political authority and the legal right to rule.

Mastery over force comes ultimately from the monopolization of the means of production, or the control over land, labor, and capital in the creation of surplus wealth. A group must have a surplus above the level of subsistence to make war, and any loss of control over the means of production diminishes its military capacity. For instance, as American Indians lost more and more of their land, a loss which was not offset by gains in other power resources, their comparative power declined.

Power must be mobilized for a group to dominate others in a system of racial stratification. This mobilization depends in part on the generality and liquidity of a group's power resources, or the degree to which a group's wealth can be converted into political authority or raw force and focused on the maintenance of inequality. The values of members of majority and minority groups alike are an important dimension in this conversion of power into the continuation of inequality. Members of a powerful group must have a taste for maintaining their privilege at the expense of others, and members of subordinate groups must be willing to accommodate themselves to the lack of privilege. From time to time, these values are transformed, however, as significant numbers of a majority group forego their privileges and fight for the rights of minorities, while

National Guardsmen and state police collar looters in Newark, N.J. in 1967. United Press International Photo.

members of minority groups demand equity. We in the United States have recently witnessed such changes in race relations.

Ethnocentrism has also been subject to change throughout American history. As prejudice toward a group has waned, that group, more often than not, has found greater opportunity in the wider society. Lyman (1974) observed that as ethnocentrism toward Chinese Americans declined during World Ward II, they benefited from opportunities never before open to them in this country. The result was a drastic improvement in the position of Chinese Americans in the nation's system of ethnic stratification (see Chapter 9). Commentary not unlike this could be made about the nation's Irish and several other Roman Catholic nationality groups. So, with changes in ethnocentrism, comparative power, and intergroup competition, the relative positions of particular groups in a system of ethnic or racial stratification will change, although as a phenomenon ethnic stratification may persist in modern society.

THE FUNCTIONAL THEORY OF ETHNIC CONFLICT

Conflict theory often leaves the impression that intergroup competition and conflict are necessarily disruptive and disintegrative in a society. That is, conflict is something a society should avoid. Is it possible that this is only one side of the coin, and that conflict can and does play a positive role in modern society? The functional theory of conflict answers in the affirmative and proposes that intergroup conflict can unite groups in a society and will not necessarily drive them further apart. Conflict contributes to the maintenance of society, for as Georg Simmel (1908/1955) put it, "a certain amount of discord, inner divergence, and outer controversy is organically tied up with the very elements that ultimately hold the group together" (pp. 17–18).

Lewis Coser, in *The Functions of Social Conflict* (1956), elaborated on Simmel's functional theme of social conflict. Occasionally groups must search for a new relationship to replace their old one, as when an established system of ethnic stratification becomes dysfunctional. This search often requires a test of the relative strength of the parties, and the outcome of this test helps determine the nature of the new relationship. In the course of conflict, the ultimate values around which groups will forge a new relationship are revitalized.

Alliances are often created in conflict, and new forms of association emerge out of it. In-group solidarity is strengthened, in-group authority is centralized, and consciousness of kind is intensified in conflict with outsiders. This means that the internal structures of conflicting parties tend to be vitalized in the course of their conflict. Another positive function of conflict is that it can prevent the buildup of tension to the point where its release would virtually wreck a society. Occasional conflict is a safety valve of sorts, and this can actually maintain rather than change the status quo.

The functional theory of conflict applies primarily to realistic conflict. Realistic conflicts "arise from frustration of specific demands within the relationship and from estimates of gains of the participants, and which are directed at the presumed frustrating object" (Coser, 1956:49). By contrast, nonrealistic conflicts "are not occasioned by the rival ends of the antagonists, but by the need for tension release of at least one of them" (p. 49). Anti-Semitism is nonrealistic conflict, "insofar as it is primarily a response to frustrations in which the object appears suitable for a release of aggressiveness. Whether this object be Jews, Negroes or some other group is of secondary importance to the aggressor" (pp. 49–50). Realistic conflict, however, is occasioned by actual rivalry.

The importance of this distinction lies in the observation that realistic conflict can be replaced by other methods for achieving the desired end. It has "functional alternatives as to means" while nonrealistic conflict has only "functional alternatives as to objects" (Coser, 1956:50). Those who are pathologically hateful will always need someone or some group to hate. By contrast, realistic conflict can bring the reintegration of society, without the need for finding another scapegoat and alienating another segment of society.

Himes (1966) found recent racial strife in this country an instance of realistic conflict, one that has had essentially positive functions for the nation. The pattern of traditional race relations in the United States was anachronistic and needed reform. Through intergroup conflict, race relations were changed in the needed direction, toward racial equity and better interracial understanding. This understanding brought the realization by members of both races that they shared in certain basic values, according to Himes. The personal identification of blacks with American ideals was strengthened, as the sense of black alienation and cynicism was reduced, and so conflict paradoxically brought the unification of black and white Americans in a single moral community. The larger point is that intergroup conflict does not always result in renewed racial stratification; several outcomes, including assimilation, can follow from conflict. Of course, the condition of a group can actually worsen in the course of intergroup conflict.

CONCLUSION

Ethnic conflict theory accentuates the role of intergroup competition, conflict, and oppression in ethnic evolution. There is in modern society more intergroup competition for a growing surplus wealth, for new kinds of jobs, political power, property, and so on. Systems of ethnic stratification rise out of this struggle, endure for a time, but ultimately

Reporter talks to a badly wounded woman during riot in Newark, N.J. in 1967. United Press International Photo.

change. What remains are the ethnic groups, who continue to exist into the modern era. This is the conflict version of ethnic evolution in the course of societal modernization.

Ethnic conflict theory is part of a larger tradition that characterizes social evolution as a process of strife and struggle. It is class struggle that the Marxists stressed, and the translation of that legacy into ethnic conflict theory has been an underlying theme of the chapter. In the Marxian tradition, ethnic conflict and stratification are viewed as parts of the larger class struggle, in which ethnocentrism plays no more than a secondary role. Other theorists have contended, however, that ethnocentrism is as important in the emergence of ethnic stratification as are economic competition and comparative power. That is, honor is considered to be an additional, significant dimension of racial stratification and conflict. Another departure from the Marxian tradition is represented by those writers who believe that the dynamics of ethnic stratification lie in the competition between labor of different races, not between capital of one race and labor of another. Workers of powerful racial groups often become an artistocracy of labor and relegate others to the bottom of the labor hierarchy.

Ethnic conflict theorists are critical of both assimiliationism and pluralism, by implication. While pluralists see an accommodation among ethnic and racial groups in modern society, the conflict theorists see strife, struggle, and the oppression of the weak by the powerful. Rather than seeing assimilation at work in modern society, conflict theorists accentuate its absence, due to racial struggle and stratification. However, there is as much evidence for ethnic and racial assimilation in America as there is for intergroup conflict and oppression. In the abstract, conflict and consensus, unity and disunity, are inseparable parts of the larger process of ethnic evolution in modern society. These three theories—assimilationism, pluralism, and conflict theory—are complementary, each making up for some of what the others lack in a fuller understanding of American ethnicity.

REFERENCES

Allen, Robert L.
   1970 Black Awakening in Capitalist America. Garden City, New York: Doubleday and Company, Inc.
Bagehot, Walter
   [1869] Physics and Politics. New York: Alfred A. Knopf, Inc.
   1948
Banton, Michael
   1967 Race Relations. New York: Basic Books, Inc., Publishers.
Barth, Ernest A. T., and Donald L. Noel
   1972 "Conceptual Frameworks for the Analysis of Race Relations: An Evaluation." Social Forces 50 (March):333–348.

Becker, Gary S.
[1957] The Economics of Discrimination. Chicago: University of Chicago Press.
1971

Blalock, Hubert M.
1967 Toward a Theory of Minority-Group Relations. New York: John Wiley and Sons, Inc.

Bonacich, Edna
1972 "A Theory of Ethnic Antagonism: The Split-Labor Market." American Sociological Review 37(October):547–559.
1973 "A Theory of Middleman Minorities." American Sociological Review 38(October):583–594.
1976 "Advanced Capitalism and Black/White Relations in the United States: A Split-Labor Market Interpretation." American Sociological Review 41(February):34-51.

Broom, Leonard, and Philip Selznick
1963 Sociology. Third Edition. New York: Harper and Row, Publishers.

Chamberlain, H.S.
1911 Foundations of the Nineteenth Century. (Translated by John Lees.) London: John Lane.

Coser, Lewis
1956 The Functions of Social Conflict. Glencoe, Illinois: Free Press.

Cox, Oliver Cromwell
1948 Caste, Class, and Race. Garden City, New York: Doubleday and Company, Inc.

Cravens, Hamilton
1971 "The Abandonment of Evolutionary Social Theory in America: The Impact of Academic Professionalization upon American Sociological Theory, 1890–1920." American Studies 12(Fall):5–20.

Cruse, Harold
1967 The Crisis of the Negro Intellectual. New York: William Morrow and Company, Inc.

Dahrendorf, Ralph
1959 Class and Class Conflict in Industrial Society. Stanford, California: Stanford University Press.

Darwin, Charles Robert
1859 On the Origin of the Species by Means of Natural Selection. London: J. Murray.

Fanon, Frantz
1963 The Wretched of the Earth. New York: Grove Press, Inc.

Frazier, E. Franklin
1947 "Sociological Theory and Race Relations." American Sociological Review 12(June):265–271.

Grant, Madison
1916 The Passing of the Great Race. New York: C. Scribner's Sons.

Gobineau, Arthur de
[1854] The Inequality of Human Races. (Translated by Adrian Collins.) New York: G. P.
1915 Putnam.

Gumplowicz, Ludwig
1899 The Outlines of Sociology. (Translated by Frederick W. Moore.) Philadelphia: American Academy of Political and Social Science.

Handlin, Oscar
1957 Race and Nationality in American Life. Boston: Little, Brown and Company.

Himes, Joseph S.
1966 "The Functions of Racial Conflict." Social Forces 45(September):1–16.

Hofstadter, Richard
1944 Social Darwinism in American Thought, 1860–1915. Philadelphia: University of Pennsylvania Press.

Horton, John
1966 "Order and Conflict Theories of Social Problems as Competing Ideologies." American Journal of Sociology 71(May):701–713.

120 / *American Ethnicity*

Key, V. O., Jr.
1949 Southern Politics: In State and Nation. New York: Alfred A. Knopf, Inc.
Kidd, Benjamin
[1894] Social Evolution. New Edition Review, with addition. New York: G. P. Putnam's
1921 Sons.
Kinlock, Graham C.
1974 The Dynamics of Race Relations: A Sociological Analysis. New York: McGraw-Hill
Book Company.
Lapouge, Georges V. de
1896 Les Sélections Sociales. Paris: A. Fontemoing.
Lenski, Gerhard
1966 Power and Privilege: A Theory of Social Stratification. New York: McGraw-Hill
Book Company.
Lyman, Stanford M.
1972 The Black American in Sociological Thought. New York: Capricorn Books.
1974 Chinese Americans. New York: Random House.
Malcolm X with the assistance of Alex Haley
1964 The Autobiography of Malcolm X. New York, Grove Press, Inc.
Metzger, L. Paul
1971 "American Sociology and Black Assimilation: Conflicting Perspectives." American
Journal of Sociology 76(January):627–647.
Newman, William M.
1973 American Pluralism. New York: Harper and Row, Publishers.
Noel, Donald L.
1968 "A Theory of the Origin of Ethnic Stratification." Social Problems 16(Fall):157-172.
Oberschall, Anthony
1972 "The Institutionalization of American Sociology." Pp. 187–251 in Anthony
Oberschall (ed.), The Establishment of Empirical Sociology. New York: Harper
and Row, Publishers.
Shibutani, Tamotsu, and Kian M. Kwan
1965 Ethnic Stratification. New York: Macmillan Company.
Simmel, Georg
1955 Conflict: The Web of Group-Affiliation. (Translated by Kurt H. Wolff and
Reinhard Bendix.) Glencoe, Illinois: Free Press.
Stoddard, Lothrop
1922 The Revolt against Civilization. New York: Scribner's.
Van den Berghe, Pierre
1967 Race and Racism. New York: John Wiley and Sons, Inc.
Vander Zanden, James W.
1972 American Minority Relations. New York: Grove Press, Inc.
Wilhelm, Sidney
1971 Who Needs the Negro? Garden City, New York: Doubleday and Company, Inc.
Wilson, Wiliam J.
1973 Power, Racism and Privilege: Race Relations in Theoretical and Sociohistorical
Perspectives. New York: Macmillan Company.
1978 The Declining Significance of Race: Blacks and Changing American Institutions.
Chicago: University of Chicago Press.
Woodward, C. Vann
[1955] The Strange Cancer of Jim Crow. Third Revised Edition. New York: Oxford
1974 University Press.

CHAPTER 5

The Psychology of Prejudice and Discrimination

INTRODUCTION

Any sociological theory is only a partial explanation of social phenomena, and each theory provides no more than a particular and incomplete perspective on society and people. Thus looking at social phenomena from several theoretical perspectives can produce a more comprehensive view of humans in society. This is essentially the position taken in this book. In the study of American ethnicity, assimilationism, pluralism, and conflict theory are each partial explanations of ethnic evolution and societal change. Each explains only part of the total relationship between ethnicity and the modernization of American society. None of them should be mistaken for a complete and unobstructed view of ethnic evolution in modern America, but some of the obstructions can be overcome, by looking at ethnic evolution from the perspectives of all three theories. Assimilationism, pluralism, and conflict theory highlight different segments of the larger process of social change, and consideration of all three can provide a more comprehensive view of ethnic evolution and societal modernization. This is not to say that the total picture of ethnic evolution emerges as a consequence. All of sociology, taken together, provides only one of several possible perspectives on ethnic and race relations.

It has been the custom to complement the sociological study of race and ethnic relations with a psychological analysis of prejudice and discrimination (e.g., Kinlock, 1974; Newman, 1973; Simpson and Yinger, 1972; Vander Zanden, 1972). Psychological explanations of ethnic and racial prejudice have been popular in sociological writings on ethnicity, due in part to an effort to round out the sociological analysis of intergroup relations with reference to psychology. American psychologists have produced a voluminous literature over the years on prejudice and discrimination in this country. After World War II, as racial protest gained momentum, the issue of prejudice and discrimination became a prominent public concern, and psychologists became interested in racial attitudes. Interest in race relations among American psychologists was also stimulated by developments within psychology itself. A classic psychological study of racial and ethnic attitudes, *The Authoritarian Personality*, published in 1950, inspired the beginning of a continuing scholarly debate concerning the psychology of prejudice and discrimination. This work is reviewed at length below.

Ethnic and race relations are implicated in individual psychology as much as in the changing social order, and racial attitudes exist as much in the psychology of the individual as they do in the broader American society and culture. To depict this relationship, social scientists began to use sociological and psychological theory together in a broader analysis of race and ethnic relations. Each type of theory compensated for some of the deficiencies of the other. The implication is that somehow social and psychological theories on ethnicity are complementary, each set of theories making up for some of what the other lacks, and together they offer a more comprehensive view of ethnicity. Thus, while sociologists were wary of psychological reductionism, they were also aware of the need to supplement a sociological analysis of intergroup relations with a psychological analysis of prejudice and discrimination.

Psychology may serve in this manner to complement all three sociological perspectives on American ethnicity: assimilationism, pluralism, and conflict theory. Study of the psychological needs behind racial prejudice can complement conflict theory's emphasis on intergroup competition and conflict at the societal level. While intergroup competition can generate racial prejudice in individuals, prejudice on the part of individuals can also exacerbate racial competition and conflict among groups. The psychological analysis of prejudice can round out the sociological view that ethnic evolution is a process of strife and struggle.

Pluralism is based on the premise that a multitude of ethnic groups can cooperate in a single society, at least to the extent that it is necessary for their continued coexistence. The issue of bigotry is thus a central concern of pluralists, for unchecked racial hostility might divide a pluralistic society beyond repair. A study of the psychology of prejudice would serve this end and thus would complement pluralism.

It is assimilationism that psychological theories of prejudice and discrimination may complement the most, however. Much of the popularity of the various psychological theories of prejudice and discrimination over the past few years derives in large measure from the fact that assimilationism has been the orthodox social theory of American ethnicity. Assimilationists found no structural reason for ethnicity in modern America, since ethnicity from the folk past was assumed to be disappearing in the process of societal modernization. This left a vacuum in sociology which a psychological explanation of racial prejudice in the modern era could fill.

Key terms and basic assumptions of the psychology of prejudice and discrimination will be presented, followed by a discussion of the major perspectives in psychology on prejudice and discrimination. The position of ethnic conflict theorists on the psychology of prejudice will also be discussed. Research on the exact relationship between prejudice and discrimination will be reviewed. The chapter ends with an assessment of this approach to American ethnicity.

KEY TERMS

Prejudice

Mack (1968:144) observed that in popular usage, prejudice has come to mean "negative attitudes about the out-group." According to Allport (1954:9), "ethnic prejudice is an antipathy based upon a faulty and inflexible generalization. . . . It may be directed toward a group as a whole, or toward an individual because he is a member of that group." In the words of Simpson and Yinger (1972:24), prejudice is defined "as an emotional, rigid attitude . . . toward a group of people." There are many more definitions of prejudice, but these examples should give a taste for the variety of ways that prejudice has been defined.

In all these definitions there is a common understanding about what prejudice is and what it is not. Prejudice is not overt behavior; it is always an *attitude*, an internal state, or a set of beliefs and feelings about some ethnic or racial group. Prejudice may predispose the individual to act in a prescribed way toward a certain ethnic group, because prejudiced people often act in a discriminatory manner, but prejudice is by definition an attitude, not an act. However, not every attitude can be considered a prejudice, for prejudice is a particular kind of attitude, one about ethnic and racial groups.

Prejudice is a set of rather rigid beliefs, often involving stereotypes and relatively strong emotions, typically negative, about a perceived group of people, which predisposes one to act in a certain way toward that group. There are three dimensions to this definition: Prejudice involves cognition, emotion, and a predisposition to act in a prescribed way, all of which is consistent with past usage (cf. Harding et al., 1969).

While the thinking that goes into prejudice may be simple or complex, it is the simplicity and rigidity of prejudicial beliefs that are most often stressed. Beliefs about ethnic and racial groups often take the form of stereotypes, which are mental pictures we all carry in our heads, simple and unsophisticated pictures about one and a thousand things. Ethnic and racial stereotypes in particular are simple generalizations about intricate variation within any racial or ethnic group. Walter Lippmann (1922:16) wrote that our life space contains "so much subtlety, so much variety, so many permutations and combinations . . . we have to reconstruct it on a simpler model before we can manage with it." For instance, a homeowner, in tending to his lawn, identifies for his convenience an almost endless variety of plants into weeds and grasses. We do this with people, too; we reconstruct human variation into simple, often rigid, and rather homogenous categories, as with racial and ethnic stereotypes. These stereotypes abound in America; who has not heard jokes about "dumb Polacks and Bohunks," "emotional" Italians, "lazy" blacks, and "greedy" Jews? The point is that stereotypes hardly allow for the realistic individual variation that occurs within ethnic and racial groups, and thus prejudices may be considered "faulty and inflexible generalization."

The emotional or affective component of prejudice refers to the fact that prejudice involves feelings or sentiments, usually negative and intense, toward an ethnic or racial group. Prejudice is not commonly considered a neutral attitude; rather, its meaning is reserved for intensely held and strongly felt sentiments about an out-group. Most often, feelings about the out-group are negative, while those about one's own group are positive. This reflects the debt that current conceptions of prejudice owe to William Graham Sumner's writing on ethnocentrism (cf. LeVine and Campbell, 1972).

The exact relationship between the emotional and cognitive compo-nents of prejudice is a subject of debate. Those in the psychoanalytic tradition tend to feel that prejudicial beliefs follow from prior feelings, specifically, from internal psychic conflict, and act much like rationaliza-tions. Cognitive theorists contend that beliefs *precede* feelings about ethnic groups, although it is acknowledged in both perspectives that beliefs and sentiments, once formed into prejudice, tend to interact and reinforce one another.

Prejudice toward certain racial and ethnic groups is thought to predispose one to discriminate against them. This is known as the *conative* component of prejudice. All attitudes imply a readiness based on beliefs and sentiments to act in a prescribed way. Prejudice implies a readiness based on beliefs and sentiments about some group to discriminate against that group. However, the exact correspondence between prejudice and discrimination, between all attitudes and overt behavior, is a matter of debate. Some students of the subject have found essentially no relationship between prejudice and discrimination, at least not an obvious one, while others argue that prejudice clearly predisposes one to discriminate. This debate will be surveyed later in the chapter, under the heading of the relationship between prejudice and discrimination.

Prejudice has been judged by psychologists and social scientists to be a corruption of rationality, justice, and human-heartedness (Harding et al., 1969). When it is assumed that modern man is rational, that he seeks accurate, correct, and complete information about himself and others, the simplicity and slantedness of prejudice is then considered a failure in rationality. This is akin to what Allport meant when he termed prejudice a "faulty and inflexible generalization." The assimilationists in sociology assumed that modern society is also a rational enterprise, and modern American society had been readied for complete intergroup assimilation. This meant the extinction of all forms of ethnocentrism, particularly, by implication, prejudice. The problem was that prejudice persisted in American society. By attributing prejudice to a failure in the psychology of individuals, to a flaw in their inherent rationality, the assimilationists could escape from the embarrassment of being wrong about ethnicity and the modernization process in society.

The idea that prejudice is a failure of justice and human-heartedness is clearly expressed in Myrdal's *American Dilemma* (1944). Prejudice was believed to be inconsistent with American ideals for justice and fair play, with the very process of societal modernization. The idea that prejudice is located in the hearts of white Americans, in their individual psyches, made the psychology of prejudice and discrimination a welcome complement to sociological assimilationism.

Discrimination

Definitions of discrimination also abound in the social scientific literature. After surveying several attempts at defining the term, Simpson and Yinger (1972:28) turned to a definition by Antonovsky (1960): "Discrimination may be defined as the effective injurious treatment of people on grounds rationally irrelevant to the situation." In a similar vein, Newman (1973:199) wrote, "discrimination may be defined as an act of differential treatment toward a group or an individual perceived as a member of a group. Moreover, the intent and/or effect of differential treatment is to create a disadvantage of some sort." Kitano (1974:66) believed that discrimination is "a barrier to prevent minority groups from equal participation in the society."

There is clearly a common theme to these various definitions of discrimination. All agree that discrimination is an act of some sort; it is overt behavior, while prejudice is an attitude and only a predisposition to action. Furthermore, discrimination is directed toward a group of people, particularly racial and ethnic groups, even though a single individual may be the object of discrimination. The individual is discriminated against because of a perceived group membership. Typically, the intent behind discrimination is to keep members of a group in their "place," usually to enforce their exclusion from full and unlimited participation in the larger society. Discrimination results in intergroup exclusion, in other words. This means that *discrimination is action which somehow limits a group's access to opportunities in the larger society, so that members of the group share only exclusively in the larger society and culture, and are likely to evolve on a course divergent from that of the larger society.* Discrimination can occur with respect to employment, adequate housing, and all sorts of public services, including education.

Most would agree that discrimination is a persistent phenomenon in American history, and it certainly has become an important concern in the study of American ethnic and race relations. Nevertheless, discrimination is hard to discern case by case. Some of the conditions specified in various definitions of discrimination are difficult to ascertain in practice. For instance, how are we to be certain that there was malicious intent behind an apparent act of discrimination? Moreover, what does the condition "on grounds rationally irrelevant to the situation" mean in actual life? Because a man or woman is denied a job on the basis of race, does this mean that such grounds were rationally irrelevant? To illustrate, if a Jew is not given a job as a loan officer for a finance company in a black ghetto because of suspected customer antipathy toward Jewish businessmen, is this rational grounds or not? Although in practice the courts appear to be the final arbitrators, who is to be the judge of whether an action is rationally relevant to the situation? The point of this chapter, however, is not the complications in proving discrimination; rather its purpose is to survey those psychological and social psychological theories that view American ethnicity from the "prejudice-discrimination axis," as Blumer (1958b: 420) phrased this outlook:

It rests on the belief that the nature of the relations between racial groups results from the feelings and attitudes which these groups have toward each other. . . . It follows that in order to comprehend and solve problems of race relations it is necessary to study and ascertain the nature of prejudice.

ASSUMPTIONS OF THE PSYCHOLOGY OF PREJUDICE

1. *Intergroup relations can be understood in the terms of the psychology of individuals.*

2. *The reasons given for prejudice vary by psychological theory, but all agree that individual prejudice rather than the nature of modern society is the cause of discrimination.*

PSYCHOLOGICAL THEORIES OF PREJUDICE

There are three major traditions within American psychology, and each gives its own set of reasons for prejudice. These are the psychoanalytic, cognitive, and psychological behaviorist traditions. What these theories share is the conviction that the prejudice of individuals causes intergroup discrimination in society, and the idea that prejudice comes from internal psychological processes as they affect beliefs and feelings about ethnic and racial groups. The internal psychological processes that underlie prejudice is the issue on which these theories differ.

The Psychoanalytic Tradition

The psychoanalytic tradition began with the work of Sigmund Freud and has continued for many years in the writings of his many followers. *The Authoritarian Personality*, for example, is an important contribution to this tradition. While it is primarily a study of ethnic and race relations, specifically the psychodynamics behind anti-Semitism, *The Authoritarian Personality* must be understood in the context of the larger psychoanalytic school.

Published in 1950, *The Authoritarian Personality*, by T. W. Adorno, Else Frenkel-Brunswik, D. J. Levinson, and R. N. Sanford, is a classic study of the psychology of prejudice and discrimination. Although this study applies several theoretical sources to the study of prejudice, as major works often do, its thrust is the psychoanalytic study of prejudice, particularly of anti-Semitism. Actually, *The Authoritarian Personality* is an expansion of earlier Freudian hypotheses on the roles of projection, frustration, and aggression in prejudice. The authors proposed that prejudice is a personality type, and while prejudice involves projection and the displacement of aggression, for instance, it is not an isolated trait or some specific defense mechanism. There is a prejudiced personality, which the authors termed the *authoritarian personality*. The authoritarian personality is an organization of interrelated characteristics or needs which lie behind ideological preferences and ethnic prejudices. These needs originate in early childhood, in the family, and are the consequence of particular child-rearing practices.

While *The Authoritarian Personality* was completed in the United States after World War II, its genesis actually was in Germany before the war (Robinson, 1969). It represents a study of the psychology behind a most horrible historical event, the extermination of millions of people in Central Europe in the course of World War II. Approximately 14 million noncombatants were systematically destroyed by the Nazis, many in extermination camps, with grim efficiency. Jews, Gypsies, and Slavic groups were the primary targets for the extermination. Adorno became interested in the psychodynamics behind the Nazi Movement while still in Germany, and when he immigrated to the United States, he continued his research with others, culminating in the publication of *The Authoritarian Personality*.

When this study was done in the United States, anti-Semitism was found to be an integrated set of attitudes about Jews, including beliefs about their "offensiveness," "threatening character," "seclusiveness," and "intrusiveness," and the desirability of segregating Jews. Aside from some surface contradictions in these beliefs—e.g., Jews are seen as both intrusive and seclusive—these beliefs tended to be highly correlated (up to .83) in the minds of anti-Semitic people. The study expanded into an inquiry about the possibility that anti-Semitism is part of a larger set of beliefs, a general rejection of all out-groups, not just Jews. This resulted in the development of an ethnocentrism scale which included subscales of attitudes about blacks, Filipinos, "Okies," Japanese, and "Zoot suiters," all minorities in California, where the study was carried out in this country. It also included attitudes about people from other countries. These subscales were found to correlate with one another, and the entire scale of ethnocentrism correlated with the anti-Semitism scale. These findings appeared to justify the theoretical premise that prejudice is part of a broad personality syndrome.

A third facet of the research was people's ideological preferences, specifically their antidemocratic or fascist attitudes. The assessment of such sociopolitical attitudes was intended to serve as an indirect measure of prejudice. This led to the development of the F scale (or Implicit Antidemocratic Trends or Potentiality of Fascism Scale). People who scored high on the F scale possessed the following characteristics: conventionalism, submission to authority, aggression toward the unconventional, opposition to the imaginative and gentle, superstition and stereotype, emphasis on power and toughness, destructiveness and cynicism, projectivity, and concern with sexual "goings-on." Examples of the items on the F scale[1] include:

---

[1] To score low on the F scale, one had to disagree with items such as these.

1. Obedience and respect for authority are the most important virtues children should learn.
2. Young people sometimes get rebellious ideas, but as they grow up they ought to get over them and settle down.
3. Homosexuals are hardly better than criminals and ought to be severely punished.
4. The businessman and the manufacturer are much more important to society than the artist and the professor.
5. Some day it will probably be shown that astrology can explain a lot.
6. People can be divided up into two distinct classes, the weak and the strong.
7. Familiarity breeds contempt.
8. Nowadays when so many different kinds of people move around and mix together so much, a person has to protect himself especially carefully against catching an infection or disease from them.
9. The wild sex life of the old Greeks and Romans was tame compared to some of the goings-on in this country, even in places where people might least expect it.

The F scale correlated with the ethnocentrism scale, although the correlation coefficients depended on the groups studied and the forms of the scales used. Clinical interviews of respondents and results from projective techniques supplemented data obtained through the attitudinal scales, and all results were interpreted as supporting the authors' basic contention that there is a prejudiced personality. This personality is characterized by the factors in the list below.[2]

1. Attitudes toward Sociopolitical Structures and Relationships
   Highly authoritarian persons:
   a. Have an emotional need for unconditional submission to authority which expresses itself in: family interaction, other interpersonal relations, political attitudes, and attitudes toward supernatural figures.
   b. Desire the polity to be ruled by a powerful, autocratic leader to whom all would grant total allegiance, unquestioning obedience, and extreme deference.
   c. Believe that obedience and respect for authority are paramount values and the most important virtues children should learn.
   d. Believe in extremely severe punishment of deviants: not only those who defy leaders but also offenders against conventional mores such as sexual restrictions.
   e. Perceive others as being deviant or committing violations against

[2]From Robert A. LeVine and Donald T. Campbell, Ethnocentrism: Theories of Conflict, Ethnic Attitudes and Group Behavior (New York: John Wiley and Sons, Inc., 1972).

conventional morality even when they are not, and view mankind generally as being potentially anarchic and immoral when not under the control of a powerful leader.

    f. Have a preoccupation with power, viewing all relations in terms like strong-weak and dominant-submissive, and admire displays of militancy, strength, and punitiveness ("toughness") by respected leaders.

2. Cognitive Style

Highly authoritarian persons:

    a. Avoid introspection, reflection, speculation, imaginative fantasy.

    b. Believe in mystical or fantastic external determinants of individual fate, that is, the operation of large, unseen powers controlling one's destiny.

    c. Think in rigid categories, believe oversimplified explanations of natural and social events, and dogmatically apply these categories and explanations to ambiguous phenomena (that is, cannot tolerate ambiguity) (cf. Rokeach, 1960).

3. Child-Rearing Practices

Highly authoritarian persons:

    a. Experienced, in childhood, fathers who were aloof, stern, and punitive.

    b. Experienced, in childhood, a good deal of physical punishment or threat of physical punishment administered by mother or father or both.

4. Family Structure

Highly authoritarian persons:

    a. Were raised in families in which husband-wife, parent-child, and sibling relations were organized along hierarchical lines, with idealization of the father as a powerful figure who is also feared.

    b. Organize their own families as adults along hierarchical lines, emphasizing the subordination of women and children, and continue to prefer this organization to "modern" egalitarian arrangements.

In keeping with the psychoanalytic tradition, the authors of *The Authoritarian Personality* sought the origins of authoritarianism in early childhood, particularly in certain types of parents and family structures. It was found that authoritarian people had parents who were extremely concerned with status distinctions and despised those below them in the status hierarchy. These same parents were seen to be harsh and rigid, and as a rule they made the expression of love for their children conditional on the children's obedience. Relationships among family members tended to be stratified into positions of dominance and submission, all but egalitarian. Duties, chores, and obligations were emphasized in the home, rather than exchanges of mutual affection and love. The result was a child forced to submit to stern, aloof authority, and rigid, arbitrary discipline, often involving physical punishment or the threat of it, and always there was the demand for obedience.

While such a child became understandably hostile toward his parents because of these experiences, he also learned that he could not express this hostility toward them. His parents were far too threatening and punitive for that. Besides, he would have felt guilty about hating his parents. Instead, he learned to repress his hostility toward his parents and thus began a pattern of submission to authority. The child grew more dependent on and unable to defy authority, first his parents and then all authority figures. Eventually, there was identification with authority and the idealization of it, all of which helped the child hold in check his natural hostility toward authority figures like his parents and political figures. Simultaneously, the child learned to displace his aggression onto substitute targets, or scapegoats. This pattern also began at home, learned from the prejudice of his parents. Not only was some of his hostility for authority ventilated in this fashion, hostility he could never express toward authority, but he also gained the approval of his parents and other authority figures for being prejudiced in this manner. Nevertheless, the authoritarian person must always defend himself against his own impulses, avoid looking too closely at himself, forever condemn the unconventional and, of course, hate the scapegoat. This is the psychoanalytic portrait of the prejudiced personality:

... the distinctive characteristics of the authoritarian personality presumably reflect defenses against the expression of repressed hostility toward authority; the major defenses are the projection of the unacceptable, frustrated impulses onto out-groups, the displacement of hostility onto the same out-groups, and the identification with the frustrating authority. (Deutsch and Krauss, 1965:160)

Such a psychoanalytic analysis of prejudice and discrimination in the United States protected the thesis of assimilationism. The assimilationists argued that America as a modern society was prepared for the full assimilation of its racial and ethnic groups. In the course of modernization, norms of achievement (whereby people are judged on competency and accomplishments, not ancestry) had replaced those of ascription in America, so talented men and women, whatever their race and ethnic birthright, would be eventually included into the larger society. Assimilation would proceed in this rational manner, and it was considered necessary for the proper functioning of a modern society. In theory, prejudice and discrimination had no place in the modern order, although in practice both were very much in evidence.

That was the problem: reality in America did not entirely conform to this assimilationist scenario. There was the phenomenon of persistent racial prejudice and discrimination in modern America. Did this mean that the assimilationists were wrong? Of course, to some extent they were. The point is, however, that a psychological analysis of racial prejudice in modern society, particularly one in the psychoanalytic tradition, might save assimilationists certain embarrassments. Prejudice was irrational, a result of inner, unseen psychic conflict, according to psychoanalytic theory, and not to be confused with contemporary social forces as part of the modernization process. Prejudice existed apart from the modern order, way off in the inner recesses of the hidden psyche. It was the murky and irrational psychology of individual white Americans that stood in the way of assimilation, not the nature of modern society. Did not Myrdal (1944), an assimilationist, identify the lack of full racial assimilation in modern society with certain outdated racial attitudes of white Americans? Prejudice in modern America was nothing so much as an externalization of psychic conflict, and the parties involved were virtually each other's inkblots. The psychoanalytic view of prejudice and discrimination filled in some of the gaps between the prediction of racial assimilation and the persistent racism in modern America. The thesis of assimilationism was protected somewhat in this manner, and this, too, helps account for the popularity of the psychology of prejudice.

The popularity of *The Authoritarian Personality* did not mean an uncritical acceptance of it. Only six years after the publication of this work, Vander Zanden (1972:148) estimated that "at least 230 publications appeared dealing with authoritarianism." Much of this commentary was critical of *The Authoritarian Personality* on a number of counts. First, critics pointed out that the people who had been studied by the authors were in no manner a representative sample of all Americans. Instead, they tended to be of the middle class, college students, members of patriotic or civic associations, and so on, and thus they were different in certain social characteristics from other segments of the nation's population. This is important because it has been found since the publication of this work in 1950 that such social characteristics as education, socioeconomic status, and age are significantly associated with authoritarianism (Pettigrew, 1958; Rose, 1966; Simpson and Yinger, 1972). For instance, among a sample of working-class men, McCord, McCord, and Howard (1960) found no significant connection between prejudice and measures of early childhood experiences, including punitive, harsh, and inconsistent treatment from parents. Moreover, Williams (1966) found regional differences in both authoritarianism and attitudes unfavorable toward racial integration, as people from the South scored higher on both scales. Whatever else these findings mean, they suggest that it is difficult to generalize from one segment of the American population to another about the level of authoritarianism in America, the dynamics behind its emergence, and its relation to prejudice and discrimination.

Another criticism of *The Authoritarian Personality* has to do with the fact that to get a low score on any one item in the original F scale, a respondent had to disagree with the item (e.g., disagree that the businessman and the manufacturer are much more important to society than the artist and the professor). Some people tend to agree with any and all statements, while others tend to disagree, possibly irrespective of authoritarianism. This tendency is one type of a response set. Several researchers have found that from 25 to 75 percent of the variance in the responses to the F scale can be explained by response set (Bass, 1955; Chapman and Campbell, 1957; Couch and Keniston, 1960; Messick and Jackson, 1957; Peabody, 1961).

A major theme of *The Authoritarian Personality* is that prejudice is part of a personality syndrome, not an isolated psychological trait. However, there is some question as to whether or not responses to the F scale do indeed represent a unified, single psychological orientation. Studies have shown through factor analysis that six or seven distinct traits are measured by the F scale, none of them very well. Simpson and Yinger (1972:81) put it this way: "If the compound of conventionality, rigidity of mind, cynicism, tendencies toward aggression and projection, and the like, is not stable—if the separate parts can vary independently of one another—one cannot measure them by a single scale nor think of them as a single personality characteristic."

The authors of *The Authoritarian Personality* also identified authoritarianism solely with right-wing (fascist) political ideology. A recurrent criticism of this work is that authoritarianism is just as likely to be found on the political left as on the political right. That is, extremists on both the left and the right may share in authoritarianism.

Nevertheless, *The Authoritarian Personality* contains valuable insights on ethnic and race relations. It, along with other psychological theories, complements a sociological analysis of race and ethnicity by bringing the individual's beliefs and feelings into the picture. Individuals and society are only arbitrarily separable, for in reality one cannot exist without the other. Intergroup relations always involve individuals, and individuals are always involved in these relations. Intergroup exchange impacts the minds of ethnic group members, on the one hand, as the thoughts and actions of individual group members affect intergroup exchange, on the other. Sex, aggression, and the entire notion of inner psychic conflict, along with power and economics, comprise the dynamics behind intergroup relations. When intergroup competition is mixed with the elements of psychic conflict, it can be transformed into irrational hatred. By helping locate the prejudice-prone, psychology can ameliorate the irrational fears and hatreds that flash in intergroup contact and competition. Thus the psychoanalytic lore is a valuable addition to the study of American ethnicity, although it is not a complete explanation of it.

Cognitive Tradition

Authoritarianism can be found across the entire political spectrum, not only on the political extremes, according to Milton Rokeach (1956; 1960).

It can be associated with any political ideology and is not unique to a right-wing or left-wing political orientation. Communists may be as authoritarian as fascists, and political moderates may be as authoritarian as those on both political extremes. Furthermore, people may be as authoritarian about their religion, philosophy, and scientific viewpoints as they are about their political attitudes. In other words, the authoritarianism analyzed by the authors of *The Authoritarian Personality* is seen by Rokeach as a single instance of a more general phenomenon, that of dogmatism and opinionation, or closed-mindedness. Closed-mindedness can be found in all political camps and connected with nearly any viewpoint. This means that one may be dogmatically unprejudiced as well as prejudiced, dogmatically tolerant as well as intolerant.

The term *dogmatism* means "(1) a relatively closed cognitive organization of beliefs and disbeliefs about reality, (2) organized around a central set of beliefs about absolute authority which, in turn, (3) provide a framework for patterns of intolerance and qualified tolerance toward others" (Rokeach, 1956:3). The dogmatic person has a closed belief system, meaning that he rejects a far wider range of beliefs and opinions than he accepts, makes little effort to keep consistent his central and peripheral beliefs, and is categorical in his opinions, showing little flexibility and awareness of situational nuances. That is, the dogmatic and opinionated person tends to view the world from a single perspective, rejects essentially all viewpoints other than his own, and is unconditional in his judgments about people and their actions, whatever the circumstances. By contrast, the open-minded individual views the world from a variety of vantage points, is more flexible in his judgments, attempts to maintain better consistency between his central and peripheral beliefs, and is less likely to reject as out of hand the opinions of others.

Dogmatic people also tend to see history from a single, fixed point in time. They may be past oriented, as are fascists; present oriented, like psychopaths; or future oriented, as are some religious enthusiasts. Regardless of the time perspective favored, the dogmatic individual tends to see the flow of events through time from only that one perspective, and thus the present is blurred with the past and the future. A fascist, for example, would see the present and the future only in terms of the past, while a religious enthusiast would view the past and the present as only leading up to the future, toward salvation. Open-minded people clearly distinguish among these time frames and appreciate the fact that the human condition can be viewed from all three perspectives.

Rokeach argued that all belief systems, dogmatic or not, have three levels: primitive, intermediate, and peripheral. Primitive beliefs are basic ideas about the nature of the world. The dogmatic person sees the world as threatening, while the open-minded person views the world as basically friendly. With respect to intermediate and peripheral beliefs, the dogmatic individual has the habit of making reference to some authority behind them, implying somehow that authority is absolute, categorical, and correct in all cases. People who are open-minded are less likely to believe in absolute authority and do not appeal to it as often in their more specific beliefs.

Rokeach's formulation represents an extension of Gestalt psychology. Gestalt psychology goes back to German intellectual traditions in the past century, as does the psychoanalytic tradition. Both of these schools were reactions against psychological associationism, another tradition in psychology known today as S–R theory, or behaviorism. Psychoanalytic theory and Gestalt psychology view humans as whole beings, as psychological systems, rather than bundles of specific reactions to specific stimuli, as does behaviorism. Gestalt psychology postulates that man is basically a cognitive being who needs to know the world around him. Through perception and cognition he organizes this world into coherent and balanced wholes, and his feelings about the world follow from his knowledge of it. Not only are people's beliefs at various levels mutually consistent, but there is also a balance between thought and sentiment. This is the picture of the open-minded person.

The portrait of the closed-minded individual, in contrast, reproduces the essentials of the authoritarian personality as found in the psychoanalytic tradition. Dogmatic beliefs follow from feelings, specifically from the need to ward off threat, not from the need to know. Inconsistencies between primitive and peripheral beliefs are kept in isolation, as if in defense. That is, there is no attempt to maintain balance between the various parts of the larger belief system. Morever, dogmatism and opinionation involve identification with absolute authority. Rokeach does not locate the causes of racial prejudice in inner psychic conflict, however; he favors the cognitive perspective that prejudice follows rationally from certain beliefs about other races.

Prejudice in this view is a function of perceived *belief similarity-dissimilarity* between races, rather than a result of deep-rooted, internal psychological turmoil. Prejudice follows from the dissimilarity a person perceives between his own values and those he associates with members of other racial or ethnic groups. The greater is this dissimilarity, the greater is the prejudice he feels, which is especially true when basic values and important beliefs are involved.[3] Prejudice does not necessarily imply a

---

[3]This view of prejudice appears consistent with our own view on race and ethnic relations at the group level; the greater the evolutionary divergence between two groups, the more likely is belief dissimilarity to be perceived. The two can form a vicious cycle.

rejection of another person on the basis of race or ethnicity per se. Rather, the rejection is based on the perceived discrepancy between that person's values and one's own, although this perception may be unreal and based on racial stereotypes. Presumably, there will be no prejudice when it is evident that members of different races share the same basic values.

Some writers object to Rokeach's position that all racial prejudice is belief prejudice; their studies show that there is both conventional and belief prejudice (Triandis, 1961; Triandis and Davis, 1965). Conventional prejudice is not necessarily the sort that follows from inner psychic conflict; it simply means that the rejection of the other is indeed based on his ethnicity or race per se. In support of Rokeach's position, other studies attest to the existence of belief prejudice (Hendrick, Bixenstine, and Hawkins, 1971; Insko and Robinson, 1967; Rokeach, 1960; Rokeach and Mezei, 1966; Rokeach, Smith, and Evans, 1960; Smith, William, and Willis, 1967).

The findings of Stein, Hardyck, and Smith (1965), like those of many other researchers, illustrate the workings of both belief and conventional prejudice. White teenagers in this study were first asked about their own values, values considered by the authors to be relevant to adolescents. From the same set of values, value profiles of four hypothetical teenagers were constructed by the researchers. Two of the hypothetical teenagers were white and two were black, and their values were fabricated to be either similar or dissimilar to the values of each of the respondents. In other words, the values of the hypothetical teenagers were matched with those of each respondent and made either similar or dissimilar. Thus for each respondent, the hypothetical teenagers formed a four-cell table: black and similar, black and dissimilar, white and similar, and white and dissimilar. In this way the weights given by respondents to race and belief in their acceptance or rejection of the hypothetical teenagers could be ascertained. Respondents' attitudes toward the hypothetical teenagers were measured by a social distance scale, that is, in terms of how friendly they anticipated they would be with the hypothetical teenager in various social settings. Some of these settings were quite formal and implied some of the traditional distance between the races, while others were informal and intimate (e.g., date my sister or brother).

Analysis of the responses showed that these white teenagers weighted belief similarity-dissimilarity more heavily than race in their anticipated friendliness/unfriendliness toward the four hypothetical peers. This was true except for certain "sensitive" items, in settings that implied intimacy. In the intimate settings the respondents weighted race of the hypothetical teenager more heavily than beliefs. We see here the working of both belief and conventional prejudice; belief prejudice stops with intimacy, where conventional prejudice begins. Moreover, when these respondents knew nothing of a hypothetical teenager, except for race, they anticipated that a black teenager would have values unlike their own, while the values of a white peer were expected to be similar to their own. This suggests that in the absence of information to the contrary, whites will think blacks are essentially dissimilar to themselves. Stein et al. (1965:289) concluded:

The data presented strongly support Rokeach's theory that the variable of belief congruence accounts for a major portion of the variance in prejudice, if it does not tell the "whole truth" about it. The teen-age subjects in this study, when given extensive information concerning the belief systems of stimulus teenagers, react primarily in terms of similarity of beliefs and only very secondarily in terms of race. This was the case in an analysis of total scores on a social distance scale, and in an analysis of "friendliness" responses. Strong "race effects" were obtained on "sensitive" items on the social distance scale, perhaps reflecting institutionalized areas of prejudice, and on total social distance scores when information concerning belief systems was not provided.

The Psychoanalytic vs. Cognitive Debate on Prejudice

The debate between psychologists in the psychoanalytic and cognitive traditions is over the nature of the relationship between prejudicial beliefs and feelings. Those in the psychoanalytic tradition emphasize that inner feelings, rooted in unconscious, psychic conflict, are externalized onto minority groups. The result is prejudice. Beliefs about a minority group are then formed in the service of these ego defense mechanisms. For instance, anti-Semitism as a set of beliefs about Jews is explained as the repression of hostility toward parents and its displacement onto a scapegoat. Cognitive theorists see the roles of beliefs and feelings as being reversed. Prejudice as a sentiment follows directly and sometimes rationally from one's beliefs about a minority group. For example, Rokeach argues that prejudice for most people is simply a result of their perception that they and minority group members are essentially different, implying that we dislike those unlike us. However, how does this explain the fact that prejudicial beliefs often appear irrational, narrow and overly stereotypical? Emotion distorts logic, those in the psychoanalytic tradition answer. From the cognitive point of view, Henri Tajfel (1969) explains that stereotypes can result from purely cognitive processes, particularly the *assimilation-contrast principle* of Gestalt psychology. Tajfel made a most emphatic statement on the need to recognize the cognitive element in prejudice and commented on the long neglect in doing so. The psychology of prejudice has been dominated, according to Tajfel, by the "blood and guts" approach, as he puts it, particularly the psychoanalytic perspective. In this approach, prejudice is irrational, even representing a reversion to man's more primitive past. It is implied that prejudice is atavistic, a survival of a more primitive time which is now out of its proper historical period.

Tajfel objected to the blood-and-guts formulation of prejudice and argued that it can be fully understood as a cognitive and rational process. No recourse is necessary to unconscious motivation or to man's evolutionary past in order to explain prejudice in modern society. Prejudice is simply a function of three cognitive processes: categorization, assimilation/contrast, and the search for coherence. Like all perception and cognition, prejudice represents an attempt to bring perceptual order to an otherwise chaotic world.

People categorize what are actually continua in the real world into distinct types or categories. For example, imagine what you would see if the world's people stood shoulder to shoulder in a single line and you rode past them in a car, as if in a military review. Would you not see a single continuum of color? There would be no clear and distinct racial categories; one race would not abruptly end and another begin. However, in our mind's eye we tend to see people belonging to one distinct racial group or another. Indeed, we categorize virtually everything in this manner, which helps bring some order and definition to our world. This process is called *perceptual grouping* in Gestalt psychology (Deutsch and Krauss, 1965). It is also seen as an essential psychological process in other forms of cognitive theory, such as the works of Piaget (cf. Flavell, 1963).

Once we categorize our world, we proceed to emphasize the differences between members of different categories and simultaneously to accentuate the similarity among members of the same category. The similarity of the members of a single category becomes greater, while the dissimilarity between members of different categories is accentuated. Members of one racial group come to look all the same, and basically different from members of other groups. This is known in Gestalt psychology as the assimilation/contrast principle: "Thus, perceptual organization is, in a sense, bipolar—it will either be directed toward minimizing stimulus differences so that the perceptual field becomes homogenous or toward accentuating them if the stimulus differences exceed a certain level or if there is an abrupt discontinuity between parts of the visual field" (Deutsch and Krauss, 1965:18).

Values and beliefs are also attributed to members of the different categories in the process of categorization. These attributes, too, undergo the dual phenomenon of assimilation/contrast. People in one category become essentially similar in their beliefs and values, while people in different categories become essentially dissimilar. This is the stuff of racial stereotypes. It also reminds us of the study by Stein et al. (1965): In the absence of information to the contrary, a member of one race will believe those of another have identical values, and they are essentially different than his own. Stereotypes are learned in childhood, Tajfel noted, when they are often taken as fact, due to the child's developmental inability to question the authority behind the stereotype (Kohlberg, 1968; Piaget, 1932). This alone can result in racial prejudice.

The theme of cognitive theory is that prejudice is a rational process. We learn to categorize people into different races or ethnic groups and to attribute values and beliefs to them on this basis, and in the process members of one group come to appear more like one another and unlike members of another group. Once we know that a member of another race or ethnic group is not different from us, however, we tend to like that person. In other words, prejudice is a rational consequence of assumed belief dissimilarity, but once we know that such dissimilarity is not the case, we rationally change and like someone of a different race because of the values shared. Research has found that much of the racial prejudice in America is just such belief prejudice. In some situations, however, race is more important than is belief similarity-dissimilarity. In situations involving interracial intimacy, whites tend to reject blacks on the basis of race rather than belief similarity-dissimilarity (Stein et al., 1965).

While Tajfel (1969) is correct that the cognitive component of prejudice had been ignored in the blood-and-guts school, he appears to err in the opposite direction, overlooking the emotional element in prejudice. All cognitive theorists may overstate the role of cognition and rationality in prejudice. All prejudice does not neatly follow from belief similarity-dissimilarity, as we already know. Years ago, Merton (1957) observed that in-group virtues may be out-group vices. For instance, members of one ethnic group may consider their own striving for success as appropriate ambition, a case of honest effort, but find the same behavior in another group to be pushiness, an indication of greed. In Merton's (1957:428-429) words:

The very same behavior undergoes a complete change of evaluation in its transition from the in-group Abe Lincoln to the out-group Abe Cohen or Abe Kurokawa. . . . Did Lincoln work far into the night? This testifies that he was industrious, resolute, perseverant, and eager to realize his capacities to the full. Do the out-group Jews or Japanese keep these same hours? This only bears witness to their sweatshop mentality, their ruthless undercutting of American standards, their unfair competitive practices. Is the in-group hero frugal, thrifty, and sparing? Then the out-group villain is stingy, miserly, and penny-pinching.

It is not clear how cognitive theorists can explain such beliefs, which on the surface appear to be irrational and made to conform with prior feelings about one's own kind and others. How can a rational person judge the same traits in his group and in the out-group to be essentially different? Beliefs about other ethnic and racial groups may at times be in the service of one's feelings or emotional needs.

The cognitive and psychoanalytic approaches to prejudice proceed from very different assumptions on the basic psychology of humankind. Cognitive theory simply proposes that prejudice is based on perceived belief dissimilarity, unlike the more complicated Freudian explanation of instincts, psychic conflict between those instincts and morality, and the externalization of that conflict onto members of minority groups. Prejudice is a rational process from one viewpoint and irrational from the other. Research shows that prejudice is both rational and irrational, based on beliefs and in the service of strong emotions. These two theories, when considered together, make it clear that both cognition and emotion play important roles in the psychology of prejudice.

The Behaviorist Tradition

Behaviorism is the third great tradition in American psychology, one that began in the past century in both the United States and Europe. As Pavlov and Bekhterev were doing early and important work on conditioning in Russia around the turn of the century, Guthrie, Thorndike, and Watson were laying the foundations of modern behaviorism in this country. Behaviorists assume that man is rational and hedonistic, that he can learn from his environment and will select from his behavioral repertoire those actions that will bring him reward. Behaviorists also prefer to depict human psychology solely in terms of observable stimuli and overt responses. Thus behaviorism is often known as S–R (stimulus-response) theory.

This S–R aspect of behaviorism presents somewhat of a problem in the study of prejudice. Prejudice is typically defined as an attitude, an internal state of beliefs and feelings which only predisposes people to respond in certain overt ways, and is usually not considered the response itself. Discrimination is the response. However, since behaviorists prefer not to deal with internal psychological states like attitudes, they must recast the meaning of prejudice. The ethnic and racial groups toward whom prejudice is directed are seen as stimuli, and prejudice itself is seen as some sort of overt response.

Leonard Doob (1947) showed us how this might be done. He defined attitudes, including prejudice, as "an implicit, drive producing response considered socially significant in the individual's society" (p. 136). Prejudice is thus a response, although an implicit one, that is evoked by some stimuli and produces some sort of drive, perhaps one to discriminate. The bond between the stimulus and the response of prejudice is learned, and like anything else that is learned, it undergoes the dual phenomena of generalization and discrimination. One can learn to generalize prejudice to several ethnic and racial groups, or learn to distinguish among these groups and direct prejudice toward only a selected few.

As an implicit response, an attitude like prejudice is "within the individual and not immediately observable to an outsider" (Doob, 1947:136). An attitude precedes, even anticipates, overt behavior and thus acts as a mediating link between the initial stimulus and the overt response. Itself an implicit response evoked by an external stimulus, an attitude then stimulates another response, an overt one, and thus it links or mediates between an observable stimulus and an overt response. This formulation is in line with the mediationist school of behaviorism, which depicts the stimulus-response bond not simply as S–R but as ES→IR→IS→ER, where ES and ER are an external stimulus and response, respectively, and IR and IS are internal counterparts, a stimulus and response within the individual. In other words, prejudice is an IR and IS, in this view, and thus it mediates between the stimulus object of a certain ethnic or racial group and one's overt response toward that group.

Prejudice is learned, meaning that the bond between the stimulus object and the overt response to that object is acquired, not innate. Behaviorists believe that there are two basic learning methods. Learning may occur through either classical or instrumental conditioning, because of either association or reinforcement. Ivan Pavlov, the early Russian behaviorist, paired a bell with meat powder and conditioned dogs to respond to the bell in a way they had to the meat powder. In this classical-conditioning paradigm, the bell is the conditioned stimulus and the meat powder is the unconditioned stimulus. The response to the bell is the conditioned response, while the original response of salivation to the meat powder is the unconditioned response. The learning of the conditioned response follows from the pairing of the conditioned and unconditioned stimuli. The second paradigm of learning in behaviorism is instrumental or operant conditioning, which is closely connected with the works of B. F. Skinner. A pigeon in a Skinner box, for instance, learns to respond, so as to attain a reward, by pecking in the right place for a pellet of food. The response is instrumental, or an operant, for obtaining a reward, and learning in this case conforms to the law of reinforcement rather than the law of association.

PREJUDICE AND CLASSICAL CONDITIONING A study by Staats and Staats (1958) illustrates how prejudice can be learned through classical conditioning. In classical conditioning two stimuli are paired, the conditioned (CS) and unconditioned stimuli (UCS). After several of these pairings, even animals learn to respond (CR) to the conditioned stimulus as they had to the unconditioned stimulus (UCR). In the Staats and Staats experiment, college sophomores were told that they were being tested on their ability to learn two lists of words simultaneously. One list of words which contained names of nationalities was presented visually. Immediately after each of the visual words was presented, another word was spoken to the subjects from a second list. Words from this second list had strong evaluative meaning, both positive (e.g., *beautiful*) and negative (e.g., *ugly*). The visual words from the first list were the conditioned stimuli, obviously, and the spoken words were the unconditioned stimuli.

It was predicted that the subjects would eventually learn to respond to names of nationalities from the first list as they had responded to the evaluative words from the second list. The subjects were asked to rate the names of nationalities on pleasant-unpleasant semantic differential scales. It was found that nationalities paired with negative words, such as *bitter*, *ugly*, and *failure*, were rated as more unpleasant than nationalities paired with positive words, consistent with the prediction. This study suggests that prejudice is a conditioned response to a stimulus—a racial or ethnic group—which has been paired in someone's mind with a noxious stimulus (see Figure 1).

PREJUDICE AND INSTRUMENTAL CONDITIONING   In instrumental conditioning, the correct response is learned in order to obtain a reward. This response is termed an *operant*. The stimulus is considered to be some drive or need, and one learns the operant that reduces the drive or satisfies the need. One can learn to avoid punishment in this manner as well as to obtain pleasure. A pigeon can be trained to escape from a shock on signal, as well as be conditioned to press a bar for food.

Classical and instrumental conditioning represent different models of learning which go back to early behaviorism. Pavlov innovated the paradigm of classical conditioning when he observed that dogs could be

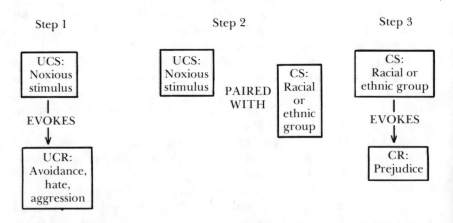

Figure 1 *Steps to the learning of prejudice through classical conditioning.*

conditioned to salivate in response to the bell as they had to meat powder. For a long time, he considered classical conditioning the model for all learning. Then, later in his career, he discovered that the consequences of a response, reward or punishment, were also important in the learning process. This principle he termed the *law of reinforcement* (Shaw and Costanzo, 1970).

In both classical and instrumental conditioning, prejudice is a response, just as Doob (1947) said it was. Prejudice is a response to a conditioned stimulus in classical conditioning, specifically to an ethnic group that has been associated in one's mind with negative traits—Jews with greed and blacks with laziness, for instance. Prejudice is an operant in instrumental conditioning, however, a means to obtain reward or avoid punishment. That is, the strength of the bond between the stimulus object of black people and the response of prejudice is a function of the reward that prejudice brings. This is Pavlov's law of reinforcement. More recently, Skinner has shown that reward need not be continuous; the bond between the stimulus and the response is actually stronger when reward is periodic or intermittent. If a child learns that prejudice brings reward from his parents or others significant to him, or if it allows him to avoid punishment, even if this is only occasional, he will become prejudiced, in accord with the principles of instrumental conditioning. Figure 2 illustrates this process.

PREJUDICE AND IMITATION We all have seen children imitate adults. Children playing "dress up" try to look like mommy or daddy, a practice we often find cute and even charming. We may be embarrassed by our own children, however, when they go so far as to mock the quirks of their mother or father. Imitation is actually a serious part of the social learning process. By imitating adult models, for instance, children begin to learn about the adult roles they will eventually be expected to play. Children

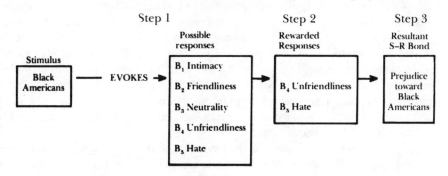

Figure 2 *Steps to the learning of prejudice through instrumental conditioning.*

learn one and a thousand things about society by imitating the grown-ups around them, and prejudice and discrimination are among the things that a child can learn in this way. A girl may learn prejudice by imitating her mother as she sees such feelings expressed in the privacy of the home or in public. That the mother is infrequently, if ever, reprimanded for being prejudiced is also noticed by the child. This serves as a model for the development of the girl's own racial and ethnic attitudes, which may ironically come as something of a surprise to her parents.

The role of imitation in the learning process might be illustrated by Bandura and Walters' studies of children imitating adult aggression (cf. Bandura, 1962). Young children were exposed to a variety of models, adults in person, adults on film, and cartoon characters on film, who were either aggressive or nonaggressive. It was found that the children who viewed aggressive models responded in an aggressive manner, when later frustrated, by punching and kicking a plastic Bozo doll. Children who had not been exposed to aggressive models did not respond to frustration with aggression. If children can learn aggression in this way, then they also learn prejudice through imitation. Prejudice is simply a product of imitating prejudiced models. Moreover, parents may be unintentional models, and the children need not be directly rewarded for imitating the prejudice of their parents in order for prejudice to develop.

Once prejudice is learned as a correct response to a certain class of stimulus objects, say black athletes while watching televised sports, it may then generalize as a response to all black Americans, possibly to all people of color. It might come to include members of other minority groups, whatever their color. This process is called *generalization*. The scope of generalization is a function of how closely related, in either a physical or thematic sense, additional stimulus objects are to the original stimulus object. Of course, prejudice toward a given minority group may be directly learned and not be a function of the generalization of prejudice toward some other group. The opposite side of generalization is *discrimination*, whereby one learns to differentiate responses to different classes of stimuli. A child who learns to be prejudiced toward black athletes may also learn that prejudice is not the proper response to other classes of black Americans, and certainly not to members of other racial groups. The dual phenomena of generalization and discrimination help determine toward whom one learns to be prejudiced, from the perspective of S–R theory.

Like all learning, prejudice can be reversed, or unlearned, a process the behaviorists call *extinction*. Through extinction, response strength diminishes; for instance, the probability that one will respond with prejudice toward black Americans becomes less. Extinction can occur with counterconditioning or through the manipulation of reinforcement schedules. Through counterconditioning the connection between the conditioned stimulus, some ethnic group, and the noxious unconditioned stimulus is broken, possibly by pairing the ethnic group with other positive stimuli. Prejudice diminishes as a consequence. If we assume that prejudice was originally learned as an operant, a means of securing reward, then prejudice should diminish if it is not rewarded. Doob (1947) considered prejudice a cue- and drive-producing response, one that could arouse other responses such as discrimination. As a learned drive, prejudice must compete with other drives, including those evoked by the same stimuli. The stimulus object of black Americans, as an example, may arouse both prejudice and sympathy, thoughts of both aversion and of the American Creed. Prejudice toward blacks may be partially extinguished by making prominent these other drives.

All psychologists are not happy with the behavioral model of prejudice, particularly those who are not behaviorists. A basic criticism of the behavioral formulation is that prejudice is not a response, implicit or explicit. It is discrimination that is the response; prejudice is the attitude behind it. Chein (1948) observed that responses come and go, while attitudes such as prejudice endure. Prejudice toward a certain ethnic group may last a lifetime, and it is hard to imagine how such an attitude is actually a response. Doob (1947) stated that an attitude once learned can also be "drive producing." This might account for the persistence of an attitudinal response over time, except that drives are stimuli, not responses, for they initiate behavior and are not behavior itself. Doob suggested that attitudes are also habits. Is prejudice all three, a response, a stimulus, and a habit? It clearly cannot be all three, and it may be none of these.

The definition of an attitude as only an implicit response is no help in clearing up this ambiguity. As Chein rightfully noted, there is no sharp distinction between explicit and implicit; both lie on a single continuum, and the difference is more subjective than objective. Just how observable must prejudice be before it becomes a response and not an attitude? The basic problem in the behavioral formulation that an attitude is a response, as Chein sees it, is that an attitude is a type of response set, not a response. Like any response set, prejudice selects one response from among a repertoire of possible responses to some stimulus. It is this selective function of attitudes which is important. The prejudice of a person may predispose her or him to select discrimination from among a set of possible responses to members of another ethnic group, or it may not, but it is never discrimination itself. Chein (1948:197) says that "in playing up the response aspect of attitude, Doob is missing the boat." Furthermore, an attitude like prejudice may exist without a response like discrimination, for it can happen that prejudiced people find themselves unwilling or unable to discriminate. Aside from these criticisms, it is obvious that prejudice can be learned through conditioning and imitation, and behaviorism adds to understanding of the psychology of prejudice.

THE FUNCTIONAL THEORY OF PREJUDICE: A SYNTHESIS?

Three perspectives on the psychology of prejudice have been reviewed, the psychoanalytic, cognitive, and behavioral theories. Each of these has certainly something to say about the psychological roots of prejudice, even about prejudice in the generic sense, but each also has its shortcomings. Here again we are faced with a plurality of perspectives on a single phenomenon, none of which seems to be a complete explanation. A fuller view of the psychology of prejudice may emerge, however, when these theories are used together in a complementary manner.

This is what Daniel Katz (1960) suggested in his call for a functional approach to the study of attitudes, including prejudice. Writers have taken one of two basic approaches to the study of attitudes, Katz observed, one based on the irrational model of man and another based on the rational model of man. The first approach posits that prejudice is an outcome of irrational and emotional forces, unconscious in its origins. In our review, it has been represented by the psychoanalytic theory of prejudice, including the version found in *The Authoritarian Personality*. The second approach to attitudes is based on the rational model of man, which explains prejudice as an essentially rational process, a product of conscious and even deliberate thought. Attitudes are part of the larger process by which man adjusts to his surroundings. This approach is seen in both behaviorism and the cognitive theory of prejudice. Prejudice is either a rationally conditioned response or an operant for reward, from the perspective of the behaviorists, and it brings a semblance of order to an otherwise chaotic world, according to cognitive theorists.

The complementarity of these three theories becomes clear when we consider the many psychological needs that attitudes like prejudice can serve. Katz (1960:167) stated that

... by concerning ourselves with the different functions attitudes can perform we can avoid the great error of oversimplification—the error of attributing a single cause to given types of attitudes. . . . not only are there a number of motivational forces to take into account in considering attitudes and behavior, but the same attitude can have different motivational bases in different people.

Katz argued that attitudes serve four classes of psychological needs; that is, they perform four major functions for an individual.

First, attitudes have an *instrumental, adjustive, or utilitarian function*, facilitating the attainment of rewards from the external environment:

Both attitudes and habits are formed toward specific objects, people, and symbols as they satisfy specific needs. The closer these objects are to actual need satisfaction and the more they are clearly perceived as relevant to need satisfaction, the greater are the probabilities of positive attitude formation. (Katz, 1960:171).

Hyman and Sheatsley (1954) have shown that prejudice can bring acceptance from one's own kind, for instance, when prejudice is a norm of that group. The utilitarian function of attitudes is stressed by the behaviorists.

The *ego-defensive function* of attitudes is to somehow protect the individual from basic but threatening truths about himself. Prejudice of the authoritarian personality is a means to displace one's hatred and hostility away from parents and onto a scapegoat. The authority personified by the parents is idealized in the process, protecting the individual even further from facing any guilt over hating his own parents. It is the psychoanalytic tradition that stresses this ego-defensive function of prejudice. From this perspective, prejudices:

. . . proceed from within the person, and the objects and situation to which they are attached are merely convenient outlets for their expression. . . . The point is that the attitude is not created by the target but by the individual's emotional conflicts. And when no convenient target exists the individual will create one. (Katz, 1960:172-173).

The *value-expressive function* of attitudes refers to the fact that one's attitudes can express to others one's basic beliefs and central values. Prejudice can serve as an assertion of self, a statement on one's world view and self-identity. This perspective on prejudice is evident in the cognitive approach, particularly in the view that prejudice follows from assumed belief dissimilarity. The very process of rejecting the dissimilar out-group confirms the values of one's own group, and thus one's self-worth. This function of attitudes would also be accented in ego psychology, and in any psychology on self-concept and self-realization.

Finally, Katz said, attitudes have a *knowledge function.* Prejudice, like any attitude, can provide some order and clarity in a chaotic and complex world. Tajfel (1969) stressed this very function of ethnic and racial stereotypes. If Katz is correct, and attitudes do serve a variety of needs, a variety that has been merely suggested by reference to these four personality needs that prejudice can serve, then the different theories on the psychology of prejudice seem to be complementary. While each theory stresses only one or two major needs met by prejudice, each one, in its narrow emphasis, makes up for some of what the others lack in their equally narrow points of view. Together they give a fuller understanding of the psychology underlying prejudice. Oversimplification in the psychological study of prejudice can be avoided to some extent by using these theories in a complementary manner.

PREJUDICE AND DISCRIMINATION: WHAT IS THE RELATIONSHIP?

The debate over the relationship between prejudice and discrimination revolves around a larger issue, the nature of the relationship between all attitudes and any kind of behavior. Some believe that there is a basic consistency between attitudes and behavior, a belief that is based on what is called the *latent process* conception of attitudes, which postulates that attitudes function within the individual, intervene between stimulus and response, and give direction and consistency to the response (DeFleur and Westie, 1963).

The "latent process view" is probably the most popular conception of prejudice, although the behaviorist conception of prejudice as an implicit response has its many followers too. It is in the former view that the issue of consistency between prejudice and discrimination arises. But is there a basic consistency between prejudice and discrimination? Do prejudiced people always discriminate, and do nonprejudiced people always act in accord with their attitudes by not discriminating?

Since 1934 there has been published evidence that no such consistency between prejudice and discrimination exists. LaPiere (1934) and a Chinese couple took long motor tours of the United States in the early 1930s, during a period of intense and widespread prejudice toward the Chinese in this country. From notes he took on these trips, LaPiere concluded:

In something like ten thousand miles of motor travel, twice across the United States, up and down the Pacific Coast, we met definite rejection from those asked to serve us *just once.* We were received at 66 hotels, auto camps, and "Tourist Homes," refused at one. We were served in 184 restaurants and cafes scattered throughout the country and treated with what I judged to be more than ordinary consideration in 72 of them. (p. 232; italics added)

That is, there was only one instance of discrimination during this series of extensive motor trips. Later, LaPiere wrote to the 250 hotels and restaurants where he and the Chinese couple had been served, asking "Will you accept members of the Chinese race as guests in your establishment?" In answer, 92 percent of restaurants and cafes and 91 percent of the hotels, auto camps and tourist homes replied no. The remainder replied "Uncertain; depends on circumstances" (p. 234).[4] Only one proprietor, a woman who had remembered the Chinese couple and had liked them, answered yes.

---

[4] 128 of the 250 establishments answered the questionnaire.

LaPiere identified the proprietors' responses to the questionnaire as prejudice, of which there was a considerable amount, and their actual receptions of the Chinese couple and LaPiere with discrimination, of which there was almost none. He concluded that there is no inherent consistency between attitudes and action, at least when the former is measured by responses to a questionnaire, as it usually is, while the latter is measured by observed behavior in real settings.

A similar study was done by Kutner, Wilkins, and Yarrow (1952). The two measures of prejudice and discrimination used in this study are nearly identical to those LaPiere used. Discrimination (or lack of it) was measured by the following procedure:

Three young women, 2 white and 1 Negro, all well-dressed and well-mannered, entered 11 individual restaurants in a fashionable North-eastern suburban community, Subtown. In each case, the white women entered first, asked for a table for three and were seated. The Negro woman entered a short while later, informed the hostess or head waiter that she was with a party already seated, found the table and sat down. (p. 649)

The Negro woman was never refused service; there was no discrimination. But when the establishments were subsequently asked if they would accept reservations for a group which included Negroes, five managers reluctantly agreed and six refused to book the group. These responses were taken as indicators of prejudice. When no mention was made of the race of the guests in calls to these same establishments, ten managers promptly made the reservations.

Another study often cited in support of the contention that there is no correspondence between prejudice and discrimination was done in the Pocahontas Coal Field by Minard (1952). Minard observed a basic inconsistency in the behavior of whites toward blacks; during working hours there was racial cooperation in the mines, while prejudice was prevalent off the job and outside the mines, in the larger community. He described the situation as follows:

The boundary line between the two communities is usually the mine's mouth. Management assists the miners in recognizing their entrance into the outside community with its distinctions in status by providing separate (racially segregated) baths and locker rooms. . . . There is a difference in men, and not all of them adjust to the shift in community patterns outside the mine in the same way. Probably about 20 per cent of the men have favorable attitudes toward Negroes reasonably free from prejudice both within and without the mine. There are another 20 per cent whose attitude both inside and outside the mine is strongly prejudiced and changes little with shift in community relationship. It is the remaining 60 per cent who tend to shift their role and status upon passing from the mine's mouth into the outside world. . . . (p. 31)

After reviewing these and other studies, Wicker (1969) concluded that on the average only about 10 percent of the variance in behavior can be attributed to people's attitudes about the object of their behavior. This would mean that there is essentially no relationship between prejudice and discrimination. But this may be an oversimplification of the issue.

Robert Merton (1949) devised a typology of four kinds of persons who combine prejudice and discrimination in different ways. This typology is useful in showing how the connection between prejudice and discrimination can vary from person to person and from one situation to the next. The unprejudiced nondiscriminator, or all-weather liberal, adheres to the American Creed in both belief and action. This type of person will act in accord with his beliefs in nearly all situations, by not discriminating, save for those instances where there is strong cultural support for discrimination. The unprejudiced discriminator, or fair-weather liberal, is a person of expediency who will act in accordance with his own beliefs only insofar as nondiscrimination is the easier and more profitable course of action. Thus, this person will act inconsistently with his beliefs when there is either weak or strong cultural support for discrimination. Merton added that this person often suffers from guilt and shame for having deviated in action from his beliefs in the American Creed.

The prejudiced nondiscriminator, or fair-weather illiberal, is a reluctant conformist to the American Creed. He does not discriminate because he fears that such an action would be costly and painful; for instance, as a merchant he would lose minority group customers. Like the fair-weather liberal, this is a person of expediency. The basic difference between these two types of people, however, is that the fair-weather illiberal is under a strain when he conforms with the American creed, while the liberal is under strain when he deviates from it. The prejudiced discriminator, or all-weather illiberal, is consistent in his beliefs and actions in nearly all situations, by discriminating consistently except in those instances where there is strong cultural support for nondiscrimination. This typology of persons and situations is illustrated in Figure 3, where inconsistency between belief and action is shown in the area of poor prediction.

Of course, it is too simple to think that prejudice alone determines people's behavior. Prejudice alone does not determine whether people discriminate or not. Even common sense tells us that we all consider many things in deciding how to act in a given situation. For one thing, we reflect on the possible consequences of our actions before acting. Even a highly prejudiced person is likely to demur from discriminating when that action is against the law, and he knows he would get caught at it. A second consideration people often make in decisions about interracial contact is just how intimate the contact between them and members of another

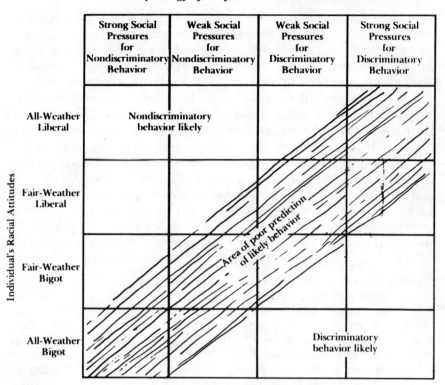

	Strong Social Pressures for Nondiscriminatory Behavior	Weak Social Pressures for Nondiscriminatory Behavior	Weak Social Pressures for Discriminatory Behavior	Strong Social Pressures for Discriminatory Behavior
All-Weather Liberal	Nondiscriminatory behavior likely			
Fair-Weather Liberal				
Fair-Weather Bigot		Area of poor prediction of likely behavior		
All-Weather Bigot			Discriminatory behavior likely	

(vertical axis label: Individual's Racial Attitudes)

Figure 3 *The relation between prejudice and discrimination.*

Source: Adapted from L. G. Warner and M. L. DeFleur, "Attitude as an Interactional Concept," *American Sociological Review*, Vol. 34 (April 1969), p. 168.

group will be. It is much easier for a nonprejudiced person to act in accord with his professed feelings, his lack of prejudice, and not to discriminate when the contact with members of another group is impersonal rather than intimate. Even relatively unprejudiced people often attempt to avoid intimate contact with members of other races. People also bring competing attitudes and motives into any action situation, which was described as part of Myrdal's (1944) American dilemma in chapter 2. All of these possibilities have been researched, and it has been found that the correspondence between prejudice and discrimination does indeed vary in accord with these additional considerations.

When people consider the consequences of their actions and thus decide whether they should act on their true feelings or not, they often take into account how visible their actions will be and who is likely to see them. For instance, is it not reasonable to expect that unprejudiced members of a community which is generally opposed to racial integration would act more in line with their beliefs, in a nondiscriminatory manner, when they believe that their behavior will be kept confidential, unknown to other members of the community? Prejudiced people in such a community, however, should act on their true feelings when they believe that their behavior will be made public, known to their neighbors. The prejudiced people would anticipate pleasant consequences for acting on their convictions in public, while the unprejudiced would not.

Research shows that this is a consideration people commonly make. DeFleur and Westie (1958) first ascertained the racial attitudes of college students. The 23 students who scored in the top quartile and 23 who scored in the bottom quartile on the verbal prejudice test were matched on background characteristics and selected for further study. These subjects were shown "colored photographic slides showing interracial pairings of males and females," and then they were presented with an opportunity to act, either in accord with or against their previously expressed beliefs:

To present the overt action opportunity, the interviewer told each subject that another set of such slides was needed for further research. The subject was first asked if he (or she) would be willing to be photographed with a Negro person of the opposite sex. . . . Then . . . the subject was presented with a mimeographed form and informed that this was "a standard photograph release agreement, which is necessary in any situation where a photograph of an individual is to be used in any manner." The photograph release agreement contained a graded series of "uses" to which the photograph would be put . . . , ranging from laboratory experiments, such as they had just experienced, to a nationwide publicity campaign advocating racial integration. They were to sign their name to each "use" they would permit. In American society, the affixing of one's signature to a document is a particularly significant act. The signing of checks, contracts, agreements and the like is clearly understood to indicate a binding obligation on the part of the signer to abide by the provisions of the document. (DeFleur and Westie, 1958:670)

The correspondence between verbal attitude (verbal prejudice test) and overt behavior (number of permissions for release of photograph) is shown in Table 1. Fourteen of the subjects (the 5 and the 9 cells) behaved inconsistently with their verbal attitudes, while the majority of students were consistent in their beliefs and actions. The results suggest that the unprejudiced students perceived their environments as somewhat supportive of discrimination, similar to our earlier example.

People also consider before they act the intimacy implied in the contact with someone of another race or ethnic background. Intimacy presents a particular problem for the liberal. A social distance often surrounds the contact between members of different racial and ethnic groups, one that is a reflection of the larger system of ethnic stratification. Bogardus and his

Table 1 Relationship between Racial Attitude and Willingness To Be Photographed with a Negro of the Opposite Sex

Behavioral Measure \ Attitude Measure	Prejudiced	Unprejudiced
Prejudiced	18	9
Unprejudiced	5	14

Source: Adapted from M. L. DeFleur and F. R. Westie, "Verbal Attitudes and Overt Acts," *American Sociological Review*, Vol. 23 (December 1958), p. 671.

followers have shown the presence of social distance in the minds of the American public over several decades (see Chapter 3). Social distance can structure and even make smooth the interaction between members of different groups, if all know their place, dominant and subordinate alike, and abide by it. The status difference between subordinate and superordinate can thus be maintained in the course of intergroup contact at the interpersonal level, meaning that the contact conforms to rather than challenges the larger system of ethnic stratification. The social distance between the races can be undermined, however, by intimate contact.

It is in just such situations that the unprejudiced person finds it most difficult to act in accord with liberal racial or ethnic attitudes. This presents a dilemma. The liberal person may be willing to act in what appears to be a completely nondiscriminatory manner when the contact with a person of different race is impersonal, that is, when it maintains the traditional social distance between the races. But he often reverses himself when the relationship implies intimacy, or the reduction of the traditional distance. Recall the research of Stein et al. (1965), which found that white teenagers anticipated friendliness or unfriendliness toward a hypothetical black peer more on the basis of their value similarity-dissimilarity than race, at least until the relationship became "sensitive" or intimate, when race became more important than value similarity-dissimilarity. The prejudiced person faces no such dilemma.

Warner and Rutledge (1970) studied the combined effects of the visibility of interracial action and its implication for social distance on students' willingness to engage in interracial contact. The racial prejudice of the students was first measured, and later they were dichotomized into prejudiced and unprejudiced people, above and below the median. The prejudiced subjects were willing to engage in nondiscriminatory actions with blacks, apparently inconsistent with their racial attitudes, when they and their behavior remained anonymous. If their behavior was to be made public, however, they acted in accord with their racial attitudes. Apparently these students felt the prejudice was expected of them by some significant others. The unprejudiced subjects acted inconsistently with their attitudes, on the other hand, when the social distance between the races was reduced, regardless of how public the action was. Again, we find that the liberal's dilemma centers around intimacy in intergroup contact.

While action may be inconsistent with a single racial attitude, it may nevertheless be consistent with other attitudes the person holds, ones that he perhaps holds more strongly. For instance, relatively unprejudiced homeowners may act inconsistently with their racial attitudes by fighting against the racial integration of a neighborhood. This inconsistency might be explained by the fact that they have most of their savings tied up in their property, the value of which they believe will fall as a result of blacks moving into the neighborhood. The observation that several attitudes may be involved in a single action is often made by those who also find a basic consistency between attitudes and behavior. As an indication of how several attitudes may bear on a single act, Liska (1974), in his commentary on the attitude-behavior controversy, turned to an earlier analysis of voting in presidential elections:

In the American Voter study (Campbell et al., 1960) attitudes during the 1952 and 1956 presidential elections were measured toward the following political objects: the personal attributes of Eisenhower, the personal attributes of Stevenson, groups involved in politics, domestic politics, foreign policy, and the comparative record of the two parties in managing the affairs of government. On the basis of the attitude toward Eisenhower, 75% of the sample's voting was correctly predicted. On the basis of attitudes toward Eisenhower and domestic issues, 79% of the sample's voting was correctly predicted, and on the basis of all six attitudes, 86% of the sample's voting was correctly predicted. Generally, through the use of multiple attitudes, the percentage of attitude-behavior inconsistents was reduced from 25% to 14%. (pp. 264–265)

Presumably, this observation also applies to the correspondence between prejudice and discrimination; prediction of discrimination improves by considering other attitudes of a person, in addition to prejudice. Merton contended that we must also consider the social support for discrimination or its absence. As Liska himself notes, the point of his review of the attitude-behavior controversy returns to an early statement by Hyman (1949:40): "If our aim is to predict a given kind of behavior in a given social setting, we should design our tests so that they incorporate the fundamental aspects of the setting into the test." Among these fundamental aspects are not only people's prejudices, but also their perception of the possible consequences of their actions, including the situational support for a given course of action, their competing attitudes and motives, and, in the case of prejudice and discrimination, their consideration of how intimate the contact with out-group members will be. These are some of the factors, in addition to prejudice or the lack of it, that help account for discrimination or its absence.

Some observers of the attitude-behavior controversy feel that attitude-behavior inconsistency is a "strawman" issue. It is an issue of little substance, based on the false premise that while there is only an imperfect correspondence between people's attitude and behavior, there is somehow a perfect correlation between people's behavior in one situation and that in another. But "the problem of correlating attitudes and behavior is no different from the problem of correlating behavior in one situation with behavior in another situation" (Kiesler, Collins, and Miller, 1969:27). While it is true that people sometimes act inconsistently with their true beliefs and feelings, is it not equally true that people behave inconsistently from one situation to the next, quite apart from their attitudes? Actually, when trying to determine the correspondence between measures of prejudice and discrimination, for instance, are we not simply asking about the correlation between two types of behavior in different situations?

To illustrate, let us reexamine the LaPiere (1934) study. LaPiere took proprietors' responses to a questionnaire as an indication of their racial attitudes. Is not the answering of a questionnaire about serving Chinese a type of behavior, rather than an attitude, to be considered just as much a behavior as checking a Chinese couple into a hotel or waiting on them in a restaurant? The issue in LaPiere's study is not so much an inconsistency between attitudes and action as it is an inconsistency between actions in different situations. The problem with this study is that it is clearly easier to discriminate against Chinese when answering a questionnaire than it is when a well-dressed Chinese couple show up with a European at the front desk of a hotel, seeking accommodations for the night with poise and self-assurance. In the parlance of psychology, these responses have different thresholds, holding constant the underlying attitude. A psychologist, D. T. Campbell (1963:160), explained: "But this is no evidence of inconsistency. Inconsistency would be represented if those who refused face to face accepted by questionnaire, or if those who accepted by questionnaire refused face to face. There is no report that such cases occurred."

Moreover, note that the stimulus objects, those to which the managers and clerks responded, change in LaPiere's study. On the questionnaire, they were asked, "Will you accept members of the Chinese race as guests in your establishment?" But, on the "behavioral" measure, the managers and clerks responded to more than a cultural stereotype; they responded to all sorts of things about a particular Chinese couple and their European companion. LaPiere (1934:232) admits as much:

> In the end I was forced to conclude that those factors which most influenced the behavior of others towards the Chinese had nothing at all to do with race. Quality and condition of clothing, appearance of baggage . . . , cleanliness and neatness were far more significant for person to person reaction in the situations I was studying than skin pigmentation, straight black hair, slanting eyes, and flat noses. . . . My Chinese friends were skillful smilers, which may account, in part, for the fact that we received but one rebuff in all our experience. Finally, I was impressed with the fact that even where some tension developed due to the strangeness of the Chinese it would evaporate immediately when they spoke in unaccented English.

But only race was salient on the questionnaire. If these observations apply to the research of LaPiere, they also apply to the studies of Minard (1952) and Kutner et al. (1952).

It seems that what Minard found was not so much an inconsistency between attitudes and action, between prejudice and discrimination, as it was an inconsistency between behaviors, discrimination or the lack of it, in different situations, on and off the job. As another indication of the same phenomenon, Killian (1953) found that while southern whites in Chicago would readily physically expel a black from their "hillbilly" bar if one entered, they commonly ate lunch alongside blacks in a nearby restaurant, and at work they shared restrooms and dressing rooms with blacks. In other words, they behaved inconsistently across these settings, not unlike what Minard observed in the Pocahontas Coal Field. This inconsistency occurred even though Killian found that most of the whites were racially prejudiced, preferring the southern pattern of race relations to that of Chicago. This sort of phenomenon is not limited to race and ethnic relations in the United States. It has been reported that when African miners are on the job, tribal identities and animosities are subordinated to transtribal cooperation and allegiances, such as trade union membership. In more private settings away from work, however, tribal identities and prejudices dominate life, segregating one miner from another along ethnic lines (Mitchell, 1956). This observation is not unlike that of Minard. All these findings are at least consistent with the pluralist position on ethnicity in modern society, that assimilation often stops at primary relationships. Pluralists would see no inconsistency in these findings (see Chapter 3).

Improvements in the measurement of attitudes and behavior may help resolve the attitude-behavior controversy. The reliability and validity of measures of both attitudes and behavior underlie this controversy. Without reliable and valid measures of both behavior and attitudes, we cannot learn much about the true nature of the relationship between the two by correlating our measures of them. So the first methodological task is to build good measures of attitudes and behavior; as the student can see, however, this task has not been completed. Next, the measures of attitudes and behavior must be matched so that they assess about the same range of events along the underlying continuum. One measure cannot be a sounding of one extreme on this continuum while the other probes the opposite extreme, if the two measures are to be correlated. In a sense, this is what happened in the LaPiere study, when it was made so easy to refuse service to Chinese on the questionnaire, yet so hard to do so on the "behavior test." Kiesler et al. (1969:33) refer to another common mismatch between measures of attitudes and those of behavior:

Most of our behavioral measures of attitude make relatively few discriminations along the attitudinal continuum; typically, persons are divided into 2, 3, 4, or 5 categories. Pencil and paper measures, on the other hand, are typically more nearly continuous—making many fine discriminations along the attitude continuum. Two persons who may fall in separate, narrow categories on the pencil and paper measure may fall in the same, broad category on the behavior measure.

Some researchers believe that the intensity and certainty with which one holds an attitude must be included in attitudinal measures before behavior can be acccurately predicted from these measures. Intensity refers to how strongly a person feels about the object of an attitude. With prejudice, it is how strongly one dislikes the out-group. It is the intensely prejudiced person who consistently discriminates, even in the face of unpleasant consequences, and who is undeterred by competing attitudes and motives. This is consistent with the observations that Merton made in 1949. Certainty refers to how convinced a person is about the truth of his beliefs about an out-group. Sample and Warland (1973) found that they could predict far better the behavioral intentions of students (in voting) who were certain about their attitudes toward student government than those who were not so certain. By analogy, the more certain one is about one's prejudicial beliefs, the more consistently is one predisposed to discriminate.

The controversy over the consistency between attitudes and behavior, and thus that between prejudice and discrimination, belongs primarily to a theoretical tradition in American psychology called *cognitive consistency theory*. Actually, cognitive consistency theory is a collection of theories, all of which share in the conviction that people attempt to keep in balance the ways they perceive, think, evaluate, and then act in their environment (cf. Brown, 1956: Deutsch and Krauss, 1965; Fishbein, 1967; Insko, 1967). When people experience an inconsistency or imbalance in their perceptions, cognitions, feelings, and actions, they will take steps to restore the balance, making the world as they see it into a coherent whole again. We touched on this tradition earlier in the chapter, in regard to the cognitive approach to prejudice.

Leon Festinger (1957; 1964) formulated a theory of cognitive dissonance which is part of the larger cognitive tradition. He made an important distinction in this theory, one that is surely worth noting here. There are two types of dissonance, he wrote; one is predecision dissonance and the other is postdecision dissonance. The former precedes any given action, while the latter follows and is in a sense a consequence of prior action. It is his focus on postdecision dissonance that made Festinger's theory new and different. Festinger observed that dissonance often follows from making a decision, any decision, although not all decisions arouse dissonance. "On the whole, the evidence is clear that simply making a decision does not guarantee the onset of dissonance-reduction processes" (Festinger, 1964:156). One must voluntarily commit oneself to a course of action, having freely chosen among alternatives, and this course of action must have real and lasting consequences, as long as one sticks to the decision, before dissonance over a decision is experienced. Buying a car is often given as an example of such a decision.

To validate his choice and simultaneously reduce any dissonance aroused by thinking about passed-over alternatives, a person will often accentuate the attractiveness or worth of his chosen course of action—after he has already set out on it. That is, a person will try to bring his attitudes into line with his actions, after, not before, he has acted. He may do this in a number of ways, for instance, by systematically avoiding exposure to any information critical of his choice. A new owner of a car might refrain from reading anything complimentary about cars other than his own, others he might have bought, but which are now passed-over alternatives.

Festinger's point is that once action is taken and a decision is made, that choice may sometimes set into motion pressures for a person to rationalize the course of action as attractive, valuable, or at least the best alternative possible. Might not this be the relationship between prejudice and discrimination, or more correctly, between discrimination and prejudice? Because of the felt need to discriminate, or because the person or those dear to him have done it in the past, a person might become prejudiced to vindicate the discrimination. Because a person has discriminated in the past, and seemingly has made the decision to do so, he may feel the need for prejudice so as to validate the course of action on which he is already set. He elevates the value of discrimination by being prejudiced, and simultaneously depresses the value of the rejected alternative. This is consistent with the view of sociological conflict theory on the psychology of prejudice. It also appears to be consistent with the stand of the Supreme Court and the federal government with respect to racial integration and affirmative action programs. Discrimination is being dealt with, and it is assumed that attitudes will subsequently fall in line.

SOCIOLOGICAL THEORY AND PREJUDICE

Sociological theory contends that groups struggle for wealth, power, and privilege in modern society, and this often brings discrimination and ethnic stratification. From this perspective, members of ethnic groups become prejudiced toward one another by simply pursuing their respective self-interests. That is, "prejudice appears to be one of the results rather than a cause of intergroup conflict" (Bernard, 1951:248). According to Glenn (1965:110), whites understand that "important interests of whites are served by the subordination of Negroes. . . . Keeping Negroes down in the occupational structure keeps whites up. . . . Low earnings of Negro males . . . force many Negro females into the labor force, thus increasing the supply and reducing the costs of domestic servants." Glenn adds that for whites, "the economic losses from discrimination are more diffuse, less direct, and less obvious than the gains" (p. 110). Prejudice on the part of the majority can justify its subordination of the minority by making it seem that the minority got what they deserved, or by making it appear that the condition is the fault of the minority. Prejudice vindicates a course of action on which people are already set, one of blatant self-interest in dealing with a competitor, and it serves to reduce dissonance over having taken this course of action.

Perhaps it is Herbert Blumer (1958a) who has most forcibly formulated this sociological view of prejudice. From the sociological perspective, prejudice is a set of beliefs and feelings about racial and ethnic groups. It can include feelings of superiority, beliefs about innate racial traits, claims to certain privileges and prestige, and fear and mistrust of the minority group. Moreover, prejudice is a predisposition to action, for it can motivate behavior: "It guides, incites, cows, and coerces" (Blumer, 1958a:5).

In this perspective prejudice is also a sense of group position and "fundamentally a matter of relationship between racial groups" (Blumer, 1958a:3). Its origins belong to the historical relationship between groups, not to the personality composition of a single, contemporary individual. Prejudice is a social phenomenon. It waxes and wanes with public sentiment and through the transmission of information. As race relations become a public issue, at least in a pejorative sense, as political leaders focus on the intergroup struggle for wealth and power, as racial stereotypes are invigorated and sharpened, prejudice intensifies and becomes more widespread. "It is this *sense of social position* emerging from this collective process of characterization," Blumer concludes, "which provides the basis of race prejudice. . . . The dominant group is not concerned with the subordinate group as such but it is deeply concerned with its position vis-à-vis the subordinate group" (p. 4).

The contrasts between the sociological and psychological perspectives on prejudice is illustrated in their respective explanations of anti-Semitism in Nazi Germany. It is explained in *The Authoritarian Personality* that anti-Semitism is a product of internal psychic conflict. This conflict begins with harsh and rigid discipline in the home, representing authority which the child comes to hate. Over the years, however, the individual learns to displace this hostility away from parents and toward out-groups. Historically, Jews have been such a target in the minds of their oppressors. Note that in this version of prejudice, Jews have only a shadowy existence, like inkblots, being merely passive objects in the tormented minds of others. This seems to reduce intergroup relations not only to psychodynamics, but also to the relation between members of only one group and their distorted imaginations.

From the sociological perspective, German prejudice toward Jews was a sense of group position activated by the leaders of the Nazi movement. Jews were a middleman minority in Central Europe, playing a social and economic role that can bring a group into conflict with many powerful sectors of the surrounding society. Their ethnic solidarity enables the middleman minority to undercut their competitors, and "the result is a tremendous degree of concentration in, and domination of, certain lines of endeavor" (Bonacich, 1973:587). This can antagonize business interests, organized labor, and the general public in the larger society. Prejudice, from this perspective, is a tactic in trying to dislodge the middleman minority from its economic position. Blumer (1958a:5) wrote that the source of prejudice is a felt challenge to a sense of group position, and "it may be in the form of encroachment at countless points of proprietary claim; it may be a challenge to power and privilege; it may take the form of economic competition." Bonacich (1973:592) took an extreme view when she wrote:

The difficulty of breaking entrenched middleman monopolies, the difficulty of controlling the growth and extension of their economic power, pushes host countries to ever more extreme reactions. One finds increasingly harsh measures, piled on one another, until, when all else fails, "final solutions" are enacted.

The point is that psychology is hardly a full explanation of intergroup relations, even anti-Semitism, and the student must keep this in mind. Ideally the psychological and sociological perspectives complement one another, each making up for some of what the other lacks.

Some writers in sociology go so far as to say that discrimination has essentially nothing to do with prejudice. Knowles and Prewitt (1969) wrote that much of the racism in American society exists in societal institutions, not in the psychology of individuals. Indeed, such institutional arrangements as racial discrimination in hiring and school admissions and racially biased I.Q. tests, require neither prejudice nor commitment to discrimination. They require only people's conformity to such practices.

The position taken in this book, however, stops short of such sociological determinism. Our own view on ethnic evolution is complemented best by cognitive dissonance as theory, although we feel that virtually all schools in sociology and psychology can be used together in a fuller understanding of the dynamics behind ethnic evolution. Discrimination is rooted in intergroup competition in modern society, from our own sociological perspective, and not in the psychological traits of individuals.

Discrimination does produce prejudice, however, as it simultaneously results in intergroup exclusion and oppression. Prejudice is a way a group reduces for its members any postdecision dissonance over their discrimination against others, along the lines of cognitive dissonance theory. Discrimination sets into motion two types of drift. One is at the societal level, the divergence between the evolutions of the minority and majority group, and the other is psychological, the perceived belief dissimilarity between members of the diverging groups. The latter process follows the principles of postdecision dissonance reduction and assimilation/contrast effect, but it is also grounded in the social reality of evolutionary divergence. That reality often includes increasing social distance, even physical distance, between members of diverging groups, so that stereotypes and prejudicial feelings are not checked by close and continuous human contact and can expand in a vacuum of ignorance. The result is sharply contrasting stereotypes of in-group and out-group members. These stereotypes are easily learned by each succeeding generation, through deliberate conditioning or unintentional modeling and imitation, and the out-group can serve for some as an inkblot for their own internal turmoil. Prejudice formed in this manner can lead to more discrimination, perpetuating the discrimination and its results, which appear more and more to support the original discrimination and subsequent prejudice. Cause and effect blur, and a vicious cycle forms.

CONCLUSION

That intergroup relations in the United States can be understood in terms of the psychology of individual Americans is the thesis of the psychology of prejudice and discrimination. Prejudice serves certain psychological needs, arising as it does out of the need to know, the need to have an orderly view of the world, the need for affiliation, the need to displace certain psychic conflicts onto out-groups. It is learned in many ways, through conditioning and modeling, for example. These are among the reasons for prejudice in modern American society, none of which have much to do with the nature of intergroup relations in modern society. Once prejudice is formed, however, it helps shape the character of intergroup relations in society. Prejudiced people are predisposed to discriminate, an action which, if it is on a large enough scale, can lead to intergroup exclusion and evolutionary divergence. This can and does occur, even though modern society is supposedly ready for ethnic and racial assimilation. The role for the psychology of prejudice and discrimination in the academic study of American ethnicity in recent years has been to explain prejudice and discrimination in a society in which it should not occur.

Psychological perspectives complement the broader sociological theories on ethnic and race relations. By their reference to subjective states of mind such as prejudice, and by their contention that these subjective states are the dynamics behind race and ethnic relations, the psychological perspectives round out the sociological emphasis on objective conditions of society as the true forces behind intergroup relations. Assimilationism is complemented the most in the psychological approach, although it can certainly complement other sociological theories on ethnicity as well. The assimilationists have argued that the evolution of American society would mean an end to ethnicity, including prejudice and discrimination. That has not happened, of course, but the idea that prejudice and discrimination in the modern era are due to the psychology of individual Americans, who unfortunately lag behind the evolving nature of society, helped explain their stubborn persistence. Psychology can be used with conflict theory, too. For instance, the psychological thesis that prejudice causes discrimination complements the reverse contention of sociological conflict theory that discrimination causes prejudice. This contradiction suggests that objective competition and subjective feelings can reinforce one another; both are merely parts of a larger whole. Thus the psychology of prejudice and sociological conflict theory are complementary, together providing a more comprehensive view of ethnic and race relations.

We must always be mindful that the psychology of prejudice is only a partial explanation of intergroup relations. Its emphasis on subjective, internal, and psychological states as the dynamic but often hidden forces behind intergroup relations must always be counterbalanced by the sociological perspective, with its emphasis on the objective conditions of intergroup relations, and an understanding of how the social reality of these relations shapes the internal psychological states of the people involved. Writers in both psychology and sociology have tried from time to time to reduce the study of intergroup relations to their own perspective. The dynamic exchange between proponents of these perspectives can be a positive stimulant to the study of ethnic and race relations, in our view, and psychology will always have a role in the larger study of American ethnicity. In this chapter on the psychology of prejudice and discrimination, we should allow a psychologist (Gordon Allport, 1962) to have the last word:

In order to improve relationships within the human family it is imperative to study causes. One valuable and valid approach lies in an analysis of social settings, situational forces, demographic and ecological variables, legal and economic trends. . . . At the same time, none of these social forces accounts for all that happens—in technical terms, for all the variance in group relations. Deviant personalities, if they gain influence, can hasten, alter, or retard social forces. What is more, these forces in and of themselves are of no avail unless they are channelized through the medium of conforming personalities. Hence to understand the full causal chain, we require a close study of habits, attitudes, perceptions and motivation. (pp. 129–130)

REFERENCES

Ackerman, Nathan, and Marie Jahoda
   1950 Anti-Semitism and Emotional Disorder. New York: Harper and Row, Publisher.
Adorno, T. W., E. Frenkel-Brunswik, D. J. Levinson, and R. N. Sanford
   1950 The Authoritarian Personality. New York: Harper and Row, Publisher.
Allport, Gordon W.
   1954 The Nature of Prejudice. Reading, Massachusetts: Addison-Wesley Publishing Company, Inc.
   1962 "Prejudice: Is It Societal or Personal?" Journal of Social Issues 18(2):120–134.
Antonovsky, Aaron
   1960 "The Social Meaning of Discrimination." Phylon 11(Spring):81–95.
Bandura, Albert
   1962 "Social Learning through Imitation." Pp. 211–269 in M. R. Jones (ed.), Nebraska Symposium on Motivation. Lincoln: University of Nebraska Press.
Bass, Bernard M.
   1955 "Authoritarianism or Acquiescence." Journal of Abnormal and Social Psychology 51(November):616–623.
Bernard, Jessie
   1951 "The Conceptualization of Intergroup Relations with Special Reference to Conflict." Social Forces 29(March):243–251.
Blumer, Herbert
   1958a "Race Prejudice as a Sense of Group Position." Pacific Sociological Review 1(Spring):3–7.
   1958b "Research on Racial Relations: The United States of America." International Social Science Bulletin 10(1):403–447.
Bonacich, Edna
   1973 "A Theory of Middleman Minorities." American Sociological Review 38(October):583–594.
Brown, Roger
   1956 Social Psychology. New York: Free Press
Campbell, A., P. E. Converse, W. E. Miller, and D. E. Stokes
   1960 The American Voter. New York: John Wiley and Sons, Inc.

Campbell, D. T.
1963 "Social Attitudes and Other Acquired Behavioral Dispositions." Pp. 94–172 in S. Koch (ed.), Psychology: A Study of a Science. New York: McGraw-Hill Book Company
Chapman, Loren J., and Donald T. Campbell
1957 "Response Set in the F Scale." Journal of Abnormal and Social Psychology 54(January):129–132.
Chein, Isidor
1948 "Behavior Theory and the Behavior of Attitudes: Some Critical Comments." Psychological Review 55(May):175–188.
Couch, Arthur, and Kenneth Keniston
1960 "Yeasayers and Naysayers: Agreeing Response Set as A Personality Variable." Journal of Abnormal and Social Psychology 60(March):151-174.
DeFleur, M. L., and F. R. Westie
1958 "Verbal Attitudes and Overt Acts: An Experiment on the Salience of Attitudes." American Sociological Review 23(December):667-673.
1963 "Attitude as a Scientific Concept." Social Forces 42(October):17-31.
Deutsch, Morton, and Robert M. Krauss
1965 Theories in Social Psychology. New York: Basic Books, Inc., Publishers
Dollard, John
1937 Caste and Class in a Southern Town. New Haven, Connecticut: Yale University Press.
Dollard, John, Neal Miller, Leonard Doob, et al.
1939 Frustration and Aggression. New Haven, Connecticut: Yale University Press.
Doob, Leonard W.
1947 "The Behavior of Attitudes." Psychological Review 54(May):135-156.
Festinger, Leon
1957 A Theory of Cognitive Dissonance. Evanston, Illinois: Row, Peterson
1964 Conflict, Decision, and Dissonance. Stanford, California: University Press.
Fishbein, Martin (ed.)
1967 Readings in Attitude Theory and Measurement. New York: John Wiley and Sons, Inc.
Flavell, John H.
1963 The Developmental Psychology of Jean Piaget. New York: Van Nostrand Reinhold Company
Freud, Sigmund
1900 The Interpretation of Dreams. Standard Edition, Vols. 4 and 5. London: Hogarth Press 1953
1915 Instincts and Their Vicissitudes. Pp. 60–83 in Sigmund Freud: Collected Papers, Vol. 4. New York: Basic Books, Inc., Publishers, 1959.
1917 A General Introduction to Psychoanalysis. Garden City, New York: Garden City Publishing Company, 1943.
1930 Civilization and Its Discontents. London: Hogarth Press.
1933 New Introductory Lectures on Psycho-analysis. New York: Norton, 1933.
Glenn, Norval D.
1965 "The Role of White Resistance and Facilitation in the Negro Struggle for Equality." Phylon 26(Summer):105-116.
Hall, Calvin S., and Gardner Lindzey
1957 Theories of Personality. New York: John Wiley and Sons, Inc.
Harding, John, Harold Proshansky, Bernard Kutner, and Isidor Chein
1969 "Prejudice and Ethnic Relations." Pp. 1–76 in Gardner Lindzey and Elliot Aronson (eds.), The Handbook of Social Psychology. Second Edition. Reading, Mass.: Addison-Wesley Publishing Company, Inc.
Hendrick, C., V. E. Bixenstine, and G. Hawkins
1971 "Race versus Belief Similarity as Determinants of Attraction: A Search for a Fair Test." Journal of Personality and Social Psychology 17(October):250–258.

Hyman, H. H.
  1949 "Inconsistencies as a Problem in Attitude Measurement." Journal of Social Issues 5(Summer):38–42.
Hyman, Herbert H., and Paul B. Sheatsley
  1954 "The Authoritarian Personality: A Methodological Critique." Pp. 50–122 in Richard Christie and Marie Jahoda (eds.), Studies in the Scope and Method of the Authoritarian Personality. Glencoe, Illinois: Free Press.
Insko, Chester A.
  1967 Theories of Attitude Change. New York: Appleton-Century-Crofts.
Insko, C. A., and J. B. Robinson
  1967 "Belief Similarity Versus Race as Determinants of Reactions to Negroes by Southern White Adolescents: A Further Test of Rokeach's Theory." Journal of Personality and Social Psychology 7(March):216-221.
Jones, Ernest
  1961 The Life and Work of Sigmund Freud. New York: Basic Books, Inc., Publishers.
Katz, Daniel
  1960 "The Functional Approach to the Study of Attitudes." Public Opinion Quarterly 24 (Summer):163–204.
Kiesler, Charles A., Barry E. Collins, and Norman Miller
  1969 Attitude Change. New York: John Wiley and Sons, Inc.
Killian, Lewis M.
  1953 "The Adjustment of Southern White Migrants to Northern Urban Norms." Social Forces 33(October):66-69.
Kinlock, Graham C.
  1974 The Dynamics of Race Relations: A Sociological Analysis. New York: McGraw-Hill Book Company.
Kitano, Harry H. L.
  1974 Race Relations. Englewood Cliffs, N.J.: Prentice-Hall, Inc.
Knowles, Louis L., and Kenneth Prewitt (eds.)
  1969 Institutional Racism in America. Englewood Cliffs, N.J.: Prentice-Hall, Inc.
Kohlberg, Lawrence
  1968 "Stage and Sequence: The Cognitive-Developmental Approach to Socialization." Pp. 347–480 in D. A. Goslin, Handbook Socialization Theory and Research. Chicago: Rand McNally and Company
Kutner, B., C. Wilkins, and P. R. Yarrow
  1952 "Verbal Attitudes and Overt Behavior Involving Racial Prejudice." Journal of Abnormal and Social Psychology 47(July):649-652.
LaPiere, R. T.
  1934 "Attitudes vs. Actions." Social Forces 13(March):230–237.
LeVine, Robert A., and Donald T. Campbell
  1972 Ethnocentrism: Theories of Conflict, Ethnic Attitudes and Group Behavior. New York: John Wiley and Sons, Inc.
Lippmann, Walter
  1922 Public Opinion. New York: Harcourt, Brace Jovanovich, Inc.
Liska, Allen E.
  1974 "Emergent Issues in the Attitude-Behavior Consistency Controversy." American Sociological Review 39(April):261–272.
Mack, Raymond
  1968 Race, Class, and Power. Second Edition. New York: Van Nostrand Reinhold Company
McCord, W., J. McCord, and A. Howard
  1960 "Early Familial Experiences and Bigotry." American Sociological Review 25(October):717-722.
Merton, Robert K.
  1949 "Discrimination and The American Creed." Pp.99–126 in Robert M. MacIver (ed.), Discrimination and National Welfare. New York: Harper and Row.
  1957 Social Theory and Social Structure. Revised Edition. Glencoe, Illinois: Free Press.

Messick, Samuel, and Douglas Jackson
1957 "Authoritarianism or Acquiescence in Bass's Data." Journal of Abnormal and Social Psychology 54(May):424–427.
Miller, Neal E., and Richard Bugelski
1948 "Minor Studies of Aggression: II. The Influence of Frustrations Imposed by the In-Group on Attitudes Expressed Toward Out-Groups." Journal of Psychology 25:437–442.
Minard, Ralph D.
1952 "Race Relationships in the Pocahontas Coal Field." Journal of Social Issues 8:29–44.
Mitchell, J. Clyde
1956 The Kalela Dance. Manchester: Manchester University Press.
Myrdal, Gunnar
1944 An American Dilemma: The Negro Problem and Modern Democracy. New York: Harper and Row, Publishers.
Newman, William A.
1973 American Pluralism. New York: Harper and Row, Publishers.
Peabody, Dean
1961 "Attitude Content and Agreement Set in Scales of Authoritarianism, Dogmatism, Anti-Semitism, and Economic Conservatism." Journal of Abnormal and Social Psychology 63(July):1–11.
Pettigrew, Thomas F.
1958 "Personality and Sociocultural Factors in Intergroup Attitudes: A Cross-National Comparison." Journal of Conflict Resolution 2(March):29–42.
Piaget, Jean
1932 The Moral Judgment of the Child. London: Kegan Paul.
Robinson, Paul A.
1969 The Freudian Left. New York: Harper and Row, Publishers.
Rokeach, Milton
1956 "Political and Religious Dogmatism: An Alternate to the Authoritarian Personality." Psychological Monographs 70(18):1–43.
1960 The Open and Closed Mind. New York: Basic Books, Inc., Publishers.
Rokeach, Milton, and L. Mezei
1966 "Race and Shared Belief as Factors in Social Choice." Science 151:167–172.
Rokeach, M., P. W. Smith and R. I. Evans
1960 "Two Kinds of Prejudice or One?" Pp. 132–168 in Milton Rokeach, The Open and Closed Mind. New York: Basic Books, Inc., Publishers.
Rose, Arnold M.
1966 "Prejudice, Anomie and the Authoritarian Personality." Sociology and Social Research 50(2):141–147.
Sample, J., and R. Warland
1973 "Attitude and Prediction of Behavior." Social Forces 51(March):292–304.
Shaw, Marvin E., and Philip R. Costanzo
1970 Theories of Social Psychology. New York: McGraw-Hill Book Company.
Simpson, George Eaton, and J. Milton Yinger
1972 Racial and Cultural Minorities. Fourth Edition. New York: Harper and Row, Publishers.
Smith, C. R., L. William, and R. H. Willis
1967 "Race, Sex, and Belief as Determinants of Friendship Acceptance." Journal of Personality and Social Psychology 5 (February):127–137.
Staats, Arthur W., and Carolyn K. Staats
1958 "Attitudes Established by Classical Conditioning." Journal of Abnormal and Social Psychology 57(July):37–40).
Stein, D. D., J. A. Hardyck, and M. B. Smith
1965 "Race and Belief: An Open and Shut Case." Journal of Personality and Social Psychology 1(April):281–289.
Tajfel, Henri
1969 "Cognitive Aspects of Prejudice." Journal of Social Issues 25:79–99.

Triandis, Harry C.
  1961 "A Note on Rokeach's Theory of Prejudice." Journal of Abnormal and Social
       Psychology 62(March):184–186.
Triandis, H. C., and E. E. Davis
  1965 "Race and Belief as Determinants of Behavioral Intentions." Journal of Personality
       and Social Psychology 2(November):715–725.
Vander Zanden, James W.
  1972 American Minority Relations. New York: Ronald Press Company.
Warner, Lyle G., and Melvin L. DeFleur
  1969 "Attitude as an Interactional Concept: Social Constraint and Social Distance as
       Intervening Variables between Attitudes and Action." American Sociological
       Review 34(April):153–169.
Warner, Lyle G., and Dennis M. Rutledge
  1970 "Prejudice versus Discrimination: An Empirical Example and Extension." Social
       Forces 48(June):473–484.
Wicker, A. W.
  1969 "Attitudes Versus Actions: The Relationship of Verbal and Overt Behavioral
       Response to Attitude Objects." Journal of Social Issues 25(1):41–78.
Williams, J. Allen, Jr.
  1966 "Regional Differences in Authoritarianism." Social Forces 44(June):443–454.

CHAPTER 6

Ethnic Evolution: Toward Theoretical Complementarity

INTRODUCTION

Is it possible that in the process of societal modernization there are forces for the inclusion of some ethnic groups into modern society and the exclusion of others from it? Is it possible that there are forces for the convergence of some groups with the very process of modernization and the divergence of others? The possibility that there are two trends in modernization—one that brings the assimilation of some ethnic groups into modern society and another that results in the exclusion of other groups, either in some form of pluralism or in a system of stratification—was presented in the preceding chapters as a correct depiction of ethnic evolution and societal modernization.

The assimilationists have argued that modernization results in the fusion of ethnic groups into a unitary society. Groups integrate, acculturate, and finally fuse into a single structure and common culture. According to conflict theorists, on the other hand, groups unceasingly compete for societal resources, a competition that they say actually grows more intense in the process of societal modernization. Powerful groups oppress weaker ones, excluding them from wealth, power, and privilege.

There is no final fusion between the powerful and the weak; their evolutions diverge, since they share unequally in the modern society. The pluralists also see the continuation of ethnic diversity into modern society, that is, a changing but persistent accommodation among ethnic and racial groups in the course of societal modernization. Psychologists add that ethnic prejudice and discrimination also continue, for largely psychological reasons, into the modern era.

The modernization of American society has brought the inclusion of some ethnic groups into the larger society and the exclusion of others. This is the position taken in this chapter. The task is to identify the historical forces behind the dual phenomena of intergroup inclusion and exclusion. The variable impacts of these historical forces on American Indians, Mexican Americans, black Americans, and Asian Americans will be examined in Part III.

KEY TERMS

Ethnic Evolution

Ethnicity is an evolving or emergent phenomenon, and groups, their relations with one another and with the larger society, change in the course of ethnic evolution. In the modernization process, groups can be better integrated into a larger society, or they can be excluded from it. Thus the evolutions of some ethnic groups converge with the modernization process, while others diverge from it. These dual dimensions of ethnic evolution in the course of societal modernization will be emphasized in this chapter.

Intergroup Inclusion and Exclusion

The inclusion of an ethnic group into a larger society is evident when that group shares with others a common culture, similar socioeconomic characteristics, and societal resources by virtue of its nonexclusive participation in the secondary institutions of the larger society, at least those that transmit the national culture and distribute societal resources, and by virtue of its ethnically nonrestrictive social participation. The complete loss of ethnic identity, or full assimilation, is not a necessary correlate of intergroup inclusion, in our view. *Intergroup exclusion is evident when an ethnic group does not share with others a common culture, similar socioeconomic characteristics, and societal resources because of its exclusive participation in the secondary institutions of the larger society, and by virtue of its ethnically restrictive social participation.* It is by degree that any ethnic group has been either included into or excluded from American society. At one extreme of this continuum is the full assimilation or fusion of an ethnic group with others into the wider society, and at the other extreme is the complete and permanent exclusion of a group from society, possible only through its extermination or forced emigration.

The instances of intergroup inclusion and exclusion in American history, however, typically fall somewhere between these two extremes.

Evolutionary Convergence and Divergence

Both society and its ethnic and racial groups evolve, and the evolution of any one group may converge or diverge with that of the larger society. *Evolutionary convergence is evident when the history of an ethnic or racial group flows into the evolutionary trend of the larger society.* For instance, the modernization of American society has meant, among other things, the multiplication of white-collar work and the expansion of public education. If the evolution of an ethnic group has converged with this evolutionary trend in American society, then its material welfare has improved, its educational and occupational status increased, and its subculture blended with modern idioms and other subcultures in the larger national ethos. *Evolutionary divergence is evident when the history of an ethnic or racial group does not flow into the evolutionary trends of the larger society.* This means that its material welfare and its educational and occupational status have not kept pace with changes in the larger society, and its subculture has not blended with the larger national culture. While some groups have been swept up in the trend toward white-collar work and a college education in this nation, others have not, or at least not as rapidly, and thus for a time their histories have diverged from these evolutionary trends in the larger society. It is by degree, however, that evolutionary convergence and divergence occur, and the evolutions of ethnic groups in America typically fall somewhere between the extremes of complete convergence and divergence.

ETHNIC EVOLUTION IN AMERICAN SOCIETY

Intergroup inclusion and exclusion, and evolutionary convergence and divergence, have all occurred in the modernization of American society. Some groups more than others have kept pace with the modernization of American society. The series of six propositions which comprises the balance of this chapter sets forth reasons for the dual phenomena of intergroup inclusion and evolutionary convergence, and intergroup exclusion and evolutionary divergence.

> *Proposition 1:* Ethnic groups in America have evolved with a changing society, particularly in connection with the modernization of American society. This evolution has involved the intergroup exchange of land, labor, and capital.

Theories should place intergroup relations in the context of the larger society in which they occur. This advice is often given by social scientists (Bernard, 1951; Lieberson, 1961; Newman, 1973; Van den Berghe,

1967). Moreover, society is frequently considered a process in sociology, or a social and economic network that is continuously changing (e.g., Buckley, 1967; Olsen, 1968). The social evolutionists of the past century focused specifically on the process of societal modernization, a focus that has been continued into the present century by assimilationists, pluralists, and conflict theorists alike. The plan of this book is similar: to analyze ethnic evolution in the context of a changing American society, and specifically in connection with the modernization of American society.

Ethnic evolution and the modernization of America have both been implicated in the intergroup exchange of land, labor, and capital. The phenomena of intergroup exchange and societal change are really inseparable. The exchange among the nation's ethnic and racial groups of land, labor, and capital is the content of both ethnic evolution and the modernization of American society. There was first the exchange of land between American Indians and white settlers on the frontier. The settlers eventually expropriated all but small parcels of Indian land, transplanted a European market economy to it, made capital improvements on it, and otherwise brought the land into the production of surplus wealth. This can be considered the initial phase of the modernization of American society, the agrarian phase. From this point forward the evolutions of American Indians and the larger American society have diverged.

Expropriation of Indian land and the transformation of its use led to the need for immigrant labor in America. Immigrant groups first settled on the land and took up work in American agriculture. Later in the nation's evolution toward an industrial society, the stream of immigrants began to flow into the industrial centers. Many of the children and grandchildren of the immigrants would in the 20th century evolve into a class of white-collar workers with college educations. Immigrant groups have evolved as America has changed from an agrarian to an industrial and then postindustrial society and its labor needs have changed, either converging with or diverging from these evolutionary trends in the larger society. It is in the context of the country's changing labor needs that the evolutions of its immigrant groups must be set.

While the evolution of ethnic groups is significantly implicated in the economic order, ethnic and racial groups are not equivalent to economic classes. Economic classes result from man's relation to production, while ethnic groups are products of commonalities in race, culture, and nationality, all of which are theoretically independent of the economic order. Ethnic groups can exist prior to their entry into any given economic order, while economic classes cannot. Nevertheless, once ethnic groups enter into production or otherwise become implicated in an economic order, their evolutions are shaped by economic change. Ethnic evolution in the course of the modernization of American society—agrarian, industrial, and postindustrial—is shown in Figure 1.

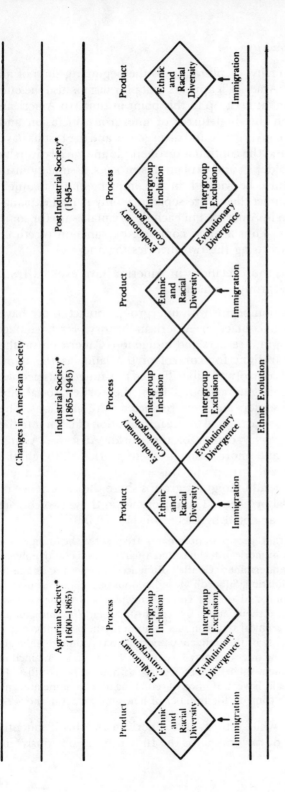

Figure 1 *Societal change and ethnic evolution.*

*Dates are approximations only. Industrial society is identified with the building of urban industrial centers and growth in industrial, blue-collar work, while postindustrial society is identified with the expansion of white-collar work.

Ethnic and racial diversity, or pluralism, is the beginning state of all ethnic evolution, and in America it appears that pluralism is also the end state of ethnic evolution, at least up to this point in time. In American history there have been the dual forces of intergroup inclusion and exclusion, evolutionary convergence and divergence, and the results have been both assimilation and the continuation of ethnic and racial diversity in American society. To depict and explain this process, assimilationism and conflict theory must be viewed in a complementary manner. Assimilationism and conflict theory are separately only partial explanations of ethnic evolution in America, but each theory makes up for some of what the other lacks. Thus a more complete explanation of ethnic evolution can emerge by using the two theories together.

Proposition 2: Intergroup relations in America have evolved from two types of intergroup contact.

While all ethnic evolution begins with intergroup contact, there have been two kinds of such contact in American history. First, contact occurred between immigrant settlers and indigenous Americans on the frontier. Following their fight for control of the land, as the more powerful settlers gained control and subordinated the indigenous people, native Americans were largely excluded from the revised social and economic system of the settlers and were restricted to reservations. The second type of contact was occasioned by the immigration of labor into the country from virtually every corner of the world. Africans, Asians, Europeans, Mexicans, and more came here to work. Although the experiences of immigrant groups in this country vary, and these variations are significant, all immigrant groups share the experience of meeting the country's labor needs. The difference in these two contact situations is significant, as noted by Lieberson (1961:906):

In areas where the migrant group is dominant, frequently the indigenous population suffers sharp numerical declines and their economic and political institutions are seriously undermined. Conflict often accompanies the establishment of migrant superordination. Subordinate indigenous populations generally have no alternative location and do not control the numbers of new ethnic populations admitted into their area. By contrast, when the indigenous population dominates the political and economic conditions, the migrant group is introduced into the economy of the indigenous population. Although subordinate in their new habitat, the migrants may fare better than if they remained in their homeland. Hence their subordination occurs without great conflict. In addition, the migrants usually have the option of returning to their homeland and the indigenous population controls the number of new immigrants in the area.

The conflict between white settlers and American Indians frequently was reduced to the use of raw force, for the Indians were obviously not predisposed to accept the legitimacy of white-settler rule. Anglo-Saxon settlers initially took land from native Americans by force, gradually assumed control of the frontier, and ultimately transformed that force into legitimate political rule (cf. Glazer, 1954). Later immigrants were comparatively willing to accept Anglo-Saxon cultural, political, and economic hegemony when they entered the country on the other side of Lenski's (1966) political cycle—force, legitimate rule, force (see Chapter 4).

> *Proposition 3:* Relations between America's immigrant and indigenous people evolved out of their conflict over land proprietorship and use on the frontier. As the more powerful immigrants transplanted their market economy and a European legal system onto American soil, the indigenous peoples were either excluded from the revised economic and social order or found some measure of accommodation to it at the bottom of the labor hierarchy. Both involved intergroup exclusiveness between the immigrants and indigenous people, and this exclusiveness has meant a divergence between the evolutions of America's indigenous groups and that of the larger society.

There was conflict between American Indians and white settlers on the frontier over land use and proprietorship. The settlers expropriated Indian land, established a market economy and European political system, and brought the land into the production of a surplus. To European settlers, but not to American Indians, land represented a tool of production and a means to create wealth. Surplus wealth was extracted from the land, distributed through a system of markets, and consumed at points distant from its production. Investments of capital and labor were required to bring the land into production and build a distribution system, and European notions of private property were established on the frontier with a settler-based political hegemony to protect these investments. This first stage of the modernization of American society, the agrarian phase, made it impossible for settlers and indigenous people to share the land in mutual subsistence.

As their wealth and numbers grew, the settlers became the superior military power in North America. From a position of power, settlers expropriated more and more Indian land and became more powerful and wealthier in the process. Thus, land in America was converted to new uses and ownership which were consistent with the principles of a market economy and a European system of law and land proprietorship.

Although great labor needs were created in the course of these changes, native Americans were largely bypassed as a potential source of labor. Instead, the country turned almost solely to immigrant labor, and

American Indians were excluded for generations from the wider social and economic order. Some might wish to put it more strongly by saying that the American Indian was nearly exterminated. American Indians were certainly isolated on reservations, out of the way, where they have stayed on an evolutionary course which was divergent from that of the larger society. Even today, evidence for this divergence can be found in the relatively low rates of Indian participation in the labor force, low levels of education, and high rates of mortality and morbidity.

Proposition 4: Immigrants came to this country as labor, and as the nation's labor needs have evolved so have the immigrant groups.

Immense numbers of immigrants came to the United States in the 18th, 19th and 20th centuries—more than 42 million, either as free individuals or slaves—to meet the labor needs of a growing country. It was the largest migration of people in the history of the world. During this era, the southern plantation economy with its slave labor expanded from the Atlantic Coast to the Mississippi Delta, and the larger frontier finally reached from Maine to the Pacific Coast. This huge expanse of land absorbed thousands of immigrants and native-born settlers alike; one need only recall the Louisiana Purchase of 1803, the Treaty of Guadalupe Hidalgo in 1848, and the Homestead Act of 1862 to sense the scale of the national policy for populating the frontier with immigrant settlers. The expansion of the frontier for settlement and the expropriation of Indian land were simply different sides of the same coin.

After the Civil War, in the second half of the 19th century, America became an industrial nation. The opposition of southern planters to measures required for great industrial growth had been nullified, and hundreds of factories, foundries, mills, and packinghouses were built after the war. This industrial growth pulled literally millions of immigrants into the country and put them to work. Immigrants by the thousands worked on building the railroads, one of the great construction endeavors of the era, and labored in industries in the nation's cities. While many people stayed on the land and in agriculture past the second half of the 19th century, the percentage of farmers and farm workers to the total labor force declined from this point forward, going down to only 3 percent of the labor force in 1970.

American agriculture played a critical role in the nation's industrial development. Agriculture and extraction processes provided industry with the raw materials for production, with the foodstuffs for an urban labor force, and with an expanding domestic market for industrial goods. Agriculture and extraction also furnished much of the investment capital for the construction of the country's industrial base. The construction of industrial plants and transportation systems required large sums of

Spring plowing. This man illustrates how his group has helped meet the labor needs of the nation. Lange; Library of Congress.

capital, and since prosperous American farmers had accumulated modest savings by early in the 19th century, they, along with wealthy merchants, were in a position to help finance American industry. While the savings of individual farmers and merchants were modest, corporations later concentrated these individual holdings into larger pools of venture capital, achieving a scale of investment necessary to build an industrial nation. Money still had to be borrowed from foreign nations, however, and American agriculture played an important role in these international dealings as well. Agricultural and mineral surpluses, even the land itself, were used as collateral in these foreign loans, and the sale of the surplus to foreign countries helped America retire these debts.[1] The expropriation of the Indian land, the conversion of this land into the production of a surplus, the sale of this surplus in a market economy, and the demand for industrial goods created by this transformation were all important in the growth of American industry in the 19th century.

From 1870 to 1950 the nation's labor force grew fivefold, from 13 to 65 million workers (Hauser, 1964). Many of these workers were immigrants who, with their children, have met the nation's growing and changing labor needs. As the country's labor needs expanded in the past century, they also changed from farming to industrial work, and the stream of immigrants was shifted away from settlement on the frontier to the nation's industrial cities. While only 17 percent of the nation's labor force was engaged in manufacturing in 1820, nonfarm blue-collar workers represented over 40 percent of the labor force in 1920, and the number of agrarian workers to the total labor force declined from 80 to 35 percent in this same period (Hauser, 1964). The transformation of America from an agrarian into an industrial society was the second phase of the modernization of American society.

The experiences of many immigrant groups, people from all over the world, converged in this country to meet its labor needs in agriculture and extraction and then in industry. There were German and Scandinavian farmers in the Midwest, African slaves in the agrarian South, Irish construction workers and industrial laborers in the Northeast, and Chinese miners and construction workers in the West; all of these groups and others shared experiences in the labor market. All provided manual labor, more or less. The histories of these many immigrant groups converged with the evolution of the larger American society toward an industrial society.

There was also evolutionary divergence, however, as some groups were

[1] It is said, tongue in cheek, that the reason trains in the United States run on the wrong side of the tracks, on the north when going east and on the south when going west, as the British drive, is that capital from Great Britain built the American railroads.

sooner than others to enter the urban, industrial labor market. For example, black Americans would not take positions in industrial labor in significant numbers until much later, in the 20th century. It was the European immigrants who first entered the industrial order of the North, in the 19th century. The significance of this evolutionary divergence became clear only later, in the present century, when the modern institutions for the greater inclusion of immigrants and their children first appeared in the northern cities.

The structure of 19th-century American society permitted only a limited measure of intergroup inclusion. The process of intergroup inclusion is facilitated greatly by the presence in a society of secondary institutions that enable immigrants to enculturate quickly, disperse throughout a variety of jobs and geographical settings, and come into frequent contact with members of other ethnic groups and with the cultural symbols of the society at large. Secondary institutions for such integration and acculturation of the masses simply did not exist in the past century, although they came into being in 20th-century America.

The occupational structure of a society is one institution for intergroup inclusion. The broader and more diverse that structure is, the greater are the chances for the intergroup inclusion of the masses. There is a greater potential for the occupational mobility of all when a goodly portion of a nation's total jobs are at the middle and upper levels. The more diverse is a nation's occupational structure, the greater is the chance for the occupational diversification of any of its ethnic and racial groups. If, in addition, much of the work requires schooling, as white-collar jobs do, then the chance is greater for the enculturation of any immigrant group. None of this was true, however, for 19th-century America.

The occupational structure of 19th-century America was not broad, nor was it diverse. Rather it was narrowly confined to manual labor, the bulk of which was in unskilled work. The chances for occupational mobility and thus the occupational diversification of ethnic groups was limited to some members moving up to skilled trades and not much further. Missing from the labor market in the past century was the multitude of white-collar jobs now found in the occupational structure. In the 19th century manual workers, skilled and unskilled, rural and urban, were not, in the course of their work, put in touch with a national culture and the larger society. Thus they could exist easily in ethnic subsocieties and subcultures, without penetrating the larger society. Their work required neither schooling nor enculturation in the general sense; by way of illustration, children in the last century typically attended school for only five or six years and then took on a job apprenticeship.

All of this would change in the 20th century with the proliferation of white-collar jobs. Because white-collar workers require prolonged

Child miners. The force of enculturation is restricted when children are in the labor force rather than in school. Hine; Library of Congress.

education (often through college) and must constantly manipulate cultural symbols, they are put in touch with the national culture. Combined with the effects of the spread of education, literacy, mass communication, and patterns of mass consumption in the present century, the growth of white-collar jobs has resulted in a greater capacity to assimilate diverse ethnic groups, in potential if not in practice. This observation is obviously consistent with the theme of social evolutionism, the theoretical premise in assimilationism.

Moreover, it was typical in the past century for unskilled, manual laborers to work in ethnically homogenous gangs. This tendency was certainly the case in the construction of railroads in the West and in agrarian labor in the South and Southwest, and it was also evident in factories and foundries throughout the country. In the construction of the transcontinental railroad, for instance, Chinese gangs laid track from the west, the Irish laid it from the east, and the two met only in Utah. In the South, around the turn of the century, blacks were cultivating the land for white planters, while white labor was working at the mills in the towns. At the same time, in New England Anglo-Americans were the managers, the Irish were the foremen, and the Polish were the common laborers in the textile mills (Collins, 1946). Work done in this manner kept the contact of immigrant groups with one another on the job at a minimum, and this slowed the rate of their assimilation as it maintained their ethnic diversity. Labor needs and the organization of work fostered segregation on and off the job, in other words, and this segregation was reinforced in the patterns of social participation of the era.

The isolation of immigrant farmers in rural areas and the urban concentration of immigrant workers in ethnic enclaves near factories circumscribed people's patterns of social participation to participation with their own kind. This also had the effect of maintaining ethnic pluralism in 19th- and early 20th-century America. For instance, industrialization fostered ethnic segregation in the nation's industrial cities from late in the 1800s to World War II (Yancey, Erickson, and Juliani, 1976). Because of the need of factories for enormous pools of labor, and in the absence of rapid transportation or the widespread use of the automobile, immigrant workers concentrated in large numbers in neighborhoods near their work. Neighborhoods near packinghouses were for years ethnic enclaves; my own roots are in just such a neighborhood. Many of these neighborhoods achieved institutional completeness, so that nearly all of the needs of immigrant residents were met within these segregated areas (Breton, 1964). The residential isolation of ethnic groups in rural and urban areas reinforced intergroup exclusiveness in the past century.

The 19th-century lack of mass public education played a role equal to

Bethlehem, Pennsylvania. Immigrants worked here in American industry.
Evans; Library of Congress.

that of the occupational structure in maintaining ethnic diversity in America. It is primarily through mass education that ethnic groups are enculturated into the larger national culture. Of course, the occupational structure and educational system of a society are thematically related. So long as labor needs in America were confined to manual and unskilled work, capital and society at large took little interest in the education and enculturation of immigrant labor. What need had an immigrant for a formal education when virtually all the nation's jobs required nothing more than motor skills? Only bodies were needed, not minds. Moreover, children exited from education and became part of the labor force at an early age. In the absence of the white-collar work that characterizes the current labor market in America, the government, private capital, and organized labor had little interest in mass public education, that is, in the enculturation of immigrant labor, and the minimal investments made at the time in public education attest to this indifference. There was no large-scale mechanism for ethnic groups, either in industry or on the land, to adopt a common culture rapidly. This mechanism would come in the present century with the evolution toward white-collar work.

The causes for intergroup exclusiveness and ethnic diversity in the past century were limited neither to the nation's occupational structure nor to the lack of mass public education. In this era, many members of ethnic groups were first-generation immigrants in this country who had strong and relatively fresh memories of their homelands and the old ways. This alone made for ethnic pluralism. Nevertheless, ethnic diversity persists in a society when its institutions for the absorption of immigrants are limited in scope, and this was the case in 19th-century America. Although Anglo-Saxons controlled the cultural, economic, and political apparatus of the larger society, including that on the frontier, their control was significantly circumscribed by the nature of the nation's labor needs. The nation needed field hands and factory workers; there was no need for the systematic and thorough enculturation of immigrant labor, nor for their occupational mobility. This allowed for the continuation of immigrant subsocieties and subcultures in 19th-century America. The national character of America did not begin to take shape until the 20th century (Handlin, 1973), the result, we argue, of changes in the country's labor needs.

Some mobility was certainly possible in the past for immigrant labor, with advancement primarily attainable through crime, politics, and the labor movement (see Chapter 2). Immigrants could also become enterpreneurs, either businessmen or farmers. But this was possible for only a few people, and careers in crime, business, politics, and organized labor brought people back into contact with their ethnic roots as much as with the larger society. This is illustrated by the Irish labor boss and by the lack of assimilation on the part of Chinese businessmen in the past century (see Chapter 9). Nevertheless, these mobility routes were important in the preparation of a group for changes in the 20th century which permitted greater intergroup inclusion. Groups which were able to establish "turfs" successfully in business, crime, politics, and the trade unions could take better advantage of the growth of white-collar work and the expansion of education in the present century.

The limits to intergroup inclusion in the past century are only comparative and a matter of degree. Relative to the mechanisms for the absorption of ethnic groups which exist in the present century, there were few secondary institutions for intergroup inclusion in 19th-century America. If the experiences of the immigrant groups in the 19th century are compared with the exclusion of the American Indians in the same period, however, it would seem that there was ample opportunity for the inclusion of immigrants. Our point is that the opportunity for the inclusion of immigrant labor expanded as American society modernized.

> *Proposition 5:* Because of the rise of white-collar work and the corresponding expansion of public education, strong forces for intergroup inclusion were set into motion in 20th-century America. The evolutions of many immigrant groups in this period have converged with that of the larger society and culture.

There have been two great changes in the labor needs of this country; the first was the growth of industrial, blue-collar work in the past century, and the second was the rise of white-collar work in this century. These changes represent the second and third phases of the modernization of American society, the transformation of America into an industrial and then a postindustrial society. White-collar workers represented less than 18 percent of the nation's labor force in 1900, but by 1970 these workers comprised 48 percent of the country's labor force. Employment in agriculture has continued to decline, from nearly 38 percent of the labor force in 1900 to only 3 percent in 1970. The proportion of nonfarm blue-collar workers to the total labor force has remained stable in the 20th century, although the percentage of unskilled workers has declined. There has been a trend toward mental and cultural work in this century, in both blue-and white-collar work, as shown in Table 1.

The growth in white-collar work has meant a growing number of clerks, teachers, medical specialists, engineers, and salaried managers in large public and private organizations. Trow (1966:438) comments on these changes:

Since the Civil War, and especially in the past fifty years [since 1900], an economy based on thousands of small firms and businesses has been transformed into one based on large bureaucratized organizations characterized by centralized

Table 1   Occupational Distribution from 1900 to 1970

Occupation	1900	1910	1920	1930	1940	1950	1960	1970
White Collar.........	17.6%	21.3%	24.9%	29.4%	31.1%	36.6%	43.3%	48.1%
Professional and technical........	4.3	4.7	5.4	6.8	.5	8.6	11.8	14.8
Managerial, official, professional.........	5.8	6.6	6.6	7.4	.3	8.7	8.8	8.3
Clerical............	3.0	5.3	8.0	8.9	.6	12.3	15.1	17.9
Sales.................	4.5	4.7	4.9	6.3	.7	7.0	7.6	7.1
Blue Collar...........	35.8	38.2	40.2	39.6	.8	41.1	38.6	36.0
Craftsmen.........	10.5	11.6	13.0	12.8	.0	14.1	14.2	13.9
Operatives.........	12.8	14.6	15.6	15.8	.4	20.4	19.4	17.6
Laborers (except farm)	12.5	12.0	11.6	11.0	.4	6.6	5.0	4.5
Services.................	9.0	9.6	7.8	9.8	.7	10.5	11.6	12.8
Private households.................	5.4	5.0	3.3	4.1	.7	2.6	2.8	1.5
Farm workers.......	37.5%	30.9%	27.0%	21.2%	17.4%	11.8%	6.4%	3.1%

Source: Sar A. Levitan and William B. Johnston, *Work Is Here to Stay, Alas* (Salt Lake City, Utah: Olympus Publishing Company, 1973).

decision-making and administration carried out through coordinated managerial and clerical staffs.

When small organizations grow large, papers replace verbal orders; papers replace rule-of-thumb calculations of price and profit; papers carry records of work flow and inventory that in a small operation can be seen at a glance on the shop floor and materials shed. And as organizations grew, people had to be trained to handle those papers—to prepare them, to type them, to file them, to process them, to assess and use them. The growth of the secondary-school system after 1870 was in large part a response to the pull of the economy for a mass of white-collar employees with more than an elementary school education.

With the two transformations of the American occupational structure, from an agrarian to an industrial and then to a postindustrial society, there have been accompanying changes in American public education. Thus the history of American education also consists of three distinct phases, as shown in Figure 2.

When the American economy was agrarian, only a small fraction of the American labor force needed a high school or college education, and only a small fraction were so educated (around 2 percent). Later, as America became an industrial and urban nation, still only a minority of eligible Americans were enrolled in the nation's high schools and colleges. No more than 10 percent of the eligible youth were attending high school in 1900, and only 2 or 3 percent were enrolled in college. As long as the nation's labor needs were manual and its occupational structure was

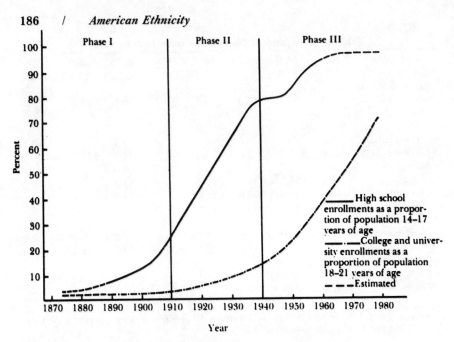

Figure 2 *The history of American education.*
Source: Martin Trow, "The Second Transformation of American Secondary Education," pp. 437–448 in Reinhard Bendix and Seymour Martin Lipset (eds.), *Class, Status, and Power,* 2nd ed. (New York: Free Press, 1966).

confined in large measure to physical and blue-collar work, and as long as the nation needed bodies rather than minds, America had little in the way of public education. More generally, it offered little in the way of social services to encourage the large-scale enculturation of immigrant labor.

However, the need for educated and enculturated labor did come later in the 20th century. The number of white-collar workers has grown phenomenally in this century; their number nearly tripled in proportion to the total labor force, from 18 percent in 1900 to 48 percent in 1970. First, the number of clerks expanded at an extraordinary rate: a 28-fold increase in clerks has occurred since 1900. Later in the century, after World War II, there was a great growth in the number of professional, technical, and kindred workers: "between 1950 and 1960 the total labor force increased by only 8 percent; but the number of professional, technical, and kindred workers grew by 68 percent and these, of course, are the occupations that call for at least some part of a college education" (Trow, 1966:442–443). Not surprisingly, college enrollments have increased tremendously in the past 30 years. Correlated with the increasing educational needs of American labor have been two transformations of American education in the 20th century, one

Graduation exercise. The force of enculturation expanded during the 20th century. Courtesy of Paddock Publications, Arlington Heights, Illinois.

associated with the training of clerks and another with the education of professionals and technicians.

First, the private academies, where a small number of elite students had been given a classical liberal education in the 19th century, were replaced by public high schools, where a mass of students were vocationally trained for clerical work. Until 1950, the high school diploma was for most students a terminal degree. After 1950 college enrollments climbed, and the nation's technical and professional workers were educated in colleges and universities (see Figure 2). This was the second transformation of American education. Trow (1966:441) summarized these two changes in American education:

The period 1870–1980 with which we are dealing falls naturally then into three phases. In Phase 1 secondary and higher education were by and large offering an academic education to an elite minority. Phase II, between roughly 1910 and 1940, saw the rapid growth of mass terminal secondary education, with higher education still offered to a small but slowly growing minority. Since 1940, or more precisely since World War II, we are (in Phase III) seeing the rapid growth of mass higher education.

The rise of white-collar work and expansion of education are the 20th-century institutions that have provided a greater potential for intergroup inclusion in American society. The occupational structure of America has become relatively broad and presently permits more occupational mobility for the nation's ethnic and racial groups. Children and grandchildren of immigrants can now move into a greatly expanded stratum of work, namely, the white-collar jobs. Moreover, children from diverse ethnic backgrounds have gone to public schools together for the first time on a mass scale in the 20th century, and they now stay together in school for longer and longer periods. They initially learned skills suitable for clerical work—reading, writing, and arithmetic—and later in the century they learned the more advanced skills for carrying out the complex functions of engineers, professionals, and technical workers. Students were also enculturated in the process; they were Americanized at the very time they were learning job-related skills. As they were taught the Anglo core of American culture, the process of acculturation necessarily ran ahead of the structural assimilation of immigrant groups (Gordon, 1964). This enculturation continues for many young Americans through late adolescence and into early adulthood in the nation's colleges, especially the large state universities, which have increasingly replaced private and parochial institutions of higher learning.[2]

---

[2] While there have been attempts to shelter the young in parochial schools, some more successful than others, all of these efforts have done little to counterbalance the cultural standardization in the public schools.

Enculturation is not merely incidental to technical learning, for cultural facility is indispensable in the discharge of many white-collar duties. The middle-class style of life, its "respectability," and those verbal skills and sense of taste and discretion involved in the selling of oneself in the great salesroom—as Mills (1951) called the role of white-collar functionaries in 20th-century America—all of these enculturated traits became vital in ethnic labor's search for a livelihood in the nation's economy. Immigrants' habits, their foreign ways, the apparent backwardness of the immigrants themselves—none of these would do in the white-collar salesroom, as American conformity and other-directedness became characteristic of the era (Mills, 1951; Riesman, 1950).[3]

First with their high-school diplomas and then with their college sheepskins, many Americans from immigrant and working-class backgrounds took up white-collar work and became middle class: "moving into the middle class was 41.1 percent of the sons of skilled workers, 33 percent of the sons of semi-skilled workers, and 23.8 percent of the sons of unskilled workers" (Schneider, 1969:439). It was the offspring of the more skilled blue-collar workers who on the average moved into white-collar work, but of course middle-class children had the best chance for finding such positions. While the children of working-class origin generally found work at lower-level white-collar jobs, there has been a significant movement of these children into the upper levels of the middle class as well. For instance, Blau (1965) found that 40 percent of the salaried professionals in the early 1960s came from the working class and another 11 percent came from rural origins. Recent studies have found that without exception, members of the nation's ethnic and racial groups have moved in large numbers into white-collar work and have attained higher levels of education in this century (Abramson, 1973; Greeley, 1974). Comparing his study of occupational and income mobility in 19th-century Newburyport, Massachusetts, with similar studies of other cities in the 20th century, Thernstrom (1966:614) came to a similar conclusion:

---

[3]White-collar workers manipulate the symbols of a national culture, putting them in touch, day in and day out, with that culture, and the enterprise requires prolonged enculturation and a working familiarity with the national ethos. This is not to say that these workers are all fully assimilated, or that they are far more assimilated than blue-collar workers in all aspects of that process. Because of compulsory education, the spread of literacy, and the diffusion of mass media, all products of the modernization process, blue-collar workers are also in touch with a national society and culture. Often they show signs of greater Americanization, in their patriotism, for instance. The basic contention remains that modernization brings a greater potential for assimilation, through occupational diversification, educational expansion, and a virtual explosion in the variety of experiences that put one in touch with the larger nation.

. . . but it is surely significant that the six studies covering the 1933–1956 period show two to three times as many laborers' sons in nonmanual positions as the figures for Newburyport in the latter half of the nineteenth century and for Indianapolis in 1910. In recent decades white-collar and professional occupations have made up an ever-increasing segment of the American occupational structure, and during the same period the American educational system has become markedly more democratic. The fruits of these two developments are graphically displayed here, in the rising proportion of laborers' sons who no longer face the necessity of making a living with their hands.

The expansion of public education and the growth of white-collar work have become major mechanisms for intergroup inclusion in modern American society. These mechanisms brought by modernization have expanded the opportunity for the integration and enculturation of the nation's ethnic and racial groups. Additional changes have occurred in 20th-century America, and they, too, permit a greater degree of intergroup inclusion. Now there are mass media and the spread of a mass culture. Due to the decentralization of the workplace, the growth of the suburbs, and the increasing convenience of transportation, there has been a dispersion of ethnic groups out of the ghettos and into the metropolitan areas. That is, many immigrant groups have recently become more dispersed with respect to residence and diversified with reference to educational and occupational status.

The present century has also brought more opportunity for intergroup contact and the rise of more ethnically inclusive patterns of social participation. This process began with immigrant groups adopting American forms of social participation, particularly the voluntary association, as they turned away from Old World ascriptive patterns of participation based on blood and place (cf. Light, 1972; Treudley, 1949). As certain immigrant groups became more diversified, their middle classes, in particular, began to participate in voluntary associations which brought them into contact with people from a variety of ethnic and social backgrounds. As a consequence, the middle classes, those with higher levels of education and white-collar jobs, became exposed to a wider and more cosmopolitan range of interests and concerns (Axelrod, 1956; Babchuk and Booth, 1969; Curtis, 1971; Foskett, 1955; Wilensky, 1961). By contrast, the social participation of blue-collar workers and those with lower levels of formal education has been largely confined to family and friends in local settings, that is, to informal relations with people from essentially similar backgrounds. The participation of blue-collar workers in formal associations outside of unions and churches has been minimal (Dotson, 1951; Suttles, 1968). That is, it is the middle classes of various immigrant groups, those with white-collar jobs and higher levels of education, that have become most included into the larger society.

As modernization occurred and intergroup inclusion proceeded, the internal differentiation of immigrant groups grew. The immigrant brotherhoods in America became more heterogeneous, due to the increasing diversity of experiences among the members of these groups. Gordon (1964) has noted that the most important divisions of immigrant groups to emerge out of their modernization were the ethclasses. Immigrant groups became stratified into distinct economic classes—ethclasses—due to the different experiences among members in the changing larger society. The middle classes of ethnic groups were the first to participate in the wider American society, to adopt the homemaking methods and take up the child-rearing practices, and so on, advised by the cultural bearers of that larger society. Evolutionary convergence came sequentially to different classes of immigrant groups, in other words, first to the middle classes and only later to the working and lower classes. Thus, evolutionary convergence also meant evolutionary divergence within a single ethnic group, as the experiences among its members became diversified and the brotherhood itself became differentiated into ethclasses.

A good example is the recent differentiation of black Americans due to affirmative action programs, as well as the larger modernization process. While blacks were excluded by other immigrant groups earlier in the century, many of them are now moving into white-collar work, while others are not. The result is the differentiation of blacks into ethclasses:

On the one hand, poorly trained and educationally limited blacks of the inner city . . . see their job prospects increasingly restricted to the low-wage sector, their unemployment rates soaring to record levels . . . their labor-force participation rates declining, their movement out of poverty slowing, and their welfare roles increasing. On the other hand, talented and educated blacks are experiencing unprecedented job opportunities in the growing government and corporate sectors, opportunities that are at least comparable to those of whites with equivalent qualifications. (Wilson, 1978:151).

The immigrant groups have changed in the process. They have evolved from foreign and homogenous groups, distinct from each other and the wider community in their subcultures, to domestic and heterogenous groups which have become differentiated into ethclasses, and each ethclass has become less and less distinct from its class counterparts in other ethnic groups. Ethclasses have also become less segregated from each other in residence and social participation. This is especially true for the growing middle classes within the nation's ethnic groups. Not only have these middle ethclasses become more dispersed in the larger community, they now reflect that larger community, including its norms and values with respect to thinking, feeling, and acting. They are the most thoroughly enculturated of the ethclasses. The larger process is that the evolutions of groups swept up in societal modernization, through educational attainment and occupational diversification, have converged with each other and with that of the wider society. In a word, the ethclasses have become modern groups.

The process of evolutionary convergence has not meant the full assimilation of immigrant groups into a unitary society. First, only certain classes of any ethnic group were included in the postindustrial American society. Moreover, acculturation, or the adoption of the Anglo core of American culture, proceeded ahead of the structural assimilation of all ethclasses. Labor had to be culturally standardized for white-collar work before taking it up, and this brought acculturation before structural assimilation. Furthermore, while members of various ethnic groups have been significantly enculturated and do participate more freely in the secondary institutions of the larger society, their private lives and primary relations are still infused with some measure of their own distinct ethnicity. The survival of ethnicity in modern American society has been a matter of both voluntary choice and the exclusion of immigrant children from the "social cliques, clubs, and institutions of white Protestant America. . . . Brooks Brothers suit notwithstanding, the doors of the fraternity house, the city men's club, and the country club were slammed in the face of the immigrants' offspring" (Gordon, 1964:111-112). Anglo-America wanted immigrants and their children to serve as employees—labor—not as intimate friends and equal-rank associates.

Ethnic boundaries have become more inclusive and permeable, less restrictive and definitive, and the expression of ethnic identity is now more voluntary and is done selectively and purposefully in domestic idioms. It is a new ethnicity (see Chapter 3). Nevertheless ethnic boundaries do persist, though often only as psychological phenomena. It is evident that the existence of ethnicity is not limited to its manifestation in the residential segregation and occupational concentration of groups. Indeed, there appears to be a current resurgence of ethnicity as an egocentric expression, an assertion of self in the seemingly impersonal modern world.

Furthermore, some ethnic groups continue to be excluded from American society to some degree. Obviously, the nation's indigenous people—the American Indians—have not been absorbed as others have into the larger American society. Some immigrant groups have also been bypassed to varying degrees in the modernization of American society. The nation's ethnic and racial groups, immigrant and indigenous alike, have not been equally included into modern society, and they do not all participate openly and freely with one another in the nation's secondary institutions. Racial and ethnic stratification persists, and racial and ethnic diversity are still evident in American society. There have been two trends in the modernization of American society: one that has brought the greater inclusion and evolutionary convergence of some ethnic groups, and a second that has resulted in the exclusion and evolutionary divergence of other groups. This has meant both change in and continuance of ethnic pluralism in America.

Proposition 6: The evolutions of some groups have diverged from the modernization of American society, due mainly to intergroup competition, conflict, and exclusion.

The error of assimilationism is that while it has pointed to the forces of modernity which provide for intergroup inclusion, it has neglected other forces which are no less a part of the modernization process and which make for intergroup exclusion. These forces are rooted in the struggle for societal resources. Intergroup competition has often meant the partial exclusion of some ethnic and racial groups from modern society by more powerful competitors, and exclusion has often meant evolutionary divergence. In other words, the expansion of opportunities which can free individuals from the folk past has been counterbalanced in the modernization process by powerful groups erecting barriers to those opportunities, in effect denying to others that freedom. The products of the dual forces of evolutionary convergence and divergence are both assimilation and the persistence of ethnic and racial pluralism into the modern era. One side of the coin, intergroup exclusion and evolutionary divergence, has been neglected by assimilationism but is clearly shown in conflict theory, which hypothesizes the exclusion of the weak by the powerful. The changes brought by societal modernization create the conditions for both intergroup inclusion and exclusion and result in a divergence between the evolutions of those groups included into and those excluded from modern society.

Intergroup competition, conflict, and stratification have been evident in every phase of American history. These historical forces have often resulted in some form of intergroup exclusiveness, either the stratification or the geographical separation of the rivals. The latter took place on the frontier, when after conflict over land the powerful settlers isolated the weaker Indians on reservations, an isolation that continues to this day. No significant mechanisms were provided for the inclusion of Indians into the revised economic and social order, and few are provided now. This has meant the evolutionary divergence of American Indians (see Chapter 7).

Immigrant groups came to the country as labor, and it has been in the labor market they have competed with each other for the nation's better jobs. In the course of this competition some groups have erected for their benefit systems of stratification which split the labor market so that one group "controls certain jobs exclusively and gets paid at one scale of wages, while the cheaper group is restricted to another set of jobs and is paid at a lower scale" (Bonacich, 1972:555). Once immigrant groups established themselves in the domestic labor market, they often prevented the quick inclusion of more recent arrivals. Typically, this was done by groups out of fear that the new immigrants would undercut their wage rates. Newer immigrants have not only been excluded from job apprenticeships, they have been denied "access to general education thereby making their training as quick replacements more difficult" (p. 556), and they are politically weakened, according to Bonacich.

The exclusion of minority labor from better jobs has happened to Asians on the West Coast, to Mexicans in the Southwest, and to blacks in the South and North. The histories of these groups are developed in the following chapters, but the list of instances and groups involved in the ethnic and racial stratification of labor in America could go on and on. The condition of intergroup exclusiveness and official inattention to the enculturation of labor has lasted in some parts of the country longer than in others, as the enduring apathy toward the education of black labor in the agrarian South and of Mexican Americans in the agrarian Southwest attest.

Other racial minority groups, however, have been swept into modern society through the mechanisms of public education and white-collar work (see Chapter 8). The point here is that the stratification of the labor market is an enduring social phenomenon, one that results in continuance into the modern era of ethnic and racial subcultures. In the most recent phase of the history of this competition and exclusion, some of the nation's ethnic and racial groups have been denied access to public education and white-collar jobs, the modern mechanisms of assimilation.

Members of white immigrant groups have become professionals, managers, and proprietors, at the top of white-collar work, while blacks have become clerks and salespeople, at the bottom. In blue-collar work, whites have monopolized the skilled trades and become foremen, while blacks have been relegated to the level of operatives and laborers (Broom and Glenn, 1965; Schmid and Nobbe, 1965). "Keeping Negroes down in the occupational structure keeps whites up" (Glenn, 1965:110). While the educational gap between blacks and whites has been reduced since World War II, the economic reward for a given level of education is still greater for whites than blacks (Broom and Glenn, 1965; Blum and Coleman, 1970; Coleman, Blum, and Sorensen, 1970; Collins, 1971; Ornstein and Rossi, 1970). Ornstein and Rossi (1970:70) concluded:

These findings provide evidence concerning the systematic way in which blacks are disadvantaged in the occupational system. They receive less education; while at school they have fewer opportunities to take on full-time or part-time employment; once they enter the labor market, they are less able to transform educational attainment into occupational attainment; the longer they work, the further behind whites they fall; and, finally, the higher the educational attainment of the black man, the worse off he is compared to whites with similar training.

Findings such as these suggest that while the potential for intergroup inclusion increases in modern society, the practice of intergroup exclusion persists.

Both capital and labor have played roles in the stratification of the nation's labor market. Intergroup competition in the labor market is part of the larger class struggle between capital and labor. Capital has historically sought the cheapest labor possible, and the newer immigrant was typically the cheapest and most docile laborer. In many cases, capital turned to new immigrants as a displacement for the more expensive and better organized labor of older immigrant groups. This process took the form of strikebreaking on occasion, but often new immigrants were not completely aware of their role in the class struggle. In response the older immigrant groups erected barriers, often through their unions, to the full and rapid inclusion of the new immigrant into the labor market.[4]

Ethnic and racial stratification has been as common in business circles as it has among laboring groups. Big business corporations have assumed increasing control of the country's economy, a course of events that Collins (1975:440) described:

The history of business enterprise in America shows that the most successful industries are those that amalgamate relatively early with the largest banking interests. . . . A related tactic. . . . is for organizations to generate internally as much capital as possible, through such devices as employee stockholding, management of insurance and pension plans, and so forth. The point here is that the control of ready sources of cash at any one point in time is crucial for maintaining the political position of the organization in the system of credit, and thus for keeping it solvent; this is a precondition for continual control in the hands of a particular group.

The small ethnic entrepreneur was forced from the marketplace, and the WASP upper class took control of big business, becoming in disproportionate numbers the executives of the national and international business corporations. Newcomer (1955) found that Jews and eastern and southern Europeans, among others, have been absent from the ranks of the nation's big business executives. Many of these executives are of

---

[4] A labor caste system is not the only result of labor competition, of course; immigration restrictions, the full inclusion of the new immigrant, and a radical alliance of workers from different groups are all possible.

European origins, only their ancestry is from the west and north. When Jews and eastern and southern Europeans have broken into this circle, they have been concentrated in entertainment, merchandising, and mass communication, enclaves of enterprise in which ethnic barriers have been harder to maintain. Other studies support Newcomer's findings (Mills, 1963; Taussig and Joslyn, 1932; Warner and Abegglen, 1955). Racial minorities have been almost completely absent from the ranks of big business executives. With respect to minority businessmen, Collins (1971:1013) stated: "Those organizations more likely to be dominated by members of minority ethnic cultures are the smaller and local businesses in manufacturing, construction, and retail trade; in legal practice, solo rather than firm employment."

The picture is somewhat different in government employment. Sowell (1975:183–184) concluded that minority employment in government service fluctuates with politics, and the civil rights movement has had positive effects on the employment of blacks in the federal government:

In the military, Negroes were slightly overrepresented. In the civilian federal agencies, Negroes gained 20 percent of all new employment in a five-year period following the establishment of the equal-employment program, with almost a doubling of blacks in the top six grades during this period, and blacks often received fancier perquisites than their white counterparts as well.

Still, blacks and other racial minorities are underrepresented in certain areas of government, such as the State and Treasury departments.

The picture that emerges when conflict theory and its corroborative evidence are taken into account is one of racial stratification in the occupational structure of modern society. In the private sector of the economy, both white- and blue-collar jobs have been stratified, as whites have taken the better and blacks the less desirable positions in both job markets. While racial stratification against minorities is not as prevalent in the public sector, racial stratification in government service is still evident. This is the other side of the coin to the assimilationist version of modern society.

The assimilationists have argued that mobility for all groups increases as society modernizes. The great expansion of educational and occupational opportunity absorbs all immigrant groups alike. From the larger perspective of sociological functionalism, to which assimilationism belongs, modern society reduces racial inequality by preparing all competent individuals, regardless of group membership, to take positions vital to society. Because of the highly specialized division of labor in modern society and the growing interdependence among specialists, each specialist is increasingly vital to society and must be the most qualified and best prepared for the job. There is no room for racism in the modern order. Of course, the jobs that are most functional or most vital to society must be rewarded best. This creates stratification, obviously, but it is one based on individual achievement, not race, creed, or color. All of this can be found in Davis and Moore's (1945) classical statement on the functional theory of stratification.

Conflict theorists argue, on the other hand, that while opportunities do expand with societal modernization, they are not equitably shared by all groups. Powerful groups erect barriers against weaker rivals to the better positions in the labor market, to the better paid and more prestigious white-collar jobs in the modern era. All sorts of case studies show "the operation of ethnic and class standards in employment based not merely on skin color but on name, accent, style of dress, manners, and conversational styles" (Collins, 1971:1008). Conflict theorists see the recent inflation of educational requirements for work, blue- and white-collar alike, and the emphasis on Anglo-American cultural styles in the selection and promotion of employees as evidence of the existence of group barriers in the labor market. Employers interpret Anglo-American cultural styles not as barriers but as signs of employee motivation, maturity, and even good character. Squires (1977:445) gave the reasons college graduates were sought by job recruiters at a large Midwestern state university for sales, managerial, and junior executive positions: "a person develops a sense of *maturity* in college; we like our engineers to have a college degree not because of the specific knowledge learned in school, but for the *social skills* developed in school" (italics added). The evolutions of groups denied access to opportunity in this manner diverge from the course of societal modernization, while those of other groups converge with that of modern society, and the products are assimilation and pluralism in modern times.

Many conflict theorists argue that racial stratification has replaced ethnic stratification since World War II. This is true to some extent, but it is also true that some racial minorities have been included into the larger society through education and white-collar work. Opportunity for acculturation and structural assimilation did grow in the modern era, even for racial minorities in America. For instance Wilson (1978:19) observes that "with the passage of equal employment legislation and the authorization of affirmative action programs the government has helped clear the path for more privileged blacks, who have the requisite education and training, to enter the main stream of American occupations." The reasons that some racial minorities benefited more than others from these changes will be discussed in subsequent chapters. The point here is that assimilationism and conflict theory must be used together for a fuller understanding of ethnic evolution in American society. Societal modernization does indeed increase the potential for intergroup inclusion, but intergroup competition and stratification, with respect to land, labor, and capital, are also a part of the modernization process. This has meant the inclusion of some groups into modern society and the exclusion of others, and thus it has meant evolutionary divergence as well as convergence.

The evolutionary divergence between ethnic groups sets the context for prejudice. Our position is that discrimination sets evolutionary divergence into motion, but it is easy to believe that members of diverging groups are different and that these differences in group traits make for the evolutionary divergence, forgetting that the differences are due to historical discrimination. Divergence can translate into restricted interaction among members of the groups involved. Thus the optimistic dictum of W. I. Thomas does not always apply to the modern world: "race prejudice could be dissipated through human association" (Frazier, 1947:268).

Several of the psychological theories on prejudice can help explain the perpetuation of prejudice in such a social setting. Diverging groups can become each other's living inkblots, stereotypes can solidify in accord with the assimilation/contrast principle, and these ideas and feelings can be easily passed on through conditioning, modeling, and imitation, to succeeding generations. That is, the psychoanalytic, cognitive and behavioristic traditions all have something to say about the relationship between intergroup exclusion, evolutionary divergence, and prejudice. Evolutionary divergence is often reflected in a sense of group position in people's minds, and that mental set, when implemented into action, can perpetuate the evolutionary divergence.

Prejudice can also be generated between converging groups as they compete for the expanded opportunities modernization brings. The content of the stereotypes and prejudice in the cases of converging and diverging groups will likely be different. Converging groups who are in competition will typically see each other as threats, holding stereotypes about each other's pushiness; while diverging groups will likely view each other in superordinate-subordinate terms, infused with stereotypes of the boss man and his shiftless workers. The larger point is, however, that modernization perpetuates prejudice as much as it eradicates it, and psychology can help us understand the process.

CONCLUSION

The experiences of ethnic and racial groups in America have alternated between the poles of intergroup inclusion and exclusion, evolutionary convergence and divergence. Intergroup inclusion has become more possible in the postindustrial phase of American society, due to the rise of white-collar work and the expansion of public education. Opportunity for inclusion has grown with greater need for enculturated labor. This transformation of American society began early in the 20th century, during the time Park and Wirth wrote their natural histories of assimilation.

Because of intergroup competition over land and capital and for favorable positions in the changing labor market, as well as the persistence of ethnic and racial stratification, groups have converged at unequal rates with the larger evolutionary trend toward a modern American society. Between the powerful and the weak there have been uneven rates of evolutionary convergence with the course of societal modernization. This has occasionally resulted in collective protest. In the 1960s black Americans, among others, protested their exclusion from modern America. This protest was particularly directed at racial discrimination in education and in the work force, or at the very barriers that have excluded blacks from modern society and have caused their evolutionary divergence. During this period of protest, the bulk of ethnic conflict theory was written.

The pluralists were saying at the same time that modernization of American society would not result in the full assimilation of the nation's ethnic groups. The evolutionary convergence of some groups and the evolutionary divergence of others have sustained the ethnic and racial diversity in America. Ethnicity survives even among groups who have been comparatively included in the larger American society. It survives in people's private lives and primary relationships. Rather than having been eclipsed in modernity, the folk group has evolved into more inclusive forms, toward the psychological and more voluntary expression of ethnicity. A constant in the entire process, according to some pluralists, is the fact that ethnicity at its root is and always had been a psychological phenomenon which can be expressed in a variety of ways, and modernization has brought to some people the freedom to express their ethnicity voluntarily and variously. It is a source of personal identity which continues because the modern unitary state cannot supply a folk identity to millions of Americans. Moreover, as the nation evolves from a postindustrial society toward a welfare state, the political state might become the direct arbitrator of intergroup competition and the distributor of societal resources, and this distribution might be done in accord with ethnic quotas. If this does occur (and some pluralists argue that it will), then the political state will replace the labor needs of the nation's private economy as the main force behind ethnic evolution in the future. This should revive ethnicity and return it to some of its sociocentric forms, particularly political interest groups.

For the time being, the practice of ethnic quotas is taking on comic proportions, however, as people modify their race and ethnic affiliations so as to benefit most from these quotas. Teachers in Los Angeles are being reassigned to schools in order to achieve a racial balance in staffing, and some teachers, majority and minority, are switching their race and ethnicity on official records to avoid the shuffle. In San Francisco, 53 "white" police officers recently became American Indians, apparently to take better advantage of ethnic quotas there. But bureaucracy is up to the challenge posed by these "ethnic cheats." Ethnic review boards have been established to rule on these cases of "ethnic discrepancy." In Los Angeles, the review board for schoolteachers is composed of two members from the ethnicity people want to change from and three from the group they wish to change to. One immediately wonders who verifies the ethnicity of the review board members.

It should be apparent that each component of the sociological lore on American ethnicity is only a partial explanation of ethnic evolution. Assimilationists are correct that modernization brings assimilation, at least it brings a greater potential for integration and acculturation. Modern more than traditional society needs enculturated labor in a wide variety of work, and this means more opportunity for the inclusion of ethnic labor into the larger society. But in no manner is assimilation inevitable in modern society, and the fact is that some groups have been excluded to some degree from the modern sources of assimilation, education, and the expanded occupational structure. This fact has been overlooked by the assimilationists, and this is the reason they have given us only a partial explanation of ethnic evolution.

Both pluralists and ethnic conflict theorists point to the connection between intergroup competition and the lack of assimilation in modern society. Conflict theory is the stronger statement, contending that intergroup rivalry for societal resources intensifies as society modernizes, and this provides more reason for the oppression of the weak by the powerful. The evolutions of oppressed groups diverge from those of their oppressors and that of the larger society; there is no necessary assimilation between the powerful and the oppressed in modern society. However, because of its preoccupation with competition and oppression, conflict theory is unable to give proper focus to the increased potential for intergroup inclusion and evolutionary convergence in modern society. The need for enculturated labor in the modern era did set into motion significant forces for the assimilation of labor. Conflict theory and pluralism are thus also only partial explanations of ethnic evolution.

These three theories are complementary, however, and while each is no more than a partial explanation of ethnic evolution in modern society, each makes up for some of what the others lack. This is essentially what Hechter (1974) recently concluded about the impact of industrialization on ethnicity in England from 1885 to 1966. He found both intergroup inclusion and exclusion and evolutionary convergence and divergence in

Britain. A complete description and explanation of ethnic evolution in America, too, must start with consideration of these theories in a complementary manner. Since the process of convergence and divergence can become rooted in the psychology of individual Americans, and that psychology when manifest in discrimination can perpetuate any evolutionary drift, the psychology of prejudice and discrimination must be used to round out the sociological analysis of ethnic evolution and societal modernization. Theoretical complementarity cannot be achieved, however, by merely adding these social theories together and then adding the psychology of prejudice and discrimination. The result would be some summation that would in effect say that all theories apply with equal adequacy to all phases of American history, that all are equally true under all historical conditions, and that each explains with equal validity the evolutions of every single ethnic group in America. Rather, these theories must be used alternately, as the ethnic groups in America themselves have alternated between inclusion and exclusion, evolutionary convergence and divergence, and as the historical forces behind inclusion and exclusion have alternated from one era to another.

Niels Bohr faced the same issue in physics: The presence of two theories of matter, the "wave" and "particle" theories, each of which was only a partial explanation of matter. According to Matson (1966:132), "both formulations persisted in remaining valid for some observations, but invalid for others; each failed where the other was successful." But comprehensive knowledge of matter was possible, Bohr argued, if only "we accept both theories as valid—not simultaneously but in alternation" (Matson, 1966:132). At times and under certain conditions, matter is a particle, while under other conditions and at other times matter is a wave. Likewise, for some groups and under certain historical conditions, ethnic evolution is a process of inclusion and evolutionary convergence, while for other groups and under different conditions, ethnic evolution is a process of exclusion and evolutionary divergence.

In the following four chapters, 7 through 10, the social history of five American minority groups is examined in the framework of ethnic evolution in the course of societal modernization. These five groups share the experience of evolutionary divergence, and although all five groups are nonwhite, it is neither intended nor implied that only nonwhite groups share this experience. The problem is that Americans from Europe are so diverse, and their experiences in this country have been so varied, that it is impossible to write a chapter or two on the so-called white ethnic groups. In our opinion, Americans from Europe deserve an entire book, if only for their numbers and diversity.

In the five case studies represented in Chapters 7–9, the student will find behind the story of ethnic evolutions a dynamic mixture of class conflict and group competition for land, labor, and capital. The competition between immigrant and indigenous groups has been primarily over land, while that among immigrants has been in the labor market for the better jobs as they have emerged in the process of societal modernization. An inseparable part of this ethnic competition in the labor force is the conflict between capital and workers of different ethnic groups. While all five groups have faced prejudice and discrimination, the degree to which they have been excluded from American society and their reactions to that exclusion vary. Variation in evolutionary divergence is put into abstract form in Chapter 10, where it is argued that the maintenance of the folk community can protect members of minority groups from the full impact of prejudice and discrimination, when that communalism translates into capital formation, political mobilization, or some form of internal opportunity structure divorced from the prejudice and discrimination inherent in the larger society.

The four chapters in Part III also have implications for the psychology of prejudice and discrimination. It was argued in both Chapters 5 and 6 that discrimination historically precedes prejudice, setting into motion the psychological need to justify the discrimination. This allows those who must to use minority groups as scapegoats, and it makes minority groups into stimuli that evoke the aggression or avoidance. Discrimination results in evolutionary divergence at the societal level and brings belief dissimilarity and pressures to vindicate the discrimination at the psychological level. The social fact of evolutionary divergence can appear to justify prejudice, but only if we forget that historical discrimination brought both the divergence and the prejudice to justify it into being. These five case studies should remind us of that fact.

REFERENCES

Abramson, Harold J.
  1973 Ethnic Diversity in Catholic America. New York: John Wiley and Sons, Inc.
Axelrod, Morris
  1956 "Urban Structure and Social Participation." American Sociological Review 21(February):13–18.
Babchuk, Nicholas, and Alan Booth
  1969 "Voluntary Association Membership: A Longitudinal Analysis." American Sociological Review 34(February):31–45.
Bernard, Jessie
  1951 "The Conceptualization of Intergroup Relations with Special Reference to Conflict." Social Forces 29(March):243–251.
Blau, Peter M.
  1965 "The Flow of Occupational Supply and Recruitment." American Sociological Review 30(August):475–490.
Blum, F. D., and J. S. Coleman
  1970 "Longitudinal Effects of Education on the Incomes and Occupational Prestige of Blacks and Whites." Center for the Study of the Social Organization of Schools, Johns Hopkins University. Report No. 70.

Bonacich, Edna
  1972 "A Theory of Ethnic Antagonism: The Split Labor Market." American Sociological Review 37(October):547–559.
Breton, Raymond
  1964 "Institutional Completeness of Ethnic Communities and the Personal Relations of Immigrants." American Journal of Sociology 70(September):193–205.
Broom, Leonard, and Norval D. Glenn
  1965 The Transformation of the Negro American. New York: Harper and Row, Publishers.
Buckley, Walter
  1967 Sociology and Modern Systems Theory. Englewood Cliffs, New Jersey: Prentice-Hall, Inc.
Coleman, J. S., F. D. Blum, and A. B. Sorenson
  1970 "Occupational Status Changes for Blacks and Nonblacks during the First Ten Years of Occupational Experience." Center for the Study of the Social Organization of Schools, Johns Hopkins University. Report No. 76.
Collins, Orvis
  1946 "Ethnic Behavior in Industry: Sponsorship and Rejection in a New England Factory." American Journal of Sociology 51 (January):293-298.
Collins, Randall
  1975 Conflict Sociology: Toward an Explanatory Science. New York: Academic Press, Inc.
  1971 "Functional and Conflict Theories of Educational Stratification." American Sociological Revew 36(December):1002-1019.
Curtis, James
  1971 "Voluntary Association Joining: A Cross-National Comparative Note." American Sociological Review 36(October):872–880.
Davis, Kingsley, and Wilbert Moore
  1945 "Some Principles of Stratification." American Sociological Review 10(April):242–249.
Dotson, Floyd
  1951 "Patterns of Voluntary Associations among Urban Working-Class Families." American Sociological Review 16(October):687–693.
Foskett, John M.
  1955 "Social Structure and Social Participation." American Sociological Review 20(August):431–438.
Frazier, E. Franklin
  1947 "Sociological Theory and Race Relations." American Sociological Review 12(June):265–271.
Gans, Herbert J.
  1959 "Park Forest: Birth of a Jewish Community." Commentary 21(April):330–339.
Glazer, Nathan
  1954 "Ethnic Groups in America: From National Culture to Ideology." Pp. 158–173 in Morroe Berger (ed.), Freedom and Control in Modern Society. New York: Octagon Books, Inc.
Glenn, Norval D.
  1965 "The Role of White Resistance and Facilitation in the Negro Struggle for Equality." Phylon 26(Summer):105–116.
Gordon, Milton
  1964 Assimilation in American Life. New York: Oxford University Press.
Greeley, Andrew M.
  1974 Ethnicity in the United States: A Preliminary Reconnaissance. New York: John Wiley and Sons, Inc.
Handlin, Oscar
  1973 The Uprooted. Second Edition. Boston: Little, Brown and Company.
Hauser, Philip
  1964 "Labor Force." Pp. 160–190 in Robert E. L. Faris (ed.), Handbook of Modern Sociology. Chicago: Rand McNally and Company.

Hechter, Michael
  1974 "The Political Economy of Ethnic Change." American Journal of Sociology 79(March):1151–1178.
Lenski, Gerhard
  1966 Power and Privilege: A Theory of Social Stratification. New York: McGraw-Hill Book Company.
Lieberson, Stanley
  1961 "A Societal Theory of Race and Ethnic Relations." American Sociological Review 26(December):902–910.
Light, Ivan H.
  1972 Ethnic Enterprise in America. Berkeley: University of California Press.
Matson, Floyd W.
  1966 The Broken Image. New York: Anchor Books.
Mills, C. Wright
  1951 White Collar. New York: Oxford University Press.
  1963 Power, Politics, and People. New York: Oxford University Press.
Newcomer, Mable
  1955 The Big Business Executive: The Factors that Made Him, 1900–1950. New York: Columbia University Press.
Newman, William M.
  1973 American Pluralism. New York: Harper and Row, Publishers.
Olsen, Marvin E.
  1968 The Process of Social Organization. New York: Holt, Rinehart and Winston, Inc.
Ornstein, M. D., and P. H. Rossi
  1970 "Going to Work: An Analysis of the Determinants and Consequences of Entry into the Labor Force." Center for the Study of the Social Organization of Schools, Johns Hopkins University. Report No. 75.
Riesman, David
  1950 The Lonely Crowd. New Haven, Connecticut: Yale University Press.
Schmid, Calvin F., and Charles E. Nobbe
  1965 "Socioeconomic Differentials among Nonwhite Races." American Sociological Review 30(December):909-922.
Schneider, Eugene V.
  1969 Industrial Sociology: The Social Relations of Industry and the Community. Second Edition. New York: McGraw-Hill Book Company.
Sowell, Thomas
  1975 Race and Economics. New York: David McKay Company, Inc.
Squires, Gregory S.
  1977 "Education, Jobs and Inequality: Functional and Conflict Models of Social Stratification in the United States." Social Problems 24(April):436–450.
Suttles, Gerald S.
  1968 The Social Order of the Slum: Ethnicity and Territory in the Inner City. Chicago: University of Chicago Press.
Taussig, Frank W., and C. S. Joslyn
  1932 American Business Leaders. New York: Macmillan Company.
Thernstrom, Stephen
  1966 "Class and Mobility in a Nineteenth-Century City: A Study of Unskilled Laborers." Pp. 602–615 in Reinhard Bendix and Seymour Martin Lipset (eds.), Class, Status, and Power. Second Edition. New York: Free Press.
Treudley, Mary B.
  1949 "Formal Organization and the Americanization Process, with Special Reference to the Greeks of Boston." American Sociological Review 14(February):44–53.
Trow, Martin
  1966 "The Second Transformation of American Secondary Education." Pp. 437–448 in Reinhard Bendix and Seymour Martin Lipset (eds.), Class, Status, and Power. Second Edition. New York: Free Press.

Van den Berghe, Pierre
  1967 Race and Racism: A Comparative Perspective. New York: John Wiley and Sons, Inc.
Warner, W. Lloyd, and James C. Abegglen
  1955 Occupational Mobility in American Business and Industry, 1928–1952. Minneapolis: University of Minnesota Press.
Wilensky, Harold L.
  1961 "Orderly Careers and Social Participation: The Impact of Work History on Social Integration in the Middle Class." American Sociological Review 26(August): 521–539.
Wilson, William J.
  1978 The Declining Significance of Race: Blacks and Changing American Institutions. Chicago: University of Chicago Press.
Yancey, William L., Eugene P. Erickson, and Richard N. Juliani
  1976 "Emergent Ethnicity: A Review and Reformation." American Sociological Review 41(June):391–402.

PART III

Ethnic Evolution in America

CHAPTER 7:

American Indians and Mexican Americans

INTRODUCTION

Two kinds of intergroup contact have occurred in America. One has been contact between America's indigenous people and immigrant settlers on the frontier, and the other involves the immigration of diverse laboring groups into the country. The first type of contact is the topic of this chapter, and the study of immigrant groups follows in subsequent chapters. White settlers came into contact with American Indians across the North American frontier and with Hispanos in the Southwest, and in both cases there was conflict over land. The white settlers eventually dominated the frontier, placing American Indians on isolated reservations where they have followed a course of evolutionary divergence. The chapter begins with a history of the Indians' experiences in American society.

The accommodation of Hispanos to Anglo dominance in the Southwest was not nearly as restrictive. First, indigenous Hispanos and then immigrant Mexicans were brought into the economy of the Southwest as laborers, and the evolution of this group, like those of other immigrant groups, has been affected by the country's changing labor needs. Because Mexican Americans are both an indigenous people and an immigrant group and their history involves both land and labor, their experience represents a transition between America's indigenous people and its immigrant groups.

In the course of their dispersion throughout the world in past centuries, Europeans came to North America, subdued its indigenous people, and settled the frontier. The indigenous people came to be called Indians. It has been argued that this type of intergroup contact, between a powerful immigrant group and a weaker indigenous people, typically results in conflict and the subordination of the native population (Lieberson, 1961). Both conflict and subordination characterize the evolution of American Indians following their contact with European settlers, as indicated in Table 1.

AMERICAN INDIANS AND AMERICAN SOCIETY

Table 1   Evolution of American Indians and the Modernization of American Society

Agrarian Society (1600–1865)		Industrial Society (1865–1945)		Postindustrial Society (1945–Present)
Frontier contact and early accommodation	Conflict over land →	Land expropriation → (1784–1900)	Exclusion of Indians (1830–1934)	Present situation (1934–present)

Note: Dates are approximations only.

Frontier Contact and Early Accommodation

Upon reaching Haiti, Christopher Columbus remarked about native Americans:

. . . they are artless and generous. . . . Of anything they have, if it be asked for, they never say no, but do rather invite the person to accept it, and show as much lovingness as though they would give their hearts . . . . they are men of very subtle wit, who navigate all those seas, and who give a marvelous good account of everything . . . . (Columbus, 1906).

The characterization of American Indians by incoming Europeans would later change, as history evolved from early accommodation to conflict and the eventual conquest of native Americans. To put it abstractly, prejudice toward American Indians would follow the taking of their land, and all sorts of stereotypical beliefs about American Indians would come to share the common property that somehow the Indians did not deserve their own land.

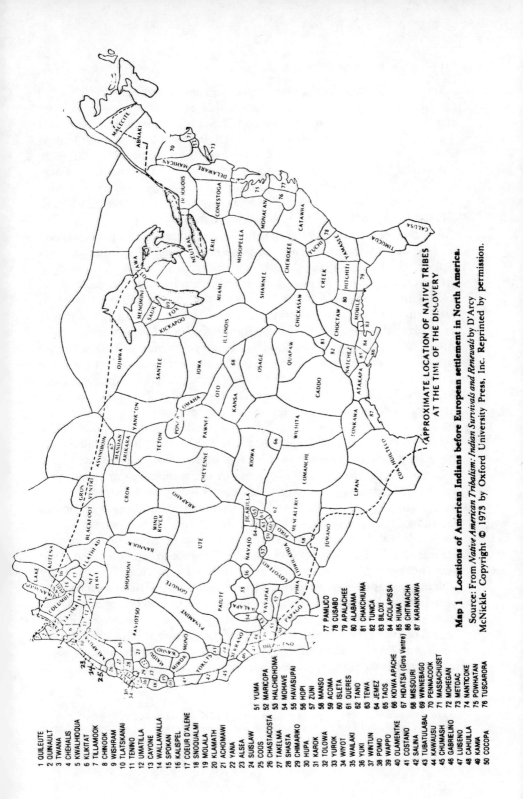

Map 1 Locations of American Indians before European settlement in North America.

Source: From *Native American Tribalism: Indian Survivals and Removals* by D'Arcy McNickle. Copyright © 1973 by Oxford University Press, Inc. Reprinted by permission.

1 QUILEUTE
2 QUINAULT
3 TWANA
4 CHEHALIS
5 KWALHIOQUA
6 KLIKITAT
7 TILLAMOOK
8 CHINOOK
9 WISHRAM
10 TLATSKANAI
11 TENINO
12 UMATILLA
13 CAYONE
14 WALLAWALLA
15 SPOKAN
16 KALISPEL
17 COEUR D'ALENE
18 SNOQUALMI
19 MOLALA
20 KLAMATH
21 ACHOMAWI
22 YANA
23 ALSEA
24 SUISLAW
25 COOS
26 CHASTACOSTA
27 TAKELMA
28 SHASTA
29 CHIMARIKO
30 HUPA
31 KAROK
32 TOLOWA
33 YUROK
34 WIYOT
35 WAILAKI
36 YUKI
37 WINTUN
38 POMO
39 WAPPO
40 OLAMENTKE
41 COSTANO
42 SALINA
43 TUBATULABAL
44 KAWAIISU
45 CHUMASH
46 GABRIELNO
47 LUSENO
48 CAHUILLA
49 KAMIA
50 COCOPA

51 YUMA
52 MARICOPA
53 HALCHIDHOMA
54 MOHAVE
55 HAVASUPAI
56 HOPI
57 ZUNI
58 MANSO
59 ACOMA
60 ISLETA
61 QUERES
62 TANO
63 TEWA
64 JEMEZ
65 TAOS
66 KIOWA APACHE
67 HDATSA (Gros Ventre)
68 MISSOURI
69 WINNEBAGO
70 PENNACOOK
71 MASSACHUSET
72 MOHEGAN
73 METOAC
74 NANTICOKE
75 POWHATAN
76 TUSCARORA

77 PAMLICO
78 CUSABO
79 APALACHEE
80 ALABAMA
81 CHAKCHIUMA
82 TUNICA
83 BILOXI
84 ACOLAPISSA
85 HUMA
86 CHITIMACHA
87 KARANKAWA

Map 1 shows the locations of America's indigenous people prior to 1540, before the European colonization of North America began with the marches of Coronado in the west and DeSoto in the east. It is estimated that in 1600 there were 850,000 Indians living in what is now the United States, but by 1850 their numbers had been reduced to 250,000 (McNickle, 1962).[1] Accommodation between Indians and whites was possible in the early years, when neither side was the military superior. The situation later evolved, however, into conflict over land and, ultimately, the conquest of America's indigenous people.

For 250 years following the first European invasions of the region that became the United States, no one people was politically dominant in it (Spicer, 1969:11). Not the British, Dutch, French, or Spanish, not even the emerging American government or the many Indian nations, could truly claim suzerainty in North America until late in the 18th century. In 1794, in what became the state of Ohio, Spicer (1969:12) notes, the triumph of the "Americans" in the Battle of Fallen Timbers gave a clear indication that they were destined for military dominance. Even after the turn of the century, the British negotiators were looking out for their Indian allies in the War of 1812 by asking for an Indian buffer state, from the Great Lakes to the Ohio River. As Vogel (1972:79) notes, however, "the stubborn resistance of the American negotiators . . . stalled the negotiations for months, and the British finally yielded the point." The American negotiators did concede to the British that there would be no more land cessions, a promise that was often made but seldom kept.

In the course of the first 250 years of their contact, immigrant and indigenous nations were rivals for control of North America. The Americans, British, Dutch, French, and Spanish all fought each other and the indigenous people for control. The conflict of the era cannot be denied. It is also beyond doubt that early contact between the indigenous nations and the European powers resulted in accommodation, since at the time Indians held the balance of power in North America. Thus the early Indian policies of the European powers and the American government were intended to be benevolent toward Indians by protecting their lands from undue settler encroachment. This intent was expressed in the Indian policy of the Spanish from the very beginning and by the British in the Royal Proclamation of 1763, and in both instances Indians were recognized as the rightful owners of land in the Americas. Land was not to

---

[1] Recently Henry F. Dobyns has estimated that the aboriginal population before contact in North America was 9,800,000. Which of these figures is more correct has, of course, important implications for the assessed destructiveness of European contact on the native population (cf. Vogel, 1972:250–255).

be taken from Indians except in fair exchange.[2] Indians were needed not only as military allies, but also as producers and suppliers, and early Indian policy reflected these hard facts. Only later did Indians become virtually useless to whites, as the American government became the unrivaled power in this land.

However, the early Indian policy of the United States, a policy largely inherited from the British, was meant to protect Indian lands from settler encroachment. McNickle (1972:84) looked to the Northwest Ordinance of 1787 as an expression of the benevolent intent to these policies:

Article III . . . The utmost good faith shall always be observed towards the Indians; their land property shall never be taken from them without their consent; and in their property, rights, and liberty, they never shall be invaded or disturbed, unless in just and lawful wars authorized by Congress; but laws founded in justice and humanity shall from time to time be made, for preventing wrongs being done to them and for preserving peace and friendship with them.

Conflict over Land

Early intentions gave way to later realities, however, and the expanding appetite of a growing number of settlers for land made competition and conflict between Indians and settlers nearly inevitable. The settlers brought a market economy to North America which gave them the capacity to generate surplus wealth, or, if you like, which produced capital. To transplant this economy on American soil, settlers obviously had to first acquire Indian land and then make investments to bring it into production. Necessary improvements required capital, labor, and technology, and the tasks included clearing the land, cultivating it, and building a system of transportation. Transportation was necessary so that agricultural and mineral surplus extracted from the land could be shipped to distant markets and sold there for a profit. To protect their investments, settlers, from a position of military superiority, established on the frontier European traditions of private property and exclusive ownership of land. This led to relatively dense white settlement on the frontier. Because the economic activities of white settlers and American Indians were largely incompatible, and because the more powerful settlers believed in the private ownership of land, settlers and Indians could not symbiotically share the land, and this meant conflict. About this phase of Indian-white relations, Prucha (1962:139) has stated that "the

---

[2] With respect to early exchange of land between Indians and Europeans, McNickle (1962:15) writes "it is reassuring to note that the Dutch were scrupulous in paying for the land and making a record of it. The first important purchase appears to be Manhattan Island in 1626 for sixty guilders, or about thirty-nine dollars at today's silver prices. This would be about 360 acres per dollar, but since the Canarsie Indians had ample acres besides, they probably considered sixty guilders in European trade goods a fair exchange."

conflict between the whites and Indians that marked American Indian relations was basically a conflict over land."

The irony of this saga is that many of these settlers had been pushed off their own land in Europe, in the transition there from feudalism to modern capitalism. Peasants were pulled into the growing industrial cities of Europe to work in factories and mills. Urban workers had to be fed somehow, creating the need for European farmers to produce a surplus. The creation of an agricultural surplus in Europe began with making land a commodity, one that could be bought and sold in the impersonal market. In this way, men with capital could first circumvent feudal notions about personal and noneconomic ties between men and land. They could buy land, consolidate their holdings into large estates, invest in labor-saving innovations for cultivation, and construct a system of transportation. Agricultural surpluses could be produced and distributed to urban workers through a system of markets. Peasants who were displaced in the process were pushed into European industrial cities or were forced to migrate to the New World, where there was still room for farmers on the frontier. In America these transplanted peasants pushed the Indians off their land, as they had been forced off their land in Europe in the transition to a market economy.

Hansen (1940) has observed that a succession of immigrants moved onto Indian lands. The Indian trader and trapper came first, followed by the frontiersman, who engaged in hunting, gathering, and some subsistence farming. These types were not permanent settlers, however, and they moved on after a short stay in one place. The effect of their encroachment onto Indian lands was to push back the frontier, allowing other settlers to locate permanently where once the trapper and frontiersman had been.

It was the permanent settler who transplanted the European market economy and brought the legacy of private property. Sizable investments of labor and capital were made by settlers, for land had to be cleared, homes and whole towns built, and a system of transportation constructed on the frontier. Hansen (1940) estimated that each homestead site required an initial investment of $1,000 to bring it into production. Private ownership of the land gave a settler some sense of security that he would realize a return on his investments, for he had legal title to the land, and the land and the improvements he made on it could not be capriciously taken from him. Public land was also converted into private holdings of big capital—the railroads, for instance—so that these corporations could secure foreign loans with collateral in the land. Thus land on the frontier became the private property of individual settlers and land speculators, real and corporate persons, and each parcel of land was under the exclusive ownership and sole control of the party who held legal

Cheyenne-Arapahoe Ghost Dance, 1891. The Ghost Dance is often considered an attempt at revitalization following conquest. Western History Collections, University of Oklahoma Library.

title to it. There was no longer room for Indians on the land; they were now trespassers.

Another fact about the contact between Indians and settlers was that their ecological uses of the land were incompatible. The modifications of the habitat required for cultivation of the land and the construction of roads and railroads seriously interrupted the ecological base of Indian life. A specific case, the near depletion of the buffalo herds during the building of the transcontinental railroad, suggests the broader scale of this disruption. The building of a market economy on the frontier had the consequence of generally undermining the Indians' ecological life-style. The transformation in land use from Indian to white purposes thus also meant conflict between settlers and indigenous people.

Indians resisted settler encroachment, engaging occasionally in open conflict which was commonly called Indian wars. East of the Mississippi River, the greatest resistance was carried on by the Creek Confederacy in the Southeast and by the Iroquois in the Northeast (Spicer, 1969). Fierce fighting occurred on the Great Plains and in the Southwest, where the Apaches held out until the 1880s. This resistance was tragic and largely ineffective, for settler encroachment eventually extended from coast to coast, at a great cost in Indian lives.

To accomplish military control over the Sioux on the Great Plains, for example, the U.S. government established a series of forts throughout the upper Missouri River area. While treaties between the Sioux and the federal government were signed, these agreements were seldom honored by either side. Gold prospectors rushed into the Black Hills (Sioux territory) around 1876, and later the Custer massacre took place in Montana. Ultimately all of the Sioux bands succumbed to the superior military force of the United States and were placed on reservations in the Dakotas and Montana. Fighting flared again later in 1890, when the U.S. Cavalry, on the advice of an Indian agent, mistook the Sioux Ghost Dance for an Indian uprising and massacred 300 Sioux at Wounded Knee Creek. Black Elk spoke to John Neihardt (1961:258) about this massacre:

Men and women and children were heaped and scattered all over the flat at the bottom of the little hill where the soldiers had their wagon-guns, and westward up the dry gulch all the way to the high-ridge, the dead women and children and babies were scattered . . . . It was a good winter day when all this happened. The sun was shining. But after the soldiers marched away from their dirty work, a heavy snow began to fall . . . . There was a big blizzard, and it grew very cold. The snow drifted deep in the crooked gulch, and it was one long grave of butchered women and children and babies, who had never done any harm and were only trying to run away.

This incident was repeated in its essentials across the frontier, as Indian land throughout North America was expropriated and Indian people were either killed or excluded to isolated reservations.

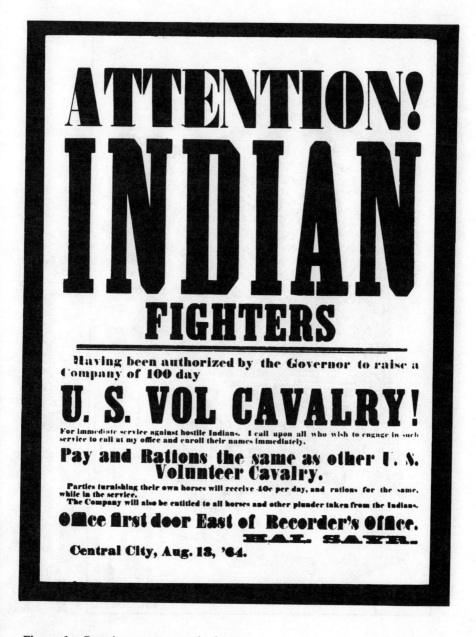

Figure 1 *Recruitment poster on the frontier.*
"Attention Indian Fighters." Civil War, Colorado Volunteers. Reprinted by
permission of the State Historical Society of Colorado.

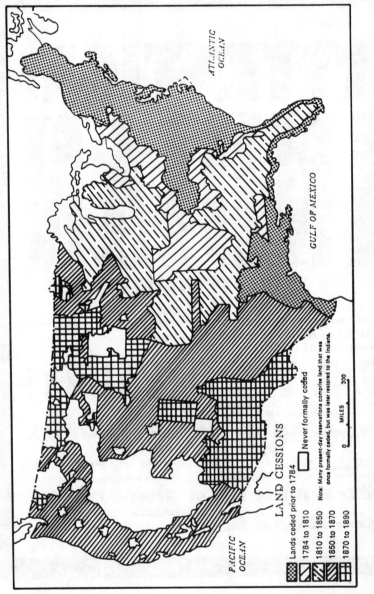

Map 2 *Indian land cessions in the United States.*
Source: "Land Cessions," map by Jean Paul Tremblay, reprinted from *The Indian Heritage of America;* copyright © 1968 by Alvin M. Josephy, Jr. By permission of Bantam Books, Inc.

Expropriation of Land

Map 2 illustrates the scale of the expropriation of Indian land over a few short years. The European powers and then the U.S. government "found it prudent to devise procedures by which title to the land could pass in an orderly manner from Indian to European [and American]" (McNickle, 1962:10). Initially, the procedure was the purchase of Indian land in fair trade; at least this was the stated purpose of European and early American Indian policy. George Washington (Vogel, 1972:75) wrote on the practicality of purchasing, instead of expropriating, Indian land: "I am clear in my opinion, that policy and economy point very strongly to the expediency of being upon good terms with the Indians, and the propriety of purchasing their lands in preference to attempting to drive them by force of arms out of their Country." However, the exchange of land in this manner proved to be a policy failure, for neither side truly understood the implications these sales had for the other. As an indication of this mutual ignorance, some members of a tribe would return to land which had been previously sold by other tribal members to settlers and would expect to share with the settlers in the use of the land. Of course the white homesteaders considered the land their private property after such sales, although these sentiments never made much sense to the Indians, for among them land had never been merchantable in the European sense. Hostilities between Indians and white settlers often resulted from this confusion over land ownership and use. It also made for ethnocentrism such as the following:

Our savage Indians had no idea of the ownership of land . . . . The idea propagated by some modern sentimentalists that in resisting the march of civilization the wild Indians were fighting for their homes and firesides belongs to fiction rather than to fact . . . . They had no home and no fireside, in the civilized sense of these terms. (Humfreville, 1964)

As the number of settlers increased, the need for land and the desire to pacify the frontier for further white settlement grew. Indian land rights were increasingly ignored by the U.S. government, and thus the precedents of earlier Indian policies such as the Royal Proclamation of 1763 and the Northwest Ordinance of 1787 were discontinued in the 1800s. First, under the discretionary powers granted to President Andrew Jackson by the Indian Removal Act of 1830, the eastern tribes were removed to lands west of the Mississippi River:

In the succeeding ten years the Atlantic and Gulf States were cleared of the Cherokees, Choctaws, Chickasaws, Creeks, and Seminoles . . . . The Ohio River and Great Lakes tribes were also rounded up and removed, with the Sauk and Fox Indians making a last desperate stand in Illinois against overwhelming numbers. All were moved—Ottawas, Potawatomies, Wyandots, Shawnees, Kickapoos,

Winnebagoes, Delawares, Peorias, Miamis, and finally the Sauk and Fox—all were sent out of their homes to strange lands beyond the Mississippi. (McNickle, 1962:40)

Some of these tribes would be forced to move again in a few years out of Iowa, Kansas, and Nebraska because of the mounting pressure for further white settlement. The Kansas-Nebraska Act was passed in 1854; then in 1862 the Homestead Act, which settled Iowa, Kansas, and Nebraska with whites, was passed. Mineral deposits were discovered even further into the frontier, in the Dakotas and Colorado, for instance, and by 1869 the transcontinental railroad linked the east and west Coasts of the country. This meant the expropriation of more and more Indian land and the removal of Indian people to even more remote corners of the frontier, out of the way of white settlement.

In 1871 Congress moved that the federal government could no longer enter into contractual agreements (treaties) with Indian tribes residing in the United States.[3] According to Spicer (1969:66-67), "The dominance of the settlers led steadily to the elimination of any conception of Indian political rights. A major step in the legal codification of this view came in 1871 when the United States Congress acted to put an end to the making of treaties with any Indian group." So ended the era of treaties; this action reversed the earlier concept of Indians as domestic nations and as the rightful owners of American land on the basis of their historical occupancy. In theory if not always in practice, Indians had been considered as self-governing political entities, capable of deciding for themselves the manner in which they would exchange land with others. Even the Indian Removal Act of 1830 had "authorized such removal only on the condition that the Indians gave consent" (Spicer, 1969:46). Actual practice had always been somewhat ahead of legal principle, but now with this legislation in 1871 and later Congressional actions, even the principle of Indian self-determination was abandoned:

So long as the Indian tribes could hold the policy makers at arm's length, as they managed to do through the treaty process, they could determine for themselves what internal controls they chose to exercise over land or any other sphere of interest. With that barrier breached in 1871, only the judicial process remained to inhibit. A countervailing legislative process was needed, and would soon be proposed. (McNickle, 1962:45)

This legislation came in 1887 with the passage of the General Allotment Act, or the Dawes Act. Under this legislation Indian families were each

---

[3] Despite this provision, Vogel (1972:163) notes, "the government found it expedient to continue the practice and did continue it, in one guise or another, into the present century."

alloted 160 acres, with titles to these allotments held in trust for 25 years by the government and "surplus" Indian land to be sold to the United States. Vogel (1972:175) notes: "No lands were to be kept in reserve for future generations of Indians, because of the assumption that their population would continue to decline." The net effect of the allotment act was to separate Indians from much of their remaining land: "In 1887, approximately 140,000,000 acres were owned in joint tenure by the Indians of the United States. The allotment law, as amended in succeeding years, set up procedures which resulted in the transfer of some 90,000,000 acres from Indian to white owners in the next forty-five years" (McNickle, 1962:49). Thus the procedures for acquiring Indian land evolved from the concept that land was to be acquired only with Indian consent and in a fair exchange, to the concept that tribal lands were held in trust by the federal government and could be sold without Indian permission. This change in legal notion facilitated land expropriation, although the practice of the unilateral grabbing of Indian land generally preceded changes in legal theory.

Whatever means settlers might have chosen to secure Indian land, they were certainly powerful enough to do it, even in the face of Indian resistance. The superior power resources of white settlers included numerical superiority, social organization, and, most importantly, surplus wealth. Settlers reached numerical superiority soon after their initial contact with America's indigenous groups, and Indians quickly became a numerical minority on their own land. This prompted a Pawnee scout, Little Warrior, to say in 1879 that "it is of no use for you to try to fight the white people. I have been among them, and I know how many they are. They are like grass . . . . If you try to fight them they will hunt you like a ghost" (Forbes, 1964:66). Not only were Indians unable to restrict the immigration of white settlers, so that the numbers of settlers grew ever greater, but their own numbers were simultaneously on the decline, due mainly to the diseases brought to America by the immigrants. While the settlers were themselves immune to the effects of many communicable diseases, those of European stock nevertheless carried smallpox and measles, for instance, which decimated the Indians at the very time the settler population was rapidly expanding. Forbes (1964:51) described two incidents of epidemics among Indians:

The natives of Massachusetts were severely weakened by an epidemic in 1633, and in the following year smallpox swept through Connecticut—at one village of a thousand persons less than fifty survived . . . . More than 200,000 Indians may have perished in California alone between 1769 and 1870 . . . . One of the most destructive sicknesses in the missions was syphilis, which virtually destroyed the native population of Baja, California, and then was introduced into California in the mid–1770s.

The settler economy generated surplus wealth, a surplus which grew as the frontier enlarged and the economy expanded. Thus, settlers possessed an increasing margin of wealth above the subsistence level, which they could and did direct in military and political efforts to expropriate more Indian land. The capacity of settlers to generate wealth was rooted in their market economy and followed from their takeover of a bountiful land. Technology helped make possible the production of an agricultural and mineral surplus and its shipment through a system of markets to various consumption centers, and thus it, too, was important in the creation of surplus wealth. The steam engine aided the transportation of crops to market, for instance, as the steel plow allowed settlers to break for the first time the rich sod of the Midwest. Technological innovations such as these provided the means for the cultivation and extraction of a surplus at a profit, stimulated settlers' desire for more land, and resulted in relatively dense white settlement on the frontier. From numbers and wealth came power, and the power of settlers was extremely liquid, since in a monetary economy surplus wealth can be easily turned into military force.

Indian resources for conflict were simply no match. Not only were Indians short of the wealth and numbers necessary for successful resistance to settler encroachment, but they never effectively mobilized the resources they did share in a united stand against invasion. Across the frontier and with few exceptions, the indigenous people were organized into small groups lacking linguistic unification and other ingredients essential for the effective pooling and easy mobilization of their power resources. Thus Indian attempts to repel encroachment were reduced to ineffective retaliation which had the net result of strengthening settlers' resolve to take more Indian land. The whites were not only more powerful, they were also better organized, having a centralized political authority and military force in the U.S. government which itself was the legacy of centuries of political evolution in Europe. The result of this mismatch in power resources is sadly evident in the surrender speech of Chief Joseph of the Nez Perces:

I am tired of fighting. Our chiefs are killed. Looking Glass is dead. Too-hul-hul-sote is dead. The old men are all dead . . . . It is cold and we have no blankets. The little children are freezing to death . . . . I want to have time to look for my children and see how many of them I can find. Maybe I shall find them among the dead. Hear me, my chiefs. I am tired; my heart is sick and sad. From where the sun now stands I will fight no more forever. (Vogel, 1972:171)

Prejudice, reinforced by the violence but rooted in the dissimilarity between European and Indian cultures, was generated in the course of the conflict over the land and helped settlers justify their expropriation of

Heap Wolves. Will Soule photo. Courtesy History Division. Los Angeles County Museum of Natural History.

it. One suspects that as settlers agitated for Indian removal, they argued that Indians wasted the potential of the land by not extracting surplus quantities from it. To settlers this was a sign of innate laziness and a convenient rationalization for Indian removal. Even when settlers met Indians who were accomplished agriculturalists, as they did in the Southwest, the stereotype of the ever-lazy and sometimes violent Indian prevailed (Spicer, 1962). The facts that several Indian cultures had been nearly destroyed and many Indians were wandering aimlessly about the frontier were undoubtedly construed as final proof in the minds of many settlers that the Indians had gotten what they deserved.

Exclusion of Indians

The fate of the American Indians eventually fell into the hands of the more powerful settlers. In their position of dominance, white settlers could have either incorporated America's indigenous people into the revised society or excluded them. The latter course was chosen, and the Indian policy of the U.S government became one of exclusion whereby Indians were isolated on reservations and removed from white settlements. This was a policy of peace through isolation. Along with their physical isolation on reservations, Indians were excluded for a great many years from any meaningful participation in the American economy or political arena, and most certainly from social networks in the larger society. This has allowed the evolutionary course of the American Indian to diverge from that of American society (see Table 1 at the beginning of this chapter).

The full-scale implementation of this exclusionary policy began with the actions of President Andrew Jackson, who apparently had the interests of Georgian settlers in mind when he ignored the opinion of the Supreme Court and executed the Indian Removal Act of 1830. Under this act, the Federal government removed Indians living east of the Mississippi River—supposedly with their consent—to reservations west of the river. It was in the course of this move that the Cherokee were forcibly marched out of the South to Indian territory in present-day Oklahoma. The tragic proportions of that march are captured in the name it is often given: the trail of tears. As Vogel (1972:70) notes: "Oklahoma, already the home of the Five Civilized Tribes of the Southeast, was soon to become a vast concentration camp into which Indians from tribes as far apart as the New York Senecas and the West Coast Modacs were to be squeezed."

Thus America's indigenous people were trapped in an evolutionary cul de sac on reservations, where, without capital and technology, they had no chance of competing as farmers and ranchers with white settlers in the new market economy. Moreover, on reservations they had virtually no access to industrial work or access of any kind into the larger society. Thus

Indians were unprepared for the later changes in American society, the evolution toward first industrial and then white-collar work. Today they are still at the bottom of America's labor and education hierarchies. At the same time, American Indians have been able to maintain their ethnic distinctiveness. The geographical distribution of reservations and major Indian tribes is shown in Map 3.

The effects of geographical isolation on American Indian evolution were compounded by those of the General Allotment Act of 1887, which had a tenure of over 40 years. Under the allotment act and its auxiliary programs, reservation Indians were expected to emulate white settlers, or at least some fancied version of settlers, by becoming farmers and tilling allotments of privately owned land. European conceptions of property rights and proper land management were forced on reservation Indians, at least on many of them, and the broader expectation was that Indians, through their experiences as a class of property owners, would eventually assimilate into American society. However, this expectation was generally contrary to Indian cultural norms, particularly those concerning the communal ownership and management of land. Equally important, it was inconsistent with the actual course of economic development—toward the consolidation of land holdings—in the regions where the reservations were located.

While Indians were scratching at small plots of arid and unproductive earth in the West, settlers of the same region were systematically consolidating their land holdings and evolving toward an economy of scale. Some of the land in this consolidation was Indian land, as Indians lost nearly two-thirds of their reservation land (90 million acres) during the tenure of the General Allotment Act. The acquisition by whites of so much Indian land was made possible by the allotment act's provisions for selling "surplus" Indian land to whites, and by the fact that Indian land had been parceled into small, unproductive, uneconomical holdings, while the trend in the larger economy was toward land consolidation and mechanization. Thus during the years of the allotment act, Indians were unable to compete with the larger and better equipped settler operations and were forced to either sell or lease much of their land to whites.[4] The

---

[4] The Meriam Report (Institute for Government Research 1928:5) adds: "In some instances the land originally set apart for the Indians was of little value for agricultural operations other than grazing. In other instances part of the land was excellent but the Indian did not appreciate its value. Often when individual allotments were made, they chose for themselves the poorer parts because those parts were near a domestic water supply or a source of firewood, or because they furnished some native product important to the Indians in their primitive life. Frequently the better sections of the land set apart for the Indians have fallen into the hands of the whites, and the Indians have retreated to the poorer lands remote from markets."

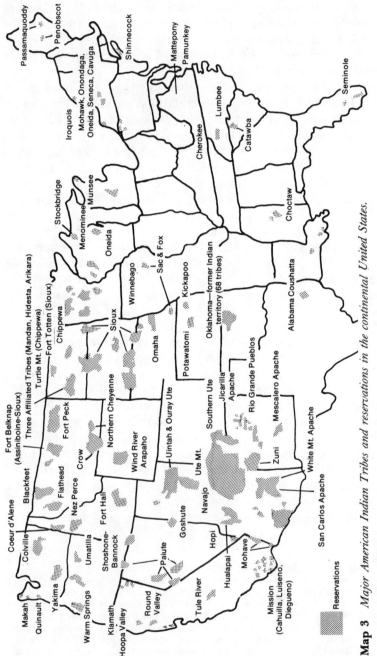

Map 3 *Major American Indian Tribes and reservations in the continental United States.*

Source: Figure 1 from *To Live on this Earth* by Estelle Fuchs and Robert J. Havighurst. Copyright © 1972 by Estelle Fuchs and Robert J. Havighurst. Reproduced by permission of Doubleday & Company, Inc.

net consequence of the allotment act was the economic and political exclusion of American Indians from the larger society, so that the evolution of Indians as a people diverged. The intent of the allotment act had been to assimilate Indians or to accomplish their inclusion into, and evolutionary convergence with, the larger society. That goal was never realized, however, and the discrepancy between intention and fact in this instance was acknowledged in later Indian policy.

Along with its provisions for land allotments, the Dawes Act of 1887 attempted to suppress native traditions in religion and education. One instance of this repression was the establishment of Indian boarding schools. Later, in 1898, the Curtis Act repudiated Indian self-determination and dissolved the governments of the so-called Five Civilized Tribes. While these measures were aimed at the enculturation of Indians, they instead had the effect of eroding the meaning and significance of native American customs and undermining traditional authority. Thus they engendered marginality and other forms of pathology on reservations. These problems were recognized a generation later in the course of the Indigenismo movement, specifically in the Meriam Survey of 1928. This recognition helped bring about the Indian Reorganization Act of 1934 (Spicer, 1969, 1972).

The ostensible reason for isolating Indians on reservations was to pacify the frontier, making it safe for further white settlement, while the apparent intent of the General Allotment Act was to somehow assimilate the Indians isolated on these reservations. But behind these reasons are more basic ones, or so say conflict theorists.

In the course of intergroup relations, groups exchange certain resources, including their land, labor, and capital, which act as assets and affect how they treat each other. Typically, the group with the larger share of such resources dominates the others, according to conflict theory. Domination can come in several forms, however, and the match between a powerful group's needs and a subordinate group's resources can greatly affect how the subordinate group is treated. If a conquered group possesses resources needed and desired by its conqueror, especially if these resources are not easily gotten elsewhere or not easily substituted for, then its domination is likely to be relatively benevolent. For instance, if Indians had been good wageworkers, and if there had been no immigrant labor in the country, American capital might have incorporated Indians into the society as labor and treated them in accord with the laws of labor supply and demand. Such assets as labor can be termed competitive resources, following Blalock's (1967) usage. A conquered group's possession of competitive resources usually brings its inclusion into the society of the conqueror.

Indians possessed few competitive resources once their land had been expropriated, as they had little in the way of labor and capital with which to influence the Indian policy of the United States. While Indians once had land, and land is potentially a competitive resource, the Indian land was obviously detachable from the Indian people and thus was not in practice a competitive resource. The tribes had virtually no other form of capital, for the Indian economies, even when intact, had generated little surplus wealth. Nor did Indians comprise an attractive labor pool. Indian numbers had declined to 250,000 people by 1850. Their physical health in the late 19th century was dreadful; there was widespread malnutrition and morbidity. So there is some question as to whether Indians were healthy enough to have been brought as labor into the revised frontier economy. Furthermore, the fragmentation of the Indian population into diverse political, cultural, and linguistic groups precluded the easy mobilization of what healthy Indian labor there was into labor pools large enough to have been useful in the labor-intense operations of the emerging economic empire in the West. Moreover, few Indians had any experience as contractual wageworkers, and potential employers were aware that earlier attempts at using Indian labor had been largely futile. Indian slaves in the South had a history of running away, and their presence "raised the danger of conspiracies with enemy Indians" (Forbes, 1964:90). Into this setting came large numbers of immigrant laborers who were cheap and relatively docile and who would work in large labor pools, as did Africans in the agrarian South, the Chinese in the construction of the transcontinental railroad in the West, and Mexicans in the agrarian operations of the Southwest. These immigrants surpassed Indians in meeting the nation's labor needs.

The exclusion of American Indians also followed from certain precedents set in the era of treaties, when they had been treated in almost all instances as political collectivities, as independent and then dependent domestic nations, and not as free, autonomous individuals. When these precedents are combined with an Indian inclination toward self-exclusion, with the fact that other people were pulled into the country's labor force as free labor, and with the Indians' low level of health, the exclusion of the American Indian from the larger society seems in hindsight nearly inevitable.

A relationship between two ethnic groups, such as that between settlers and Indians, may be affected by third parties who stand outside the dyadic relationship. Indeed, a third party may determine the relationship of the other two, as it does when two otherwise antagonistic groups ally in the face of a common enemy, a condition common in war. However, no such alliance between settlers and Indians, which might have made many Indian tribes important to the security of other Americans, was necessary on the frontier during the 19th century. Settlers and Indians rarely shared a common enemy. After Britain and France had relinquished their claims in the area early in the 19th century, the American government faced no serious foreign threats. If conditions had been different, it is possible that Indians might have been swept up in the mobilization of American society to meet an external threat.

Indians stood between a powerful group and its goal, to put it abstractly, without having either competitive resources or the protection of a third party to temper the powerful group's inclination to take the most direct and least costly route toward its goal. Thus, the U.S. government gravitated toward the legitimization of the unilateral expropriation of Indian land, catching up with actual practice as it did. Following this expropriation, neither American capital nor labor had any interest in assimilating Indians into the revised American economy. So Indians were excluded to reservations, and it was hoped that there the red man would vanish.

The Present Situation

The exclusion of the Indians has always been a partial one, and the red man did not vanish. By 1960 there were over one-half million Indians living in the United States, indicating considerable growth in Indian numbers since the 19th century. Today, more and more American Indians are living in the nation's cities, where they are attempting to make the transition into an urban, industrial laboring class. In 1940, two-thirds of the employed Indian males were farmers, but only 23 percent were so employed in 1960 (Schmid and Nobbe, 1965). Table 2 shows how American Indians are currently following the evolutions of immigrant groups, going from agrarian work to urban residence and industrial, blue-collar and even white-collar work. Note the decrease in Indians employed as farm workers since 1940, and the increasing percentage of Indians in blue- and white-collar work. Indians have remained behind other groups in this transition, however, which indicates their continued evolutionary divergence. Nevertheless, Indian evolution since 1940 has been consistent with, not contrary to, trends in the larger society.

Steps toward reversing the exclusion of American Indians began early in the 20th century. By 1920, observed Spicer (1972), it was obvious that the allotment act had failed in its intent to assimilate Indians. Realizing this, certain influential whites, including John Collier, who later became Commissioner of Indian Affairs, proposed changes in Indian policy. These suggestions were ultimately incorporated into the Indian Reorganization Act of 1934. Edward Spicer (1972) expresses the opinion that such efforts toward improving Indian welfare, which he calls Indigenismo movements, represent a later phase in a cycle of conquest which comes when the conquered people are no longer a military threat.

Table 2   Percentage Distribution of Indians and All Employed People by Occupational Groups, 1940–1970.

Occupational Group	Indians				All People			
	1940	1950	1960	1970	1940	1950	1960	1970
White-Collar Workers								
Professional and technical......................	2.6	3.2	6.2	9.8	7.5	8.7	11.1	14.9
Managers, officials, and proprietors (except farmers)......................	1.3	1.9	2.6	4.1	8.4	8.7	8.4	8.3
Clerical and sales..........	2.6	4.5	8.7	16.6	16.8	19.2	21.6	25.0
Blue-Collar Workers								
Craftsmen and foremen......................	4.6	9.1	11.2	14.1	11.3	14.3	13.5	13.9
Operatives......................	13.7	16.1	19.9	18.1	18.4	20.3	18.4	13.7
Laborers except farm and mine....................	19.8	14.4	14.7	8.6	6.8	6.5	4.8	4.5
Service Workers								
Private household..........	3.7	3.3	5.2	2.6	6.2	2.5	2.7	1.5
Other service................	4.0	7.0	11.9	16.4	6.2	7.8	8.4	11.3
Farm Workers								
Farmers and managers.	37.9	20.5	7.4	1.6	11.5	7.6	3.9	1.9
Laborers and foremen...	9.2	20.1	12.2	4.2	6.9	4.4	2.2	1.3

Sources: 1940 Census, *The Labor Force*, Table 62, p. 90; 1940 Census, *Characteristics of the Non-white Population by Race*, Table 26, pp. 83–84; 1950 Census, *Occupational Characteristics*, Table 3, pp. 29–36; 1950 Census, *Characteristics of the Nonwhite Population by Race*, Table 10, p. 32; 1960 Census, *Occupational Characteristics*, Table 2, pp. 11–20; *Characteristics of the Nonwhite Population by Race*, Table 33, p. 104; 1970 Census, *Occupational Characteristics*, Table 39, pp. 593-600.

Note: Percentages may not total 100.0 because of rounding.

He locates the initial stage of the Indigenismo movement in the United States as spanning the years 1870–1920 and being associated with formulating the assimilative intentions of the allotment act, while the second stage of this movement, begun in 1920, consists of a reappraisal of that act.

The belief behind the Indian Reorganization Act was that Indians would find their own accommodation to American society if left to themselves. This policy rationale is a reversal of common practices under the earlier General Allotment Act. The Indian Reorganization Act included a return to tribal management of reservation land, the replacement of distant boarding schools with day schools near home, and the encouragement of tribal practices, including native religions. All these measures were directed toward the reestablishment of traditional ways, the authority of which had been so badly undermined during the tenure of the Dawes Act. Many tribes became economic corporations and political entities under the Indian Reorganization Act. The intent of this act was to have Indians move into the future under their own management, and it was hoped that the process would be facilitated by the return to traditional authority patterns. The act also represents a return to the earlier principle in the Royal Proclamation of 1763, and in the rulings of Justice Marshall early in the 19th century that Indians have the right to self-determination.

Since the Indian Reorganization Act, Indian policies have steadily moved toward greater self-determination. In 1946 the federal government waived its immunity from legal suits for having inadequately compensated Indians for their land, as well as for having mismanaged tribal lands under the Dawes Act. In the 1950s the federal government even attempted to terminate its special relationship with American Indians and to dissolve essentially all of its historical obligations toward them. The passage of this legislation was blocked by Indians, on the premise that they were neither prepared nor willing to abandon their ties to the federal government and their land. Passage of the Indian Self-Determination and Educational Assistance Act of 1975 now allows tribes to provide services to their members in their own way with federal funds. At the present time several tribes are also seeking the return of their lands; the current legal suit in the state of Maine is only one instance of this broader thrust. This signals the intention of American Indians to take the offensive in finding their own accommodation to the larger society.

The Indian Reorganization Act and the legislation following it represented the cessation of the forced enculturation of Indians. The current policies of the federal government appear to be on a course of cultural pluralism for Indian people. This policy may also bring a change in the Indian subeconomy, which since the past century has been running in a direction opposite that of the large American economy. This real possibility is symbolized by the recent Alaskan Native Claims Settlement Act (1971) on our last land frontier: "Here, for the first time, very large economic resources are placed in the hands of native people with very few external controls over the way they use those resources" (Havighurst, 1977:13). Forty million acres of land were restored to Alaskan natives, and $962.5 million was promised them for land taken over by the state and federal governments. The way Alaskan natives will receive this money is also important:

The valuable thing they receive is 100 shares in one of 12 Native Regional Corporations which take title to the land and which keep for investment purposes 90 percent of the money paid under the Act . . . . The Regional Corporations were formed as quickly as possible after the passage of the Act, and have been using approximately $200 million they received from the government in the first five years to invest in productive enterprises—such as hotels, supermarkets, mineral exploration, reindeer herds, and fish canneries. (Havighurst, 1977: 13–14)

While American capital as a class was moving toward the consolidation of its holdings and economies of scale, the base of the Indian subeconomy in the past—reservation land—was being partitioned into inefficiently small holdings or was being lost under the General Allotment Act. Recent legislation might be a step in the right direction, but it has not been entirely successful in erasing the residues of earlier Indian policy, coming, as it has, many years too late. Sorkin (1971), in his commentary on the present state of Indian agriculture, captures the old and the new:

Farming is unprofitable for most individual Indians because of poor management, lack of capital, and the inefficiently small farm sizes. They often lease their land to whites because they cannot earn sufficient income from their own work. Tribal enterprises have proved more successful, since they are not subject to these disadvantages. (p. 79)

Sorkin noted too the great problems in creating jobs for Indian labor on reservations, problems other writers also see (e.g., McFee, 1972). On some reservations unemployment rates for Indian males run as high as 80 to 90 percent. Across the nation, in cities as well as on reservations, labor force participation rates for Indian males have been declining; 70 percent of the Indian males in this nation participated in the labor force in 1940, but this rate dropped to 59.5 percent in 1960. Moreover, "The median level of schooling of the Indian male in 1960 was about the same as the 1940 level of all males . . . " (Sorkin, 1971:16). Such evidence as this testifies to the continued exclusion of American Indians from major institutions of the larger society such as education and the labor force. Commentary on Indian adjustment to urban life has been pessimistic about the rapid transition of significant numbers of Indians into the ranks of urban wage earners. These observations portend an uncertain forecast for the future of American Indians.

Whatever the future brings, the present situation of the American Indian shows signs of evolutionary divergence over the past 100 years or so, Indians are still one of the least educated groups in the country and still reside more than others in rural areas. Levels of Indian health and welfare are well below national norms, and infant death rates and death due to certain infections among Indians remains the highest for any group in the nation. The level of Indian health and welfare is behind that of the nation as a whole (see Table 3). But there have been significant improvements in Indian health since the Public Health Service has taken over the administration of health care to Indians.

Table 3   Some Indicators of the Evolutionary Divergence of American Indians

Characteristics	Year in which U.S. Rate Approximates Indian 1967 Rate	Difference in Years
Birth rate	No U.S. rate on record is as high as 1967 Indian rate.	
Percentage of live births born in hospital	1962	5
Infant death rate	1947	20
Neonatal	No U.S. rate on record is as low as 1967 Indian rate.	
Postneonatal	1941	26
Maternal death rate		
Using 1967 Indian rate	1964	3
Using 1965–67 average rate	1954	12
Age-adjusted death rate, all causes	1941	26
Influenza and pneumonia death rate		
Crude	1945	22
Age-adjusted	1945	22
Diabetes death rate		
Crude	1949	18
Age-adjusted	No U.S. rate on record is as high as 1967 Indian rate.	
Tuberculosis death rate		
Crude	1952	15
Age-adjusted	1950	17
Gastritis, etc., death rate		
Crude	1938	29
Age-adjusted	1941	26
Age expectancy at birth	1939–41 period	27

Source: Reprinted from Robert L. Kane and Rosalie A. Kane, *Federal Health Care (With Reservations!)*, p. 62. Copyright 1972 by Springer Publishing Company, Inc., New York. Used by permission.

The infant death rate among Indians after 1955 went down by 48 percent, and their tuberculosis death rate went down by 70 percent (Kane and Kane, 1972). The convergence of Indian welfare with that of others might be a mixed blessing, however:

Indians in Oklahoma who have largely adopted white ways and have readier access to medical centers suffer more frequently from obesity, diabetes, hypertension, and gall bladder pathology than do the Indians of the Southwest . . . . We can anticipate that as the Indian becomes more acculturated he will inherit the right to heart attacks, strokes, and cancer. (Kane and Kane, 1972:74)

The point here, is that indicators of the current health, wealth, education, and welfare of Indians attest to their historical evolutionary divergence as a people. The current cultural idioms of Indians and the general pattern for them to restrict social participation to their own kind are also evidence of their continued exclusion and evolutionary divergence. Some assimilation of Indians has occurred, of course, but when compared with the evolutions of other ethnic groups, the inclusion and evolutionary convergence of Indians has been minimal.

This is not meant to dismiss the obvious signs of Indian assimilation. Field research on the contemporary Indian finds significant degrees of acculturation, even among reservation Indians. McFee (1972) observed that the acculturation of the Blackfeet began immediately after their conquest, and a conscious decision was made by some families to adopt white ways. Today, the different degrees of enculturation among the Blackfeet divide the tribe into two camps: Indian oriented and white oriented. Not only do these two groups have different value systems and status hierarchies, they are partially segregated from each other in their patterns of social participation. Social occasions for Indian-oriented Blackfeet and others for white-oriented Blackfeet are mutually exclusive. When the two groups do participate together in public, it is on a neutral site at a large, impersonal event. Moreover, social distance between members of the two groups is maintained in town, on shopping and business trips. The evolutionary convergence of Indians has been small, however, when compared to the evolutions of most immigrant groups.

Summary on American Indians

Frontier contact between America's indigenous Indians and white settlers evolved into conflict over land, the expropriation of Indian land, and then the exclusion of Indian people from the economic and social order of the settlers. Ethnic conflict theory and pluralism provide good interpretations of this history. Ethnic conflict theory helps explain the exclusion of American Indians and their evolutionary divergence, and thus the pluralism of Indian and white society. Historically, both groups competed for land, and because the white settlers were more powerful they were able to expropriate Indian land. The power resources of settlers included their numbers, centralized political authority, and capacity to generate surplus and fluid wealth within the framework of a market and monetary economy. The settlers' desire for Indian land followed from their intention to make permanent settlements on the North American frontier. From a position of power, the settlers transplanted a European economic, political, and social order to the frontier. Because of white ethnocentrism and the fact that American Indians had few competitive resources, Indians were largely excluded from this revised society.

As a consequence of their exclusion, American Indians proceeded along an evolutionary course divergent from that of the larger society. Today the pluralism of white and Indian societies is still evident. As the larger society evolved into one of white-collar work, urban residence, and mass public education, the American Indian was following a different evolutionary course. Indians grew more and more dependent on the federal government, as first the ecological base to their way of life disappeared, and then little was accomplished to bring their evolutionary convergence with the larger society. The evidence for the evolutionary divergence of American Indians in the 20th century is obvious.

The prospects for American Indians are far from clear, but current trends, if they persist, should bring the greater inclusion and enculturation of Indians (see Table 2 above). The nadir of the material conditions of Indian life is in all probability behind us. Their levels of health, wealth, education, and welfare should continue to improve, it is hoped, to a point of parity with those of other groups in the country. We should also expect more convergence of Indian culture with the trends in the total society. This convergence of material conditions and cultural content of Indian life will come with increased Indian participation in the secondary institutions of the larger society, in the labor force and the nation's schools, for instance, and it will be first in evidence among the young, well-to-do, urban Indians. It is ironical that the current conflict between urban Indian groups and other sectors of society might facilitate this convergence.

The historic conflict between Indians and the larger society involved military force, and it resulted in something close to the extermination of the Indian. The cycle of conflict appears to have swung away from the use of force, however, and toward the legal litigation of Indian-white grievances. This is an instance of Lenski's political cycle (see Chapter 4). Indian leadership must now adopt cultural principles from the larger society; indeed, it has done so, and more of the same can be anticipated in the future. The channeling of Indian-white conflict and Indian cultures through the institutions of the larger society, such as the courts and universities, necessitates the enculturation of many Indians into its practices and skill. This means the acquisition of language skills, the reading of law, practical experience with bureaucracy, and so on. The likely result is that more Indians will come to share with others cultural idioms, common experiences, and the same material conditions of life. The irony is that the more successful Indian leadership is, the more it will reflect the characteristics of its adversaries. Thus Indian leaders will become modern men and women with modern skills.

Moreover, to press their demands on the larger society, Indians will increasingly organize themselves into voluntary organizations, as they have already done in the National Congress of American Indians, the National Indian Youth Council, and the American Indian movement. It is significant that these associations are tribally inclusive and follow organizational principles adopted from the larger society, being established by Indians who have had previous extensive experience in the secondary institutions of the larger society such as the schools and the military. These trends can be taken as indicators of the evolutionary convergence of Indians, at least of certain Indian leaders, and they suggest that Indians might follow the ethnic evolutions of some immigrant groups. If that is so, the first level of their evolutionary convergence is the inclusion of several tribes in common organizational endeavors and the corresponding growth of a pan-Indian consciousness. It may also mean a growing divergence between Indian ethclasses. In any case, as Indians prepare themselves to negotiate with the larger society, and as they acquire competitive resources through education to do so, their evolution should converge more with that of the total society. Now that the nature of Indian-white conflict has changed, and now that Indians must become an organized political interest group, the future of American Indians should be more convergent, at least to the extent that Indians are successful at realizing their claims on American society.

Undoubtedly, traditional idioms will be rediscovered and circulated in the course of future conflict. This must be done to mobilize Indians for collective action against the larger society. While this will revitalize certain traditional themes in Indian cultures, as the Ghost Dance did in the past century, ideology for collective action must now be of a pan-Indian nature, to appeal to people from diverse tribes. The risk of the entire endeavor is that Indian ethnicity will be stripped of its tribal traditions, even its authenticity, and become contentless. That is, Indians might become just another organized political group in the modern welfare state.

Future conflict could also truly revitalize Indian identity, even tribal identity, and shore up ethnic boundaries. This could happen in those cases where single tribes pursue their land claims and return the land to its former uses, thus committing themselves and the land to the preservation of the old ways. Even tribal members living elsewhere, off tribal lands, could return home for personal succor and ethnic rejuvenation.

But more than anything else, it is the mismatch between Indian labor skills, as these exist today, and the current need for socially skilled (Anglo skills) and highly technical labor that points toward the continued divergence between the evolution of American Indians and that of the larger society. Unless this discrepancy is significantly diminished, Indian participation in the mechanisms for intergroup inclusion of postindustrial society will be minimal, and we should expect the continued evolutionary divergence of American Indians.

MEXICAN AMERICANS AND AMERICAN SOCIETY

As white settlement expanded across the western frontier, Anglo settlers eventually came into contact with Hispanos in the Southwest. It is estimated that the Hispanic community of the Southwest numbered no more than 200,000 people at the time of contact, early in the 19th century. This community was composed of three economic classes: elite landlords, who possessed large tracts of land and could trace their property rights back to early Spanish land grants in the New World; a large class of poor Mexican-Indian laborers; and a small number of middle-class merchants, small ranchers, and farmers. Then, early in the 20th century, in connection with both the growth of the Southwest as an economic empire and the Mexican Revolution (1910), the Spanish-speaking community of the Southwest was swollen with immigrants from Mexico. McWilliams (1968) estimated that fully 10 percent of the Mexican people immigrated into the United States early in this century, and the vast majority of them took up work in the Southwest. This immigration continues to this day. Thus, this nation's second largest minority group, as Mexican Americans are sometimes called, is unique among America's ethnic groups in that it is both indigenous and immigrant in character.

It was a familiar story in the Southwest. Powerful Anglo settlers came into contact with an established but weaker Hispanic community, and the powerful group wanted—and got—the land of the weaker one. Thus the frontier contact between Anglos and Hispanos is similar to that between white settlers and American Indians. However, Mexican labor was incorporated into the economy of the Southwest later in the 20th century, and so Mexican Americans—meaning Hispanos of the borderlands and immigrants from Mexico—were never excluded from the larger society to the extent that American Indians were. The evolution of Mexican Americans is outlined in Table 4.

Table 4 Evolution of Mexican Americans and the Modernization of American Society

Agrarian Society 1600–1865	Industrial Society 1865–1945		Postindustrial Society 1945–Present
Frontier Contact and ⟶ Early Accommodation (1800–1850)	Conflict over Land ⟶ (1850–1900)	Land Expropriation ⟶	Ethnic Stratification (1910–Present)

Note: Dates are approximations only.

Frontier Contact and Early Accommodation

Frontier contact between Anglos and Hispanos took place in the borderlands, from Texas in the East to California in the West (see Map 4). The initial contact betwen Anglos and Hispanos was varied enough across this region that writers usually prefer to depict it state by state (e.g., McWilliams, 1968; Moore, 1970; Stoddard, 1973). This variation in contact will be noted below. The evolution of Anglo-Hispano relations in the entire Southwest is represented in Table 4.

There was such a rapid influx of Anglos into Texas and northern California in the 19th century that Hispanos quickly became a significant minority in these areas. Anglo settlers quadrupled in number in Texas between 1820 and 1830, and the same thing occurred later in California, during the Gold Rush around 1850. Texas invited Anglo invasion, for there are no natural boundaries between Texas and territory to the north and east from which the Anglo-American immigrants came. While there are such barriers in northern California, the lure of quick riches in the gold fields brought large-scale immigration from the East. The passage of people over the Sierra Nevada Mountains in California during the Gold Rush is noted for its severe hardship.

There was an early alliance in Texas between Anglos and Hispanos. The latter had been dissatisfied for some time with Spanish and Mexican rule, since neither government had been able to provide Hispanos in the borderlands with effective protection against the Indians of the region. Unhappy with Mexico City, Hispanos of Texas turned to Anglo immigrants as allies, and together they forged a declaration of independence from Mexico in 1836.

Anglos and Hispanos also allied in Arizona against Indians. Unable to pacify the Apaches, Hispanos had been forced to concentrate in a few cities of Arizona. But, by the late 19th century, largely due to the campaigns of the U.S. Cavalry, the Indians of Arizona had been conquered and sent to reservations.

Hispanos were most firmly established in New Mexico. Unlike Texas, New Mexico was protected from Anglo invasion by natural barriers, and a numerical imbalance between Hispanos and Anglos did not occur early in their contact. More than in any other state, there has been an equitable accommodation between the two groups in New Mexico, particularly in state politics. But even in New Mexico, Anglo-Hispanic relations evolved into conflict over land.

Conflict over Land

Land in the borderlands was held privately by Hispanos of the region, of course, but the region was also a possession of Mexico early in the 19th century. Thus, in their efforts to gain control of the Southwest, Anglos came into conflict with both their Hispanic neighbors and the Mexican government, as well as the Indians of the region. Once Mexico ceded most of the Southwest to the United States, in 1848 under the Treaty of Guadalupe Hidalgo, and in 1853 with the Gadsden Purchase, Anglo settlers could turn most of their attention to the private land holdings of their Hispanic neighbors.

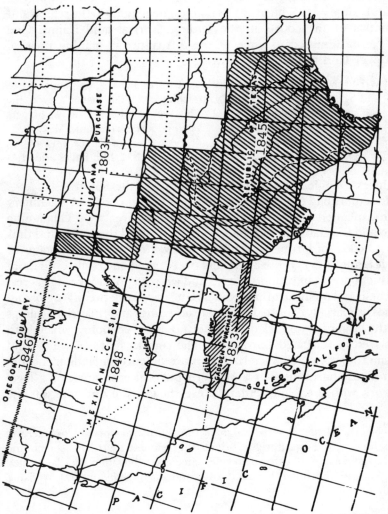

Map 4 *Mexican land cessions to the United States in the 19th century.*
Source: Carey McWilliams, *North From Mexico* (New York: Greenwood Press,
Publishers, 1968).

Both groups resorted to open violence on occasion, as occurred in the Lincoln County Wars of New Mexico, in the burning of courthouses to destroy documentation of land rights, and during the periodic range wars between cattlemen (Anglos) and sheepmen (Hispanos) throughout the Southwest. There were also lynchings of Mexican miners in California during the Gold Rush. While such incidents cannot be denied, the true character of this conflict is found more in legal and political battles over property rights, during elections and in courtrooms, than in gunfights, arson, and range wars. The issue was political hegemony in the region and thus control of the courts in the settling of rival land claims. One Anglo-Texan admitted to some of the difficulties in gaining political control over land ceded by Mexico:

Mexico! What the hell do we want of it. It isn't worth a cuss. The people are as bigoted and ignorant as the devil's grandchildren. They haven't even the capacities of my black boy [Negro slave]. Why, they're most as black as niggers anyway, and ten times as treacherous . . . . You go any further into Mexico . . . and you'll get Mexicans along with your territory; and a dam'd lot of 'em too . . . . *It'll be fifty year before you can out vote 'em.* (Olmsted, 1857:126; italics added)

Nevertheless, Anglos did get political control of the Southwest.

Anglo settlers had the advantage, for their law and political machinery were transplanted to the Southwest after the Treaty of Guadalupe Hidalgo and the Gadsden Purchase. They controlled the courts and thus the jurisdiction of property rights. This was to the disadvantage of Hispanic landowners, whose land claims were based on Spanish and more feudalistic concepts of property rights and who did not enjoy equal access to legal help and political influence. The land conflict between Anglos and Hispanos was largely confined to legal proceedings and financial dealings within the larger framework of a Western political economy, which both sides shared as relocated Europeans. The conflict between whites and American Indians was characterized by more violence and military action, since Indians shared neither a Western political economy nor a legal framework with the white settlers. Nevertheless, the outcome was the same:

In the end, the Hispanos were caught up in the meshes of Anglo-American banking, finance, and legal intrigue. Prior to the conquest, there had been no land tax in New Mexico; but, with Anglo rule, came taxes, litigation over land titles, mortgages, and the other incidents of a monetary economy. (McWilliams, 1968:76)

Expropriation of Land

With the Treaty of Guadalupe Hidalgo in 1848, most of the borderlands, including California, became the possession of the United

States, three days after gold was discovered in California. The Gadsden Purchase in 1853 brought even more of the Southwest under American political control. Once the borderlands were under this control, Anglo settlers got the upper hand in their conflict with the Hispanic landowners. Dominating the political machinery of the region, from county courthouses to territorial and state capitols and on to Congress, Anglo-American settlers typically found their legal challenges to Spanish land grants were successful in the courts of the region. McWilliams (1968:77) described the situation in New Mexico:

Many of the villagers neglected to bring their papers into court and often had lost evidences of title. Most of them lacked funds to defend titles; or, if they retained an Anglo-American lawyer, a large part of the land went in payment of court costs and fees. The confusion became so great that in 1891 a Court of Private Land Claims was established to pass upon the land grants in New Mexico. Needless to say, the members of this court were all Anglo-Americans; and, as nearly as I can determine, there was not a single Spanish-American lawyer in the territory. Litigation over land titles was highly technical and involved; cases dragged on in the courts for years; and, in the general process of settling titles, control of resources shifted to the Anglo-Americans.

In parts of Texas and California, great numbers of land squatters among the Anglo immigrants simply ignored legal niceties.

Taxation was among the more popular mechanisms by which Hispanic land was expropriated. American politicians would levy property tax rates at levels that only the largest of Spanish landholders could afford, thereby forcing small Hispanic entrepreneurs off their land and into wage labor. Such maneuvers were particularly effective during economic hard times, when first the ranchero system and then dry farming faltered because of droughts and low prices (Moore, 1970).

By 1900 American capital, particularly the railroads and agribusiness, as well as the federal government owned the Southwest. As the Hispanic economy slumped, American capital flowed into transportation, irrigation, and all the improvements needed to make the region an economic empire. King cotton moved into Texas (1890–1930) and eventually into Arizona and California. Hispanic forms of extraction in mining were improved and made more profitable with American capital and technology. The extraction industry grew in the Southwest and came to include the powerful petroleum industry. Equally important, railroad lines were built so that the surplus of foodstuffs, fiber, and minerals from the Southwest could be shipped to consumption centers in the East and North by the early 1900s.

The scarcity of water had always been a limiting factor in agricultural development in the Southwest. Steps taken at the turn of the century to offset this limitation included the National Reclamation Act of 1902. Public funds were expended to ensure an adequate supply of water for the growers in the San Joaquin, Imperial, Salt River, Mesilla, and Lower Rio Grande valleys. While the intent of the Reclamation Act was to extend the Homestead Act into the Southwest, its consequence was to provide water to large growers at public expense. Public lands were also given to the railroads, among others, with the intent of furnishing them with collateral for borrowing investment capital. Tariffs were passed at the national level to foster the economic development of the region, as was the case with the Dingley Tariff of 1897, which helped the sugar beet industry by taxing imported sugar at 75 percent of its market value (McWilliams, 1968).

An alliance of big capital and the U.S. government came to dominate the economy of the Southwest. Anglos eventually owned most of the land in the borderlands, in both private and public holdings, and the private holdings became increasingly concentrated under the ownership of the railroads and the big growers. These business interests, with governmental assistance, made capital improvements in farming and transportation (e.g., irrigation, canning operations, refrigerated cars). With the importation of Mexican labor early in the century, the economy of the region, in cotton, sugar beets, produce farming, mineral extraction, and transportation, took off. The Southwest became an economic empire with the convergence of land, labor, and capital in the 20th century.

Ethnic Stratification

Great labor needs came with this expansion in the Southwest economy. Irrigated truck farming, cotton growing, and the construction and maintenance of railroads were at this time all labor-intensive endeavors. The population of the region was not sufficient to fully satisfy these growing labor demands. The small Hispano entrepreneurs who had been forced into wage labor, along with immigrant labor from Asia, Europe, or other parts of America, could not meet the region's labor needs in the early 1900s.

The economic boom of the Southwest occurred at roughly the same time as the Mexican Revolution, however. By the second decade of the 20th century, jobs created by capital investments in farming and transportation in the Southwest were acting as a magnet to pull Mexican labor into the region's economy. Simultaneously, the turmoil of the Mexican Revolution pushed Mexican labor out of Mexico and into the borderlands. McWilliams (1968) estimated that 10 percent of the Mexican population came to work in the region. In this manner, labor came together with land and capital investment in the Southwest.

The labor demand was greatest in truck and cotton farming, railroad

Mexican field labor. These people illustrate how their group has helped meet the nation's labor need. United States Department of Agriculture photo.

construction and maintenance, and mining. Into these industries Mexican workers came, comprising two-thirds of the laborers in cotton farming and 70 percent of the section crews and 90 percent of the extra gangs on the railroads (McWilliams, 1968). Mexicans became an agrarian laboring class or otherwise filled the bottom positions of the regional labor hierarchy.

This was the point at which the evolutions of Mexican Americans and American Indians began to differ. While the treatment of Mexicans excluded them, they were a labor caste in the revised economy of the Southwest, Indians were more completely excluded from the larger society and isolated on reservations. There are several reasons for this difference in evolutionary courses.

Mexicans and Hispanos had a history of labor in farming, ranching, and mining, in both Mexico and the borderlands. They were an experienced labor class when American capital came into the region. Indians did not comprise a comparable labor pool, having had virtually no history as wage labor in agriculture, ranching, or mining. Furthermore, Indians who had earlier made the transition into wage labor had been assimilated into the Hispanic culture and community, so that by the 20th century their progeny were more often considered Mexican than Indian.

American employers were also predisposed to hire Mexican labor because the Mexicans lived in the areas of the region where the greatest labor needs arose, that is, in the fertile river valleys of the Southwest. Before the coming of Anglos, Hispano settlement in the Southwest had resembled a fan, with the people concentrated along the ribs of the fan, the river valleys of the region. Thus, Mexican labor was right at hand, and the cultural ties of these areas with Mexico acted as conduits for labor emigration from Mexico. In the same region, Indians were by the turn of the century located in isolated corners, on marginal land where a comparable labor demand never developed.

Mexican labor was also more easily organized by employers in the Southwest. Employment of Mexican labor typically took the form of the traditional padrone-peon system, in which a single labor boss bringing a gang of laborers to a grower could meet most of the grower's labor needs. For employers this was an efficient hiring method, since they needed gang labor. In its efficiency, it would not have been matched by the employment of Indians. Compared to the linguistic and cultural diversification of the region's Indians, Mexicans were linguistically and culturally integrated and thus were more easily mobilized into large but manageable labor gangs.

Mexicans faced virtually no competition from other ethnic groups for their position as an agrarian labor caste in the Southwest. Blacks did not move into the Southwest with king cotton, due to their earlier emancipation. If that labor migration had occurred, it would have most certainly meant fewer positions for Mexican labor in the agrarian economy of the Southwest. Because most Anglo labor could secure other opportunities, few of them were willing to work for long in the fields at low wage rates, at least until the Great Depression. The same may be said about European immigrant laborers, who, like the Volga Germans in the sugar beet industry, would exit after a few short years in seasonal work for better opportunities elsewhere in the economy. Moreover, Asian immigration into the country had been restricted by the early 20th century, and thus there was no adequate supply of either Chinese or Japanese field workers for southwestern agriculture. By default, then, Mexicans became the farm workers of the Southwest.

While Mexicans were incorporated into the revised economy of the Southwest as labor, unlike the historical experiences of Indians, the difference between them and Indians was not too great. Mexicans were incorporated into the agrarian economy in an exclusive manner, and this has had implications for their evolution:

The basic factor retarding the assimilation of the Mexican immigrant, at all levels, has been the pattern of his employment. . . . With few exceptions, only a *particular class* of employers employed Mexican labor in the Southwest: large-scale industrial enterprises; railroads; smelters; copper mines; sugar-beet refineries; farm-factories; large fruit and vegetable exchanges. These concerns have employed *many* Mexicans, in gangs, crews, and by families as in the sugar-beet industry. It is not the individual who has been employed but the group. (McWilliams, 1968:215)

Because they have been employed as a group and worked together in gangs, primarily in rural areas and at migratory jobs, Mexican-American workers have been isolated from workers of different ethnic backgrounds and from other potentially assimilative mechanisms in the Southwest. Thus, Mexican workers were not totally unlike Indians; they, too, took an evolutionary course divergent from that of the larger society.

The concentration of Mexican Americans in agrarian work and apart from mechanisms for their assimilation into American society lasted until the 1940s, when, with the increasing mechanization of agriculture in the Southwest and the growing urban manpower needs of a wartime economy, they migrated to the cities of the Southwest. Thus the Mexican American entered America's urban economy a generation later than even the most recent of European immigrants, those from southern and eastern Europe. In the intervening years, these ethnic groups had established their occupational turfs in the nation's cities, had organized themselves in unions, had taken advantage of cheap but good urban educational services, and had in numerous other ways prepared themselves for societal evolution toward white-collar work. When Mexican Americans arrived in the cities, they faced prejudice and discrimination from the other ethnic groups. There were even instances of violence against urban Chicanos in the 1940s, the best known being the so-called zoot-suit riots in Los Angeles. There were barriers against the entry of Mexican Americans into the institutions for intergroup inclusion—education and the white-collar labor force.

Nevertheless, the difficulties urban Mexican Americans faced in preparing themselves for the postindustrial society reached into their history, their agrarian past. While laboring in the fields in the Southwest at low wages, Mexican Americans could accumulate neither the savings nor the skills necessary to prepare themselves for white-collar occupations. Migratory work, a necessity for many Mexican agrarian workers, precluded the adequate education of Mexican-American children in the cultural skills required in the 20th-century, urban labor market. Schools for children of migratory workers have been notoriously inadequate, and inadequacy in school facilities, curriculum, and faculty has been confounded by the fact that the children of migratory workers attend school less than other children do. Children in classrooms for only a portion of the year, year after year, cannot learn as much as those who attend on a regular basis. Many children of migratory workers would quit school and enter the farm labor force at an early age to help with the family income, due to the prevailing low wage rates for field workers. What parents could not do the schools did not do; that is, prepare a generation of Mexican Americans for a new type of work in this country which required a large degree of enculturation.

Better attention to the education of children of farm workers by educators and public officials in the rural Southwest did not materialize because the tax base has been the owners of large tracts of land, the big growers and the railroads—the very interests who have opposed property taxes and have needed cheap Mexican labor. What interest did big growers, absentee landlords, and corporation comptrollers have in the education of Mexican Americans, a service which would cost them money? As a class of employers, they needed only bodies, not minds. Moreover, until recently, the Southwest never had a large, urban middle class, due to the historical marginality of urban industry in the region, or much of an agrarian middle class, due to land consolidation. Thus there was no middle class in the history of the region to invest in good schools which would have prepared Chicano children better for the realities of postindustrial society.

Such were the circumstances behind the evolutionary divergence of Mexican Americans. Barnes (1971:23) summarized the impact of such conditions in the Southwest on the historical exclusion of Mexican Americans from the larger society:

Schools, shops and civic institutions never blossomed in those parts of the South and West dominated by giant landholdings. Enormous disparity of wealth and power is rarely conducive to widespread involvement in public affairs, and is even less so when large portions of the population are emigrants, or are barred by one means or another from voting. Why, after all, should an absentee landlord spend his taxes on good public schools, when his own children go to private school and an educated work force is the last thing he wants?

One suspects that in much of the Anglo working class of the Southwest, which was composed of Americans from a variety of ethnic backgrounds, the indifference of Anglo capital toward improving the conditions of Mexican-American laborers was equally strong. Through their unions Anglo workers formed in significant respects an aristocracy of labor, particularly in construction and on the railroads. On the railroads the Mexicans, along with some Indians, laid and maintained the tracks, hard and dirty work, while whites ran the trains as engineers, firemen, and brakemen—a neat instance of ethnic stratification. Opening their craft unions to Mexican Americans and educating Chicano children would have been obviously inconsistent with the interest of the Anglo aristocracy of labor (cf. Bonacich, 1972).

To compound the exclusion brought about by their industrial concentration and their limited participation in public schools, Mexican Americans have lived apart from other Americans, segregated in the barrios of the Southwest. At work and at home, Mexicans have avoided contact with outsiders and outside social institutions, preferring instead their own kind and relying on their own ethnic services. While nearly all of America's ethnic groups have lived in ethnic neighborhoods, segregated for a time from others, Mexicans in the borderlands have lived in barrios for centuries, in close and continuous contact with the mother country of Mexico. Segregation of this sort and the proximity of Mexico have also played roles in the historical exclusion of Mexican Americans from the larger American society.

Land consolidation in the Southwest meant Mexican-American families faced nearly insurmountable barriers to buying their own farms. This mobility route ordinarily requires few cultural skills and allows for the direct application of job-related experiences; it was used by the Japanese on the West Coast at the turn of the century (see Chapter 9). However, in the Southwest, land holdings and agricultural production had become so concentrated in the hands of big growers that small farms were not competitive, and it was only the small farms that Mexican-American workers could afford to buy. For Mexican Americans this mobility route has been used only by the few families who have come to own small-to-modest truck farms and produce stands outside the cities of the Southwest and Midwest. Only a miniscule proportion of the table fruits and vegetables eaten by American families is purchased from such operations.

Some writers contend that unlike many other immigrant groups, Mexicans did not and still do not come to America with a commitment to establish themselves and work toward their assimilation (e.g., Grebler, Moore, and Guzman, 1970). Many Mexican migrants are sojourners, who work for a time in the United States and then return to Mexico with their savings. Because they are willing to work at low wage rates—dollars go further in Mexico than in the United States—these sojourners have had the effect of depressing wage rates for other Mexican families who have wanted to establish themselves in this country. While this argument has some merit, many ethnic groups who have "established" themselves in America were also sojourners (see Chapter 9).

Mexican Americans were particularly hard hit in the Great Depression. Many field workers lost their jobs, due to increased competition with Anglos from the Midwest and South and the increasing mechanization of agriculture in the Southwest. Displaced workers returned to Mexico, but many more migrated to the cities of the Southwest, and they have done so since in increasing numbers. First in the late thirties and early forties, and again in the fifties and sixties, many Mexican Americans have evolved into an urban people.

Grebler et al. (1970:71) noted the significance of this internal migration of Mexican Americans and the continued immigration of Mexican nationals in the context of the country's changing labor needs:

In the late decades of the nineteenth and the early years of this century, the American economy could easily absorb millions of unskilled Irish, Polish, Italian, and Scandinavian immigrants. But since the 1920s (when the mass immigration from Mexico began) and particularly since World War II the absorption of people with low-grade job qualifications had become increasingly difficult. The mechanization of industry, the more recent automation of manufacturing and other processes, and the growing importance of consumer and business services have placed a high premium on skills.

Table 5 shows how Mexican Americans are as a class evolving out of agrarian work and toward industrial, blue-collar and even white-collar work. In this, they are converging with the country's changing labor needs. They are still behind other groups, however, as Table 5 also shows. The discrepancy between the occupational composition of Mexican Americans and others in 1970 is greatest in white-collar work, the type of work that indicates a good degree of integration into the larger society

Table 5 Percentage Distribution of Spanish-Surname and All Employed People by Occupational Groups, 1950–1970

Occupational Group	Spanish Surname			All People		
	1950	*1960*	*1970*	*1950*	*1960*	*1970*
White-Collar Workers						
Professional and technical..........................	2.7	4.6	7.7	8.7	11.1	14.9
Managers, officials, and proprietors except farmers............................	7.4	4.1	4.2	8.7	8.4	8.3
Clerical and sales..............	10.4	14.1	19.4	19.2	21.6	20.0
Blue-Collar Workers						
Craftsmen and foremen...	10.6	12.6	14.0	14.3	13.5	13.9
Operatives............................	21.1	24.8	22.6	20.3	18.4	13.7
Laborers except farm and mine.........................	15.0	11.5	7.2	6.5	4.8	4.5
Service Workers						
Private household	3.0	3.1	1.7	2.5	2.7	1.5
Other service.....................	8.1	9.9	14.1	7.8	8.4	11.3
Farm Workers						
Farmers and managers.....	4.0	1.8	0.5	7.6	3.9	1.9
Laborers and foremen......	20.7	13.5	4.1	4.4	2.2	1.3

Sources: 1950 Census, *Occupational Characteristics,* Table 3, pp. 29–36; 1950 Census, *Persons of Spanish Surname (except Puerto Rican),* Table 6, pp. 23–39; 1960 Census, *Occupational Characteristics,* Table 2, pp. 11–20; 1960 Census, *Persons of Spanish Surname (except Puerto Rican),* Table 6, p. 38; 1970 Census, *Occupational Characteristics,* Table 39, pp. 593–608.

Note: Percentages may not total 100.0 because of rounding.

and requires a good measure of acculturation. If the evolution of Mexican Americans ever truly converges with that of other groups and the larger society, this discrepancy must be diminished.

Summary on Mexican Americans

Their concentration in agrarian wage labor or otherwise at the bottom rungs of the occupational ladder of the Southwest, their legacy of working in rural areas in ethnically homogenous gangs, their limited access to formal education, their migratory work, their residence in segregated communities, their sojourning motives and habits, their general nonparticipation in the secondary institutions of the larger American society—all of these instances of the historical exclusion of Mexican Americans have meant their evolutionary divergence. Mexican Americans have been at least a generation behind many other ethnic groups in converging with the opportunity structure of modern society, the 20th-century expansion in education and white-collar work.

Even though the divergence between the history of Mexican Americans and that of the larger society has been diminishing in the decades since World War II, the evolutionary gap between Mexican Americans and the larger society is still obvious (see Table 5 above). Grebler et al. (1970) reported an educational gap between Anglos and the Spanish-surnamed in the Southwest, particularly for people 25 years and older; a gap in the median family and individual incomes between these same groups; greater unemployment rates among the Spanish-surnamed than among Anglos; a greater tendency for the Spanish-surnamed to live in overcrowded and substandard housing; and the underrepresentation of Spanish-surnamed people in the region's white-collar jobs and overrepresentation in its low-skill, manual jobs. Moreover, there is evidence that Mexican Americans have continued use of the mother tongue longer than have other immigrants into the United States, as their proximity to Mexico would indicate in the Southwest.

While these evolutionary gaps should grow smaller in the future, it is far too simplistic to expect a linear movement toward the assimilation of Mexican Americans. Recent convergence in the evolution of the Spanish-surnamed people with that of the larger community in the Southwest is partly due to historical events which will not be repeated in the near future. There have been postwar gains in educational opportunities for Chicano servicemen, due to the G.I. Bill of Rights, and there has been a mass migration of Mexican Americans to cities and to California in recent decades. As for the future, Grebler et al (1970:202) noted what is needed to advance the evolution of Mexican Americans:

In the context of the Southwest as a whole, further increases in the relative income of Mexican Americans will require more rapid shift of people in the labor force from manual to non-manual occupations. Such a shift calls for enormous educational inputs. Only modest gains can be accomplished by moving from unskilled labor jobs into higher-wage manual occupations. The structure of employment is changing in favor of non-manual work. This change limits the opportunities for income gains from upgrading in manual jobs.

To make the transition from manual to mental work in this country, Mexican Americans must quickly acquire cultural and technical skills through formal education. But this is where a gap still exists between Anglo and Chicano children. If this gap does not close, we should expect more of the same intergroup exclusion and evolutionary divergence of the Mexican American:

Americans have thought of their country as one of the few in the world without an identifiable proletariat as a *social class,* that is, a group of people who are and feel permanently relegated to poverty and whose expectations for their children are conditioned by this hopeless outlook. Regardless of the historical validity of this view, the problems posed by a continued existence of an *ethnic* proletariat will be particularly acute in the Southwest with its two disadvantaged minorities. (Grebler et al, 1970)

Even as Mexican Americans rise with the occupational structure of American society and the Chicano middle class grows larger, there are important limits on the full assimilation of Mexican Americans into the larger American society. One limitation Mexican Americans share with many other groups in the country, and that is the use of ethnicity and particularly minority status as a strategy for the acquisition of certain resources in the welfare state. It is particularly the middle class of a minority group that benefits from quota systems; quotas are meaningless at the bottom. This will tend to keep alive ethnic identity among the Chicano middle class. The risk in this has been mentioned before, in regard to the evolution of American Indians: the use of this tactic may mean that eventually the group becomes nothing more than a contentless interest group. But will Hispanic culture grow shallow with the rise of the Chicano middle class? There is reason to believe that it will not. The exchange, including migration, between this country and Mexico, especially along the borderlands, should continuously invigorate the Hispanic subculture in this county. The prospects are for the cultural pluralism of Mexican Americans, coupled with a decreasing measure of intergroup exclusion and evolutionary divergence with respect to material life chances, the same as those for American Indians.

REFERENCES

Barnes, Peter
    1971 "The Great American Land Grab." The New Republic 164(June):19–24.
Blalock, H.M., Jr.
    1967 Toward a Theory of Minority Group Relations. New York: John Wiley and Sons, Inc.
Bonacich, Edna
    1972 "A Theory of Ethnic Antagonism: The Split Labor Market." American Sociological Review 37(October):547–599.
Columbus, Christopher
    1906 "Letter from Columbus to Luis Santangel." Pp. 264–270 in Julius E. Olson and Edward Gaylord Bourne (eds.), *The Northmen, Columbus and Cabot, 985–1503*. Early Narratives of American History Series. New York: Charles Scribner's Sons.
Forbes, Jack D. (ed.)
    1964 The Indian in America's Past. Englewood Cliffs, New Jersey: Prentice-Hall, Inc.
Fuchs, Estelle, and Robert J. Havighurst
    1972 To Live on This Earth: American Indian Education. Garden City, New York: Doubleday and Company, Inc.
Grebler, Leo, Joan W. Moore, and Ralph C. Guzman
    1970 The Mexican-American People: The Nation's Second Largest Minority. New York: Free Press.
Hansen, Marcus Lee
    1940 The Immigrant in American History. New York: Harper and Row, Publishers.

Havighurst, Robert J.
  1977 "Indian Education Since 1960." Paper presented at the Meeting of the American Sociological Association, Chicago, September 5, 1977.
Humfreville, J. Lee
  1964 "A Letter." Pp. 18–19 in Jack D. Forbes (ed.), The Indian in America's Past. Englewood Cliffs, New Jersey: Prentice-Hall, Inc.
Institute for Government Research
  1928 The Problem of Indian Administration. Under the Technical Direction of Lewis Meriam. Baltimore: Johns Hopkins Press.
Josephy, Alvin M., Jr.
  1969 The Indian Heritage of America. New York: Alfred A. Knopf, Inc.
Kane, Robert L., and Rosalie A. Kane
  1972 Federal Health Care (with Reservations!). New York: Springer Publishing Company, Inc.
Lieberson, Stanley
  1961 "A Societal Theory of Race and Ethnic Relations." American Sociological Review 26(December):902–910.
McFee, Malcolm
  1972 Modern Blackfeet: Montanans on a Reservation. New York: Holt, Rinehart, and Winston, Inc.
McNickle, D'Arcy
  1962 The Indian Tribes of the United States: Ethnic and Cultural Survival. London: Oxford University Press.
  1972 "Indian and European: Indian-White Relations from Discovery to 1887." Pp. 75–86 in Deward E. Walker, Jr. (ed.), The Emergent Native Americans. Boston: Little, Brown and Company.
  1973 Native American Tribalism: Indian Survivals and Renewals. New York: Oxford University Press.
McWilliams, Carey
  1968 North from Mexico: The Spanish-Speaking People of the United States. New York: Greenwood Press, Inc.
Moore, Joan W.
  1970 Mexican Americans. Englewood Cliffs, New Jersey: Prentice-Hall, Inc.
Neihardt, John G.
  1961 Black Elk Speaks, Being the Life Story of a Holy Man of the Oglala Sioux. Lincoln: University of Nebraska Press.
Olmsted, Frederick Law
  1857 A Journey through Texas. New York: Dix, Edwards & Company.
Prucha, Francis P.
  1962 American Indian Policy in the Formative Years. Cambridge, Massachussetts: Harvard University Press.
Schmid, Calvin F., and Charles E. Nobbe
  1965 "Socioeconomic Differentials among Nonwhite Races." American Sociological Review 30(December):909-922.
Sorkin, Alan L.
  1971 American Indians and Federal Aid. Washington, D.C.: Brookings Institution.
Spicer, Edward H.
  1962 Cycles of Conquest: The Impact of Spain, Mexico, and the United States on the Indians of the Southwest. Tucson: University of Arizona Press.
  1969 A Short History of the Indians of the United States. New York: Van Nostrand Reinhold Company.
  1972 "Indigenismo in the United States, 1870–1960." Pp. 159–160 in Seward E. Walker, Jr. (ed.), The Emergent Native Americans. Boston: Little, Brown and Company.
Stoddard, Ellwyn R.
  1973 Mexican Americans. New York: Random House, Inc.
Vogel, Virgil J.
  1972 This Country Was Ours. New York: Harper and Row, Publishers.

CHAPTER 8

Black Americans

INTRODUCTION

The exchange of land, labor, and capital has been basic to ethnic evolution in this country and to the evolution of the country as a whole. Land was a source of conflict between America's indigenous people and its immigrant groups, and the land of American Indians and Hispanos was in the end expropriated by the more powerful immigrants. This brought even more immigration to America. Once the frontier had been settled by immigrants, the rapid industrialization of the nation spurred further immigration into the industrial cities. The growing labor needs of the nation brought the immigrants, and the fate of these groups has since been implicated in the country's changing labor needs.

The history of black Americans is part of this larger legacy. Immigrants from Africa share with others a long, hard history of labor, and their evolution, like that of others, has been implicated in the evolving labor needs of the nation. The evolution of black Americans is unique, however. Only immigrants from Africa were slaves, the property of Southern planters. The history of black people in this country is more than one of labor, it also concerns an absence of capital. Black people were once treated as the property of others, and they have historically been dispossessed of their own property. The evolution of black Americans is outlined in Table 1.

Table 1 Evolution of Black Americans and the Modernization of American Society

Agrarian Society 1600–1865	Industrial Society 1865–1945	Post-industrial Society 1945–Present
Contact ➤ Southern ➤ Emancipation slavery	➤ Racial → Racial caste conflict in the South	➤ Northern ➤ Present migration, accommo- racial dation conflict, and caste

Note: Dates are approximations only.

CONTACT

It is true, of course, that the New World was richly endowed by nature with fertile soils, a great spectrum of climates, and enormous reserves of precious metals. These resources, however, were in themselves worthless. In order to farm the soil, there must be farmers, and in order to mine the earth, there must be miners. (Harris, 1964/1974:11)

This quotation makes a fundamental point; manpower was needed on the frontier to exploit fully the land expropriated from native Americans. Europeans found it difficult, however, to harness native labor in their extraction endeavors on the expropriated land. When Europeans did encounter natives in the New World who were agriculturalists and had sedentary habits, as the Spanish did in the highlands of Mexico and South America, they indeed pressed these natives into forced labor (Blassingame, 1972). But most native people were unaccustomed to hard, continuous labor, and when they were enslaved by Europeans they ran away, disappearing beyond the frontier, or they died in great numbers. Indian slaves constituted a security threat since they could ally with free natives in retaliatory raids against planters. The same may be said for whites, who could easily escape from plantations into the surroundings. African slaves could do none of these things, and their blackness became a visible sign of their bondage, eliminating for planters many of the security problems associated with enslaving other groups. There are several reasons African slaves were an attractive alternative to native labor, although they had to be imported across a great distance and at a considerable cost.[1]

---

[1]Is it too obvious to mention that Europeans were reluctant to enslave their own kind? While the practice of indentured servants from Europe was widespread in colonial America, European servants were never enslaved on the same scale as Africans. This shows the role of ethnocentrism in ethnic evolution and hints at the fact that European labor in the millions was not available for immigration until the 19th century, after Abolition. Serfdom in Eastern Europe lasted into the 19th century, and agrarian labor from the River Elbe east was not free from bondage in the 17th, 18th and early 19th centuries and was unable to migrate, voluntarily or by coercion, to the New World (cf. Blum, 1957).

First, "it is well known that slavery, serfdom and corvee were on-going institutions in many sub-Saharan African societies before European contact" (Harris, 1974:14). Moreover, Africans "probably had acquired immunities to certain common European disease organisms which were lethal to the American Indians." For these reasons and others, West Africans were a good and dependable labor pool in the absolute and comprised a superior labor supply compared to American Indians.

Africans were brought to the New World over a span of more than three centuries, from 1502 to 1860. It is estimated that 9.5 million Africans were imported into the Americas, and 6 percent of this total immigration came to the United States (Fogel and Engerman, 1974). Most of the slaves brought to the New World, 60 to 70 percent, were laborers in sugar production, another goodly number were miners, particularly in Mexico and Brazil, and the rest cultivated a diverse number of crops, including tobacco and cotton in the United States. The peak period of African immigration into the United States was between the years of 1780 and 1810, coinciding with the development of the cotton gin in this country and the rise of the British textile industry. Once slave trade ended and as slaves became increasingly valuable in the expanding plantation system, due to innovations in cotton farming and in the textile industry, living and working conditions of slaves improved. This was the period of slavery studied by Fogel and Engerman (1974).

Slaves were principally from West African agricultural tribes who had skills useful for cultivation and extraction in the New World. The West African tribes were never in a position to stop the great European powers in their slave trade. Europeans entered West Africa and fanned intertribal hostility with alcohol and other inducements, and in the resultant turmoil they took out slaves by the thousands. The European colonial powers were generally more powerful than the tribes of West Africa; specifically, the Europeans possessed gunpowder and more modern, lethal weapons of war. So, groups from the Yoruba, Dahomey, Ashanti, Ife, Oyo, and Congo tribes came to the New World as slave labor. They came in the ships sailing under the flags of the then maritime powers of Europe: British, French, Dutch, Portuguese, and Spanish. It may seem odd, but so long as African labor remained in Africa it was of little use to Europeans. African labor had to be exported to be of use to Europeans elsewhere in the world. At least this was the case until the middle of the 19th century, when the European powers eventually colonized much of Africa and could use African labor at home. At this time the slave trade finally stopped.

Slave trade was a triangular operation, according to Williams (1966). The triangle began in Europe, ran to West Africa on one side, crossed over the Atlantic to the Americas at its base, and ran up and across the

Atlantic again to continental Europe. In this triangle, the British, for example, shipped finished products to Africa in trade for slaves, transported the slaves to the New World in trade for raw materials here, and took these products home to England. In England, these raw materials were either consumed or turned into finished products, and the cycle was started again. A profit was made at each point on this triangle, and with these profits Britain helped finance its industrial revolution (Williams, 1966). Ironically, the rise of the industrial order in Britain, itself made possible by profits from the slave trade, resulted in the subsequent British attack on slave trade. It was in the interest of Britain as an industrial nation to buy raw materials from the colonies in the New World at the lowest possible price, but the sugar monopoly of West Indian planters stood in the way of this scheme. Thus, the British eventually, in the 19th century, undermined that monopoly by prohibiting slavery and thereby eliminating the planters' labor supply.

SLAVERY

Slavery is a period of American history about which much has been said and written, but it is still surrounded by debate and controversy. More often than not, accounts of slavery are a weave of hard, historical evidence, political ideology, and academic or popular fashion. Accounts of slavery fall on a continuum of being either critical or apologetic of this "peculiar institution."

Those critical of slavery present it as most inhumane and cruel, a version that has its roots in the Abolitionist movement. By this account, black slaves were regularly brutalized and reduced to beasts of burden. In the fields of the South there were grinding, hard field labor and routine physical punishment. With the whip sadistic white masters and their overseers coerced slaves into labor and often forced sexual attention on black women. Black bodies and souls alike were abused in the process. These critics of slavery disagree, however, over the degree to which black people were degraded by enslavement. Some believe that the black character and community were broken during slavery, and this condition is still evident in the modern black community (Frazier, 1949). Other critics argue that, on the contrary, the black family and community remained intact during slavery (Gutman, 1975).

The apologists of slavery portray this "peculiar institution" as one in which black slaves were humanely treated. Slaves were neither regularly brutalized nor sexually molested in any systematic way. White masters were genuinely concerned for the welfare of their slaves, and the relationship between master and slave was nothing more than one between a watchful white parent and an innocent black child. Physical brutality was no more common in slavery than it is when a father occasionally corrects his own children. It is not surprising that many of the apologists of slavery were slaveholders who tended to fashion their cultural image—what would now be called a media image—after that of a moralistic Christian father.

Both of these versions are caricatures of southern slavery and not totally correct depictions of it. Both views blend together hard evidence, political ideology, and blatant self-interest. Of course, any history of slavery is necessarily an interpretative one. Our hope is to interpret slavery sensibly from the perspective of ethnic evolution in the course of societal modernization, during which groups exchange land, labor, and capital. Slavery was a labor regimen on the southern frontier, a way to extract wealth profitably from the land, and it began for black people a long history of menial agrarian work for others, even as the labor needs of the larger nation changed. It is beyond the scope of this chapter to try to settle once and for all the controversy surrounding slavery.

Profit as a Goal of Slavery

The bottom line in plantation life was profit, in our view, and it is widely known today that the plantation economy of the South was profitable. Slavery was neither instituted nor maintained on the whim of planters' racial prejudice. It was instead an economic arrangement, as Cox (1948:332) observed:

Sometimes, probably because of its very obviousness, it is not realized that the slave trade was simply a way of recruiting labor for the purpose of exploiting the great natural resources of America. This trade did not develop because Indians and Negroes were red and black, or because their cranial capacity averaged a certain number of cubic centimeters; but simply because they were the best workers to be found for the heavy labor in the mines and plantations. . . .

Southern planters were agrarian capitalists, and by most accounts they were as a class successful entrepreneurs, first in tobacco in Virginia and Maryland and then in cotton on the southern frontier. Slavery was a way to organize labor in this enterprise, and slave labor certainly played a part in making the endeavor profitable. The slave represented a good investment and an important tool of production, and this was the basis of the relation between white master and black slave.

Slavery was also a perverse extension of the concept of private property. With the rise of capitalism, the feudal obligations between lord, land, and labor were replaced with the concept that land and labor were mere commodities in an impersonal marketplace. Land and labor once purchased became the private property of their owners, and their use was restricted only by the law of supply and demand. At least this was the theory of laissez-faire capitalism. Land was considered a commodity by nearly all European settlers in America, and southern planters took the additional step of viewing the slave, a human being, as a piece of private property.[2] Themselves the property of others, slaves were forbidden to accumulate any property of their own, and this also greatly affected the evolution of black Americans (Gutman, 1975).

Current estimates of the profitability of the plantation system give every indication that southern plantations and slave labor were good economic investments. It has been recently estimated that the rate of return on investment in slave labor of both sexes and all ages was 10 percent (Fogel and Engerman, 1974). Investment in Northern textiles in the same period yielded about the same rate of return, while investment in southern railroads brought a smaller return of 8.5 percent. Comparisons within agriculture itself tell the same story. Southern agriculture was 35 percent more efficient in 1860 than was northern agriculture, due in large measure to the economies of scale made possible by cheap slave labor (Fogel and Engerman, 1974). Plantations with slave labor were 28 percent more efficient than were farms in the South using free labor. Slaveholders were in a position to force small, independent farmers off the best land in the South and to control the market for staples by price cutting (Bonacich, 1975:608). The economic advantage in southern agriculture enjoyed by slaveholding planters was rooted in their monopolization of cheap slave labor and their economy of scale.

Another indication of the relative economic value of slave labor is found in the fact that while one-third of the free population at the time of slavery were active participants in the nation's labor force, at least two-thirds of the slaves were in the labor force. Virtually all the slaves worked, women and children as well as men, and they worked for less than did free labor. Spero and Harris (1931) wrote that while free labor cost capital at least $106 per year, slave labor cost as little as $75 per annum. Bonacich (1975:603) cited another example of the slave's labor value for capital from Linden (1940): a mill in DeKalb, Georgia, reported that a slave cost $75 a year, while a white operative cost $116. Slave labor was also flexible. Planters frequently rented slaves to enterprises off the plantations, particularly during the slack seasons, to serve as construction workers and skilled workmen such as carpenters, masons, and tailors. This obviously added economic value to slave labor. As for certain extra costs in the surveillance of slave labor, the southern states often picked up most of

---

[2]This, we argue, is the essential truth of slavery, even though planters liked to fashion themselves as having a feudal sense of noblesse oblige toward their black slaves. As capitalism evolved toward industrial capitalism, pressures arose to free labor from the land, out of slavery in the South and serfdom in Europe, so that workers could migrate to industrial cities. Black Americans, however, would not become part of that trend until the 20th century.

these costs by providing police, militia, and court services with public money (Sowell, 1975).

Slaves as Tools of Production

To planters, slaves represented nothing so much as capital investments and tools of production in a labor-intensive, agrarian economy. Next to land, the purchase of slaves was the planter's largest investment. Moreover, in labor-intensive endeavors, profits are won or lost by the cost of labor. Thus the price and productivity of slaves was a prominent concern of planters as a class of entrepreneurs, and this concern set parameters to the planters' treatment of their slaves. If this is so, then we should expect that slaves were physically well maintained, like any significant capital investment or tool of production. Brutality and the sexual abuse of slaves were necessarily checked by the degree to which such excesses interfered with the discipline and productivity of slave labor. Nevertheless, brutality and abuses of all sorts did occur on southern plantations; enslavement alone is abusive, and some slaveholders were particularly barbarous. However, some planters were benevolent masters. Thus abuse and kindness both were meted out. We should expect, therefore, that slaves were treated as capital investments and a class of labor for whom there was no better substitute. The sadism, sexual mistreatment, or kindliness of white masters were all secondary to their utilization of slave labor in the southern plantation economy. Slaves were a planter's largest capital investment, after his land, and certainly his most important tool of production. It was these hard economic facts that affected the use and treatment of slaves on southern plantations.

Evidence indicates that concern for the physical welfare of slaves was at least equal to and in some instances exceeded that of free labor in the 19th century. From records kept by planters on their daily operations, Fogel and Engerman (1974) found that the diet of some slaves exceeded modern recommendations on the daily intake of chief nutrients, and it surpassed by a wide margin the dietary levels of the entire population of the United States of the time. By even a wider margin, the slave diet exceeded that of the average white Southerner in the past century. Slaves experienced less crowded housing than some classes of free men did, especially the urban, industrial workers of the early 19th century. It is not surprising that southern slaves had longer life expectancies in the 19th century than did free industrial labor in America and Europe.[3]

Another indication of the quality of physical maintenance of black

---

[3]Fogel and Engerman (1974) tend to compare the material conditions of slave life with some of the worst conditions faced by free industrial workers of the era. Also, records kept by planters were probably self-serving.

slaves in the United States is found in their rate of natural increase. Their birth rates were the highest of any slave population anywhere in the New World. While only 6 percent of the African slaves imported to the New World ever arrived in the United States, by 1825, 36 percent of the slave population living in the Western world was in this country (Fogel and Engerman, 1974). This comparison is strengthened by the fact that slaves were continuously imported into the Caribbean and South America to offset the high mortality rates of slaves there. According to Van den Berghe (1976:535), "The mines of Brazil, especially in the eighteenth century, were undoubtedly the greatest consumers of black flesh in the New World, with mortality rates up to 40 percent a year." In this country slaves increased their numbers, an indication that they were maintained as valuable property and tools of production. W. E. B. Du Bois (1935:9), a black leader and scholar, seemed to agree with the essentials of this interpretation of slavery:

The slavery of Negroes in the South was not usually a deliberately cruel and oppressive system. . . . The victims of southern slavery were often happy; had usually adequate food . . . and shelter sufficient for a mild climate. . . . when the mass of their field hands were compared with the worst class of laborers in the slums of New York and Philadelphia . . . the black slaves were as well off and in some particulars better off. . . . their [slaves'] hours were about the current hours for peasants throughout Europe. They received no formal education, and neither did the Irish peasant, the English factory-laborer, nor the German *Bauer;* and in contrast with these free white laborers, the Negroes were protected by a certain primitive sort of old-age pension, job insurance, and sickness insurance. . . .

However, Du Bois noted, "no matter how degraded the factory hand, he is not real estate" (p. 10). Du Bois helps us express our feelings about southern slavery, reminding us also that slavery must be judged in the context of the treatment of all labor in the era, including industrial workers and the serfs of eastern Europe.

While there were definite economic limits to the physical mistreatment of slave labor, some slaves were certainly overworked. This was often true in cases of absentee landowners, when the management of a plantation was turned over to an overseer. This "enabled the planter to place between himself and the black slave a series of intermediaries through whom bitter pressure and exploitation could be exercised and large crops raised" (Du Bois, 1935:36). An overseer tended to drive slaves in their work. He was paid in proportion to the current year's crop, rather than the average crop over several years, and his wages and attractiveness to other planters, and thus his career mobility, were all tied to short-term production (Sowell, 1975). These labor bosses seldom cared about the eventual costs of such practices, which included the exhaustion of both land and labor, since they did not share in these costs. The economic interests of overseers rested solely in the maximization of short-term production, which often led to the exploitation of slave labor.

Both rewards and punishments were used as inducements to ensure the productivity of slave labor. On most plantations there was a system of rewards for hard work which included incentives such as bonuses, prizes, and opportunity for occupational mobility. Bonuses for hard-working slaves ranged up to $1,000 in 1974 dollars, according to Fogel and Engerman (1974). Opportunity existed for ambitious slaves to move into skilled trades and even into managerial and professional work on many plantations. At the end of the Civil War, 1865, 83 percent of the mechanics and artisans in the South were black.

Slaves in the cities, particularly, were engaged in a variety of work: "Our butchers are Negroes; our fish-mongers Negroes; our vendors of fruit, vegetables, and flowers are all Negroes; and generally slaves" (Wade, 1964:29). In Richmond, Virginia, slave labor was used extensively in the tobacco and iron industries, and much of this work was highly skilled. Slaves were also used in the building of railroads in the South, as well as in the construction of other means of transportation. Black slaves were dockworkers in many southern seaports. Slaves were also naval carpenters, tailors, bakers, and tanners. Positive inducements such as bonuses and the promise of occupational mobility insured labor productivity and maintained slave discipline in the South. Fogel and Engerman (1974) went so far as to conclude that the occupational structure of slavery was not unlike that of free labor of the period.

Gutman (1975) has objected to much of the detail in this portrait of slavery. He specifically has questioned the proposition that the occupational structure of slavery was comparable to that for free labor and the corollary suggestion that slaves were nothing so much as black Horatio Algers. Fogel and Engerman make slavery sound like a Skinner box, Gutman complained; that is, through the use of stimuli, cues, and reinforcement schedules, Africans were made over into black Anglo-Saxons, complete with the Protestant ethic for hard work. Gutman argued that this is an overly mechanistic and simplified depiction of slavery. In his view, slavery was as much rooted in the realities of property ownership in the South and in the informal system of slaves as it was in any formal inducements for labor productivity.

The Slave Subculture

When men and women work together, their work and the meaning it has for them and their lives off the job are elaborations on what is required by their bosses. Out of the formal organization of labor evolves an informal system of workers, one that may or may not conform to the formal rules and regulations. Thus neither slavery nor any other organization of labor is like a Skinner box. Even in total institutions like concentration camps (and slavery has been likened to a total institution), where it might appear that life is totally governed by routine and official orders, unique, self-initiated adjustments are often made by inmates. On occasion these adjustments can seriously subvert the operation, meaning, and purpose of the formal institution (Goffman, 1961). Goffman called the informal system of a total institution its underlife.

There was an underlife to slavery everywhere it was found. It was organized into family bonds and allegiances among friends, crystallized into values and roles unique to slaves, and manifested in the habits and personal styles of slaves. It was the black subsociety and subculture of the South. The subculture of slaves was primarily an oral tradition which was passed from one generation to the next by word of mouth. The perpetuation of this black subsociety, rooted in West Africa, was largely the result of the exclusion of blacks from the dominant white society. Slaves did not share in certain privileges with planters, nor were they welcomed in the subsociety of white workers and farmers in the South. We will trace the evolution of this subculture through the stages of the larger history of black Americans.

The slave subculture was in part due to the labor needs of the planters. It has been observed that slavery is suited only for the organization of labor for crude physical work. Forced labor is less practical and efficient for work that is more complex, skilled, and mental in nature. Thus slaves were necessarily concentrated in manual labor. If capital's labor needs are largely confined to manual work, as with the planters, little investment is made in the systematic enculturation of labor (see Chapter 6). The subculture of slaves was a direct outcome of planters' labor needs. They had no need for enculturated slaves, and it was also in the interest of white labor to keep slaves largely uneducated, save for instruction in the manual arts. Furthermore, the vast majority of slaves worked and lived in isolated rural areas, and three out of every four slaves toiled in all-black work gangs, often under black supervision. Most slaves had only occasional and asymmetrical contact with whites, and as a result black-white cultural pluralism prevailed in the antebellum South. Of course, in this era of American history there were few mechanisms for the enculturation of any laboring group, slave or free.

The planters in every practical sense controlled the Old South, both its economic and political systems, although they comprised only 7 percent of the population of the region. Plantations were the central economic institution of the southern economy, and planters exercised virtual mastery over the land, labor, and commodity markets in the South. Property qualifications for the voting franchise and the outright restriction of public office to members of the planter class also gave planters political domination over the Old South (Spero and Harris, 1931). Du Bois (1935:33) noted:

Into the hands of the slaveholders the political power of the South was concentrated, by their social prestige, by property ownership and also by their extraordinary rule of the counting of all or at least three-fifths of the Negroes as part of the basis of representation in the legislature. It is singular how this "three-fifths" compromise was used, not only to degrade Negroes in theory, but in practice to disfranchise the white South.

The three-fifths rule ensured planter control over state capitols and their domination of labor, black and white. It also meant that there would be no tax monies for the social services necessary for the enculturation of labor. Because of the power and prestige of the planter class, their economic interests were the context in which a slave subculture was established and evolved.

There was a class of free blacks who before the Civil War constituted approximately 11 percent of the black population of the country. In fact, Sowell (1975) considers this figure to be an underestimation, and Meier and Rudwick (1970:99) found that "Free Blacks monopolized barbering, practically controlled the building trades, and were prominent among the shoemakers and butchers." There was also a small class of free black professionals. As older immigrants have been generations ahead of more recent arrivals from the Old World, free blacks have been ahead of slaves with respect to education, family stability, and economic position. Sowell observed that the free-black business class in northern cities had been, by most indicators, rather comfortable, at least until the 20th century, when the black migration to the North inflamed the racial prejudice of white clients and business fell off. The descendants of this class, along with the children of black families in the South who were fortunate enough to have acquired land or a profession after Emancipation, made up the bulk of black college students well into the present century. The "talented tenth," as they have been called, has been moving closer than the black masses to intergroup inclusion in and evolutionary convergence with the larger society.

The exclusion and evolutionary divergence of the black masses during slavery can be overemphasized. There are many indications that there was some racial assimilation in the South. First, the material welfare of slave labor was at least equal to that of white labor in the South, which suggests some measure of evolutionary convergence in material living conditions. There was also cultural blending. On their part, black slaves in this country converted in great numbers from pagan beliefs and Islamism to Christianity, although in parts of Brazil blacks remained essentially

Islamic (Harris, 1974). Slaves also adopted Anglo names, both voluntarily and as a result of force, and mother tongues from West Africa were lost. The perpetuation of Africanisms was more difficult in this country than elsewhere in the New World. Here the plantations were smaller, and thus there was seldom a critical mass of slaves from a single tribe on one plantation, which is necessary for the survival of tribalisms. Slavery saw the beginnings of the assimilation of tribal identities into a single social entity, black Americans, which was American as well as African.

By the same token, white Southerners adopted many aspects of African culture. The ingredients and preparation of southern cooking are more West African than English. Rice, grits, yams, okra, greens, and hot spices are not staples of the British diet but are common in the dishes of West Africa. The British prefer rather blandly prepared meats, particularly roast beef and mutton stews. Southern cooking consists of highly seasoned casseroles and meat dishes that are fried, baked, or barbecued—anything but bland. I know of a white woman, formerly of Georgia, who bought her first standing rib roast and promptly boiled it—so much for her British ancestry. She was much taken with a party dish which included black-eyed peas, several meats, and spices and which had been literally envisioned in a dream of a Yoruba woman. The woman from Georgia exclaimed that she had not enjoyed such cooking since leaving the South.

In the preparation of food and other domestic practices, and in music, African idioms have been diffused throughout the South and the entire nation. These were the corners of the larger labor market in which black creativity was allowed to flourish. As musicians and cooks, blacks have been expected to entertain and serve whites, and along these lines African styles have crossed over and into the white community.

We are not suggesting that blacks and whites imitated each other in the antebellum South, however. Their assimilation of each other's ways was interpretative and selective, and the adoptions each made were translated into their own respective idioms. Black Christianity is no mere copy of the worship of whites; the rite of baptism, for example, was filtered through memories of Dahomey river-cult ceremonies. Black dialect is no mere regional patois; English was translated through West African semantics and phonetics as slaves adopted it. Full-scale racial assimilation was severely limited in the South because of the social distance between planter and slave and the competition between black slave and free white workers. This made for a good measure of racial exclusion during slavery and permitted the evolution of a black subculture in the South.

While white planters and black slaves were allied in a sense against white labor during slavery, the social distance between planter and slave prohibited the full inclusion of blacks and thus their evolutionary convergence with the society of planters. Racial assimilation in this manner was not on the agenda of the powerful planters. Moreover, the antagonism between slaves and poor whites, workers and small farmers, prevented assimilation at the level of labor. Slaves were an ever-present threat to the economic position of white labor, for capital always had the option of displacing white workers with cheaper black labor. White workers in the cities of the South were aware that their employers could always turn to cheaper slave labor, perhaps renting slaves as hirelings and avoiding the purchase price of a slave. White yeomen on the land also knew that they were subordinate to the planters, since only large planters could afford the best land and control the staples market (Bonacich, 1975). The dominance of planters resulted from their reduced labor costs in slavery and the savings of scale in their large operations. This made for a great deal of resentment on the part of poor whites, not only toward planters but toward slaves as well. Thus the assimilation of slaves, both vertically into the society of planters and horizontally into the society of white workers, was restricted.

In the course of slavery, poor whites made little headway in competition with white planters and slave labor (Spero and Harris, 1931). Capital had the ultimate weapon, of course; it could flood the labor market by setting free approximately 4 million slaves (Harris, 1974). Thus there were mutual exclusion and enmity between black and white labor during slavery. If significant assimilation occurs between groups, it typically comes when class counterparts in different ethnic groups converge, but this did not happen between black and white labor in the antebellum South. Moreover, if the day ever came (and come it did) that planters could no longer protect blacks from hostile poor whites, then the spirit of whites such as the one Cash (1960:52) describes could be turned loose in full-blown racial conflict:

to stand on his head in a bar, to toss down a pint of raw whisky at a gulp, to fiddle and dance all night, to bite off the nose or gouge out the eye of a favorite enemy, to fight harder and love harder than the next man, to be known eventually far and wide as a hell of a fellow—such would be his focus. To lie on his back for days and weeks, storing power as the air he breathed stores power under the sun of August, and then explode, as that air explodes in a thunderstorm, in a violent outburst of emotion—in such fashion would he make life not only tolerable but infinitely sweet.

EMANCIPATION, RACIAL CONFLICT, AND CASTE

It surely seemed at the time that Emancipation would hasten the inclusion of blacks into the larger American society. While Emancipation might not have been the fundamental issue of the Civil War, at least at first, the issue of slavery was always part of the conflict. Moreover, the shortage of labor created by the war meant that the South had to rely more and more on black labor behind the battle lines. Blacks by the thousands took up positions in industry and transportation that had been vacated by whites serving the Confederacy. This signaled some progress for black labor, but the trend collapsed at the end of the war with the wholesale destruction of southern industry. Blacks also served the Union; there were at least 186,017 black troops in the Union Army, and their losses during the war numbered 68,178 (Du Bois, 1935).

After the Civil War, moreover, there were plans and possibilities for bringing ex-slaves into the larger society. There was the possibility of their resettlement in either the North or the West. Black workers could have migrated north and taken up positions in the emerging industrial order of that region, or they could have gone west, becoming homesteaders on the frontier. There was also a plan for land redistribution in the South, so that ex-slaves could become independent farmers and property owners with "forty acres and a mule." This was the plan of Thaddeus Stevens, an antislavery leader and one of America's great commoners. Its theory was similar to that of the General Allotment Act for Indians (see Chapter 7)—assimilation through property ownership. This was a fundamental theme of the era, by the way, the thought that capital acquisition was the route to civilization, if not salvation. The point is that there was a potential for black people to evolve into either a class of industrial workers or independent farmers after the Civil War, thereby converging with the evolutionary trend of 19th-century American society.

The Racial Caste System

When none of these plans saw fruition, race relations took a turn for the worse, entering into a period of prolonged conflict that is remembered as one of the ugliest periods of American history. The outcome of Emancipation was racial strife and stratification, with black people on the bottom in agrarian tenancy and domestic service. A racial caste system, the product of racial competition, class conflict, the superior power of antiblack forces, and a growing racial ethnocentrism, replaced slavery in the South in the latter half of the 19th century.

After Emancipation, or more specifically, after the withdrawal of federal protection of blacks with the Compromise of 1876–77, the racial caste system was established and had essentially the same effect on the evolution of black Americans as had slavery. It continued the exclusion of blacks from American society and perpetuated their evolutionary divergence. Bonacich (1972:555) sees caste as "essentially an aristocracy of labor . . . in which higher paid labor deals with the undercutting potential of cheaper labor by excluding them from certain types of work." Furthermore, "caste systems tend to become rigid and vigilant,

Field labor, Greene County, Georgia, 1937. Lange; Library of Congress.

developing an elaborate battery of laws, customs and beliefs aimed to prevent undercutting." According to Bonacich, the success of one laboring group involves the acquisition of certain essential skills and denial to another group of access to general education and political power: "the solution to the devastating potential of weak, cheap labor is, paradoxically, to weaken them further, until it is no longer in business' immediate interest to use them as replacements" (Bonacich, 1972:556). The racial caste system that followed Emancipation meant the exclusion of cheap black labor from nearly all trades save agrarian labor and domestic service, the segregation and exclusion of blacks from decent education, and the almost complete exclusion of blacks from the political process in the South. This caste system was an extensive form of ethnic stratification.

With the passage of "Jim Crow legislation" in the 1880s and 1890s blacks were disfranchised in southern states, segregated in public accommodations and on common carriers, and curtailed in their access to due process of law. With the *Plessy* vs. *Ferguson* decision of the U.S. Supreme Court in 1896, they were also segregated in public education (Miller, 1967). Blacks were made powerless, in a word, and set up as targets for white hostility, which also helped keep in check any black challenge to the racial caste system. The effect of this racial caste system showed up in the evolutionary divergence of blacks (cf. Bonacich, 1975; Fogel and Engerman, 1974; Johnson, 1939; Sowell, 1975; Spero and Harris, 1931). After the Civil War, black life expectancy actually declined by 10 percent, black morbidity increased by 20 percent, and the gap between the wages of blacks and whites in comparable occupations grew. In 1880 for the first time a decline was noted in the absolute number of black artisans, although at this time the black population was growing. Blacks were becoming more concentrated than ever in agrarian labor and domestic service. By 1900, 58.3 percent of the gainfully employed black males in the country were engaged in agriculture and another 23.7 percent were employed in domestic and personal service (Schmid and Nobbe, 1965). Spero and Harris (1931:33) summarized the effects of this period on the evolution of the black worker: "The emancipation of the slaves in the perspective of the labor movement produced the following results. The major portion of the Negro labor supply was shunted away from the labor movement and industrial employment into agriculture and domestic service." Thus, after Emancipation the evolution of blacks diverged from the trend in the larger society toward industrial work and settlement on the frontier, and blacks lost ground to other immigrant groups.

The triangle of capital, white labor, and black labor was the shape of the forces behind the formation of the racial caste system in the South. Before the Civil War, planters had been in the position to undercut both white and free black workers with cheaper slave labor. However, the situation changed after the war. The planters lost much of their power, for they had suffered a military defeat, the South was occupied by Yankees, and the franchise had been extended to labor, black and white. Du Bois (1935) likens the Reconstruction era to a dictatorship of the proletariat. Of course, the war had been a disaster for the entire South, not just for the planters, and southern conservatives were aware of the widespread desperation. According to Cash (1960:176), the planter class read the times in these terms:

. . . that the South was hurrying fatally, was indeed already distinctly coming into a time when there wouldn't be room enough on the plantation to take care of both the main body of the blacks and this always multiplying army of white candidates—when these whites would be hurled, not only into competition with these blacks, but into the most naked and brutal competition—into a struggle to the death for the means of subsistence.

"Who could not see, in a word, that here was chaos?" Cash asked.

Chaos was certainly evident in race relations: the lynching, burning, beating, and shooting of blacks were commonplace during the era. The Ku Klux Klan and other organizational versions on the same racist theme were on the rise. Cash described the period in harsh terms:

The final great result of Reconstruction . . . is that it established what I have called the savage ideal as it had not been established in any Western people since the decay of Medieval feudalism, and almost as truly as it is established today in Fascist Italy, in Nazi Germany, in Soviet Russia—and so paralyzed Southern culture at the root. (p. 137)

The conviction grew in the minds of the Southern leadership that the resolution lay in progress, in the Yankee formula of industrialization: "Let us introduce the factory in force. Let us, in particular, build cotton mills, here in the midst of the cotton fields. Let us build a thousand mills—and more than a thousand mills, and erect the South into a great industrial and commercial empire" (Cash, 1960:177). With industry came the compromise between southern capital and white labor, and the relegation of blacks to a class of agrarian laborers and domestic servants. For both white capital and labor, some class interests were served by this compromise, while it was black labor that lost the most in the process. Both parties in the compromise had ideal outcomes in mind.

The planters sought the cheapest possible agrarian labor, and in those days black meant cheap. However, the planters could not forge anew their historical alliance with black labor against white workers. Blacks were no longer the private property of the planters and were free to enter into alliances of their own making. A Populist alliance of free slaves and white poor was particularly feared by the planters. This was a serious threat to political control of the South by planters in the late 19th century, when labor, black and white, might have gotten the upper hand in the class struggle in the South. Black and white labor had to be divided if capital was to stay in control. In other words, capital was as concerned with the Populist alliance as with racial antagonism and possible chaos, and the planters eventually turned to the white poor with a deal.

White labor sought at least some protection against its displacement by cheaper black labor, and in some quarters it hoped for nothing less than a class revolution in the South. In addition to the release of 4 million slaves, the ranks of white labor had been swelled since the War as the yeomanry were forced into wage labor by the economic catastrophe that followed the war. Cash (1960) located the quandary of the small farmers in the lack of capital in the South which resulted in credit arrangements with "supply merchants" that all too often brought bankruptcy and the dispossession of their land. White workers and small farmers were in a desperate condition and in an ugly mood, and capital had to compromise with these poor whites.

Whites took up positions in the mills and in unionized trades or otherwise came to monopolize the better jobs in the labor hierarchy of the South. Most of the labor for the southern cotton mills was obtained from "two classes, the tenant farmers and the mountaineers, as well as from the lowest class, known as *poor whites*" (Hawk, 1934:479). At the close of the Civil War five out of every six artisans in the south (83 percent) were black, but by 1900 their numbers had been reduced to approximately 5 percent. (Landry, 1977). Many whites became an aristocracy of labor in the new industrial order of the South, while others located on the land, either as peasant proprietors or, like blacks, agrarian tenants (Vance, 1939). Blacks remained bereft of land and largely excluded from industrial work, and they continued as a propertyless class of agrarian laborers and domestic servants. In 1890, when the Census Bureau first gathered data on Negro occupations, almost 90 percent of Negro workers were engaged in agriculture or domestic and personal service (Broom and Glenn, 1965:107).

This was the deal Southern capital gave poor whites. Blacks were forced to the bottom of the region's labor hierarchy, disfranchised and pushed out of the Southern political arena, and segregated in public services, including education. Du Bois (1935:611) saw the meaning of the end of Reconstruction for black people in their relationship to the land: "The German and English and French serf, the Italian and Russian serf, were, on emancipation, given definite rights in the land. Only the American Negro slave was emancipated without such rights and in the end this spelled for him the continuation of slavery." The entrapment of blacks in

Children near Wadesboro, N.C., 1938. Wolcott; Library of Congress.

agricultural and domestic service continued into the 20th century, in a racial caste system which served the interests of both capital and white labor. As white labor evolved into industrial work and land proprietorship it realized some security against the economic threat of cheaper black labor, although poor whites did not get the upper hand in the class struggle with southern capital. It was the planters who benefited the most; they kept their cheap black labor and gave the Southern industrialists (many of whom were Yankees) the higher priced white labor.[4] Moreover, they broke the Populist alliance between black and white labor, and the "Bourbon Democrats," as Key (1940) called the political party of the planters, thereby maintained their political and economic control over the South.

There were several reasons external to the South for the failure of Reconstruction. One is that the United States began a venture in international colonialism late in the 19th century, using racism as it did. This represented a moral corruption of northern liberals, the political force behind Reconstruction, a hypocrisy that southern conservatives turned to their advantage. Most importantly, however, immigrant labor in the North was opposed to the migration of black labor out of the South, fearing that black labor would undermine their economic position, as slave labor had been detrimental to white workers in the South. Thus landowners in the South were left free to virtually reinstitute slavery; there was no effective intervention by a more powerful outside party.

Scientific racism (Social Darwinism) became a popular ideology regarding racial inferiority during this era (cf. Chapter 4). This conveniently justified the racial caste system as it added to the irrational frenzy of Southern racism. Nevertheless, violence and cruelty toward blacks occurred in the South because it was allowed, and it was allowed because it served the rational ends of the compromise between the planters and poor whites. All along the line, according to Woodward (1966:81), "signals were going up to indicate that the Negro was an approved object of aggression. These 'permissions-to-hate' came from sources that had formerly denied such permission." This reinforced the caste status of blacks and thus satisfied the rational interests of the planters and white workers. Sowell (1975:48) commented on the effect of the caste system on black evolution:

The economic realities of white land ownership, near-monopoly of technical and business skills, and control of financial institutions meant that blacks had to work

---

[4]Reasons that southern planters won out over their class counterpart, Yankee industrialists, can be found in Woodward (1966): The withdrawal of federal troops, the identification of Yankee capital with carpetbaggers, and the fact that the planters were the most respected class in the eyes of much of the southern populace.

for whites on whatever terms were available. A form of sharecropping came into being in which the sharecropper was kept perpetually in debt to the local merchants . . . and so tied to the soil in de facto peonage. Severe vagrancy laws and harsh enforcement by local police and courts made it very difficult for many Negroes to get free even momentarily and to change their occupations.

The caste system also meant educational deprivation for blacks, most of whom lived in the South following Emancipation. The majority of blacks in the United States were illiterate in the past century, and the rates of illiteracy among blacks far exceeded those of whites (see Figure 1). Only 31 percent of blacks 5 through 20 years of age were enrolled in school in 1900, compared to 54 percent of the country's white population. The significance of the inequality of educational services offered to blacks and whites in the past century would become manifest later, as the nation's labor needs moved toward mental-oriented, white-collar work and blacks had to make up the tremendous gap between their educational level and that of other groups.

This is not to say that black people at this time had no resources of their own, and that there was neither integrity nor sweetness in their lives. The fact is that there was a viable black community, a subsociety and a subculture. Black subculture continued to evolve as an essentially oral, folk tradition, along the lines it had followed during slavery. It celebrated and soothed the soul, giving a melancholy meaning to the economic reality of black life in the South, and it continued to cross the race line into the larger world as entertainment and an art form. The black subsociety included a wide network of interlocking institutions—benevolent societies, fraternal associations, burial societies, cultural groups, and, most importantly, churches and schools. After Emancipation, black people established a network of colleges, including Fisk, Howard, and Tuskegee, which has trained the bulk of the black middle class well into the present century (Sowell, 1975). Black scholars in this era made important technical and cultural contributions to American life, achievements which are often personified by George Washington Carver. The black church helped its parishioners, mostly common people, face a harsh reality:

A primary function of the church was to nourish and maintain the souls of black folk by equating them with the essence of humanness. Religion was molded into an adaptive mode of resistance to the dehumanizing oppression, degradation, and suffering of slavery. The black church developed as the institution which counteracted such forces by promoting self-worth and dignity, viable identity, and by providing help in overcoming fear. (Holt, 1972:189)

There was also the black family, of course, and all these institutions— family, fraternal organizations, mutual aid societies, schools, and

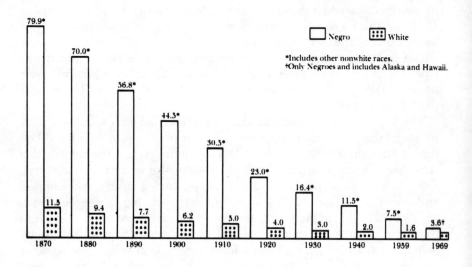

Figure 1 *Percentage of persons 14 years old and older classified as illiterate, by race, United States, 1870–1969.*

Source: Bicentennial Edition of Historical Statistics of the United States (Washington, D.C.: U.S. Bureau of the Census, 1976).

*Includes other nonwhite races.

+Only Negroes, and includes Alaska and Hawaii.

churches—constituted a community in which people came to understand the meaning of their life.

An exodus of blacks out of the South after the Civil War might have been expected, but such a migration did not materialize until later in the 20th century. After Emancipation, there was opportunity elsewhere in the nation. Cheap and plentiful land was available in the West as a result of the Homestead Act, and the North was just entering a period of rapid industrial growth (cf. Chapter 6). There were attempts to resettle slaves by the Bureau of Refugees, Freedmen, and Abandoned Lands, for instance, but these efforts failed for lack of necessary support. Indeed, there was active resistance in many northern and western states against any immigration of freed slaves into those areas (Bonacich, 1975). Instead, the opportunities elsewhere in the country were taken up by immigrants from Europe and Asia, and it was not until European and Asian immigration had virtually stopped in the 20th century that blacks moved out of the South.

The failure of the resettlement of freed slaves is possibly the most significant nonevent in black American history. In the South, where they stayed, blacks were essentially trapped in an evolutionary cul de sac as a result of the compromise between southern capital and white labor. Unlike other immigrant groups, blacks did not benefit from the union movement for industrial labor until much later in the 20th century. While blacks remained on the land in the South, they never came to own much of it, and many of them were caught in debt peonage. Thus in the early thirties Charles Johnson heard this tale from a black tenant in Macon County, Alabama:

Last year I drawed $10 to the plow [meaning $10 a month for from four to six months for each 20 acres cultivated] but I ain't getting but $7 this year. I rents the whole place [400 acres] and then subrents it, and pays 4 bales of cotton for rent. But I don't never make nothing offen it. Didn't clear nothing last year. I paid out $200 last year. Interest steps on me time I pay my rent [for money borrowed from the bank] and interest cost 15 cents on the dollar. I haven't made nothing since 1927. I clears $210 then and ain't cleared nothing since. I got 21 cents for cotton that year. (Johnson, 1934:110)

Through the 19th century blacks were the majority of the labor force in the rural South, from 71 percent in 1860 to approximately 50 percent in 1900, but they never owned more than a small fraction of the region's farms, no more than 6 percent (Vance, 1939), and these were typically small operations on marginal land. Furthermore, there was little in the way of a class of black businessmen in Southern cities, although there were prosperous black entrepreneurs in several northern cities (Sowell, 1975). Thus black labor was almost without exception at the mercy of more

Instruction at home, Louisiana, 1939. Lee; Library of Congress.

powerful parties in the economic and political arena, and these parties had agreed to establish a racial caste system.

Du Bois (1935:626) summarized the larger meaning of the failure of Reconstruction:

The white capitalist of the South saw a chance of getting rid of the necessity of treating with and yielding to the voting power of fully half the laboring class. It seized this opportunity, knowing that . . . the United States, instead of marching forward through the preliminary revolution by which the petty bourgeois and the laboring class armed with the vote were fighting the power of capital, was disfranchising a part of labor and on the other hand allowing great capital a chance for enormous expansion in the country. And this enormous expansion got its main chance through the thirty-three electoral votes which the counting of the full black population in the South gave to that section. It was only necessary now that this political power of the South should be used in behalf of capital and not for the strengthening of labor and universal suffrage. This was the bargain of 1876.

In the 19th century, great changes occurred in American society. Indian land was expropriated, the frontier was settled by immigrant groups, and the industrial base of the nation was built. All of these were important elements in the larger process of societal modernization. These changes largely bypassed black people, however, resulting in their evolutionary divergence. Blacks did not resettle on the frontier, nor did they migrate North, into industrial work. Instead, they stayed in the South, where in the context of a larger class struggle they were forced into a caste of propertyless agrarian workers and domestic servants. Black people were excluded from the modernization of American society, in other words, and this is the essential meaning of the failure of Reconstruction from our perspective.

MIGRATION AND RACIAL COMPETITION

In 1910, almost 90 percent of the blacks in the nation lived in the South. By 1970 only 52 percent of black Americans were located in the South, and now the majority of black people live in the nation's cities. In 1970 fully 55 percent of the blacks vs. 28 percent of the whites lived in the nation's central cities, comprising four-fifths of the blacks in the North and two-fifths of the blacks in the south. This represents a most significant migration during which blacks moved not only regionally, but also moved off the land and into cities. In the process, blacks have evolved from a largely uneducated class of agrarian and domestic workers toward a class of industrial blue-collar and white-collar workers.

The bulk of this migration has occurred since 1940. The percentage of blacks living in the South went from 89 percent in 1910, to 77 percent in 1940, to only 52 percent in 1970. Each year since 1950, 150,000 blacks have left the South. Broom and Glenn (1965:159-160) have described this migration in some detail:

During the decade following 1910, the great migration of Negroes from the rural South began with the push of a depression in Southern agriculture and the pull of new opportunities for industrial employment in the North. . . . World War I reduced immigration [of Europeans] and increased the demand for new workers, thus creating a labor vacuum into which thousands of Southern workers could move. The northward migration subsided during the depression of 1920–1921, resumed by 1924 when the heavy flow of European immigrants was permanently stopped, and subsided again during the Great Depression of 1929–1939. The Negro exodus from the South reached a new high during World War II and the period of postwar prosperity, but in this later migration large numbers of Negroes joined the movement to the West.

Blacks were first pulled into the industrial North, in connection with World War I and the cessation of European immigration, and only after World War II did they move in significant numbers to the West. This migration has been likened to the crossing of the river Jordan sung about in Negro spirituals, or the passing over to the Promised Land. Detroit was a rather gray Jordan, and the entire North was a somewhat cheerless and certainly cold Promised Land. But it was economics that brought blacks to the North; there were jobs in Mr. Ford's place in Detroit. Henry Ford announced in 1914 that none of his workers would earn less than $5 per day, the same year he began to hire blacks, and word of this spread among poor blacks throughout the South (Jones, 1963). Blacks entered many of the old heavy industries in the North: steel in Pittsburgh and Gary, metal trades in Detroit, brick making in Newark, and meat packing in Chicago and East St. Louis. Blacks also entered coal mining in Pennsylvania, corn refining in Chicago, longshore work on the eastern seaboard, and numerous other trades in the nation's industrial order. In this way black history began to converge with the trend toward an industrial nation.

Black labor was not only pulled into the North and later into the West, it was also pushed out of the South. The southern compromise that followed Emancipation had meant severe social and economic hardship for blacks. Blacks were bypassed in the process of bringing industry to the South; they were disfranchised, segregated in public services, and, in a word, weakened. The racial caste system served the interest of capital and white labor and was maintained as much in lawlessness and violence as it was by the law. There were approximately 100 lynchings in the South each year for over 20 years, in the 1880s and 1890s (National Advisory Commission on Civil Disorders, 1968). The North symbolized to the southern black personal safety for him and his family, schools for his children, and some semblance of dignity, as well as economic opportunity (Palmer, 1967).

Economic factors were nonetheless the primary forces for pushing blacks out of the South. Around World War I, a combination of inflated farm prices and damage done to cotton by the boll weevil freed black tenant farmers from debt peonage in one sense and forced them off the land in another. Many fled North. However, it was not until after World War II that the push of black labor out of the South took on truly mass proportions. According to Wilhelm (1971:182), the full impact of industrial technology was not felt by the black farm worker until the postwar era, when " 'factories in the fields' took over the production of farm produce and displaced the Negro farm hand in the process." More specifically:

A virtual revolution took hold in Southern agriculture because there was a dramatic shift from preindustrial to industrial technology. For the 20-year period from 1940 to 1960, the farm labor dropped from 4.2 million to 1.7 million; crop acreage declined from 111 million to 81 million for the same time. Average farm size increased by 1960 to twice the acreage of the 1930s, but in spite of the expansion, owners employed less than half the amount of labor required twenty years earlier. (Wilhelm, 1971:183)

Black labor in the South was becoming obsolescent, due to the mechanization of southern agriculture, which pushed black agrarian workers to the North and the West.

The old southern formula was behind the entry of black labor into the industrial North around World War I. Industrial capital sought in the black worker a more tractable and cheaper alternative to white labor, who were becoming increasingly militant and organized into labor unions. That is, capital sought to counter the growing labor movement by bringing black workers north. Moreover, with the end to mass European immigration later in the 1920s, migrating southern blacks became northern capital's last alternative to high-priced union labor. Blacks were specifically used as strikebreakers in many industries and at several locations in the North and Midwest (see Table 2), and generally the intention was for blacks to displace unionized white workers (Bonacich, 1976; Spero and Harris, 1931). In this era employers brought black workers north in cattle cars (Jones, 1963); my grandfather, in this country for only a few years, first saw black Americans in significant numbers as they exited from cattle cars to break a strike in the meat-packing industry in East St. Louis, Illinois. Such a scene was not uncommon earlier in the century in industrial centers throughout the North and Midwest.

To many white workers, southern blacks appeared to be the lackeys of capital and scabs being used to destroy the white worker. Southern blacks were equally suspicious of white workers and tended to avoid involvement in labor unions. Instead, there was a paternalistic and protective

Table 2 Strikes in Which Blacks Were Used as Strikebreakers, 1916–1934

Industry	Year	Locality	Source
Aluminum.............	1917	East St. Louis	Rudwick, 1964:19
Brick making.........	1923	Newark	Spero and Harris, 1966:141
Building................	1919	New York	Franklin, 1936:299
Coal mining..........	1922	Pennsylvania	Wesley, 1927:280
	1925	Northern West Va.	Spero and Harris, 1966:225
	1927	Western Pa.	Spero and Harris, 1966:225
	1928	Ohio	Spero and Harris, 1966:232
	1934	Birmingham	Cayton and Mitchell, 1970:323
Corn refining.......	1919	Chicago	Tuttle, 1970a:102
Fig and date packing..............	1926	Chicago	Spero and Harris, 1966:141
Garment industry	1917	Chicago	Chicago Comm., 1922:414
	1920	Chicago	Chicago Comm., 1922:415
Hotel industry......	1918	Chicago	Tuttle, 1970a:99
Longshore work...	1916	Baltimore	Spero and Harris, 1966:193
	1923	New Orleans	Spero and Harris, 1966:188
	1929	Boston	Reid, 1969:168
Meat packing........	1916	East St. Louis	Fogel, 1970:32
	1919	Chicago	Tuttle, 1970a:109
	1921	Chicago	Herbst, 1932:59-66
	1921	Widespread	Fogel, 1970:34-5
Metal trades.........	1921	Detroit	Widick, 1972:26
Railroads..............	1916	Chicago	Tuttle, 1970a:109
	1922	Unspecified	Reid, 1969:166
Restaurants...........	1920	Chicago	Chicago Comm., 1922:427
Steel.....................	1919	Widespread	Foster, 1920:207

Source: Edna Bonacich, "Advanced Capitalism and Black/White Relations," *ASR*, Vol. 41, Vol. February 1976, p. 41.

relationship between white capital and black labor which was reminiscent of arrangements in the Old South between planter and field hand. Employers often formed company unions for black workers, and black preachers were known to take the occasion of a Sunday sermon to advocate the alliance of black labor with capital against white labor. Competition between white and black workers in this era can, however, be overstated. Many black workers did join with whites in labor unions or took only jobs that had been vacated by whites. Moreover, many of the strikebreakers were white, themselves migrants from the rural South. Blacks were not the only migrants serving as replacements for unionized workers; it just seemed that way.

Racial Differences in the North

The competition between white and black labor in the North, some of it real and some of it fancied, brought racial conflict in the North just as it had in the South. Race riots were evident as early as the 1860s in Cincinnati and New York City, for instance. But it was after the turn of the century, with the acceleration of black migration North, that race riots took place with some regularity in the region. Around World War I, there were race riots in Chicago, Philadelphia, Washington, D.C., Omaha, and East St. Louis, Illinois. Riots occurred again in connection with black migration during World War II, in Harlem, Detroit, and throughout the country.

The competition between black and white labor was not settled by street violence in Northern cities, however. There was an accommodation between black and white workers in the North that was not unlike the old Southern caste system. Blacks and whites split the labor market. Whites took the better white-collar and blue-collar jobs, the professions, technical work, crafts and skilled trades, for instance, leaving vacant for blacks jobs at the bottom of the labor hierarchy:

During and since the war [World War II], hundreds of thousands of new jobs have been created at intermediate and upper levels, and many Negroes have been able to move up without displacing whites. . . . Between 1940 and 1960, the total number of employed white-collar workers increased by nearly 12 million, or 81 percent, while the total employed labor force increased by only 37 percent. Hundreds of thousands of white workers have moved into new higher-level jobs, leaving vacancies at intermediate levels that could be filled by Negroes. (Broom and Glenn, 1965:108)

In white-collar work, whites were the professionals, proprietors and managers, while most blacks in white-collar work were employed in sales and as clerks. Blue-collar work was also split; whites monopolized the skilled trades and positions of foremen, and blacks became operatives and laborers (Schmid and Nobbe, 1965). At least this was the trend until recently.

The split labor market in the industrial cities of the North was accompanied by racial segregation in public education for much of the 20th century. Despite the decision of the U.S. Supreme Court in 1954 that "rigid and arbitrary separation of the races in the public schools solely on the basis of race is no longer legal" (Simpson and Yinger, 1972:549), the equal opportunity report by Coleman et al. (1966) found that in 1965 80 percent of white children in the nation attended schools that were from 90 to 100 percent white. Around 65 percent of the nation's black children attended schools where 90 percent of the students were black. Furthermore, the research showed that as a class, black students across the nation scored below whites on academic achievement tests which included standardized measures of verbal and math ability and reading comprehension. As indicators of racial differences in preparation for the skills necessary in white-collar occupations, these tests are related to the racially split labor market.

While the factors involved in academic achievement are many and complex, the Coleman Report gave special attention to the impact of racial integration in the schools on the academic achievement of black students:

. . .the general pattern is an increase in average test performance [for black students] as the proportion of white classmates increases, although in many cases the average for Negro students in totally segregated classes is higher than the average for those in classes where half or less of the students were white. (Coleman et al., 1966:331)

It was also found that black students who attended integrated schools in the early grades showed slightly higher achievement scores than those who attended integrated schools only in the later grades. This relationship, while not strong, held when controlling for the family backgrounds of the students.

With respect to the relationship between the racial composition of classrooms and the academic achievement of black students, Pettigrew (1967:287) proposed that "Many of the consequences of interracial classrooms for both Negroes and whites are a direct function of the opportunities such classrooms provide for cross-racial self-evaluation." When black students are accepted by their classmates, are expected to do well academically, and can publicly express their competence before whites, they overcome their sense of futility, raise their academic self-concept, and perform well. Coleman et al. (1966) concluded that childhood and family experiences primarily accounted for black students' attitudes toward academic achievement. Pettigrew suggested that interracial interaction in classrooms intervenes between family background and black students' attitudes toward education, and the sooner black children are introduced into interracial classrooms the stronger and more positive effect this has on their academic achievement. If this is so, racial segregation in the nation's schools helped perpetuate the racially split labor market.

The Beginnings of Convergence

Nevertheless, the 20th-century migration of blacks to the urban North and West regions was a significant step toward the inclusion of black Americans in the larger American society. It was the first time that blacks in significant numbers were included in industrial blue-collar trades and white-collar work. The inclusion was not complete, however; blacks were still at the lower levels of the labor hierarchy in blue- and white-collar work. But until this migration, and before the middle of the 20th century, the vast majority of black people were far more extensively excluded from the larger American society. Not only were they concentrated in one region of the country, a region which itself lagged behind the evolution of the rest of the nation, but they had been restricted to agrarian labor and domestic service and completely segregated in public education. In the rural South, black culture had continued as an oral folk tradition, and the material living conditions of the black masses remained divergent from those of many citizens of the nation. However, as black workers swung into industrial jobs and the lower levels of white-collar work, the material living conditions of black people began to converge with those of other industrial and white-collar workers. Indicators of health, wealth, education, and welfare showed tremendous improvement in the material base of black life in 20th-century America (Broom and Glenn, 1965; Levitan, Johnston, and Taggart, 1975; Schmid and Nobbe, 1965; Sowell, 1975). These gains were somewhat overshadowed by the even larger gains made by other ethnic groups, such as Asians and Jews. There was improvement, nonetheless. Black cultural traditions also changed in the process, and they too converged with those of the larger society.

Black folk traditions were intellectualized, their circulation was rationalized, and their expression was professionalized in the 20th century. A Negro press emerged in northern cities which exists to this day; dozens of newspapers and several magazines give testimony to the modernization of black folk culture. Black art, theater, literature, and music have all become professional pursuits in the cities, where they have been made into consumable products that can be bought by all. For instance, the folk tradition of blues music, which began in slave work songs, became the "race record" in the North. Because of its consumer appeal, the Columbia Record Company roamed the South in a mobile unit to record "people like Barbecue Bob, Peg Leg Howell, Blind Willie Johnson . . . Aaron T-Bone Walker, and many other singers who sang what was essentially folk material" (Jones, 1963:116-117). The works of contemporary black musicians are now available to virtually everyone in American society. Black protest too was rationalized along the lines of organizations in the larger society and became structured into voluntary associations like the NAACP, with full-time directors and professional staffs. Even the cultural image of blacks changed. The black male, for instance, was transformed from the stereotypical field hand to the equally stereotypical streetcorner hipster or militant, about whom so many recent books have been written. It was a categorical imperative for these cultural types to have nothing but contempt for the old "Toms" down South. Jones

(1963:118) saw the evolutionary convergence of blacks even in the Great Depression and observed that this convergence brought costs as well as benefits:

The Depression was the first real economic crisis—an economic crisis experienced by the Negro, based on the general fortunes of the entire society. Before the Depression, it is quite easy to see how in the paternalized stratum of American society inhabited by Negroes an economic crisis would be of no great importance. The movement by Negroes into the mainstream of American society had also placed them in the path of an economic uncertainty that they had never known before.

While black people early in the 20th century were moving toward evolutionary convergence with the larger society, their divergence was still evident. Fein (1965) found that the median education of nonwhite adults, 25 years and older, was 8.2 years in 1960, while that of white adults had reached 8.7 years in 1940, a gap of 20 years. In 1964, the median income of black families was $3,839, but the median income of white families had reached $3,800 in 1951. Black males had a life expectancy of 61.5 years at birth in 1959–61, a level that had been reached by white males in 1931–33. The rate at which black children were born in a hospital in 1962 was reached for whites in 1946, a 16-year gap. While black-white occupational gaps are closing, they are also still evident. If discrimination against blacks does indeed end, it will still take several years for these gaps to close (Lieberson and Fuguitt, 1967).

PRESENT ACCOMMODATION

The racial caste system in the North did not last nearly as long as the old one in the South. Beginning with legislation under Roosevelt's New Deal, the alliance of capital and cheaper black labor was assailed by "making it illegal for employers to use blacks as strike-breakers or 'strike insurance,' denying the legitimacy of the company union and taking away the advantage to be had in paying blacks lower wages for longer hours" (Bonacich, 1976:45). Although the intent of this legislation was not immediately realized, it still signaled the start of a new era in northern race relations.

The immediate effect of the New Deal legislation was to strengthen the hand of labor in its struggle with capital. Bonacich (1976) noted that union membership expanded in the 1930s and up to World War II, and this expansion included a goodly increase in black union membership. But the long-term effect of equalizing the wage rates and general treatment of black and white labor in major industries has been something else again. American capital faced for the first time an alliance between black and white labor, one backed by the federal and state governments. After

World War II capital sought an alternative to expensive union labor, black and white.

One option capital pursued was the relocation of some of its labor tasks overseas, to take advantage of cheap labor outside the United States in the so-called Third World (Bonacich, 1976). This process reversed the historical practice of importing cheap labor into the country and has been referred to as the "runaway shop." The ability of American capital to relocate labor needs overseas was undoubtedly aided by the international position of the United States after World War II, when American political influence made American investments there secure.

Capital also relocated its labor force within the country, generally away from the expensive union labor in the North to cheaper nonunion labor in the South. As the meat-packing industry took up this practice in the 1950s and 1960s, black men in the North lost their jobs, while black women in the South, among others, found employment in the relocated packing operations. Expensive union labor was also displaced by mechanization and automation, and blacks were disproportionately hurt in the process. They were concentrated in jobs with low technological content, in industries that were economically inert, had declining labor needs, and were easily automated (Baron, 1971). At the same time, blacks by the thousands were being displaced by the mechanization of southern agriculture (Wilhelm, 1971).[5]

All of this has meant black unemployment, according to Edna Bonacich (1976). Sometime in the 1930s, in connection with the passage of the National Recovery Act in 1933, the unemployment rates of blacks and whites underwent a reversal. Contrary to what is commonly understood, until 1940 white unemployment rates in this nation had always exceeded those of blacks. After 1940, black unemployment began to exceed white jobless rates, and it climbed rapidly to the current two-to-one ratio (Bonacich, 1976:35). As this trend continues, it is black youths who are hurt the most. Inner-city black youths have little access to industries in the suburbs and so are unable to undercut labor costs there and as a consequence they find no work at all.

Little reference is made in Bonacich's argument to active discrimination against black workers, much of it in the skilled trades and white-collar work in the private sector of the economy. This discrimination persisted in northern cities long past the New Deal and World War II. Nevertheless, her argument is insightful; it ties black evolution to changes in the larger American society, which she sees as on a course of advanced capitalism.

---

[5]Mechanization is now moving into white-collar jobs, of course, and clerks, secretaries, and technicians are being displaced by the computer.

The essentials of her argument are illustrated in the life cycle of my home town, East St. Louis, Illinois, since World War II.

This city was a meat-packing center and a heavy industrial complex until recently, up to the early 1960s. In East St. Louis and throughout the nation, a stockpile of investment capital and personal savings had been accumulated during World War II. These savings created a great postwar demand for consumer goods by the American public, who had been starved for such possessions during the war. People bought cars, homes in the suburbs, appliances, clothing, and meat; the per capita consumption of meat in this country tripled after World War II. All of this created jobs, and there was an economic boom.

Because of this boom, the old plants in East St. Louis, with their outdated production processes and expensive union labor, were in full production after World War II. East St. Louis was a vibrant place, if a bit corrupt and rough and tumble. It was a good place for a working man to be, and southern blacks by the hundreds moved into the city. The good times did not last long, however, as plants began moving out of town in the 1950s to avoid antiquated production processes, expensive labor, and "union troubles." Nevertheless, southern blacks continued to move into East St. Louis. The town "died" as an industrial center in the 1960s, and these people were trapped. Unlike the earlier European immigrants to this city, the black migrants on the average did not benefit as much from the better days and had less of a chance to prepare their children for technical and professional employment. Today many of them live in East St. Louis, essentially jobless, amid the rubble left from the riots of the 1960s.

Fortunately, unemployment is only part of the current picture of black America. There has been considerable occupational mobility for many black Americans in recent years:

Blacks moved into better paying and higher status jobs. The proportion employed as managers and administrators, professional and technical workers, and craftsmen and kindred workers—the three highest paying occupations—almost doubled between 1958 and 1973, while the proportion employed in service work, nonfarm, and farm labor—the three lowest paying occupations—fell by one-third. Occupational patterns of whites did not change as much, so that non-whites caught up somewhat. . . . (Levitan et al., 1975:44)

Connected with these recent changes in the occupational composition of blacks was a 370 percent increase in the number of black college students between 1960 and 1973.

Table 3 shows the occupational changes of black Americans over the past three decades. Note the decline in black household servants and farm workers, reflections of the old racial caste system, and the increase in black

Table 3 Percentage Distribution of Black and All Employed People by Occupational Groups, 1940—1970

Occupational Groups	Blacks				All People			
	1940	1950	1960	1970	1940	1950	1960	1970
White-Collar Workers								
Professional and technical	2.7	3.2	5.2	8.3	7.5	8.7	11.1	14.9
Managers, officials, and proprietors except farmers	1.1	1.7	1.6	2.2	8.4	8.7	8.4	8.3
Clerical and sales	1.8	4.6	8.1	16.0	16.8	19.2	21.6	25.0
Blue-Collar Workers								
Craftsmen and foremen	3.0	5.6	6.7	9.1	11.3	14.3	13.5	13.9
Operatives	10.4	19.2	21.5	18.0	18.4	20.3	18.4	13.7
Laborers except farm and mine	14.3	16.8	13.7	9.3	6.8	6.5	4.8	4.5
Service Workers								
Private household	22.9	14.8	16.1	8.3	6.2	2.5	2.7	1.5
Other service	11.4	15.4	18.4	20.0	6.2	7.8	8.4	11.3
Farm Workers								
Farmers and managers	15.0	9.1	3.0	1.0	11.5	7.6	3.9	1.9
Laborers and foremen	17.5	18.9	5.8	2.5	6.9	4.4	2.2	1.3

Sources: 1940 Census, *The Labor Force,* Table 62, p. 90; 1950 Census, *Occupational Characteristics,* Table 3, pp. 29-36; 1960 Census, *Occupational Characteristics,* Table 2, pp. 11-20; 1960 Census, *Occupational Characteristics,* Table 3, pp. 21-30; 1970 Census, *Occupational Characteristics,* Table 39, pp. 593-608.
Note: Percentages may not total 100.0 because of rounding.

white-collar workers. These trends have continued since 1970, although parity with others has not been reached. The historical absence of black proprietors and entrepreneurs, as well as business managers, public officials, and elected politicians, should also be noted. With a rising number of black public officials and politicians in recent years, this picture is changing somewhat, but not by an increase in the number of black capitalists. The history of black people is not only one of people laboring for others, it is almost totally devoid of entrepreneurs and property holders. The effect is that black labor has had no economic alternative to working for whites, and thus no option to facing the prejudice and discrimination of others at work.

Evolutionary Trends of Black Americans

The recent occupational gains point toward a gradual evolutionary convergence of some black Americans with the larger society. Current mobility among blacks is most striking for the young and for black women. Working black women now make 90 percent of the income of their white counterparts, up from 62 percent in 1959 (Levitan et al., 1975). More than ever, black women are playing an important and even dominant economic role in the black community. When both partners of a young black family work, they now make 90 percent of the income of their white counterparts. In all of these comparisons, it has been the better educated blacks who have made the greatest gains. Educated blacks now find opportunities in white-collar work, particularly in the public sector of the economy, that is, in governmental bureaucracies and publicly regulated industries (Sowell, 1975). The impact of racial quotas in hiring and promotion is most evident in the sectors of the nation's economy under direct or indirect governmental control. Of course, political reaction to black protest would first show up in these parts of the economy. Modern black families in which both partners have good educations and both partners work now converge with others in material well-being and cultural values.

The evolutionary convergence of black Americans began before the racial protest of the 1950s and 1960s and was to some extent a cause of that protest. The acculturation of blacks into the broad, consumptive American society preceded their inclusion into its opportunity structure. Blacks developed the taste for the "good life," or middle-class status and life-styles, before they acquired the resources to support those styles. Having migrated out of the rural South, blacks found themselves surrounded in northern cities by postwar prosperity, but it was the whites who prospered the most. The whites lived in the best suburbs, possessed modern appliances, sent their children to good schools, and experienced economic security and personal safety. Black migrants acquired a taste for these elements of the good life as black children were becoming better prepared for white-collar jobs, the route to this life.

Intergroup inclusion ran behind enculturation, due in large measure to racial discrimination. Through discrimination, other groups were protecting their own positions in the skilled trades and white-collar work, trying to perpetuate the black-white split-labor market. The organized, nonviolent protest of the 1950s and early 1960s was directed at the barriers faced by aspiring middle-class blacks. It was an ethclass movement aimed at realizing the good life. The subsequent street riots appear to have been cries of frustration from working-class and underprivileged black youth, unprotected from unemployment due to mechanization and automation. The skills of these youths were obsolescent in a technical society, and they were not only discontented with American society, they were also alienated from middle-class blacks. Their protest was unstructured, violent, and expressive rather than goal oriented, and it was void of black middle-class leadership. Black leaders have discovered their political voice, however, and now there are political pressures for the full evolutionary convergence of black people, at least for middle-class blacks.

Farley (1977) found that the evolutionary trends of black Americans, those begun in the 1960s, have continued largely uninterrupted in the 1970s. On the one hand labor force participation rates for black males continued to decline, while, on the other hand, blacks are still making gains into the middle class through educational and occupational mobility. Farley (1977:206) concluded:

During the prosperous 1960s, racial differences in education, occupation and income generally declined. We investigated whether this trend continued into the 1970s and concluded that the gains of the 1960s apparently were not solely attributable to the prosperity of that decade, since racial differences in status narrowed in the 1970s as they did in the previous decade. Blacks and whites, especially the young, are more alike in years of school completed than ever before. Racial differences in the occupations of employed workers continue to decline. The income gap separating black and white families has remained constant, but this is largely a consequence of the sharp rise of female-headed families among blacks. Indexes describing the income of specific types of families or the earnings of individuals generally reveal that racial differences moderated during the early years of the 1970s.

There appears to be a growing inclusion of a black middle class into the larger American society, while a black proletariat remains economically stagnant.

Black workers in nearly every occupational category are still underrepresented at the top of the category. While the proportion of employed black workers who are professionals, managers, administrators, and technical workers rose from almost 7 percent in 1960 to 14 percent in 1973, blacks in 1973 were at the lower levels of this occupational category (Levitan et al., 1975). Black professionals in 1973 were concentrated in precollege teaching, nursing, medical technology, social work, personnel, and labor relations. This is only one illustration of the general trend for blacks to be concentrated at the lower rungs of certain labor hierarchies, while at the same time they have made considerable progress in recent years. The picture is complete only when we add that labor force participation rates for blacks are declining, especially for poor, young male blacks.

Furthermore, the social participation of black Americans tends to be ethnically restrictive. Recent research has shown that blacks tend to participate almost exclusively with other blacks in voluntary associations, in churches, fraternal organizations, proethnic organizations, and neighborhood improvement associations (Williams, Babchuk, and Johnson, 1973). It is obvious to most Americans that blacks tend to limit their informal associations to their own kind, even in predominately white settings. The intergroup inclusion of even middle-class black Americans falls far short of their full assimilation. Of course, many blacks do join with others in some organizations—labor unions, for instance—and this is a function of the degree that they are included in the secondary institutions of the larger society.

The breakdown in the nation's racial caste system has brought greater inclusion of a growing black middle class into the larger society, to be sure, but it has also meant a widening stratification within the black community. By the late 1960s, income distribution was more unequal between wealthy and poor black families than it was between wealthy and poor white families (Wilson, 1973). More than ever, black America is now stratified into ethclasses, although class divisions among blacks go as far back as that between freedman and slave. The black middle class will probably keep abreast of changes in the occupational structure of American society and will come to be a class of professionals, managers, and property owners. On the other hand, there will be a rather permanent black proletariat in this country, composed of people whose skills are obsolescent or who have been pensioned off (Allen, 1970). The critical issue is whether the black middle class will ally with poor blacks or will join with their white counterparts in the pursuit of class interests and the quest for material comfort.

CONCLUSION

The mechanisms for intergroup inclusion and the chances for the evolutionary convergence of ethnic groups have increased in the modernization of American society. The nation changed from an agrarian to an industrial society, beginning in the middle of the past century, and then evolved into a postindustrial society in the present century. This evolution has brought changes in the nation's labor needs, first from agricultural to industrial blue-collar work and later, in the 20th century, to white-collar work. White-collar work requires an enculturated labor force, and there has been an expansion of public education along with the multiplication of white-collar occupations. These two changes in particular, white-collar work and mass public education, have meant increased opportunity for intergroup inclusion and the evolutionary convergence of ethnic groups with one another and with the larger society.

But these opportunities have not been shared equally by the nation's ethnic groups, due in large measure to intergroup competition and the persistence of ethnic stratification. While some groups have been so included into the larger society, others have continued to be excluded, and while the evolutions of some groups have converged with one another and with these societal trends, those of other groups have diverged from the trends of American society. Much of the history of black Americans illustrates the latter course of ethnic evolution in this country.

For longer than nearly any other ethnic group in the country, black Americans have been a class of agrarian laborers and domestic servants, well into the 20th century. During the agrarian phase of American society, most blacks were slaves and regarded as property, not free labor. Since it was impossible in the southern plantation economy for slaves to own property or practice entrepreneurial skills in any systematic way, blacks had little chance to develop a class of capital within their own ranks, save for a small class of freed black entrepreneurs in northern cities. Nor was black labor welcomed in the subsociety of white workers in the South. Slavery is best characterized as an extreme form of ethnic stratification, and it was never meant to be a mechanism for assimilation. Nevertheless, some black-white assimilation did occur during slavery with respect to language, religion, cooking, music, and so on, and it followed along the lines where blacks came into contact with whites in the course of their work. The assimilation of blacks was severely limited during slavery, however, by the nature of the planters' labor needs as well as the antagonism between slaves and white workers.

After Emancipation of the slaves, as the nation entered its industrial phase, black labor was excluded once again, this time from the emerging industrial order of the nation and from resettlement on the frontier. The historical antagonism between white workers and freed slaves surfaced in widespread acts of violence in the post-Reconstructionist South. There was at the same time, however, the possibility of an alliance between black and white labor in the Populist movement. Southern capital feared both chaos and the Populists, and it struck a compromise with white labor which resulted in a racial caste system. Blacks were largely excluded from industrial work, remained propertyless, and stayed for another two or three generations on the land under the domination of the southern planters. This they did as the rest of the nation followed a course of industrialization. Thus the evolution of black Americans continued to diverge from those of other immigrant groups through the 19th and into the 20th centuries.

In the 20th century, however, there began a mass migration of blacks out of the rural South and into the industrial North and West. Black workers again faced a racial caste system, this time in the industrial North, although the northern version did not last nearly as long as had the southern caste system. So in many ways, the migration of black Americans out of the rural South has been a significant step toward their greater inclusion in the larger society. Black labor has been transformed in the 20th century from a class of uneducated, agrarian workers and domestic servants into a better educated class of blue- and white-collar workers. In the process, the black subculture changed from an oral folk tradition into an urban expression which has made significant intellectual contributions to the larger national culture. The Harlem renaissance in the 1920s and recent protest art symbolize this change and these contributions.

The inclusion of blacks in white-collar work has been particularly significant in recent years, since the black protest of the 1960s. But this tells only half the story. There is also a growing black proletariat in this country, as indicated by the increasing number of black women on welfare and the declining labor force participation rates of black males. The labor skills of these people have been made obsolescent by the simultaneous mechanization and automation of southern agriculture and northern industry. There is no reason to predict the inclusion of the black poor into the larger society in the near future, given the current discrepancy between their skills and the evolving technology in the nation.[6] Their future rests on political decisions, particularly those that bear on welfare and income redistribution, rather than the economics of labor needs and property ownership. The evolution of the black middle class will probably converge with that of its white counterpart, limited by barriers to interracial intimacy and the use of race as an identity badge and strategy in resource competition.

The history of black people in this country brings to mind the lyrics of Langston Hughes in "The Negro Speaks of Rivers" (1958).

> I've known rivers:
> I've known rivers ancient as the world and older than the flow of
> human blood in human veins.
>
> My soul has grown deep like the rivers.
> I bathed in the Euphrates when dawns were young.
> I built my hut near the Congo and it lulled me to sleep.
> I looked upon the Nile and raised the pyramids above it.
> I heard the singing of the Mississippi when Abe Lincoln went down
> to New Orleans, and I've seen its muddy bosom turn all
> golden in the sunset.
> I've known rivers:
> Ancient, dusky rivers.
>
> My soul has grown deep like the rivers.

---

[6]If the energy crisis forces us to return to human power in industrial and agricultural production, then all bets are off with respect to this prediction.

REFERENCES

Allen, Robert L.
    1970 Black Awakening in Capitalist America. Garden City, New York: Doubleday and Company, Inc.

Baron, Harold
  1971 "The Demands for Black Labor: Historical Notes on the Political Economy of Racism." Radical America 5(March–April): 34–38, esp.
Blassingame, John W.
  1972 The Slave Community: Plantation Life in the Antebellum South. New York: Oxford University Press.
Blum, Jerome
  1957 "The Rise of Serfdom in Eastern Europe." American Historical Review 62(July):807–835.
Bonacich, Edna
  1972 "Theory of Ethnic Antagonism." American Sociological Review 37(October): 547–559.
  1975 "Abolition, the Extension of Slavery, and the Position of Free Blacks: A Study of Split Labor Markets in the United States, 1830–1863." American Journal of Sociology 81(November):601–628.
  1976 "Advanced Capitalism and Black/White Race Relations in the United States: A Split Labor Market Interpretation." American Sociological Review 41(February):34–51.
Broom, Leonard, and Norval Glenn
  1965 Transformation of the Negro American. New York: Harper and Row, Publishers.
Cash, W. J.
  1960 The Mind of the South. New York: Vintage Books.
Coleman, James S., et al.
  1966 Equality of Educational Opportunity. Washington, D.C.: U.S. Government Printing Office.
Cox, Oliver C.
  1948 Caste, Class, and Race. Garden City, New York: Doubleday and Company, Inc.
Du Bois, W. E. B.
  1935 Black Reconstruction. New York: Harcourt, Brace and Company.
Farley, Reynolds
  1977 "Trends in Racial Inequalities: Have the Gains of the 1960s Disappeared in the 1970s?" American Sociological Review 42(April):189–208.
Fein, Rashi
  1965 "An Economic and Social Profile of the Negro American." Daedalus 94 (Fall):815–846.
Fogel, Robert William, and Stanley L. Engerman
  1974 Time on the Cross: The Economics of American Negro Slavery. Boston: Little, Brown and Company.
Frazier, E. Franklin
  1949 The Negro in the United States. New York: Macmillan Company
Goffman, Erving
  1961 Asylums. Garden City, New York: Doubleday and Company, Inc.
Gutman, Herbert G.
  1975 Slavery and the Numbers Game. Urbana: University of Illinois Press.
Harris, Marvin
  [1964] Patterns of Race in the Americas. New York: W. W. Norton and Company, Inc.
  1974
Hawk, Emory T.
  1934 Economic History of the South. New York: Prentice-Hall, Inc.
Holt, Grace Sims
  1972 "Stylin' Outta the Black Pulpit." Pp. 189–204 in Thomas Kochman (ed.), Rappin' and Stylin' Out. Urbana: University of Illinois Press.
Hughes, Langston
  1958 The Langston Hughes Reader. New York: George Braziller, Inc.
Jones, Le Roi
  1963 Blues People. New York: William Morrow and Company.
Johnson, Charles S.
  1934 Shadow of the Plantation. Chicago: University of Chicago Press.

1939 "Race Relations and Social Change." Pp. 271–303 in Edgar T. Thompson (ed.), Race Relations and the Race Problem: A Definition and Analysis. Durham, North Carolina: Duke University Press.

Key, V. O., Jr.
1949 Southern Politics: In State and Nation. New York: Alfred A. Knopf, Inc.

Landry, Bart
1977 "The Economic Position of Black Americans." Pp. 50–108 in H. Roy Kaplan, American Minorities and Economic Opportunity. Itasca, Illinois: F. E. Peacock Publishers, Inc.

Levitan, Sar A., William B. Johnston, and Robert Taggart
1975 Still A Dream: The Changing Status of Blacks since 1960. Cambridge, Massachusetts: Harvard University Press.

Lieberson, Stanley, and Glenn V. Fuguitt
1967 "Negro-White Occupational Differences in the Absence of Discrimination." American Journal of Sociology 73(September):188–200.

Linden, Fabian
1940 "Repercussions of Manufacturing in the Ante-Bellum South." North Carolina Review 17(October):313–331.

Meier, August, and Elliot Rudwick
1970 From Plantation to Ghetto. Revised edition. New York: Hill and Wang, Inc.

Miller, Loren
1967 The Petitioners: The Story of the Supreme Court of the United States and the Negro. New York: World Publishing Company.

National Advisory Commission on Civil Disorders
1968 Report of the National Advisory Commission on Civil Disorders. New York: Bantam Books, Inc.

Palmer, Dewey H.
1967 "Moving North: Migration of Negroes During World War I." Phylon 28:52–62.

Pettigrew, Thomas F.
1967 "Social Evaluation Theory: Convergence and Applications." Pp. 241–319 in Nebraska Symposium on Motivation, Vol. 15. Lincoln: University of Nebraska Press.

Schmid, Calvin F., and Charles E. Nobbe
1965 "Socioeconomic Differentials among Nonwhite Races." American Sociological Review 30(December):909–922.

Simpson, George Eaton, and J. Milton Yinger
1972 Racial and Cultural Minorities: An Analysis of Prejudice and Discrimination. Fouth Edition. New York: Harper and Row, Publishers.

Sowell, Thomas
1975 Race and Economics. New York: David McKay Company, Inc.

Spero, Sterling D., and Abram L. Harris
1931 The Black Worker: The Negro and the Labor Movement. New York: Columbia University Press.

Van Den Berghe, Pierre
1976 "The African Diaspora in Mexico, Brazil, and the United States." Social Forces 54(March):530–545.

Vance, Rupert B.
1939 "Racial Competition for the Land." Pp. 97–124 in Edgar T. Thompson (ed.), Race Relations and the Race Problem: A Definition and Analysis. Durham, North Carolina: Duke University Press.

Wade, Richard C.
1964 Slavery in the Cities: The South, 1820–1860. New York: Oxford University Press.

Wilhelm, Sidney M.
1971 Who Needs the Negro? Garden City, New York: Doubleday and Company, Inc.

Williams, Eric
1966 Capitalism and Slavery. New York: Capricorn Books.

Williams, J. Allen, Jr., Nicholas Babchuk, and David R. Johnson
  1973 "Voluntary Association and Minority Status: A Comparative Analysis of Anglo, Black, and Mexican Americans." American Sociological Review 38(October):637–646.
Wilson, William J.
  1973 Power, Racism and Privilege: Race Relations in Theoretical and Socio-historical Perspectives. New York: Macmillan Company.
Woodward, C. Vann
  1966 The Strange Career of Jim Crow. Second Revised Edition. New York: Oxford University Press.

CHAPTER 9

Chinese Americans and Japanese Americans

INTRODUCTION

The Chinese and Japanese share a legacy with black Americans; all were immigrant laborers, and as racial minorities all have experienced color prejudice and discrimination in this country. There are important differences, however, between the experiences of these racial minorities. Asian Americans, unlike blacks, became entrepreneurs and proprietors, middleman minorities which, through their own subeconomies, could circumvent to some extent the economic discrimination and color prejudice of others. Furthermore, in the second half of the 20th century both Asian groups were rapidly being included into the wider American society, at least a generation before there was a similar inclusion of blacks into the postindustrial society. The Asians were brought into the larger society through the modern mechanisms for intergroup inclusion, mass public education, and white-collar work. Now the American-born Chinese and Japanese are among the best educated and most middleclass of the nation's ethnic groups, giving evidence of their evolutionary convergence.

The study of these Asian Americans is important for students of American ethnicity. It forces us to examine closely the contention that color prejudice and racial discrimination have made the evolutions of people of color in this country similar and uniquely different from those of other ethnic groups. Asian Americans do not conform to the rule that racial groups face everlasting exclusion to the bottom strata of American society.

CHINESE AMERICANS AND AMERICAN SOCIETY

Table 1   Evolution of Chinese Americans and the Modernization of American Society

Agrarian Society 1600–1865	Industrial Society 1865–1945	Postindustrial Society 1945–Present
Immigration and contact ⟶ Early accommodation ⟶ (Peak years, 1848–1882) (1848–1870)	Intergroup competition, ethnic stratification, ⟶ and exclusion (1870–1940)	Middleman minority ⟶ Toward intergroup inclusion (1870–1940) (1945–)

Dates are approximations only. Moreover, there has been recent Chinese immigration, since 1965, and the history of these new Chinese immigrants has just begun.

Contact

It is estimated that 409,439 Chinese immigrated into the United States between 1820 and 1961, although all these immigrants did not settle permanently here. The peak years of Chinese immigration were between 1848 and 1882, a period that began with the Gold Rush in California, continued with the construction of the transcontinental railroad, and ended with the first Chinese Exclusion Act of 1882. While the first Chinese Exclusion Act was meant to be temporary and to be in force for only 10 years, it was renewed in 1892 and made permanent in 1904. While these acts had loopholes, which permitted the entry of certain classes of Chinese into the country, these were closed with the Immigration Act of 1924, the tenure of which ran essentially unchanged up to 1965. With the recent changes in immigration laws since 1965, Chinese immigration into the country jumped from 105 to 142,108 people per year between 1965 and 1972 (Light and Wong, 1975). (See Table 1.)

The immigration of Chinese into the United States in the past century was a part of a larger movement of people (cf. Park, 1926/1950). In the course of European expansion, as Europeans settled throughout the world, including the Pacific basin, they used the Chinese, among others, in the construction of their settlements. Eventually, Chinese emigrants ringed the Pacific Ocean. Chinese labor located in Canada, the United States, Mexico, and Central and South America in the Western Hemisphere and settled throughout Southeast Asia in the Eastern Hemisphere. In this country, the Chinese joined with blacks, other Asian groups, Mexicans, and the many European nationalities in the building of American society.

Virtually all of the early Chinese immigrants, those who came to this country in the past century, originated from seven districts of southern China, in the province of Kwangtung, and in the vicinity of the city of Canton (Light, 1972). The vast majority of these immigrants were males who had been peasants in China and whose lives had been woven into a social fabric of clan, village, and dialect groupings. This social network was reconstructed by Chinese immigrants on American soil, and virtually every immigrant was integrated into an ethnic moral community, an immigrant brotherhood. In the face of their exclusion from the larger American society, an era that began in the past century and lasted well into the present one for these immigrants, the Chinese turned inward into their immigrant brotherhood. Through this communal network they evolved out of a class of wage laborers and into a middleman minority, and eventually toward their inclusion into the larger society.

Early Chinese immigrants to the United States were sojourners who sought work and wages in this country with the intention of quickly returning home to China with their savings. Poverty pushed peasants out of southern China, and paradoxically it pulled them back again. Emigration was an escape from the poverty of China, but it also meant that emigrants with savings earned elsewhere could return to China and live well. With this in mind, Chinese immigrants to the United States willingly suffered hardships at work on the West Coast, thereby undercutting the working conditions and wage rates of other ethnic groups in California and invoking their wrath. According to Lyman (1974:75), "Labor tended to identify Chinese immigrants as the tools of a consortium of monopoly capital that would drive the white workingman to utter degradation." At least the actions of Chinese immigrant labor gave the appearance of an alliance with capital. Realistically, Chinese immigrants undercut the economic position of whites unknowingly, for they were generally ignorant of the prevailing wage rates on the West Coast, often having contracted the terms of their employment while still in China. Furthermore, neither the Chinese immigrants nor China itself was in any position to complain about the exploitation of Chinese labor by American employers. The poverty of China made her and her emigrees powerless to prevent such exploitation in America. These were the conditions when the Chinese first entered the rough-and-ready atmosphere of California during the Gold Rush.

Early Accommodation

The Chinese came to America to work, meeting labor needs mainly on the West Coast, particularly in mining, railroad construction, and agrarian wage labor. Labor demand was great and its supply was short when the Chinese entered the economy of 19th-century California. This made for an early accommodation between the Chinese and other laboring groups; there was initially little labor competition. The situation changed, however, as more and more people moved to California and as the area experienced a post–Civil War economic recession. Competition between Chinese and white labor became common, and the Chinese were forced first out of mining, then out of railroad work, and eventually out of agrarian wage labor. The Chinese then migrated to the cities on the West Coast and other regions, and there they established their own subeconomies and evolved into a middleman minority.

Chinese males were nearly one-quarter of the wage laborers of California in the 1870s (Saxton, 1971). Many of the early Chinese immigrants to California initially found their way to the gold fields of northern California. In the census of 1860 for California, more than two-thirds of all Chinese were found in the mining regions of the Sierra Nevada and Trinity Alps (Saxton, 1971:3). While never popular from the first with white miners (including the American-born and Irish, German, and Scotch-Irish immigrants), the Chinese nonetheless worked claims alongside them. As soon as the good claims became scarce, the Chinese were forced to either work abandoned claims or to provide personal services for others. Later, as miners became wage labor, the Chinese were forced out of mining altogether and barred from the miners' unions.

As the good claims petered out railroad construction picked up, and thousands of Chinese were put to work building the western half of the nation's transcontinental railroad. The decision to hire Chinese was taken in 1865, when the Central Pacific found itself far behind schedule, that is, behind the pace of the Union Pacific Railroad, which was laying track from the east. This was a serious problem for the Central Pacific, since Congress in 1862 had made land grants and posted financial bonds for the two railroads on the basis of the miles of track each constructed. Competition between the two railroads in the 1860s was very keen, and the High Sierra was not yet in sight of the Central's construction crew in 1866, while the crews on the Union Pacific were laying a mile of track per day (Saxton, 1971:62).

Not only did the Central Pacific secure Chinese labor from the mining districts of California, it also contracted labor out of China as well. One such labor contractor boasted that he alone had brought 30,000 Chinese into California (Saxton, 1971). There was no competition between Chinese and white workers over railroad work, contrary to what had been happening in mining. Saxton explained that white workers were in short supply, and the mining districts offered attractive alternatives. Therefore the hiring of Chinese resulted not in the displacement of whites but in their upgrading. Further, Saxton says, "No man who had any choice would have chosen to be a common laborer on the Central Pacific during the crossing of the High Sierra" (p. 63).

After the golden spike was driven into the ground at Promontory, Utah, in 1869, finally linking the nation by rail, some Chinese stayed with the railroads and laid track off the trunk line in southern and northern California. Others became agrarian wage laborers for California ranchers or began to concentrate in the trades, domestic services, and urban manufacturing, moving into urban Chinatowns in California, particularly San Francisco. Although competition and conflict between the Chinese and other laboring groups were not totally absent in the early years, this era is best characterized as one of accommodation. Because of the initial shortage of labor on the West Coast there was little reason for labor competition. But the situation soon changed, into one of competition, conflict, and the eventual stratification and exclusion of the Chinese.

Intergroup Competition, Conflict, Ethnic Stratification, and Exclusion

Chinese immigrants took up a variety of work, but they were initially concentrated in mining, railroad construction, and then agrarian wage labor. So long as there was no labor competition in these endeavors, the Chinese were able to manage an accommodation of sorts with white labor. However, mining became quickly competitive, railroad construction tapered off, and eventually the Chinese even faced competition as field labor from white labor unions and immigrants from Japan and Mexico.

Competition became heated first in the gold fields of California, and in the end the Chinese were compelled to assume a noncompetitive posture. They were relegated to such service jobs as laundrymen and gatherers of firewood in the gold fields or took over from white miners undesirable, worked-over sites. This was the first stage of ethnic stratification of the Chinese in mining. As mining evolved from a collection of small operations, primarily in placer mining, to the capital-intensive large-scale endeavor of deep-shaft mining, miners too changed. They became wage laborers instead of small, independent entrepreneurs. White miners subsequently organized themselves in unions, from which they excluded Chinese, thereby excluding them from mining itself, all with the consent of absentee capital. In 1870 there were 27,045 Chinese miners and laborers in the country and by 1920 only 151 Chinese miners remained (Yuan, 1963).

Chinese were excluded from mining by a variety of techniques, including local ordinances prohibiting Chinese from working area sites, discriminatory taxation of Chinese miners (e.g., the California Foreign Miners' Tax), closed-shop arrangements, and mob violence. Chinese in the mining regions of California, the Pacific Northwest, and the Rockies were beaten, burned, lynched, and shot by mobs with some frequency in the last half of the 19th century.

As the Chinese were forced from mining, and then as railroad construction fell off after 1869, Chinese labor took up other lines of work, two of which stand out. As experienced construction workers, great numbers of Chinese began building an agrarian empire in California. They diked, ditched, drained, irrigated, and otherwise made fields in California ready for production, and they also harvested the crops for white growers. Chinese were first welcomed by California growers and ranchers as a source of relatively cheap and experienced labor, in the context of a critical labor shortage in that state. But as the Chinese population grew older and the supply of Chinese labor correspondingly diminished, due to the restrictions on further Chinese immigration, Chinese field workers became understandably more militant about wage rates and working conditions. This turned growers cool toward the Chinese, and they began to look elsewhere for labor. Lyman(1974:74) observed that "a series of racially-based strikes, occurring from 1893 to 1894, dealt the final blow to extensive employment of Chinese in agriculture. . . . the Chinese were removed from the agricultural scene by a violent campaign that united independent growers and the thoroughly Sinophobic urban labor unions."

Before this time, however, Chinese had begun to concentrate in urban areas, particularly in San Francisco, taking up work in manufacturing, trade, and most significantly, domestic service. By 1900, 57 percent of the gainfully employed Orientals in the United States (including Japanese as well as Chinese, but the bulk of the Japanese immigration came after 1900) were engaged in domestic service, whereas only 40 years before, nearly two-thirds of the Chinese were miners (Light, 1972; Saxton, 1971).

While Chinese were being relegated to the bottom of the labor hierarchy, in manufacturing (sweatshops) and domestic service (as houseboys), their immigration into the country was being restricted as well. The first Chinese Exclusion Act passed Congress in 1882 and was renewed twice and made "permanent" between 1904 and 1965. It was through politics, mainly, that the foes of the Chinese managed to force them out of desirable jobs and restrict their entry into the country (Daniels, 1969). In the 1870s, America was in a long postwar depression, and the matter of Chinese labor competition was a serious political issue, especially on the West Coast. Political parties there had anti-Chinese planks in their platforms, and the California Constitutional Convention

Filipinos follow the Chinese in lettuce fields. Lange; Library of Congress.

expressed sentiment for Chinese exclusion in its articles, at the insistence of white labor unions. Moreover, California experimented for more than three decades with immigration restriction, including a number of pieces of legislation known collectively as the passenger acts (Lyman, 1974:63). These acts had little immediate success, since the U.S. Supreme Court declared unconstitutional California's attempt to engage itself unilaterally in international relations.

Ultimately, pressure was felt in Washington, however, and President Chester Arthur signed the first Chinese Exclusion Act into law in May 1882 (Daniels, 1969; Lyman, 1974). This act provided that no skilled or unskilled Chinese laborer or miner could enter the United States for ten years, but it exempted certified merchants, students, and itinerants (Lyman, 1974:66). The exclusion of Chinese was extended in 1892 under the Geary act for another ten years, and this act went so far as to deny bail to Chinese in habeas corpus proceedings and to require all Chinese labor in this country to carry identity cards, as is now done by native labor in South Africa. The exclusion of Chinese immigration was extended again in 1904, and certain loopholes in the previous acts were closed with the Immigration Act of 1924, which remained essentially in force until 1965.

The Chinese have been historically excluded from American society. They were forced to assume a subordinate position in the nation's system of ethnic stratification, on the one hand, and restricted in their entry into the country on the other. Competition between the Chinese and white workers, demands of the Chinese on white growers in California, the superior political power of their Sinophobic foes, especially on the West Coast—all these set into motion the forces for Chinese exclusion. This history is obviously consistent with ethnic conflict theory. The foes of the Chinese controlled the legislative and political process, and through it they got the upper hand in their conflict with the Chinese. The Chinese were virtually powerless in politics; Chinese aliens in the United States could not vote, and China, because of its weakness in world politics, was unable to protect her nationals in this country. Her notes of protest simply went unanswered.

The Chinese as a Middleman Minority

Excluded from the wider society, the Chinese evolved into a middleman minority, thereby maintaining over several generations their distance from the larger American society. Equally important, this gave the Chinese an alternative to facing the discrimination and prejudice of others. Bonacich (1973:583) says middleman minorities "tend to concentrate in certain occupations, notably trade and commerce, but also other 'middleman' lines such as agent, labor contractor, rent collector, money lender and broker. They play the role of middlemen between producer and consumer, employer and employee, owner and renter, elite and masses." She has suggested that the common denominator to middleman minority status is the liquidity of the occupations such groups choose. They concentrate in jobs which provide a portable or easily liquidated livelihood, as personified by the trader, truck farmer, and independent professional, consistent with sojourning motives.

The Chinese began to concentrate in commercial trades and services late in the 19th century. As Chinese labor withdrew from mining, railroad construction, and agrarian wage labor, they went into "middleman" jobs and became segregated in Chinatowns. Lee (1960) referred to this evolutionary period of Chinese Americans as one of reconcentration in which the Chinese moved to the nation's larger cities and there established their subeconomies and Chinatowns. Between 1870 and 1920 there was a 280 percentage increase of Chinese in domestic and service work, and a phenomenal 960 percent increase in the number of Chinese traders and dealers (Yuan, 1963). In the process a class of Chinese capital emerged which provided Chinese Americans with employment without prejudice and discrimination. The establishment of an ethnic subeconomy and opportunity structure is an important event in the evolution of any ethnic group, especially for one facing restricted opportunity in the larger society. An ethnic subeconomy does not necessarily mean any better treatment of employees by employers, however; the exploitation of labor in the sweatshops of this nation's Chinatowns is sad and legendary. But it did mean that the Chinese were able to avoid the full impact of anti-Oriental prejudice and discrimination.

The Chinese middleman minority position took shape in the nation's Chinatowns around the turn of the century. Self-employed Chinese at this time were concentrated in hand laundries, import outlets, restaurants, and retail grocery stores. The bulk of the salaried Chinese were employed in Chinese firms, including manufacturing as well as commercial outlets. Outside their subeconomy, Chinese laborers were domestic servants and gardeners in the larger labor market. The exclusion which marked Chinese participation in the labor force is dramatically illustrated by the fact that fully 50 percent of the nation's salaried and self-employed Chinese in 1920 were in hand laundries or restaurants (Light, 1972).

The occupational concentration and residential segregation of the Chinese meant their effective exclusion from the larger American society. There were no horizontal alliances between the Chinese and their class counterparts in the wider society, capital or labor. Instead, Chinese employers and employees were vertically integrated into their own subeconomy and subsociety, secluded from others. Antagonism toward

the Chinese drove them further into their own separate ethnic
community:

One of the accusations frequently made by non-Chinese against their Asiatic
fellow workers was that they were too docile, too slavelike, to be able to stand on
their own feet in a free society. But the greater the pressure from the outside, the
more cohesive became the vertical structure of the Chinese establishment, and the
more unlikely any horizontal cleavage within it. (Saxton, 1971:10)

Antagonism against Chinese capital was equally great. Chinese businessmen enjoyed a competitive edge in certain industries, in part due to their
access to cheaper Chinese labor, and this created ethnic hostility in
business circles. This paralleled hostility in the ranks of labor, because of
the refusal of Chinese labor to join the union movement. The ethnic
solidarity of the Chinese and the antagonism toward them were merely
different sides of the same coin.

Chinatowns were organized along Old World lines, into clans (*Tsu*), *Hui
Kuans*, secret societies (tongs), and trade guilds. Clans were surname
associations which originated in the lineage communities of southeast
China. They enforced endogamy until recently and were typically
organized around a leading merchant's store. While clans had definite
economic functions, their purpose was primarily fraternal and welfare. It
was the clans that reminded the sojourner of his obligations to village and
family back in China and thus acted *in loco parentis*.[1] However, for the
third- and fourth-generation Chinese Americans these obligations have
diminished in saliency, and the functions of clans have been curtailed
(Lyman, 1974).

Hui Kuans were ethnic divisions within the larger Chinese groups,
composed of those who spoke the same dialect and hailed from the same
region of China. They were similar to the *Landsmannschaft* Louis Wirth
observed in the Jewish ghetto of Chicago (see Chapter 2). Lyman (1974)
wrote that *Hui Kuans* were most important in incorporating immigrants
into American Chinatowns, serving as caravansaries, credit and loan
societies, and employment agencies. Members of a *Hui Kuan* would
normally employ only their own kind, as trade guilds and commercial
establishments were organized around these dialect groups. *Hui Kuans*
exercised control over labor, commerce, debts, and disputes, and thus
their communal control over economic exchange in Chinatowns and the
integration of immigrants into this subeconomy was absolute.

Membership in both clan and *Hui Kuan* was ascriptive, based on
birthright. Secret societies, or tongs, were voluntary associations in which
membership was on the basis of mutual interest rather than birthright.

---

[1]See Rose Hum Lee (1960) for some not so flattering latent functions of Chinese clans.

Chinatown, San Francisco. Genthe; Library of Congress.

Tongs recruited members from those who were either ineligible or ostracized from Chinatown's more powerful clans and *Hui Kuans*. The economic function of these secret societies centered around the provision of illegal goods and services, such as prostitutes for homeless Chinese males.[2] Tongs included professional killers who were known as hatchetmen for their use of small hatchets in that trade. Some observers believed that there were as many as 30 tongs in San Francisco alone in 1900, although a government survey in the same era listed only 16 tongs across the entire nation (Light, 1972). Regardless of their number, secret societies provided a check on the power of prominent clans and *Hui Kuans* and offered opportunity to outcasts from these other organizations in the Chinese community.

Trade guilds drew their membership not only from people in the same trade or line of work but also from a particular clan or *Hui Kuan*. Trade guilds represented an extension of the economic control of powerful clans and *Hui Kuans*. Laundrymen, cigar makers, restaurateurs, clothing manufacturers from one clan, *Hui Kuan*, or another—all had their trade guilds. Internal competition was regulated, rules of location and compensation were enforced, and violators of the rules were punished through the trade guilds. Of course, employers in a trade guild would hire their own clansmen or members of their own *Hui Kuan*. The paternalism between Chinese capital and labor was rooted in these Old World blood ties and communal obligations.

This was the state of the Chinese in America up to World War II. They had evolved into a middleman minority, a pattern of ethnic evolution also common to Chinese emigrants elsewhere, not only in this country. It is a course of evolution very different than that of black Americans (see Chapter 8). The Chinese concentrated in certain businesses and built an ethnic subeconomy in the nation's Chinatowns, where they provided opportunity for their own kind. The result was the further exclusion of the Chinese from American society and their evolutionary divergence, at least the continuation of a foreign Chinese subculture in America's Chinatowns. The past unification of Chinese capital and labor in a single subeconomy and ethnic community, one separated from the larger society economically and culturally, was reinforced by the fact that there was not a significant American-born generation of adult Chinese until World War II. In short, the inclusion of Chinese into American society was minimal just 40 years ago.

---

[2]Because of the restrictions on Chinese immigration and the sojourning motives of Chinese males, Chinese women did not join their men in America, and this delayed the birth of an American-born generation of Chinese until the 20th century. This had the effect of further isolating the Chinese from the larger society.

By the same token, the Chinese were better prepared than many other ethnic groups for the changes in the nation's labor needs that followed World War II. They as a group possessed the economic base for investments in the education of their young, a prerequisite for mobility into higher levels of white-collar work. Because of the historical solidarity of the Chinese community in this country, there was also a network of mutual aid that distributed economic resources to the American-born generation. Thus this generation of Chinese Americans would carry a sense of ethnic pride and achievement into the nation's universities and great work bureaucracies in the second half of the 20th century.

Toward Intergroup Inclusion

The percentage of white-collar workers in the total labor force increased from 31 percent in 1940 to 48 percent in 1970, representing the growth in professional and technical workers that followed World War II. There have been thousands of new teachers, medical specialists, researchers, and engineers in the labor force since 1940, to mention only a few examples. Between 1940 and 1950, the number of engineers in the country doubled, and the number of research workers increased by 50 percent (Trow, 1966:442). College enrollment has increased tremendously in the process, and in the past 30 years the percentage of the age cohort 18–21 who attend college has grown from 15 to almost 50 percent. In the midst of these changes in the larger society, significant numbers of American-born Chinese evolved out of a middleman minority status and toward inclusion into the secondary institutions of the larger society.

Table 2 indicates how the inclusion of the Chinese into the wider society has progressed. The percentage of Chinese employed in professional and technical fields increased from 7.2 in 1950 to 19.2 in 1960. By 1970, over 26 percent of the employed Chinese were in these upper levels of white-collar work. Corresponding with the increasing number of Chinese in professional and technical work there has been a decreasing number of Chinese proprietors and household servants. Taken together, this indicates the evolution of many Chinese Americans out of the economic niche of a middleman minority and into the professional and technical fields of the postindustrial American society. The occupational composition of the Chinese people in 1970 compares favorably with that of the entire labor force.

Only 3 percent of the male Chinese Americans 25 years and older possessed a college education in 1940, while in 1960 19 percent of them had at least four years of college. This put them as a group ahead of all other ethnic groups in educational attainment. Four percent of the adult Chinese females in the country had a college education in 1940, and by 1960, nearly 15 percent of them had at least four years of college, placing

Table 2 Percentage Distribution of Chinese and All Employed People by Occupational Groups, 1940–1970.

Occupational Groups	Chinese				All People			
	1940	1950	1960	1970	1940	1950	1960	1970
White-Collar Workers								
Professional and technical......................	3.0	7.2	19.2	26.5	7.5	8.7	11.1	14.9
Managers, officials and proprietors except farmers...........	14.7	20.0	13.6	8.9	8.4	8.7	8.4	8.3
Clerical and sales..........	12.0	16.2	21.9	21.2	16.8	19.2	21.6	25.0
Blue-Collar Workers								
Craftsmen and foremen......................	1.4	2.9	5.5	5.4	11.3	14.3	13.5	13.9
Operatives......................	23.3	17.3	16.1	13.8	18.4	20.3	18.4	13.7
Laborers except farm and mine....................	2.0	1.7	1.4	2.3	6.8	6.5	4.8	4.5
Service Workers								
Private household.........	7.0	2.6	1.1	0.8	6.2	2.5	2.7	1.5
Other service.................	31.6	29.2	20.1	19.6	6.2	7.8	8.4	11.3
Farm Workers								
Farmers and managers.	1.3	1.2	0.7	0.3	11.5	7.6	3.9	1.9
Laborers and foremen.	3.0	1.4	0.5	0.3	6.9	4.4	2.2	1.3

Sources: 1940 Census, *The Labor Force*, Table 62, p. 90; 1940 Census, *Characteristics of the Nonwhite Population by Race*, Table 32, pp. 95–96; 1950 Census, *Occupational Characteristics*, Table 3, pp. 29–36; 1950 Census, *Characteristics of the Nonwhite Population by Race*, Table 12, p. 42; 1960 Census, *Occupational Characteristics*, Table 2, pp. 11–20; 1960 Census, *Characteristics of the Nonwhite Population by Race*, Table 35, p. 111; 1970 Census, *Occupational Characteristics*, Table 39, pp. 593-608.

Note: Percentages may not total 100.0 because of rounding.

them behind only Filipino females among the nation's ethnic groups in educational attainment (Schmid and Nobbe, 1965). These figures attest to a great change in Chinese Americans in a short time span, a change that has brought their greater inclusion into American society, and one that is consistent with our view on the increased potential for intergroup inclusion in modern society (see Chapter 6).

The Chinese became engineers, architects, physicians, dentists, optometrists, pharmacists, accountants, and college teachers. Lyman (1974:137) found that of 1,124 Chinese employed in American colleges and universities in 1960, 648, or more than half, were teaching engineering and physical or natural science and 108 were in medical science; only 254 were employed in the humanities or social sciences. Thus the Chinese selected a narrow range of white-collar work. They opted for work that gave them prestige, high income, free choice of clientele, and independence from professional peers, and jobs which did not demand interpersonal skills and facility in English. The Chinese circumvented many potential competitors and barriers for the better white-collar jobs by selecting fields that were to be the growth occupations after World War II and required technical expertise rather than skillfulness in Anglo-American cultural styles. These fields also represent portable skills and are reminiscent in this sense of the occupational choices made by the earlier Chinese sojourners and middleman merchants. Not every Chinese person could satisfy all of these criteria in job choice, of course, but these were some of the occupational goals sought by the Chinese as a class.

There were other changes in the Chinese community after World War II which were connected with their educational and occupational achievements. Lyman (1974:147) observed that:

Chinese Americans often wish to ratify their newly acquired middle-class status by moving to better residences, purchasing their own homes, and relocating outside Chinatown. . . . when Chinese did remove to the suburbs they often reconstituted their community and reestablished an ethnic enclave in the supposedly cosmopolitan and raceless regions of American residences.

Community development by middle-class and suburban Chinese was not unlike that of suburban Jews in the Chicago area (see Chapter 3). Typically, suburban Chinese-American communities were organized around a Chinese language school, and the people's interest in the school fostered a wider form of organization (Lyman, 1974:149). This suggests a continuation of cultural pluralism among middle-class Chinese Americans. The recent occupational diversification of Chinese Americans has not been so great as to mean their full assimilation into American society. It does mean, however, that divisions between Chinese ethclasses are greater than ever before. There is a growing class of Chinese poor in this country, due to renewed immigration, as the American-born Chinse are simultaneously included more into the larger American society.

There were several reasons for the greater inclusion of the Chinese into the larger society after World War II. China was an ally of America in the Pacific, and the propaganda about the courageous Chinese peasant meeting the Japanese onslaught moderated domestic prejudice against Chinese Americans. Besides, the country was preoccupied at the time with hatred for another Asian group, the Japanese. Opportunities were made available for the first time to Chinese Americans, as a consequence, and many of the young began to pass through doors previously shut to the Chinese. The concentration of Chinese in urban areas and on the West Coast, where many of these opportunities occurred, also helped. This all coincided with the fact that the first large generation of American-born Chinese came of age during the war years.

However, the roots of the inclusion of the Chinese during the postindustrial phase of American society go back to their exclusion in an earlier era. The Chinese had managed to build an ethnic subeconomy and maintain themselves as a communal group in the course of their exclusion. The formation of this subeconomy was facilitated by the original sojourning motives of the early Chinese immigrants and by the ethnic solidarity within clans and *Hui Kuans.* The result was the integration of Chinese capital and labor into one economic endeavor, tied together economically and socially, through the overlapping bonds of economic interdependence, clan, and *Hui Kuan* membership. This had the effect of preserving the immigrant brotherhood and simultaneously precluding the assimilation of the Chinese with their class counterparts in the larger society. When it came time to prepare an American-born generation for work in the wider society, however, both the economic resources and the mechanism for their distribution were present. Wealth and its distribution through the mutual obligations of clans and *Hui Kuans* provided the means for financing the education of the young and thus their entry into professional and technical fields.

Bonacich (1973:593) speculated on an economic reason for the Chinese turning their attention to the inclusion of their young into the wider American society: "one important factor seems to be changing economic conditions (the development of chain stores, supermarkets, etc.), making the family firm less viable, and driving the younger generations to seek employment in higher-paying non-ethnic firms." That is, the Chinese were forced out of their middleman economic roles by the growing scale of business in this country after World War II, while at the same time opportunities in the larger economy were expanding for the Chinese. Furthermore, China underwent a political revolution after World War II, making the eventual return home of the sojourner now virtually impossible. The second-generation Chinese were Americanized, and among them the Old World regional societies and ascriptive obligations lost much of their saliency. These patterns were partially replaced by participation in voluntary associations. Recently, ethnic interest groups have grown pan-Asiatic and include both American-born Chinese and Japanese, along with those from the other Asian groups in the country. All of this indicates the evolutionary convergence of the middleclass, American-born Chinese in recent years.

Nevertheless, half of the Chinese in the nation's labor force remained in manual work during this same period, and over half of these were employed in service work as waiters, busboys, and domestics. This is traditional work for Chinese labor in the country, and many of these workers have stayed in Chinatowns, while the better educated and more mobile ones have moved to the nation's suburbs. Populations in Chinatowns have been inflated by the Chinese immigration into the country since 1965. Many of these recent immigrants appear to be trapped in menial work, perhaps unable to duplicate the evolutionary course of the earlier Chinese immigrants.

Unlike the earlier immigrants, these newer immigrants come not from a single region of China but from diverse origins, and they have conflicting ideological orientations, especially on the issue of China and Taiwan. In view of the role of communal allegiances in the climb of the older Chinese immigrants out of menial wage labor, it is difficult to predict that the new immigrants will follow in their footsteps. Moreover, while the consumer demand for certain Chinese goods and services still exists among immigrants and in the larger society, the era of small mom-and-pop stores and restaurants has peaked and is on the decline, as they are replaced by supermarkets and fast-food chains. The rapid inclusion of these new immigrants into white-collar work is also problematic. Chinatowns are now portrayed as areas of festering resentment, alienation, labor exploitation, unemployment, and nascent rebellion (Light and Wong, 1975; Lyman, 1974). Light and Wong believe that these problems have not been publicized in the wider society because elites in Chinatown fear that social protest will inhibit tourism. The Chinese in America are now stratified into three ethclasses: Those who have evolved into the American middle class, at least with respect to their education, occupation, residence, and forms of secondary association; those who are uneducated and still in domestic service and menial work; and powerful merchants in the nation's Chinatowns. The Chinese in America are now more diversified and dispersed; they are a modern ethnic group which is stratified into ethclasses.

All three theories of the sociological lore on American ethnicity must be taken into account to understand the history of the Chinese in this country. Labor competition led to the exclusion of the Chinese by more powerful and Sinophobic groups in a direct application of conflict theory. The Chinese then evolved into a middleman minority in the nation's Chinatowns and formed their own subeconomy. At this point the role of capital became important in the evolution of the Chinese. It meant the isolation of Chinese capital and labor from their class counterparts in the larger American society, resulting in the cultural and structural pluralism of the Chinese community. It also meant the continuation of intense prejudice against the Chinese, distilled into stereotypes of their clannishness and shrewdness, and made for the social distance other Americans have historically expressed toward the Chinese. Thus the psychology of prejudice helps explain the social context of the image of the Chinese in the larger society and how this image contributed in perpetuating the exclusion of the Chinese. Forces for the inclusion of the Chinese came later, with the postindustrial phase of American society.

White-collar work provided opportunity for American-born Chinese in the wider society, while the changing picure of enterprise in America simultaneously meant the reduction of small-scale ethnic businesses. The gains that had been made in these businesses also helped in the preparation of the American-born generation for white-collar positions. The result is that Chinese Americans are now a much more diverse group, stratified into ethclasses. The student should realize that theoretical complementarity enhances our understanding of Chinese Americans, and this applies to Japanese Americans as well.

JAPANESE AMERICANS AND AMERICAN SOCIETY

The history of the Japanese in America is similar to that of the Chinese in this country. Both Asian groups were initially laborers on the West Coast, on the bottom of the labor hierarchy, and both then became middleman minorities. Furthermore, the second-generation Japanese (Nisei) were included into the larger society after World War II, like their Chinese counterparts, through mass public education and white-collar work. Unlike the Chinese, however, the Japanese have also been independent farmers over the years, particularly in California. Land and agriculture play important roles in the history of Japanese Americans. In addition, the Japanese were placed in internment camps during World War II, making their evolution in America unique, not just different from that of the Chinese. The evolution of the Japanese in America is shown in Table 3.

Table 3   Evolution of Japanese Americans and the Modernization of American Society

Agrarian Society 1600–1865			Industrial Society 1865–1945		Post Industrial Society 1945–Present
Immigration and contact → (1890–1924)	Early accommo- dation → (1890–1910)	Intergroup competition, Ethnic stratification and exclusion ———→ (1910–1942)	Middle man minority (1910–1942)	Intern- ment (1942–45)	Toward intergroup inclusion (1945–)

Note: Dates are approximations only.

Contact

It is estimated that less than 300,000 Japanese had immigrated to the mainland of the United States by 1924, the year that further Asian immigration was virtually stopped. The majority of the Japanese immigrants arrived here between 1900 and 1924 (Daniels, 1969; Petersen, 1971). Many of these immigrants to the mainland had immigrated earlier to Hawaii, and from Hawaii they later came to the West Coast. The intention was for the Japanese to replace the aging

Chinese in the fields of California, although many of these immigrants also found work on the railroads, in mining, and as domestic servants.

Most of the Japanese immigrants came from the southern prefectures of Hiroshima, Kumamoto, Wakayama, Fukuoka and Yamaguchi (Kitano, 1969:10). Emigration from Japan began in the year "Meiji One," or 1868, when 148 contract laborers went to Hawaii (Petersen, 1971:9). Most of the emigrants had been farm laborers or small farmers in Japan. As a class they held the agricultural arts and land ownership in high regard, values which were to prove significant in the later evolution of the Japanese in America. Economic depression and social unrest in Japan pushed these people out of their homeland, at the same time as the labor needs in Hawaii and on the West Coast pulled them here.

Like the Chinese before them, the Japanese immigrants to the United States were sojourners of sorts who were willing to suffer severe hardships in this country, working for less than others and sticking to themselves. Many returned to Japan after a short stay in America. But, on the average, the Japanese immigrants were better prepared than the Chinese for their entry into the United States. First they were better informed about working conditions on the West Coast and in Hawaii, a state of readiness that the Japanese government nurtured in its emigrees. Furthermore, unlike China, Japan was a powerful enough country to have her notes protesting the mistreatment of her nationals taken seriously in this country. Japan was a power in the Pacific at the turn of the century, and President Roosevelt was not indifferent to Japanese protests about the discrimination against their nationals in California (Daniels, 1969). As a consequence, Japanese immigrants were less vulnerable than the Chinese had been to acts of outright discrimination and unscrupulous exploitation in America.

Japanese immigration to the United States came to a virtual halt in 1924 with the passage of the Immigration Act of that year and did not pick up again until later in the century. Agitation for the restriction of Japanese immigrants actually began early in the 20th century, shortly after their arrival on the West Coast. In 1907–8 the United States and Japan signed a gentlemen's agreement stipulating that Japan would issue passports good for the continental United States only to those Japanese who were once residents of this country or who were the parents, wives, or children of U.S. residents. The United States meant to restrict significantly further Japanese immigration into the country with this legislation, but its intent was circumvented by the Japanese practice of "picture brides." A Japanese male in the United States would arrange for a marriage with a woman in Japan by proxy, knowing her only by her photograph, and these brides then could legally enter the country, after the signing of the gentlemen's agreement. The Japanese population on the West Coast continued to grow, as a consequence, to the horror of anti-Oriental factions in the state of California (Daniels, 1969). Later legislation plugged this loophole.

Early Accommodation

It seemed that at the turn of the century Japanese immigrants would make a rather easy transition into agrarian labor in California, given the shortage of Chinese labor there. Were not the Japanese simply replacements for the aging Chinese in the fields of California? According to Daniels (1969:8),

This is an oversimplification. California . . . was in the throes of the most prolonged panic of the century. The earliest Japanese labor gangs were in direct competition with the remaining Chinese, and had to resort to wage cutting to get employment. . . . Japanese were working for 50 cents a day. . . . The normal scale for Chinese had long been established at a dollar a day.

Everyone would not agree with this assessment of the early accommodation of the Japanese in California: "Seldom have other classes been discharged in large numbers to make room for the Japanese; on the contrary, Japanese have usually been employed to fill places vacated by others" (Petersen, 1971:28).

Whatever the level of competition between the Japanese and others in the early days, it would grow greater in succeeding years. At first, Daniels (1969:9) says, employers welcomed the early Issei (first-generation Japanese) recruits to the ranks of American agriculture, particularly since the Chinese were using their rapidly diminishing numbers to try to raise wages. Working at a lower wage scale than the Chinese, Japanese farmhands reduced significantly the labor costs of growers; for example, the sugar beet harvest price was reduced from $1.20 to 70 cents per ton (Daniels, 1969:8). Later, as the Japanese began to buy their own land, they became competitors with California growers, their former employers, and the growers joined the chorus of anti-Oriental agitation on the West Coast.

Initially, the Japanese were concentrated in agrarian wage labor, although they were also to be found in mining, on the railroads, in general construction, and in domestic service. Fully 40 percent of the Japanese immigrants in the United States were working as farm laborers in 1911 (Petersen, 1971). They were funneled into farm work through their version of the padrone system. In response to the historical need of California growers for gang labor, along the Pacific slope clusters of boardinghouses run by Issei who doubled as small-scale labor contractors rapidly developed (Daniels, 1969:7). The boardinghouse keepers and hotel managers attracted a clientele of newly arrived immigrants from the

Ken [prefecture in Japan] of the owner-proprietor, who then became the employment agent of Kenjin residing with him (Light, 1972:66). The boardinghouse keepers had connections with the Japanese labor bosses who placed Japanese crews into the fields of California. This funnel moved immigrant laborers fresh off the boat directly into the fields.

Within a few years, however, many of these immigrant workers had bought land of their own and become independent farmers. In this development the padrone system was also important. The role of the Japanese labor boss in the rise of many Japanese people out of agrarian wage labor and into the status of landowners is so important that it is worthwhile to quote Light (1972:74–75) at length on the subject:

In their contractual relationships with the growers, agricultural bosses were outspokenly mercenary on behalf of their crews. . . . and unhesitantly allocated their crew to whichever rancher offered the men the best terms. . . . The Japanese boss system constituted an embryonic form of trade unionism. . . . Moreover, boss and crew typically shared a loyalty to ken, dialect, religious sect, and circle of friends. . . . The boss was thus. . . . induced to take on the role of representative of his crew. . . . The contract labor system became "the central instrument" of the Japanese rise from agricultural day labor to independent farming. Prefectural control of the labor supply and of the contractor enabled Japanese farm hands to extract maximally favorable terms from white ranchers and so expedited the development of widespread proprietory status.

The Japanese value commitment to farming and land ownership and their skills at labor-intensive agriculture must also be counted among the reasons for their rapid mobility out of field labor. The Japanese typically bought marginal land, often swamps and marshes, drained them, and cultivated crops from their homeland. This required hard, continuous, intelligent effort. When the Japanese immigrants became independent farmers, they continued to use their network of Ken ties for their mutual advantage and economic growth. The Japanese in the process became increasingly competitive with white growers in California, which ushered in the era of intergroup competition, ethnic stratification, and exclusion of the Japanese.

Intergroup Competition, Ethnic Stratification, and Exclusion

Japanese immigrants were welcomed at first by California growers and ranchers, among other employers, as a source of cheap, reliable labor. The Japanese as a group did not remain for long in wage labor, however, at least not for white employers. They soon acquired farms and businesses of their own, which meant competition with their former employers. Moreover, the Japanese movement out of agrarian wage labor had been preceded by strikes, and other instances of their labor militancy which had begun to turn growers cool toward the once-favored Japanese immigrant.

Obviously, it meant for the growers a loss of a once-dependable labor pool. This brought pressure to prevent the Japanese from becoming a class of land proprietors and independent farmers. Certain interests in the large society wanted the Japanese restricted to particular stations in the labor force, that of docile agrarian workers and domestic servants, mainly, and when the Japanese did not comply with these wishes, agitation grew for the restriction of further Japanese immigration.

Observers of the Japanese in America are all struck by the rapid rise of the Issei, the first generation out of wage labor and into entrepreneurship. Japanese immigrants began buying their own land in the agricultural valleys of California within a few years after their arrival in this country. Light (1972:72-73) writes about this remarkable transition:

> . . . Japanese farm laborers began to work and lease land as contract, share, and tenant farmers, and ultimately began to purchase substantial amounts of land outright. . . . Japanese were exceptionally advantaged by their acquaintance with traditional Japanese methods of intensive cultivation. . . . They introduced new crops, notably rice, in the cultivation of which by dint of enormous effort they were able to make use of the most barren wastelands. Thus, the Japanese began to branch out of agricultural wage-labor by purchasing small tracts of barren land at very low prices. Since they were able to cultivate this land more successfully than others had anticipated, they began to make money in agriculture.

The Japanese version of the padrone system, the network of field laborers and labor bosses tied to one another by regional affiliations (*Kenjinkai*), was critical in this movement into independent farming. The unswerving advocacy of the labor bosses for their crews meant favorable wage rates for Japanese farm laborers, but the labor bosses made even faster progress for themselves. Daniels (1974:219) wrote about the career of one very exceptional labor boss, a Mr. Shima:

> By 1909 the press was referring to him as the "Potato King" of California. By 1913, when a Japanese graduate student surveyed his holdings, Shima controlled nearly 30,000 acres directly, and, through marketing agreements, handled the produce raised by many of his compatriots. By 1920 it was estimated that he controlled 85 percent of California's potato crop, valued at over $18 million that year.

As Japanese immigrants became independent farmers, they increasingly came into competition with their former employers, the white growers and ranchers of California. There were two dimensions to this competition. First, Japanese farmers now competed directly with white growers in some of the produce markets of California, in which they had a competitive edge because of their ethnic marketing associations. Light (1972) maintains that this applied to only a few markets, in truck vegetables, berries, and flowers, and in only a few cities in California. Second, the evolution of the Japanese into a class of independent farmers meant a corresponding decline in the supply of cheap Japanese field labor for white growers, and it must be remembered that this occurred before the influx of Mexican farm workers into California. Light believes that it was this loss in their labor supply which antagnoized white ranchers the most against the Japanese. In any case, white growers took steps to exclude Japanese from agrarian proprietorship in the form of the alien land laws, and they would eventually find a replacement for the Japanese field hand in the Mexican farm worker.

In 1913, an Alien Land Bill was passed in California, with the object clearly being "to drive the Japanese out of agriculture, and perhaps out of California" (Kitano, 1969:17). However, the Japanese easily circumvented the intent of this legislation:

It was quite simple for the attorneys who represented Japanese interests in California to evade the alleged intent of the law in many ways. The simplest was through incorporation so that control was ostensibly held by whites. For the growing number of Issei who had American-born children, things were even easier; they simply transferred the stock or title to their citizen children whose legal guardianship they naturally assumed. (Daniels, 1974:226)

Japanese agriculture in California actually prospered after the passage of the Alien Land Law, due in large measure to the increased demand for farm produce during World War I. There was also the immigration of 70,000 Japanese aliens into the country between 1910 and 1920, many of whom provided cheap and dependable labor for a growing number of Japanese agriculturists.

The Alien Land Law of 1913 was amended in 1920, in an act "designed to prevent the Issei from acting as guardians for the property of a native-born minor if the property could not be held legally by the alien himself" (Kitano, 1969:17–18). By plugging such loopholes in the earlier legislation, it was hoped in exclusionist circles that the Alien Land Law of 1920 would produce the effect intended all along, to drive the Japanese out of farming in California. How much of a hindrance the Alien Land Laws proved to be to the Japanese is a matter of some debate. Petersen (1971:53) said that "According to Iwata (1962), the law 'did much to discourage the Japanese from entering farming or expanding their operation.' " On the other hand, Daniels (1969:88) termed the 1920 law "an empty gesture, an ineffective irritant; it caused much litigation, but in no wise significantly affected land tenure in the state." Light (1972:74) reports that Japanese land holdings declined from 458,026 acres in 1920 to 330,053 in 1923 and 304,966 in 1925.

Some Japanese were "banished from the soil" and moved to the cities of the West Coast (Light, 1972:74). This was only a trend, however, for many Japanese immigrants had initially settled in cities on the West Coast and many others continued in farming, so that by 1941, they raised 42 percent of California's truck crops (Kitano, 1969:18). Unlike the Chinese, a significant minority of the Japanese remained on the land in the face of anti-Oriental agitation on the West Coast. By 1940, only 55 percent of the Japanese as compared to 91 percent of the Chinese were urban residents in this country, excluding Alaska and Hawaii (Schmid and Nobbe, 1965).

The Japanese in the cities at first competed with white workers but eventually had to withdraw to noncompetitive positions in the urban labor market, particularly on the West Coast, due to pressures from organized labor. They fell back to jobs in domestic service and gardening or retreated from the larger labor market altogether, by folding back into the emerging Japanese urban subeconomy. This subeconomy came to include retailing, wholesaling, and service establishments, such as restaurants, hotels, laundries, barber shops, and shoemakers, not unlike that of the Chinese. Thus much of the Japanese labor excluded from the urban labor market found work with Japanese employers. Employers would typically hire their own kin or *Kenjin*, which solidified through ties of blood and origin the bond between Japanese capital and labor. The same principle applied to the relationship between Japanese farmers and farmhands. The relations between Japanese capital and labor and their class counterparts in the larger society were kept at a minimum in the process. The social distance between Japanese domestics and gardeners and those whom they served was also observed at this time, all of which meant the cultural and structural pluralism of the Japanese. It also meant that the Japanese to some extent circumvented the economic discrimination and color prejudice.

Agitation for the restriction of further Japanese immigration picked up where movements for the exclusion of Chinese had left off. According to most writers, these two movements were merely different sides of the same set of anti-Oriental sentiments on the West Coast. Nevertheless, the movements were in one important way dissimilar. In the face of the Asiatic Exclusion League and other quarters of the anti-Oriental movement in California, the Theodore Roosevelt administration tried to keep the issue of Japanese immigration cool, having in mind the power of Japan in the Pacific. By contrast, the federal government played only a passive role in the mistreatment of Chinese aliens in California.

On October 11, 1906, the San Francisco School Board issued a directive for the segregation of Japanese children in the schools of that city, during a period of Asiatic phobia in California. This action became front-page news in Japan, and the Japanese government protested against the segregation of its nationals in the United States. The protest greatly disturbed President Roosevelt in Washington, and he dispatched a Cabinet member to California to look into the matter while he privately assured the Japanese government that the school segregation of Japanese children would be corrected. He also publicly denounced the school board decision in his annual message of December 2, 1906:

Roosevelt thus differentiated sharply between Chinese and Japanese. As we have seen, he signed the Chinese Exclusion Act of 1902, and strongly reiterated his opposition to Chinese immigrants in 1905. The reason Roosevelt discriminated between Orientals was because of the different relative military strengths of China and Japan. (Daniels, 1974:223–224)

After the Japanese victory in the Russo-Japanese War of 1905, Japan was a power to be reckoned with in the Pacific, while China was weak. Roosevelt took this into account in his concern for Asian residents of this country.

However, Roosevelt was powerless to truly protect Americans of Japanese ancestry. In the specific case of school segregation, separate but equal facilities for children of different races was the law of the land, due to the *Plessy* vs. *Ferguson* decision in 1896. So Roosevelt attempted to reach an agreement with Japan, which would restrict immigration of Japanese into this country and thus assuage anti-Oriental sentiments on the West Coast. The outcome of these negotiations with Japan was the gentlemen's agreement signed in 1907–8 which was discussed at the beginning of this section. As the practice of picture brides among resident Japanese ensured the continued immigration of Japanese into this country, the Japanese population in California grew, and so did the cry for their exclusion. This helped bring the Immigration Act of 1924, which established immigration quotas for various nationalities. These quotas favored Europeans from west and north Europe, and allowed absolutely no quota for Japanese. The Japanese were excluded in two senses. They were forced to assume a subordinate position in the nation's system of ethnic stratification, on the one hand, and their immigration into the country was restricted, on the other. The foes of the Japanese had gotten the upper hand through politics, as they had with the Chinese, for, like the Chinese alien, the Japanese immigrant did not have the franchise.

The Japanese as a Middleman Minority

Facing barriers in the larger economy, the Japanese evolved into a middleman minority, concentrating in retail sales and personal services in the cities on the West Coast. In this way they followed the evolutionary lines of the Chinese, who also had become a middleman minority in urban areas. Unlike the Chinese, however, many Japanese continued as a class of agrarian entrepreneurs on the West Coast. Bonacich (1973:585) observed that the middleman minorities

tend to concentrate in certain occupations, notably trade and commerce but . . . other easily liquidated or transportable occupations . . . are also found among so-called 'middleman" groups. Among them are the independent professions, . . . *truck farming specializing in crops that have rapid turnover, found among* . . . the Japanese in California; and various skilled trades. In other words, the term "middleman minorities" is really a misnomer. The more general occupational characteristic of these groups is liquidity. (Italics added)

The search for liquidity in occupations on the part of middleman minorities is tied to their sojourning motives, according to Bonacich. Japanese and Chinese selected such economic positions and established their own ethnic subeconomies, with the idea of accumulating portable wealth for their eventual return home.

Japanese farm laborers used a version of the padrone system to their advantage in their rise to a class of independent farmers, and this kind of ethnic cooperation continued among the independent farmers:

According to the California Board of Control, in 1920 there were nineteen local affiliates of the Japanese Agricultural Association of Southern California and thirty-six associations in northern and central California affiliated with the Japanese Agricultural Association and the California Farmers Cooperative Association. Almost every Japanese farmer belonged to some Japanese agricultural organization. These associations were organized along the familiar lines of the trade guild, taking as their purpose the marketing of members' produce, control of prices and wages, regulation of labor disputes and of internal competition, protection of farmers' interests, and guardianship of the social welfare of members' families. (Light, 1972:75–76)

This amounts to extensive communal self-regulation among Japanese farmers, which is best indicated in their common practice of dumping a portion of their produce to keep prices up. Farmers involved in this practice would be reimbursed by the Japanese Cooperative Farm Industry, a marketing mechanism connecting Japanese farmers, wholesalers, and retailers to the point of the consumer. This network of Japanese growers, wholesalers, and retailers was so extensive as to vertically integrate some aspects of the truck farming industry in California before the giant food corporations of our era moved in that direction.

This communal regulation was also evident among urban Japanese businessmen. "Urban self-employment absorbed the energies of Japanese men who faced discriminatory barriers . . . in the urban labor market. By 1919, for example, 47 percent of hotels and 25 percent of grocery stores in Seattle were Japanese owned. The census of 1940 reported that 40 percent of Japanese men in Los Angeles were self-employed" (Light, 1972:10). In 1929, Japanese owned one and one-half times as many businesses per thousand people as did other residents of the United States (Daniels, 1969).

Family and regional ties reinforced the economic interdependence between Japanese businessmen and farmers and their employees and field hands. Because Japanese businessmen typically hired members of their own family or *Kenjin*, in most cases the relationship between employer and employee was more than simply economic; it was one of blood and regional loyalty as well. Moral obligations to family and *ken* tied employers and employees to one another, checking the tendency in a purely economic exchange for each party to seek only self-interest. The mutual loyalty between Japanese capital and labor was further strengthened in the common practice of Japanese employers setting up their employees in businesses of their own after an apprenticeship had been served. Because of the self-regulation among Japanese businessmen, the employer in these cases was assured that he was not launching a competitor. Competition among Japanese in the same business or trade was regulated communally, through trade guilds or other cooperative arrangements, based on ethnic and family loyalty. The infusion of blood ties and ethnic loyalties into economic exchange among the Japanese united capital and labor, rich and poor, into a common economic effort and a single moral community. In this manner the Japanese immigrant brotherhood evolved as a middleman minority through the industrial phase of American society, protecting its members from prejudice and discrimination as it did.

It was common for the small farms and grocery stores, restaurants, cleaning establishments, and florists of the Japanese Americans to be run by members of the same family. In these operations, of course, there is no clear line between labor and capital, employee and employer. Families were also the first source of relief and welfare, since seeking public assistance was a sign of disgrace among the Japanese. The next level of communal obligations concerning employment and assistance was the prefectural associations, *Kenjinkai*, which were ascriptive associations with origins in the provinces of southern Japan. Nearly all the Japanese immigrants to this country were eligible for membership in one of the *Kenjinkai*. When an employer for any reason could not secure sufficient labor from within his own family he would typically turn to his own *ken* for labor. *Kenjinkai* functioned as employment agencies for the urban Japanese, just as they had earlier for immigrant Japanese field labor. Moreover, just as the *ken* affiliations between Japanese field hands and their labor bosses were important in the mobility of both into the ranks of agrarian entrepreneurs, they also helped urban Japanese workers into their own businesses. Japanese employers would often help finance employees into businesses of their own, an unusual arrangement made possible by *Ken* affiliations and the mutual obligations they implied. While the exploitation of Japanese employees by Japanese employers was not completely eradicated, ethnic and family ties did bring a mutual commitment and sense of fraternity to their relationship. This meant that Japanese employees often were more loyal to their employers than to the labor movement, and Japanese businessmen with access to cheap and dependable ethnic labor had an important edge over their competitors. This often brings the charge that the middleman minority is clannish and unfair in business competition, a charge that can be used as a rationalization for a direct attack on the middleman minority (Bonacich, 1973).

Japanese businessmen in urban areas were also organized in trade guilds. These guilds regulated internal competition between Japanese in the same trade (e.g., shoemakers), while they assisted Japanese in their competition with outsiders. The same principle applied to Japanese farmers, who were organized in ethnic agricultural associations. Membership in these trade associations overlapped with *ken* and family obligations, integrating the Japanese into an ethnic subeconomy and subsociety:

In sum, middleman community organizations, combined with thrift, enable middleman firms to cut costs at every turn, so that they can compete effectively with other enterprises in the same line. Add to this a preference for liquidable occupations, and the result is a tremendous degree of concentration in, and domination of, certain lines of endeavor. (Bonacich, 1973:587)

Japanese businessmen and farmers were in competition with several powerful sectors of the larger society. The irony is that while communal effort in an ethnic subeconomy can mean the economic advancement of a group, it can also result in competition and conflict with certain interest groups in the wider society. Because of the communal and noneconomic ties between Japanese employers and their employees, Japanese workers generally rejected efforts toward their unionization and willingly worked longer hours for less money. Because of this same ethnic solidarity, Japanese businessmen and farmers, with their reduced labor costs and ethnic marketing associations, could undercut their competitors, in some cases driving them out of the market. This meant in some instances the vertical integration by the Japanese of an entire market, from production to the consumer. The result was hostility toward the Japanese in both business circles and labor unions. According to Bonacich (1973:591), it is labor in the larger society which stands to lose the most from competition with a middleman minority:

Host management has some interest in opposing middleman cheap labor, as we have seen. But management can use this as a weapon against labor by arguing that, if labor insists on higher wages and better work conditions, both will lose. Labor is caught in a bind: either improve its position and accept the possibility of losing the job altogether, or accept a low standard of living and middleman work conditions.

The solution for organized labor would have been to incorporate Japanese labor into the union movement, reducing the threat of wage undercutting and deterioration in working conditions. However, this was improbable for two reasons. There had been a history of antagonism, ethnocentrism, and forceful exclusion of the Japanese from the broader labor market on the West Coast. Given this history, alliance of Japanese and white labor under the banner of the union movement was virtually impossible. Japanese labor also rejected unionization because, as members of a middleman minority, they were "more closely tied to their co-ethnic employers than to the working class. . . . Besides, most see their position in the 'working class' as a temporary status; a gateway to a business of their own" (Bonacich, 1973:591).

White customers and clients of Japanese businessmen could also understand the anti-Oriental sentiments of some business groups and labor unions, given the suspicions that usually surround transactions between merchants and their customers. Thus the public could unite with certain self-serving interest groups on the issue of presumed Japanese clannishness and unfair business practices, and could even suspect their patriotism. This hostility in the host society can flare up against a middleman minority, if only some precipitating event ignites it. The war with Japan was that event in American history.

The Internment

On Sunday morning, December 7, 1941, the Japanese launched a surprise attack on the U.S. Pacific Fleet at Pearl Harbor, Hawaii. President Franklin Delano Roosevelt declared war on Japan the following day. The entry of America into a war with Japan began a chain of events within the country that eventually led to the forcible relocation of Japanese aliens and Japanese-American citizens from their homes on the West Coast to War Relocation Centers further inland.

Immediately after the attack on Pearl Harbor, the FBI detained enemy aliens throughout the country, Germans and Italians as well as Japanese. The backdrop to this roundup of "enemy aliens" was the widespread fear of fifth-column activities in the country. The West Coast was particularly vulnerable to sabotage. "Nearly half the U.S. military aircraft output was concentrated in the Los Angeles area. Naval yards and port facilities from San Diego on the south to Puget Sound in the north were essential to the launching of any counterattack. The fleet depended heavily on oil pumped from California's coastal fields" (Hosokawa, 1969:258).

Among the Japanese aliens detained in the early weeks following the attack on Pearl Harbor, only one was ever convicted of any wrongdoing, and he was sentenced to a term of two to six months for not having registered as a foreign agent "because one of his customers was the

Japs Keep Moving, Los Angeles. United Press International photo.

Japanese government" (Petersen, 1971:67). Nevertheless, there was considerable public sentiment for evacuating all Japanese on the West Coast, particularly among certain political interest groups and patriotic organizations in the region. The idea of an evacuation of the Japanese was first dismissed as undemocratic and impractical, even by the same officials who would later implement the order. For instance, Lt. General John L. DeWitt, commander of the Western Defense Command, firmly opposed in December of 1941 the evacuation of Japanese and justified his opposition to Major General Allen W. Gulion, Provost Marshal General in Washington, in these words: "An American citizen, after all, is an American citizen. And while they may not be loyal, I think we can weed the disloyal out of the loyal and lock them up if necessary" (Hosokawa, 1969:259-260).

Later, in 1943, after he had directed the evacuation of the Japanese, General DeWitt would say before a Congressional committee: "A Jap's a Jap. . . . You can't change him by giving him a piece of paper [American citizenship]" (Hosokawa, 1969:260). The relocation of the Japanese on the West Coast, alien and citizen alike, was mandated on February 19, 1942, when President Roosevelt signed Executive Order 9066. The western half of the three Pacific Coast states and the southern third of Arizona were designated as military areas in the order, and the Secretary of War was authorized to remove "any or all" persons from these areas.

All the people removed were of Japanese ancestry. On March 2, 1942, General DeWitt issued an order to evacuate all persons of Japanese ancestry. More than 110,000 of the 126,000 Japanese in the United States were affected by the order, and two-thirds of these were U.S. citizens (Kitano, 1969:33). The evacuation proceeded in two phases. People were first taken to temporary assembly centers on the West Coast, in the summer of 1942, and later were relocated to more permanent camps inland. These relocation camps located in Arizona, Arkansas, California, Colorado, Idaho, Utah, and Wyoming, were administered by a civilian agency, the War Relocation Authority, first under the directorship of Milton S. Eisenhower and then Dillon S. Myer.

The temporary assembly centers had been hastily converted from other uses: livestock exposition halls, fairgrounds, racetracks. The conditions Japanese families faced in these centers reflected the haste of the conversion. Mine Okubo writes of her first impression of her new home at one of these centers:

The guide left us at the door of Stall 50. We walked in and dropped our things inside the entrance. The place was in semidarkness; light barely came through the dirty window on either side of the entrance. A swinging half-door divided the 20 by 9 ft. stall into two rooms. . . . The rear room had housed the horse and the front room the fodder. Both rooms showed signs of a hurried whitewashing. Spider webs, horse hair, and hay had been whitewashed with the walls. Huge spikes and nails stuck out all over the walls. A two-inch layer of dust covered the floor, but on removing it we discovered that linoleum . . . had been placed over the rough manure-covered boards. We opened the folded cots lying on the floor of the rear room and sat on them in the semidarkness. We heard someone crying in the next stall. (quoted in Hosokawa, 1969:329–330)

The more permanent relocation centers were in isolated regions of the United States, many in the arid expanse of the western states. One of these camps might be home to as many as 20,000 people. Accommodations consisted of tarpaper-covered barracks, the rooms of which were furnished with only a stove, one droplight, and Army cots and mattresses. To each room one family was assigned. Latrines substituted for sanitary facilities in the barrack rooms, and mess halls took the place of family kitchens. The camps were surrounded by barbed-wire fences and guard towers. Though the residents would try to beautify the camps by planting shrubs and flowers, anything that would grow in the arid climate, the centers still gave the appearance of concentration camps despite such amenities. However, concentration camps they were not. Thousands of the Japanese, especially the Nisei (second generation), were eventually released through work programs, resettling in the Midwest and East, and early in 1943 the Army began to recruit among the Nisei.

Both the work-release program and the Army draft required clearances for loyalty. The loyalty of camp inmates was ascertained in the form of three clumsily conceived questions: (1) Are you loyal to the United States, abjuring allegiance to the emperor? (2) Do you hope the United States wins the war? (3) Would you serve in the combat forces of the United States wherever ordered? (Haak, 1970:28). As an indication of their insensitiveness to the conditions faced by many Japanese evacuees, the first question required an alien Issei, ineligible for American citizenship, to forswear allegiance to the only country wherein his citizenship was assigned. While the wording of this question was later changed, the manner in which various Japanese people answered these questions on loyalty divided the camps, often along generational lines. Between 80 and 90 percent of the eligible camp inmates were later cleared for loyalty, and Nisei draftees went on to serve their country with great distinction.

Hosokawa (1969) wrote that before the internment, even before the war, the Issei realized that they had planted roots in this country, a fact they saw in the faces of their children. The Nisei naturally adopted American habits and mannerisms and blended them with the traditional ways. They ate peanut butter and jelly sandwiches as well as fishcakes, celebrated American holidays along with the traditional Japanese New Year's Day, and otherwise combined Japanese and American customs.

The Issei saw this and were even willing to send their sons into the service of the United States after hearing of Pearl Harbor.

While the Issei may have encouraged the entry of their offspring into the larger society, the middleman subeconomy might have just as naturally pulled many Nisei toward the old ways if it were not now gone, lost in the evacuation and never to be regained. The Japanese would never be fully compensated for the loss of their businesses, farms, and other economic assets. The parental authority of the Issei also declined, due to their loss of wealth and economic function, and it shrank further in the relocation camps as the Nisei assumed the leadership roles and went off to war or work elsewhere, outside the subeconomy of their parents.

It is understandable that so many Americans have asked who was responsible for the internment of the Japanese. The constitutional rights of 110,000 residents of the country, two-thirds of them U.S. citizens, were unilaterally suspended. This was done in the absence of any substantial evidence as to the disloyalty of Japanese Americans. Mindful of the fact that the Japanese Americans were essentially innocent victims, the nagging feeling this historical episode leaves is the question: Can it happen again, and could it happen to any of us?

Everybody was responsible for the internment of the Japanese, essentially is the answer of Ten Broek, Burnhart, and Matson (1954). They argued that responsibility for evacuation and internment of the Japanese must be shared by many groups. These groups include the various branches of government, at both the state and national levels, numerous interest groups, and the general public, especially people on the West Coast. Kitano (1969:43) amplified the argument for wholesale responsibility and added that it was racism that united these various groups in the country against the Japanese: "It is difficult to avoid the conclusion that the primary cause of the wartime evacuation was West Coast racism." Petersen (1971:73) chose to focus on the absence of a liberal counterattack and the obvious conservative interests served by the removal of the Jaanese from the West Coast: "The most interesting clue to the influence of pressure groups, as in the Sherlock Holmes story, is the dog that did not bark." Not only were liberals not barking at the conservative groups over the issue of Japanese evacuation, but they were in the vanguard of the agitation for the evacuation and internment. The liberal columnist Walter Lippmann was four days ahead of the conservative columnist Westbrook Pegler in calling for the mass evacuation of Japanese Americans from the West Coast. Petersen believes that the liberal support for the evacuation stemmed from the control the Communist Party exercised at the time over the American political left. The American Communist Party had shifted to all-out support of the war against the Axis powers, once Nazi Germany broke the Stalin-Hitler Pact in 1941.

Some may still feel that war hysteria united Americans, liberal and conservative alike, in their support of the mass evacuation and internment of the Japanese. But this "mass panic" thesis has never adequately accounted for the fact that the Japanese of Hawaii were never interned, uprooted from their homes, and deprived of their livelihood, though there had also been agitation for the evacuation of Japanese on Hawaii, and the islands were more vulnerable to Japanese invasion and sabotage because of their location and greater number of Japanese residents. It was only the Japanese on the West Coast who were interned for the stated reason of national security.

The Japanese on the West Coast were a middleman minority, largely bereft of political allies. They were in direct competition with white growers and businessmen and indirectly competed with organized labor over the issue of nonunion Japanese labor. Because the Japanese in Hawaii had faced less discrimination than on the mainland, they were more occupationally diversified and politically involved. They also had political allies who spoke out against Japanese evacuation there. The Japanese on the West Coast had no such allies, and because of their concentration in middleman economic roles, they were seen as clannish and beyond assimilation by their competitors and by the general public. This brought accusations commonly made against middleman minorities: "middleman minorities are disloyal to the countries in which they reside," and "middleman groups drain the host society of its resources" (Bonacich, 1973:591). On the basis of such fears, people on the West Coast clamored for the evacuation of the Japanese.

The irony is that before the war the Nisei on the mainland had been gradually moving toward inclusion in the larger society, following the pattern of the Japanese in Hawaii. The first generation of any immigrant group typically stays to itself, and the Issei were no exemption. These first-generation Japanese had compounded the effects of their cultural isolation with the affects of being a middleman minority. The Nisei had begun, however, to make political and social friends in the wider society before the war, as Hosokawa (1969:200) observed:

The *Nisei* of this period were just beginning to feel their way into the involved world of politics and pressures outside their communities. Of those days, Mary Oyama Mittwer has written: "Between wienie bakes and the beaches and dances, *Nisei* would gather at church and JACL meetings to ponder ways of getting out the *Nisei* vote, planning ways of putting up Japanese American candidates for political offices, mixing more into the larger American community . . . "

But there were simply too few adult Nisei before the war for the Japanese to have accomplished much in the way of political influence on the West Coast. In 1930 fewer than 4,000 Nisei in the entire United States were of voting age (Hosokawa, 1969:152), which suggests that the perceived clannishness of the Japanese also followed from the absence of an adult generation of Nisei. The decision to intern was a political one, which had always been the most successful line of attack on Japanese and Chinese Americans.

Toward Intergroup Inclusion

As the Nisei left the internment camps, a new era in the evolution of the Japanese American began which brought greater inclusion into American society. American society was just entering its postindustrial phase, and the evolution of the Nisei converged with the larger trend toward college education and professional and technical work. By 1960, 26 percent of the Japanese males in the nation's nonfarm labor force were engaged in technical work and the professions, compared to only 12.5 percent of the white males. For Japanese Americans, that proportion had been only 5 percent in 1940. In the same period, 1940–60, the percentage of Japanese males in the nonfarm labor force who were proprietors, managers, and officials declined from 23 to 13 percent, and the percentage of the Japanese in farm work declined from 43 to 26 percent (Schmid and Nobbe, 1965).

Table 4 tells the same story for both Japanese males and females. Note the increase in professional and technical workers in the past decades and the decrease in Japanese proprietors. Also observe the falloff in the percentage of Japanese men and women in farming. The occupational composition of the Japanese in 1970 compares favorably with that of all employed people in the country. This indicates that the Nisei evolved away from a middleman minority in urban commerce and agrarian enterprise, and toward technical and professional work in the larger postindustrial society.

A college education was a requisite in this evolution of the Nisei into the technical and professional fields, and for many postgraduate study was necessary. Around 6 percent of the nation's Japanese males and 4 percent of the females (25 years and older) had a college education in 1940. By 1960, over 18 percent of the men and 8 percent of the women had at least a college education. In contrast, just over 10 percent of the nation's white males had a college education in 1960 (Schmid and Nobbe, 1965). Petersen (1971) studied the files of the Nisei at the University of California's placement bureau for signs of their occupational selection and found that their degrees were almost never in liberal arts, but rather were in business administration, optometry, engineering, or some other middle-level profession. For them, "education was obviously a means of acquiring a salable skill that could be used either in the general

Table 4 Percentage Distribution of Japanese and All Employed People by Occupational Groups, 1940–1970.

Occupational Groups	Japanese				All People			
	1940	1950	1960	1970	1940	1950	1960	1970
White-Collar Workers								
Professional and technical......................	3.0	6.8	14.2	19.0	7.5	8.7	11.1	14.9
Managers, officials, and proprietors except farm...................	11.4	7.1	7.7	8.4	8.4	8.7	8.4	8.3
Clerical and sales..........	11.3	15.4	22.8	26.4	16.8	19.2	21.6	25.0
Blue-Collar Workers								
Craftsmen and foremen.............................	2.0	5.5	12.9	11.6	11.3	14.3	13.5	13.9
Operatives....................	7.3	13.2	13.5	9.7	18.4	20.3	18.4	13.7
Laborers except farm and mine..........	18.4	9.5	4.0	6.3	6.8	6.5	4.8	4.5
Service Workers								
Private household.........	7.6	6.5	3.6	1.7	6.2	2.5	2.7	1.5
Other service................	7.3	8.7	8.1	11.4	6.2	7.8	8.4	11.3
Farm workers								
Farmers and managers.	14.7	11.1	7.9	2.0	11.5	7.6	3.9	1.9
Laborers and foremen...	16.3	16.2	5.3	1.9	6.9	4.4	2.2	1.3

Sources: 1940 Census, *The Labor Force*, Table 62, p. 90; 1940 Census, *Characteristics of the Nonwhite Population by Race*, Table 38, pp. 107–108; 1950 Census, *Occupational Characteristics,* Table 3, pp. 29–36; 1950 Census, *Characteristics of the Nonwhite Population by Race,* Table 11, p. 37; 1960 Census, *Occupational Characteristics,* Table 2, pp. 11–20; 1960 Census, *Characteristics of the Nonwhite Population by Race,* Table 34, p. 108; 1970 Census, *Occupational Characteristics,* Table 39, pp. 593–608.

Note: Percentages may not total to 100.0 because of rounding.

commercial world or, if that remained closed, in a small personal enterprise" (p. 116).

After the internment experience, the Nisei evolved away from the middleman minority status of their parents, first by going in goodly numbers to college and then by entering the growing technical and professional fields. They avoided direct competition with others over white-collar work by steering away from jobs that put a premium on interpersonal skills and language mastery. Instead, they chose the technical fields and independent professions, choices which are also reminiscent of the middleman's gravitation toward portable skills. For this accomplishment, this generation of Japanese Americans has been called America's *model minority.*

The role that internment played in the accomplishments of the Nisei is a matter of some debate. One argument is that the internment experience lessened the control of the Issei over the Nisei allowing the latter to break out of the Japanese subeconomy and the mobility trap of small farming and business. Petersen (1971:126) spoke to this argument:

The occupational traps of the young *Nisei* tending vegetable stands in Los Angeles, the seemingly unreasonable control that *Issei* exerted in their families, the restrictive life in a Little Tokyo—these elements of prewar existence were reduced in importance or eliminated, together with the agricultural economy, the Japanese Association, consular authority, and much of the informal community solidarity. This is what is meant by the preposterous statement that, in one version or another, is found in several accounts of the internment—that today many Japanese "are grateful for the evacuation experience."

Petersen agreed that the internment experience and the subsequent collapse of the Japanese subeconomy forced the Nisei on the mainland out into the mainstream of society. The demise of the Japanese subeconomy was due to both the evacuation of the Japanese on the West Coast and the increasing scale of business and agriculture in this country after World War II. Many small Japanese firms and farms were made obsolete. The Japanese in Hawaii, on the other hand, could and did continue in their parents' businesses after the war, or could go into the lower and middle rungs of the state's civil service:

In Hawaii . . . the impetus to rise was to some degree countered by the pressure to take over one's father's retail store, to follow one's father in his skilled trade. And if, as has been hypothesized, the electoral gains in the islands were accompanied by similar increases in the proportion of Japanese in the lower and middle ranks of the state's civil service, this was another relatively easy route to modest financial security. On the mainland, the postwar rule had to be the famous slogan of the 442nd, "Go for broke"—all or nothing; for there were no easy routes to middle-level status. (Petersen, 1971:126)

A second argument is that the mobility of the Nisei into white-collar work was a direct application of traditional Japanese values for success, the transmission of which was uninterrupted, even intensified, by the internment experience. Haak (1970:30-31) says they responded with

. . . an ancestral reflex pattern of self-sacrifice and cooperation with no reward in sight. . . . What helped them most. . . . was the way they chose to earn recognition by performance. . . . They simply worked and endured until their performance overwhelmed, without contentiousness, society's negative definitions of their worth. . . . The *Nisei* with whom I spoke were all active Buddhists. The more articulate spoke of resolving conflict through cooperation, invoking the higher synthesis of yin and yang, rather than savage partisan dues to the social death.

The traditional communal network of Japanese helped translate the equally traditional values into new forms of success. Petersen (1971) noted that the Nisei students at the University of California often had letters of reference from Japanese professors in unrelated fields and frequently had part-time jobs in Japanese-owned establishments. The historical solidarity of the Japanese continued to play a role in the evolution of the Japanese, it appears, even after the loss of much of their property and wealth.

The third generation, Sansei, have continued in the same evolutionary direction as the Nisei and now are something of an elite among the later native-born generations of the nation's immigrant groups. From data on a national sample of three generations of Japanese in the country, Levine and Montero (1973:45) observed, "Whereas 57% of the Nisei respondents have at least some college training, 88% of the Sansei had as much. . . . Further, fully 92% of the Sansei intend to become professionals." Upwardly mobile Japanese tend to live in mostly Caucasian neighborhoods and have frequent, even intimate, contact with whites. Kikumura and Kitano (1973:79) concluded that the Japanese in this country "are no longer a group that marries their own." The rate of outgroup marriage among the Sansei has reached 50 percent in many parts of the country. Kikumura and Kitano (1973:79) speculated that "this rate will continue to grow with each new successive generation, so that in time there may no longer be a pure Japanese American group." This means continued evolutionary convergence and intergroup inclusion for the Japanese in the future.

A COMPARISON OF ASIAN AND BLACK AMERICANS

The evolutions of Asian and black Americans run along similar lines up to a point, and then diverge. Both are immigrant groups whose evolutions have been implicated in the nation's changing labor needs. Asian and black Americans are also racial minorities in the United States, and both have been objects of racial discrimination and color prejudice. They competed with other immigrant groups and were forced in the course of this competition to the bottom of the labor hierarchy, where they were expected to work at menial jobs, in field labor and domestic service. The immigration of Asians was also restricted, nearly to the point of complete exclusion. While Asians were not brought to this country as slaves, many came as contract laborers, perhaps a difference of degree rather than kind. Moreover, Asians and blacks alike have been prohibited from owning land and other forms of capital necessary for their mobility out of menial wage labor. In short, both Asian and black Americans have faced racial stratification and color prejudice in this country.

However, this is where the similarities end. The Asian groups evolved into middleman minorities, circumventing racial barriers and building subeconomies of their own. Blacks did not do this, remaining employed instead in domestic service and agrarian wage labor. Moreover, Asian Americans converged shortly after World War II with the trend toward a post industrial society, while blacks only recently have made significant steps toward improving their inclusion into modern society.

There have been several attempts to explain the evolutionary differences between these two racial minorities. Racism alone cannot account for these differences, since both blacks and Asian Americans have been objects of color prejudice and discrimination in this country. Some writers point out that special consumer demands among Chinese and Japanese helped establish Asian businessmen, and no comparable special needs existed among black Americans. Chinese and Japanese immigrants were restricted by language barriers and ethnic preferences to certain consumption patterns, to be sure, and this resulted in a ready-made clientele for Chinese and Japanese businessmen. Black shopkeepers have always had to compete with the better financed operations in the larger society, since black customers have not been restricted in this manner, either by language barriers or foreign preferences.

While this is all true, it is an inadequate explanation. Light (1972) noted that non-Asians apparently consumed one-half of the food and one-quarter of the dry goods sold by Oriental businesses. He concluded that the consumer-demands explanation is but one part of a larger, sociological explanation (p. 108). This explanation begins by emphasizing the sojourning motives of the Chinese and Japanese immigrants in this country. According to Bonacich (1973:585), "Sojourning is not a sufficient condition of the middleman form in that there are sojourners who do not become middlemen; but it is a necessary one, with important economic and social consequences directly related to the pattern." These consequences include a " tendency toward thrift" and a "concentration in certain occupations." Black slaves were never sojourners, of course; they neither elected to come to this country nor could hope to accumulate savings here and return to Africa.

Sojourners concentrate in occupations that provide a portable or easily liquidated livelihood, intending all along to return home with their savings. In addition, since they plan to return, "sojourners have little reason to develop lasting relationships with members of the surrounding host society" (Bonacich, 1973:586). This enhances the cohesion of the middleman minority, a solidarity that for Asian immigrants was rooted in their transplantation of Old World familial and regional loyalties to the United States. Ethnic solidarity, communal regulation of internal competition, and cooperation between Asian capital and labor provided them with a competitive edge in urban commerce and agrarian enterprise. It gave Chinese and Japanese businessmen access to cheap and dependable labor from within their own groups, and it gave them access to internal sources of credit, making possible the establishment of businesses and the purchase of property. Ethnic solidarity also facilitated the marketing of goods and services. Bonacich (1973:586) observed:

Solidarity is interjected into economic affairs in two ways: it plays a part in the efficient distribution of resources, and helps to control internal competition. Resources distributed within the ethnic community include capital . . . , credit and easier terms to purchasers, information and training, and jobs and labor.

Bonacich (1973:586) also suggested the mechanism for the translation of sojourning motives and ethnic solidarity into collective economic action: "The 'primordial tie' of blood provides a basis for trust, and is reinforced by multi-purpose formal and informal associations." The role of blood ties and communal associations in the Asian subeconomies and immigrant brotherhoods has already been noted. Primordial ties have specific, direct roles in the accumulation of capital and ownership of land by both the Chinese and Japanese. In the movement of a group from the bottom of society to a position of middleman minority, it must accumulate savings and effectively distribute this capital to members of the group. Asians accomplished this pooling of capital largely through rotating credit associations. Members of such an association agree to make regular contributions to a common fund, to be given in total or in some fixed proportion to each contributor in rotation. For example, ten Chinese immigrants might agree to contribute $10 monthly to a common fund, to be distributed to one of the members each year until each contributor had received a share. This is a general model of a rotating credit association; there were many variations on this common theme. For instance, while the Japanese rotating credit associations in this country, variously called *ko*, *tanomoshi*, or *mujin*, did include unrelated persons, the Chinese *hui* did not (Light, 1972). The importance of rotating credit associations is that they serve to capitalize small businessmen who, for many reasons, including racism in the case of minority groups, cannot readily turn to banks or other financial institutions in the larger society for funding. Moreover, banks and other formal financial institutions owned by racial minorities have been notoriously unstable in the history of this country, an observation that applies to both Asian and black Americans. Immigrant Chinese and Japanese engaged in rotating credit arrangements on an informal basis, however, while black Americans did not, at least not to the same degree.

Chinese and Japanese brought their rotating credit associations with them to the United States and transplanted these "Old World traits" in this country. Light (1972) noted that the Japanese had probably adopted this tradition from the Chinese back in the 13th century. The risk involved in rotating credit associations is that members may default on their obligations to one another, but the high level of interpersonal trust and communal control among immigrant Chinese and Japanese eliminated much of this risk. For instance, extended kin often honored the financial obligations of someone who might have otherwise failed to meet his obligation to other members. Overlapping primordial ties took much of the risk out of these transactions, without which the Chinese and Japanese could not have accumulated capital and property to the extent that they did at a time when they were denied credit in the larger society.

There is no positive evidence for the existence of such practices among black Americans. Evidence does indicate, however, that a tradition of rotating credit associations did exist in West Africa. Among the Yoruba, the rotating credit association was known as *esusu*, and it existed among them as early as 1843. Thrift clubs were also in practice in Sierra Leone as early as 1794. Moreover, Africans brought this tradition to the New World, at least to the West Indies. It was called *asu* in the Bahamas, *susu* in Trinidad, and *partners* by Jamaicans; West Indians imported the practice into Harlem in the 20th century (Light, 1972). But there is no evidence for the existence of some variant on *esusu* among American-born blacks. Light (1972:36) concluded that "lack of reference to rotating credit associations among Negroes in the United States may be taken as prima facie evidence that such practices were not, in fact, employed. Students of the question have thus far been unable to locate any instance of rotating credit practices among American-born Negroes."

How do we account for the disappearance of this African tradition among black Americans? First, there is a possibility that the tradition of rotating credit associations began in West Africa after most slaves had already arrived in the United States. Free African labor might have introduced the tradition into the West Indies after emancipation there in 1838, and no such immigration into the United States occurred, at least not until West Indians brought the tradition to Harlem in the 20th century. Partly because of this practice, West Indians stand out as entrepreneurs among the nation's blacks and are known among American-born blacks as "black Jews." There is also reason to believe that the tradition of rotating credit associations was indeed brought by slaves to the United States, but somehow the practice disappeared here while it survived among West Indian slaves. In the West Indies, black slaves were a numerical majority who worked for absentee landlords and, most importantly, were allowed to install their own subeconomy and market system there, from production through distribution. After emancipation, blacks in the West Indies moved into the interior of those islands, removed almost completely from the political and economic domination of the white planters. The rotating credit association had almost daily relevance in this environment, and it survived.

In the United States, by contrast, blacks did not have the same measure of economic autonomy. Except for a small class of freed blacks in the North, black Americans never were able to establish a subeconomy of

338 / *American Ethnicity*

their own, as had Africans in the West Indies and Asians in the United States. Black Americans have been historically deprived of economic independence. Indeed, it was once illegal for them to own property, as they themselves were virtually nothing more than the property of others. Nor were slaves in the United States ever permitted to pursue entrepreneurial activity on their own terms. Unlike the pattern in the West Indies, plantation owners and small white farmers managed the local markets and subsistence economy of the South. After emancipation, black labor in this country remained under the economic domination of white landowners. No room was ever made for black entrepreneurial activity in the South, a critical difference from both the Asian-American and West-Indian patterns. This alone might have led to the disappearance of rotating credit associations among American-born blacks.

Tribal bonds among slaves in the South had largely disappeared by the time of their emancipation, making them bereft of those human bonds that meant so much in the rise of Asian Americans to a position of a middleman minority. Gone with these primordial ties was the degree of interpersonal trust and internal self-regulation that made such practices as rotating credit associations work for the Chinese and Japanese. Although there was always trust and love within black families, family units were too small for the effective pooling of resources, and black voluntary associations could not compensate for the absence of ascriptive solidarity among black Americans (Light, 1972). Certain entrepreneurial practices and skills and the cohesion that make them work were gone by the time black Americans had the chance to evolve as free people. Tribal integrity had been better maintained in the West Indies, due to the larger plantations there and the more frequent influx of African immigrants into those islands. Moreover, slaves in the West Indies had greater economic autonomy, and they evolved into subsistence farmers with land of their own after their emancipation. When they emigrated to this country in the 20th century, West Indians became something of a middleman minority among the nation's blacks. Thus the history of black Americans is significantly different from that of their West Indian counterparts, as well as from that of Asians in this country.

It appears that their internal structure affects how minority groups fare in their competition with others for land, labor, and capital. Asian and black Americans share prejudice and discrimination as a common experience, yet because of their different internal organizations they are very different in how they have coped with this experience. This does not deny or in any way diminish the fact that minority groups have faced restricted opportunity in Amercan society. Indeed, it is assumed that lack of opportunity is the common denominator in the minority experience in America. What makes the evolutions of minority groups variable is how they cope with prejudice and discrimination, which is at least in part affected by their internal solidarity. The Chinese and Japanese transplanted their tribal ties to American soil and then translated these loyalties into economic advancement, in spite of intense prejudice and discrimination against them. This principle can been seen in the mobility of immigrant field hands into independent farmers, through a padrone system, in the placing of *ken* into urban enterprises of their own, and in the practice of rotating credit associations. Blacks had lost their tribal bonds in slavery, however, and were thereby disadvantaged in their fight against prejudice and discrimination as free people.

This comparison of Asian and black Americans also illustrates the role of capital in ethnic evolution. Their accumulation of capital was critical in the evolution of the Chinese and Japanese out of menial wage labor and economic subordination. The internal organization of these groups enabled them to accumulate capital within their own ranks and with it build their own subeconomies, which offered their members an alternative to the prejudice and discrimination in the larger society. This point will be expanded in the abstract in Chapter 10.

The emphasis up to now has been on the relationship between societal change and ethnic evolution. The modernization of American society brought changes to the nation's ethnic and racial groups which were articulated through their exchange of land, labor, and capital. Ethnic groups have both converged with and diverged from this process of societal modernization, a view that expands on assimilationism, pluralism, and conflict theory. The nation's more powerful ethnic groups have excluded the weaker ones from full participation in modern society, causing the evolutionary divergence of the latter. Prejudice was generated to justify the exclusion, and it, too, helped perpetuate the divergence. Intergroup exclusion and evolutionary divergence mean different things for different minority groups, however, a point made in this comparison of Asian and black Americans. Variations in evolutionary divergence are analyzed further in Chapter 10.

REFERENCES

Bonacich, Edna
  1972 "A Theory of Ethnic Antagonism: The Split Labor Market." American Sociological Review 37(October):547–559.
  1973 "A Theory of Middleman Minorities." American Sociological Review 38(October):583–594.
Daniels, Roger
  1969 The Politics of Prejudice. New York: Atheneum Publishers.
  1971 Concentration Camps USA, Japanese Americans and World War II. New York: Holt, Rinehart and Winston, Inc.
  1974 "The Japanese American Experience: 1890–1940." Pp. 214–235 in Rudolph Gomez, Clement Cottingham, Jr., Russel Endo, and Kathleen Jackson (eds.), The

Social Reality of Ethnic America. Lexington, Massachusetts: D. C. Heath and Company.

Haak, Ronald O.
1970 "Co-opting the Oppressors: The Case of Japanese Americans." Society 7(October):23–31.

Hosokawa, Bill
1969 Nisei: The Quiet Americans. New York: William Morrow and Company.

Iwata, Masakuzu
1962 "The Japanese Immigrants in California Agriculture." Agricultural History 36(January):25–37.

Kikumura, Akemi, and Harry H. L. Kitano
1973 "Interracial Marriage: A Picture of the Japanese Americans." The Journal of Social Issues 29(2):67–81.

Kitano, Harry H. L.
1969 Japanese Americans: The Evolution of a Subculture. Englewood Cliffs, New Jersey: Prentice-Hall, Inc.

Lee, Rose Hum
1960 The Chinese in the United States of America. Hong Kong: Hong Kong University Press.

Levine, Gene N., and Darrell M. Montero
1973 "Socioeconomic Mobility among Three Generations of Japanese Americans." Journal of Social Issues 29(2):33–48.

Light, Ivan J.
1972 Ethnic Enterprise in America. Berkeley: University of California Press.

Light, Ivan, and Charles Choy Wong
1975 "Protest or Work: Dilemmas of the Tourist Industry in American Chinatowns." American Journal of Sociology 80(May):1342–1368.

Lyman, Stanford M.
1974 Chinese Americans. New York: Random House, Inc.

Park, Robert Ezra
1950 Race and Culture. New York: Free Press.

Petersen, William
1971 Japanese Americans. New York: Randon House, Inc.

Saxton, Alexander
1971 The Indispensable Enemy: Labor and the Anti-Chinese Movement in California Berkeley: University of California Press.

Schmid, Calvin F., and Charles E. Nobbe
1965 "Socioeconomic Differentials among Nonwhite Races." American Sociological Review 30(December):909–922.

Ten Broek, Jacobus, Edward N. Burnhart, and Floyd W. Matson
1954 Prejudice, War, and the Constitution. Berkeley: University of California Press.

Trow, Martin
1966 "The Second Transformation of American Secondary Education." Pp. 437–448 in Reinhard Bendix and Seymour Martin Lipset (eds.), Class, Status and Power. Second Edition. New York: Free Press.

Yuan, D. Y.
1963 "Voluntary Segregation: A Study of New York Chinatown." Phylon 24(Fall):255–265.
1969 "Division of Labor between Native-Born and Foreign-Born Chinese in the United States: A Study of Their Traditional Employment." Phylon 30(Summer):160–169.

CHAPTER 10:

Evolutionary Divergence: Pathology or Communalism?

INTRODUCTION

In the social sciences there are two very different depictions of American minority groups, those that have been excluded from American society and have been objects of prejudice and discrimination. One portrait has it that minority groups are typically caught in a tangle of pathology. Members of minority groups become psychologically damaged and the group itself becomes socially disorganized in the course of its exclusion from the larger society. Members of the minority group may come to hate themselves, internalizing the prejudice of the majority group, and the social fabric of the minority group may unravel at the same time, as is often seen in the disintegration of the family. Psychological damage and community deterioration can be mutually reinforcing, and thus minority group members may be trapped in a vicious cycle and downward spiral. This is what is meant by the metaphor that a minority group is caught in a tangle of pathology, a popular historical viewpoint on evolutionary divergence.

Social pathology as a perspective is no longer popular in the social sciences, since recent evidence suggests the worth of an alternative point of view on evolutionary divergence and minority groups. "In their various attempts to demonstrate the negative consequences of caste victimization, social scientists have, in their description of the Negro American, unwittingly provided scientific credibility for many white-held stereotypes of the Negro" (McCarthy and Yancey, 1971:650). This is only one of the recent criticisms of social pathology. Unfortunately, McCarthy and Yancey are right—this perspective has been disproportionately applied to black Americans and seems to support certain racial stereotypes. While social pathology has been suspected of nearly all ethnic groups, and reference to Chapter 1 and a careful reading this chapter will show that to be true, it is hard to establish a balance among groups in presenting this perspective, since so much of it deals with black Americans.

A second and more contemporary view has it that the minority group when excluded from the larger society evolves as a communal group, which preserves its integrity and thereby protects its members from the debilitating consequences of prejudice and discrimination. There is no necessary psychological damage to minority group members, nor is the social disorganization of the group itself inevitable. The minority community can pull together and become strong in the face of externally imposed hardships. Its members can find their sense of self-worth in their own community, from their own kind, quite apart from the surrounding prejudice and discrimination. In a word, prejudice and discrimination lead neither to the collapse of the minority group as a community nor to the demoralization of its members. This depiction of evolutionary divergence accentuates the communalism, consciousness, and solidarity of the minority group.

The changing ethnic community in the course of societal modernization has been the principal topic of this book. Some ethnic groups have been included into modern society, and their evolutions have converged with the course of modernization itself. Other groups have been excluded from modern society, and their evolutions have diverged from the modernization process. There are different versions of what happens to groups which are on courses of evolutionary convergence, the disagreement is over whether they lose their folk community or not. Social scientists disagree at least as much about minority groups, those that diverge from the course of societal modernization. This debate is over the exact nature of the social and psychological consequences of exclusion and evolutionary divergence. One version is that minority groups become entangled in pathology, and another has it that they evolve as communal groups. This debate is the topic of the chapter.

It must be remembered that theories on American ethnicity as a rule are only partial explanations of ethnic evolution, and social pathology and ethnic communalism as perspectives are no exception. While it is true that discrimination has resulted in the personality disorganization of minority group members and the social disintegration of minority groups, it is equally true that minority groups have endured as communal groups whose members drew together and, by dint of collective effort, often overcame the barriers of prejudice and discrimination. Both types of adjustment to exclusion have occurred in American history, and pathology and communalism as perspectives show these two sides of the same coin.

The format of this chapter is consistent with those of some preceding chapters. Key terms are defined, and basic assumptions of both schools of thought on the American minority group are identified. Samples of the pathology and communalism perspectives are then surveyed. The chapter ends with an analysis of why the evolutionary divergence of Asian Americans was a case of communalism.

KEY TERMS

Intergroup Exclusion and Evolutionary Divergence

In Chapter 5 intergroup exclusion was defined as being evident *when an ethnic group does not share with others a common culture, similar socioeconomic characteristics, and societal resources because of its exclusive participation in the secondary institutions of the larger society, and by virtue of its ethnically restrictive social participation.* Intergroup exclusion is typically a product of intergroup competition and conflict, a direct result of discrimination, and excluded groups have been traditionally called minority groups. Minority groups follow a course of evolutionary divergence, *evident when the history of an ethnic or racial group does not flow into the evolutionary trend of the larger society.* Two forms of evolutionary divergence have been identified in the social sciences: social pathology and ethnic communalism.

Pathology

The instability of the Negro family, the inadequacy of educational facilities for Negroes, the emotionalism in the Negro church, the insufficiency and unwholesomeness of Negro recreational activity, the excess of Negro sociable organizations, the provincialism of his political thinking, the high Negro crime rate, the cultivation of the arts to the neglect of other fields, superstition, personality difficulties, and other "characteristic" traits are mainly forms of social ill-health, which, for the most part, are created by caste pressures. (Rose, 1948:294).

Pathology is a condition of minority groups in the eyes of some social scientists and is assumed to be a result of prejudice and discrimination. *Pathology is thought to be a product of a minority group's exclusion from the larger society, a specific form of evolutionary divergence, one which further restricts the group's chances of inclusion into the larger society. A pathological condition makes members of a minority group appear to be so deviant or divergent from the wider norms that it impedes the inclusion of the group into society, and can make prejudice against them appear justified.* Thus, a vicious cycle of prejudice, pathology, and more prejudice is formed.

Pathology is both a social and psychological phenomenon, one that can be found in both the psychological states of minority group members and in their patterns of social organization. It has been said that black Americans, for instance, deviate from certain psychological states considered normal and healthy in American society, experiencing a crisis of identity and exhibiting low self-esteem. Comparing themselves with the generalized other, who is both white and more successful, black people often feel a sense of low self-worth, and some may even become self-prejudiced by internalizing the racial ethnocentrism of the majority group. Such pathological consequences of prejudice and discrimination have been called the "mark of oppression" by Kardiner and Ovesey (1951). The various manifestations of personal pathology might be considered cases of self-alienation, where self-alienation is a process "in which individual selves may lose contact with any inclinations or desires that are not in agreement with prevailing social patterns, manipulate their selves in accordance with apparent social demands, and/or feel incapable of controlling their own actions" (Taviss, 1969:47).

Not only can the personalities of minority group members be damaged because of prejudice and discrimination, but it is also observed that the social organization of minority groups disintegrates under the same pressures. Patterns of social organization can become abnormal and impede minority assimilation. A score of writers have analyzed the low-income black family, for instance, in terms of its social pathology (e.g., Frazier, 1939; Liebow, 1967; Moynihan, 1965; Rainwater, 1966; Shulz, 1969). The pathological characteristics of the black family are said to include matriarchy; casualness in performing household chores; marital instability; early sexual experiences, including a high rate of incest; the absence of fathers, and the lack of masculine identification for boys. Such characteristics, it is argued, hinder the inclusion of low-income blacks into the larger American society. The fact is overlooked that some of these same practices in groups who have assimilated are seen as experiments in family living.

Commentary on pathology is not confined to a single class or racial group. Nearly all minorities in American history have been considered pathological at one time or another. One can read today about the current pathology of American Indians, for instance, particularly their alcoholism. With respect to the pathology of Mexican Americans, McWilliams (1968:206–207) observed:

The data "proved" that Mexicans lacked leadership, discipline, and organization; that they segregated themselves; that they were lacking in thrift and enterprise, and so forth. A mountainous collection of masters' theses "proved" conclusively that Spanish-speaking children were "retarded" because, on the basis of various so-called intelligence tests, they did not measure up to the intellectual calibre of Anglo-American students . . . . Paradoxically, the more sympathetic the writer, the greater seems to have been the implied condescension. All in all, the conclusion is unavoidable that Mexicans have been regarded as the essence of "the Mexican Problem."

Earlier in the century it was a common belief, even in official circles, that the new immigrants, the Italians, Jews, and Slavs, among others, had innumerable pathologies. Harry Laughlin wrote that these new immigrants were characterized by high incidences of feeblemindedness, insanity, crime, epilepsy, tuberculosis, and dependency on welfare (cited in Handlin, 1957). Laughlin concluded that these tendencies were hereditary, rather than the effects of prejudice and discrimination, using committals to public institutions only as his measure of hereditary traits. Handlin (1957) remarked that groups, old and new immigrants alike, varied so much across these indicators of pathology that there was no consistent pattern of overall pathology, a point that Laughlin, in the heat of the politics of immigration restriction, apparently chose to ignore. A work like Laughlin's seemed to use science as a vindication for the racism against the new immigrants, a racism that ultimately resulted in the restriction of immigrants from southern and eastern Europe into our country. Social pathology has, nevertheless, continued to be a popular perspective on the American minority community.

Culture of Poverty

An important component of social pathology perspective is the so-called culture of poverty. *"A culture of poverty is thus a design for living within the constraints of poverty, passed down from generation to generation, thereby achieving stability and persistence"* (Lewis, 1961:xxiv). The culture of poverty can become the cultural component of the evolutionary divergence of the groups excluded from the modern society. Pathology can become ingrained in a culture of poverty, and thus passed from one generation to the next, separate from prejudice and discrimination. About the Mexican poor, Lewis (1961:xxvi–xxvii) observed, "We can recognize from the ghetto such items as gregariousness, informal credit among neighbors, a high incidence of alcoholism, the use of violence in settling quarrels, consensual unions, male desertion and a tendency toward matrifocal families, a cult of masculinity, and a corresponding martyr complex among women; these are traits from the list of components of a Mexican culture of poverty." Lewis believed that the poor the world over share in this culture of poverty.

Hannerz (1969:177) termed black ghetto life and outlook in the United States a ghetto-specific complex:

Among the components of this ghetto-specific complex are for instance female household dominance; a ghetto-specific male role of somewhat varying expression including, among other emphases, toughness, sexual activity, and a fair amount of liquor consumption; a relatively conflict-ridden relationship between the sexes; rather intensive participation in informal social life outside the domestic domain; flexible household composition; fear of trouble in the environment; a certain amount of suspiciousness toward other persons' motives; relative closeness to religion; particular food habits; a great interest in the music of the group; and a relatively hostile view of much of white America and its representatives.

The ghetto-specific complex, like the broader concept of pathology, includes peculiarities in psychological make-up, certain abnormalities in patterns of social organization, as well as a pathological culture for living with poverty. Because many of the elements of the ghetto-specific complex are considered to be out of line with the norms of the larger society, the assimilation of this or any other minority group which shows signs of it can be seriously impeded. Remember that these same traits in the majority group would not often be considered pathological.

Ethnic Communalism and Consciousness

Some social scientists find a good measure of communalism and ethnic consciousness in American minority groups. They say that minority and majority groups alike have maintained their solidarity in the process of the modernization of American society, one set of groups as it has been excluded from that process and the other as it has been swept up into modern society. Solidarity can shelter minority group members from many of the pathological consequences often associated with minority status in American society. Milton Gordon (1964) wrote that both minority and majority groups are ethnic subsocieties with distinct subcultures in modern America. An ethnic subsociety is "a network of organizations and informal social relations which permits and encourages the members of an ethnic group to remain in the confines of the group for all of their primary relations and some of their secondary relationships at all stages of the life-cycle" (Gordon, 1964:34). This network, when complete enough, can protect minority group members to a great extent from the full-blown impact of majority prejudice and discrimination. Ethnic communalism is defined here as an ethnic group was defined earlier—*a self-conscious collectivity of people, who can maintain a distinction between themselves and outsiders based on origin or a common culture. Such boundary maintenance may be manifest in circumscribed social participation or in distinctive patterns of thought, sentiment, or action. Communalism is evident when a collectivity is an ethnic group in the above sense and its members have a consciousness of kind and sense of shared societal position.*

Minority groups can and do preserve their communalism in the face of their exclusion from the larger society. Ethnic communalism represents the preservation of the folk past, whether the group is evolving into or away from modern society. It is the continuance of certain traditions, the consciousness of kind among group members, and their sense of historical continuity, all of which is structured and given organizational expression through newspapers, fraternal societies, churches, and the informal relationships among members of the group. The communalism and consciousness of minority group members may also be reinforced by their exclusion from the larger society, as prejudice and discrimination remind them almost daily that they are different from others and share the same fate. Evolutionary divergence can mean the preservation of the folk group, and it is in this community that prejudice and discrimination are comprehended and coped with.

The assimilationists have considered the ethnic community as belonging to another historical era, part of our evolutionary past—a place, a pattern of association, and a state of mind that has no function in modern society. Thus, the eclipse of the ethnic community in the course of societal modernization was predicted. As groups assimilated into the modern society through their educational advancement, occupational diversification, and residential dispersion, there would be the eventual loss of their ethnic heritage. For those groups excluded from modern society, the minority groups, there would also be a loss of the folk heritage under the pressures of prejudice and discrimination, as these groups became entangled in pathology. The predicted passage of the folk community held for the minority as well as the majority group. To the assimilationist, evolutionary convergence means assimilation and divergence means pathology, and neither entails the extension of the folk community into the modern era.

Out of conflict theory comes a second view of the American minority group. From this perspective, the minority group evolves as a *communal* group, one which can undertake collective and concerted action for the purpose of improving its position within the larger system of ethnic stratification. The same is true for the majority group; thus both the majority and minority groups are potential conflict groups. Intergroup competition is certainly part of societal modernization, perhaps growing even more intense and widespread in the process. In their struggle for societal resources, groups engage in communal action, or action "which is oriented to the feelings of the actors that they belong together" (Weber, 1966:22). The process tends to vitalize ethnic boundaries and enhance ethnic consciousness of kind and sense of societal position.

This consciousness of kind is what Brown (1931:92) had in mind when he said: "The race conscious posit their race as an entity to which they have obligations. They have a conscience about this race. They must serve it, fight for it, be loyal to it." Moreover, Brown located consciousness of kind in the ongoing struggle among groups in contemporary society for wealth, status, and power:

> Through race consciousness the members of a race become a historic group acquiring a past, aware of a present and aspiring to a future. A racially conscious group is more than a mere aggregation of individuals zoologically distinguishable from other ethnic groups. It is a social unit struggling for status in a society. *It is thus a conflict group, and race consciousness itself is a result of conflict.* (pp. 569–570; italics added)

Consciousness of kind refers to the self-consciousness of group members, their realization that they belong to the same group and have a degree of loyalty to each other, and thus their drawing a distinction between themselves and others. While consciousness of kind is most certainly rooted in people's sense of historical continuity, it is made continuously current by the persistent struggle among groups for wealth, power, and status, or, from our own conflict perspective, by the competition over land, labor, and capital. To the extent that minority groups are party to this struggle, they should manifest a consciousness of kind.

Ethnic consciousness also includes a sense among minority group members of their position in modern society or their rank in the system of ethnic stratification. While consciousness of kind is self-reflexive and the object of contemplation is one's own group, *consciousness of societal position is the awareness of the relation of one's group to other groups in the larger society, particularly within the context of ethnic stratification.* Pitts (1974:669) defined this sort of ethnic consciousness as "indicating the actor's interpretation of the stituation as representing invidious relationships, even struggle, between the races." Black consciousness was defined by Hraba and Siegman (1974:64) as "an awareness of racial barriers, deprivation, consequent discontent, as well as a commitment to black collective action addressed to this racial situation." Consciousness of kind and consciousness of societal position refer to a shared definition of their situation by minority group members, and both lie behind any collective action with respect to that situation: "Preliminary to any self-determined act or behavior there is always a stage of examination and deliberation which we may call the definition of the situation" (W. I. Thomas, 1931:41). Of course, communal action once undertaken tends to intensify conscious-ness of kind and societal position.

A communal group is an ethnic group whose members have a consciousness of kind and sense of their societal position. A communal minority group provides its members with their own set of standards, a subculture, and a context in which their divergence from the larger society is suffered and understood. It typically brings about the social alienation of minority group members, not their self-alienation, a process "in which individual selves may find the social system in which they live to be oppressive or incompatible with some of their own desires and feel estranged from it" (Taviss, 1969:46).

BASIC ASSUMPTIONS OF EVOLUTIONARY DIVERGENCE

1. *The evolutions of some of the nation's ethnic groups have converged with the modernization of American society. These groups are now considered the nation's majority group. The evolutions of other ethnic groups have diverged from the modernization of American society, and these groups are now known as the nation's minority groups.*

2. *Minority groups can lose their folk community in the course of their evolutionary divergence and be caught in a tangle of pathology. Minority groups also can retain their folk community, even under the pressures of prejudice and discrimination, and evolve as a communal group in the struggle with others for wealth, power, and prestige.*

3. *Both pathology and communalism are evident to some degree in all minority groups. The abilities of a minority group to accumulate capital, develop a subeconomy, or accomplish the political mobilization of its membership, among other factors, are critical in determining which course of evolutionary divergence it will take.*

PATHOLOGY

Pathology is a social and psychological condition of minority groups that is generally assumed to be a result of their exclusion from the larger society. It represents a particular form of evolutionary divergence whereby the ethnic communalism of a minority group disintegrates under the pressures of prejudice and discrimination. Communal solidarity dissolves and family structure becomes disorganized, diverging from family patterns in the larger society. In the process, the personalities of minority group members are damaged and deviate from the norms of mental health in the wider world. As a consequence, members of a minority group engage in deviant and self–debilitating behavior, including crime and delinquency, alcoholism and drug addiction, homicide and suicide, and are susceptible to several forms of mental illness. These are among the "marks of oppression" (Kardiner and Ovesey, 1951) which further disable the minority group from working toward its inclusion into the larger society. The pathology of minority groups appears to others as extremely deviant and thus offers a convenient rationalization for the exclusion of the group in the first place.

It is commonly understood that the ultimate cause of pathology is prejudice and discrimination, and the process of becoming pathological commences for any one individual in childhood. Minority group children learn that their own group is devalued by others, deviates significantly from others in the larger society, and frequently become self-prejudiced or self-alienated at a very early age. Thus begins a cycle of human development which is impaired from the very start.

The Evidence

Clark and Clark (1947) found in 1939 that black children (3–7 years old) preferred white dolls and rejected black dolls when asked to choose which dolls they would like to play with, which were nice, which were bad, and which were the nice color. These observations also have been made in subsequent studies utilizing a variety of testing methods and in various geographical and social settings (Asher and Allen, 1969; Frenkel-Brunswik, 1948; Goodman, 1952; Greenwald and Oppenheim, 1968; Landreth and Johnson, 1953; Morland, 1958, 1966; Radke, Trager, and Davis, 1949; Trager and Yarrow, 1952). When white children have been used as a control group, they generally have made responses favorable to the dolls of their own race. The results of the Clark and Clark study are shown in Table 1.

Table 1   Doll Choices of Black Children

Item	White Doll	Black Doll
Give me the doll that you want to play with..........................	67%	32%
Give me the doll that is a nice doll...	59	38
Give me the doll that looks bad...	17	59
Give me the doll that is a nice color......................................	60	38

Note: Individuals failing to make either choice are not included; hence some percentages add to less than 100.

Source: From *Racial Identification and Preference in Negro Children* by Kenneth B. Clark and Mamie P. Clark, in *Readings in Social Psychology*, Third Edition, edited by Eleanor E. Maccoby, Theodore M. Newcomb, and Eugene L. Hartley. Copyright 1947, 1952, © 1958 by Holt, Rinehart and Winston. Adapted by permission of Holt, Rinehart and Winston.

This long tradition of research showing a preference among black children for whites implies a history of self-prejudice on the part of black children in this country. At least this has been a common interpretation of these findings. Morland (1969:360) offered this generalization on the basis of these findings: "In a multiracial society in which there is a dominant and subordinate race, young children of the subordinate race tend to prefer and identify with members of the dominant race, while children of the dominant race tend to prefer and identify with members of their own race."

From a bad start matters get worse for minority group children, according to social pathologists. These children soon enter school, where many do not do well. Reasons for this "failure" are many, obviously, but the inadequacies of the home in preparing and supporting children in serious school work are the ones emphasized by social pathologists. Instead of academic success and preparation for careers in the professions and technical fields, there is a pattern of early pregnancy for girls, and for boys there is life on the streets:

While the feminine role is associated with respectability, dependability, the family, and the home, masculinity is more often associated with the reverse of these and its locus is the street. A boy strives to achieve a "rep" on the street because he perceives that he does not have much status in the home. He strives to assert his masculinity against almost overwhelming handicaps. His father still remembers his "place," but his mother is a recognized pillar of the family and the church and is the one who sees to it that he at least makes an effort in school. If he is in his late teens, he has seen in himself what he feared he saw all along in his father—a person ill-prepared to "go it alone." He sees himself more destined for the dependency of welfare than the independence of manhood. Coming up as a boy in the ghetto is thus a most difficult process indeed. (Schulz, 1969:59)

By the time they are adults, many members of minority groups are unprepared for entry in all but the menial levels of the occupational structure of a modern society. They lack the necessary credentials for better work and this, combined with the prejudice and discrimination they face, means more evolutionary divergence for the group as a whole. The lack of educational preparation or vocational training of adolescents eventually translates into economic and social marginality as adults—lives that are spent either at the bottom of the labor market, in unskilled work, or on welfare. This way, generation after generation, the cycle of poverty and pathology continues.

According to the research of Hess and Shipman (1965), the poor preparation at home of minority-group children, at least of those from lower class origins, begins in mother-child communication patterns. Communication between mothers and their children was characterized as either restrictive or elaborative in this study. Restrictive language codes lack specificity, relying instead on gross generalizations, including stereotypes, to conceptualize the perceived world. These codes lack flexibility to communicate situational nuances and thus blur the differences between types of situations, topics, and people. Elaborated codes, by contrast, give expression to such differences, to the uniqueness of situations, topics, and people, and thus contain more detail and communicate more meaning. Not surprisingly, elaborated codes were found to be common among well-educated and high-income black mothers, while restrictive codes were more evident among less well-educated, black welfare mothers. These two classes of women were also distinguished by the ways in which they controlled their children. Undereducated mothers made directives to their children matters of conformity and obedience, while the better educated mothers made their suggestions relevant to a child's own particular situation, explaining how and why the advice would directly help the child with the task at hand. That is, the worth of the advice was explained in the context of the specific situation and made relevant to the task, and the child was always free to take or ignore it. The advice from educated mothers was never imperative or a matter of obedience and conformity. This situation was observed in a child development laboratory as mothers assisted their children with a series of games and puzzles. Hess and Shipman concluded from these findings that the meaning of deprivation is the deprivation of meaning.

This early experience leads to later school problems, often with the result that the child drops out of school, the pathologists say. Instead of school and the preparation for a "normal" adulthood, adolescent males of minority groups turn to the peer group, the gang, and the street-corner subculture. This means delinquency in general, and school truancy, getting girls "in trouble," stealing, and fighting in particular. To break away from their mothers and in the absence of a father, boys tend to exaggerate certain features of their masculinity, not in school work but in fighting, stealing, drinking, and sex. They are on their way to becoming "bad" dudes. "Playing the dozens" represents one of the devices used to manage this break, a game whereby black adolescent males deride one another's mother's alleged disreputable behavior, particularly with respect to sex.

The existence of bilingualism in minority groups has also been seen as a hindrance to school achievement and their assimilation. Home/school bilingualism was at one time thought to interfere with the schooling of Italian and Jewish students, the children of immigrants earlier in the century. It is still a major concern among pathologists, now directed to Chicano children. Such a conclusion seems to be supported in the several studies which have found that Chicano children, like blacks, are behind white children at each step in the achievement ladder (cf. Lopez, 1976). On the other hand, Lopez (1976:244) reported that "home-school bilingualism has no necessary positive or negative effects on attainment." It can hinder educational and occupational attainment when it is considered a sign of ethnic stigma in the larger society, or it can help by identifying one as an insider and deserving of assistance from one's own kind. Lopez found that the latter function applied particularly to blue-collar Chicanos.

The dismal conclusion often offered by the pathologists is that by the time minority group children grow up, they can do little except perpetuate the cycle of poverty and pathology. Liebow (1967) wrote about low-income black men, street-corner men, they were called, who hung out at a carry-out restaurant somewhere in Washington, D.C. These men despised their own fathers for not having lived up to the mainstream model of an adult male. Their dilemma was that they themselves were fast becoming what their fathers had been, men with marginal jobs, drifters, men on street-corners. The mainstream model of manhood was the ideal for these street-corner men, Liebow said, as it was for those around them, especially their women. Men and women alike sought the mainstream ideals—for men to be good providers, husbands, and fathers—but this was impossible.

The reasons for the "failures" of the street-corner men Liebow studied go back to their childhood. These men had not prepared themselves for vocations that put a premium on cultural and technical skills, in a word, on schooling. They came into adulthood with skills qualifying them for only marginal jobs, in food service and unskilled construction work, for instance. The extremely low pay or the seasonal nature of the work meant no more than a marginal economic existence for these men and their families. Money for them was always in short supply. The result was that these men found it increasingly impossible to live by the mainstream model of the adult male, and thus they eventually turned away from their families and toward the street corner.

At home, the wives of these men appeared always ready to point to the gap between the mainstream ideals and what they really were, undoubtedly reminding each man of the conflict between his mother and father in the previous generation. These men saw in themselves their own fathers, something they had wished to avoid. Children also jogged unpleasant memories, reminding them that the cycle of poverty had been perpetuated through their own generation and would probably continue into the next.

The magic of the street corner is that vices are turned into virtues, and a man's failures become signs of a more basic and truer masculinity; failures become manly flaws. To explain the desertion of his wife and nonsupport of his children, the man on the street corner, with the consent and approval of the others, turned to the theory of manly flaws, that men have too much dog in them: "Men are just dogs! We shouldn't call ourselves human, we're just dogs, dogs, dogs! They call me a dog, 'cause that's what I am, but so is everybody else—hopping around from woman to woman, just like a dog" (Liebow, 1967:120–121). Street-corner mythmaking is dialectical; out of failure arises its opposite, success; a man fails at manhood by being too much of a man.

It was Liebow's conclusion that such street-corner mythmaking was an ex post facto rationalization of a painful reality, the fact that these men could not live by common standards expected of adult males in the larger American society at the time. These men were not prepared for anything but a low-level entry into the occupational structure of our postindustrial society, and the result was the formation of certain personal pathologies and the disruption of family life. Rainwater (1970) represented this situation as in Figure 1.

The marital instability among low-income blacks prompted Daniel Patrick Moynihan to make this controversial comment:

In essence, the Negro community has been forced into a matriarchal structure which, because it is so out of line with the rest of the American society, seriously retards the progress of the group as a whole, and imposes a crushing burden on the Negro male and, in consequence, on a great many Negro women as well (Moynihan, 1972:197).

The roots of the pathology of the black family go back to slavery, according to E. Franklin Frazier (1939). African family forms were lost by

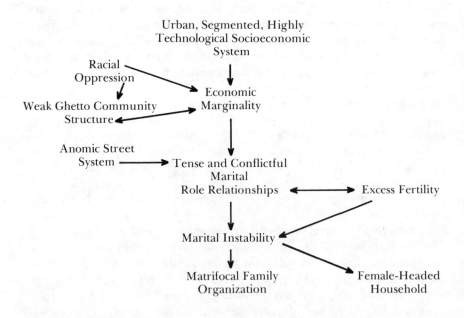

Figure 1   *The situation of low-income blacks in a technological society.*
Source: Reprinted by permission, from Lee Rainwater: *Behind Ghetto Walls: Black Family Life in a Federal Slum* (Chicago: Aldine Publishing Company); copyright © 1970 by Lee Rainwater.

the masses of black people under slavery. Stable family life was disrupted during slavery by the selling of family members separately, particularly the fathers, and by forced mating of slaves at the whim of the master and under the pressures of slavery noted in the Abolitionists' version of slave life. In other words, blacks lost the principal elements of their folk community under slavery, long before this loss occurred to other ethnic groups. The disintegration of the black family and thus of the black community continued with the 20th-century migration of blacks into the industrial cities of America. While sturdy black women found work readily as domestics and service workers in the cities, many black men took up a migratory career of living off these women, moving from woman to woman until their luck ran out or age caught up with them. This made for promiscuity, desertion, female-headed households, and the delinquency of children. At least this was the version of the black family suggested by Frazier, in the tradition of the social pathologists.

While writings on black Americans have been used as an illustration of the broader school of social pathology, it must be remembered that this perspective has been applied to nearly all American minority groups, immigrant and indigenous alike. Observers have found pathology in the Irish, the eastern and southern Europeans, and the Asians, and today they find it in American Indians, Chicanos, and black Americans. There must be hundreds of academic articles and research reports on Indian alcoholism. The pathology of Indian drinking patterns is not that Indians drink so much more than anyone else; it lies in the manner in which they consume alcohol, drinking to extreme intoxication, together, in public. The result is that police are often summoned, and arrest and incarceration follow. The reasons given for Indian alcoholism center around their material circumstances and the loss of their communal traditions (Dozier, 1966).[1] Alcohol provides a temporary release from poverty and deprivation, and can sometimes capture, if only temporarily, the old communal solidarity lost in conquest. Pathology as a perspective is one portrait of evolutionary divergence, one that reminds me of a passage describing African societies in Fanon (1963:41):

Native society is not simply described as a society lacking in values. It is not enough for the colonist to affirm that those values have disappeared from, or still better never existed in, the colonial world. The native is declared insensible to ethics; he represents not only the absence of values, but also the negation of values.

---

[1] Levy and Kunitz (1974:174) see the Navajo use of alcohol in a different light: "The level of acculturation stands in an inverse relationship to the level of involvement with alcohol. This and the nature of the difference between Navajo and white patterns of drinking raise questions concerning the definition of alcoholism as a pathology and the notion that problem drinking is the result of strains attendant upon the acculturative process."

Reasons for Pathology

Social pathology is one form of evolutionary divergence, a product of the exclusion of a minority group from the larger society. Members of a minority group become self-prejudiced, fail to develop the cultural skills of the larger society, and show signs of social disorganization and psychological deterioration. There are in the social sciences two different explanations for this pathology. One explanation has it that pathology is a direct and immediate consequence of intergroup exclusion, or prejudice and discrimination. This is blocked-opportunity theory. A second explanation is that minority groups live by a culture of poverty, one that is passed down from generation to generation, and it is this culture of poverty that prevents each generation from evolving toward its inclusion in the larger society.

CULTURE OF POVERTY "A culture of poverty is a design for living within the constraints of poverty, passed down from generation to generation, thereby achieving stability and persistence" (Lewis, 1961:xxiv). Lewis contended that all the poor share in this culture of poverty, making them distinct from the rest of the people of the world. The situations of minority groups in the United States have been analyzed as domestic instances of this worldwide culture of poverty. Ball (1968) applied this analysis to the folk subculture of the Southern Appalachians, for instance. There are two fundamentally different designs for living, one that is motivation instigated and another that is frustration instigated. We see motivation-instigated action when people take steps in a rational manner to attain their goals, and this is presumably characteristic of most Americans. But the poor of Southern Appalachia are characterized by a different mode of behavior, one that is frustration instigated. Frustration-instigated behavior is neither rational nor goal oriented in any ordinary sense: "there is no apparent goal in frustration-instigated behavior, such behavior appears senseless . . . . behavior resulting from extreme frustration may represent a terminal response to the frustration itself rather than a means to any end" (Ball 1968:887). Frustration originates in the hardships of life among the poor in this region, and its release has been institutionalized into the region's folk culture. Ball termed this folk subculture the analgesic subculture of the Southern Appalachians and likened it to a downward spiral, a descending cycle of frustration and its irrational release without any attempt to remove the sources of frustration.

The principal components of this analgesic subculture include fixation, regression, aggression, and resignation, all of which have been observed by experimental psychologists as among the responses of animals to extreme frustration. These responses have been codified in the folk culture of Southern Appalachia, so that "the young learn to anticipate defeat and to perform subcultural rituals which reduce its impact" (Ball, 1968:890). Ball found fixation in "the obstinate tradition of the Southern Appalachian folk subculture" and institutionalized regression in "the lack of aesthetic appreciation, anti-intellectualism, the preference of anecdote over abstraction, the insistence upon a literal interpretation of the Bible, the entanglement of religious fundamentalism with deep superstition, the improvident squandering which often accompanies 'pay day' or a welfare check." Moreover, "Resignation, apathy, and fatalism are rarely so prominent as among the members of the mountain folk subculture" (Ball, 1968:892).

Like the culture of poverty the world over, the analgesic subculture of the Southern Appalachians is seen as a design for living with the frustrations of poverty, passed down from generation to generation, which incapacitates these mountain folk even more from moving toward their inclusion into the larger American society. Like so many other instances of the culture of poverty in this country, it provides only for the irrational release of frustrations, without doing anything about ameliorating the conditions which cause those frustrations in the first place.

BLOCKED-OPPORTUNITY THEORY Those who subscribe to the blocked-opportunity theory argue that the behavioral and cultural traits of the poor, their design for living, cannot be explained by reference to those traits, as is done in the theory of the culture of poverty. Specifically, they take exception to the notion that a culture of poverty was formed long ago and has been transmitted over the generations to the young, so that "the young learn to anticipate defeat" (Ball, 1968:890). For instance, Liebow (1967) maintained that black street-corner men shared with other Americans the national culture, both its goals and prescribed means, but could not live by those standards due to their lack of opportunity. This resulted in their behavioral deviation from the larger cultural standards, as seen in the desertion of their wives and children. In search of some aid and comfort after such failures, these men found one another on street corners and there spun myths about their manly flaws. There was no intergenerational transmission of these myths, however; for each generation they were ex post facto rationalizations for failure to live by the cultural standards of the larger society. That is, minority group members share in the cultural values of the larger society, especially in an era of mass education and communication, and their behavioral deviations from those values cannot in any way be attributed to some culture of poverty. This latter view appears to square with Gordon's (1964) contention that ethnic groups in American society have usually been enculturated into the national ethos long before they have attained full structural assimilation into American Society.

Merton (1957) observed that American culture contains prescriptions for both the legitimate goals of life and the means of attaining those goals. One should not only strive for success but do it in a respectable way, by becoming a doctor or lawyer, for instance, not a pimp. Using only legitimate means in the pursuit of success is not always possible for members of minority groups, however; because of prejudice and discrimination they often must take deviant paths to success. Political machines, crime, prostitution, and street-corner men are among the many illustrations of this phenomenon in American history. The point is that these deviations are not necessarily evidence for a culture of poverty; they may represent alternative ways to realize goals that the poor share with the rich.

Upon reviewing the debate between the proponents of the culture of poverty and those of the blocked-opportunity theory, and after having lived for two years in a black ghetto in the nation's capitol, Hannerz (1969:182) wrote:

We have noted that the ghetto-specific male role is more in line with the economic, occupational, and educational position of many ghetto men than is the mainstreamer male role; we have established the fact that economic problems form one of the foundations of male-female conflict as generated within the ghetto household; and we have pointed out the pooling and redistribution of limited resources are functions of both flexible household composition and informal neighborhood interaction. Certainly there may be touches to these features of ghetto life which are not directly determined by poverty, but it cannot be gainsaid that they are strongly influenced by it.

In short, Hannerz locates psychological states, behavioral styles, and patterns of social organization typically thought to be pathological in the hardships of poverty, not in the culture of poverty. The culture of poverty, whenever it exists, is the result of poverty, not its cause. This is a conclusion reached in several critiques of the culture of poverty as an explanation of poverty (e.g., Roach and Gursslin, 1967; Valentine, 1968). This view is consistent with our own, which is that social pathology is one form of evolutionary divergence and a consequence of intergroup exclusion, not a product of the motivational peculiarities of the poor.

The behavioral deviations from the standards of the larger culture among minority poor represent what Hyman Rodman (1968:301) called the lower-class value stretch:

By the value stretch I mean that the lower-class person, without abandoning the general values of the society, develops an alternative set of values. Without abandoning the values placed on success, such as high income and high educational and occupational attainment, he stretches the values so that lesser degrees of success also become desirable. Without abandoning the values of marriage and legitimate childbirth he stretches these values so that a nonlegal union and legally illegitimate children are also desirable. The result is that the members of the lower class, in many areas, have a wider range of values than others within the society. They share the general values of the society with members of other classes, but in addition they have stretched these values, or developed alternative values, which help them to adjust to their deprived circumstances.

Some Negative Evidence

Although the preceding evidence seems to support the pathological premise about minority problems, a number of recent studies have cast doubt on the utility of relying exclusively on the pathological perspective as a depiction and explanation of the evolutionary divergence of American minority groups. To conclude that patterns of behavior and social organization of a minority group are pathological is ultimately a value judgment. Because members of a minority group may deviate in certain respects from the styles of the majority group does not necessarily mean that they are pathological. Is it not possible that the way of life of the *majority* group is pathological, and by deviating from it the life-style of the minority group is more normal and wholesome? Observers also often forget that members of a minority group are not homogenous—all the same—and that there is a diversity of life-styles within all minority communities. Another issue raised in recent research is to what degree members of minority groups actually deviate from mainstream standards of psychological well-being and social organizational integrity. There is a growing body of evidence that pathology in minority groups is not as widespread as once supposed and that the traditional view, social pathology, distorts the situation beyond recognition (Heiss and Owens, 1972:369).

The findings of black children's preference for and misidentification with white dolls have been traditionally interpreted as evidence of rampant self-prejudice on the part of black children, and the start of identity problems for millions of black Americans. McCarthy and Yancey (1971:658) suggested that this might be an impetuous conclusion:

It is rather a long jump in our opinion, however, from racial awareness, preference for white dolls, and assignment of inferior roles to brown dolls to self-hatred . . . . There are a number of plausible explanations for such findings which have nothing to do with self-hatred. Personality ratings accompanying one piece of research in this tradition demonstrate that the Negro children were more cheerful, more curious, more inclined toward leadership, kinder, and more sensitive . . . hardly picturesque of rampant self-hatred. In our opinion the evidence embodied in this literature is open to various interpretations, especially since much of it does not make a racial comparison . . . . We do not argue that the interpretation commonly made is necessarily incorrect. It may be correct, but the evidence remains inconclusive.

The interpretation that for black children interracial contact engenders preference for white and is the start of their identity problems stands out in this traditional literature. Some have been advocates of this position (e.g., Armstrong and Gregor, 1964; Asher and Allen, 1969; Gregor, 1963; Gregor and McPherson, 1966). Asher and Allen (1969:164) put it this way: "enhanced status will not necessarily lead to greater racial pride, but may instead contribute, through more frequent comparison with whites, to increased feelings of inferiority." Gregor and McPherson (1966:103) phrased it in another way: "Negro children tend to be more outgroup oriented the more systematically they are exposed to white contact."

Hraba and Grant (1970) tested this thesis by duplicating the Clark and Clark (1947) doll study in an interracial setting. This study was done in Lincoln, Nebraska, a city where blacks comprised approximately 1.4 percent of the population and where black children went to predominately white schools. The percentage of black children in the elementary schools of this city ranged from 3 to 18 percent. Moreover, the sample of school children studied, both black and white, demonstrated friendship patterns which substantiate the interracial nature of this setting. Sociometric choices confirmed by teachers indicated that 70 percent of the black children had white friends and 59 percent of the white children had black friends. In short, these black children could not and did not avoid systematic contact with whites.

Did they show self-prejudice as a consequence? No, to the contrary, these black children demonstrated a belief in "black is beautiful," generally preferring and identifying with the black dolls. White children also preferred and identified with the dolls of their own race. Children of both races also made responses favorable to the other race, reflecting the interracial nature of the friendships (Hraba, 1972). The racial preferences of these children, black and white, and a comparison with the Clark and Clark data are shown in Table 2.

In the traditional view, black children develop into psychologically damaged adults, beginning with early self-hatred, doubt, and identity crises. But often there was no explicit and formal comparison of the psychological states of blacks with those of whites. McCarthy and Yancey (1971:656) turned to Kardiner and Ovesey's *The Mark of Oppression (1951)* as an indication of this tendency:

If we compare the self-hatred of any social grouping with an ideal personality state—as the neo-Freudians are fond of doing—we can do nothing more than find what we seek—a discrepancy .... Kardiner and Ovesey .... draw generalizations concerning the effects of prejudice and discrimination from twenty-five intensive case studies of Negro Americans. The only obvious comparison being

Table 2 Comparison of Data in Hraba and Grant (1970) and Clark and Clark (1947)

Item	Clark & Clark (1939 data) Blacks	Hraba & Grant (1969 data) Blacks	X² (1939-1969) Blacks	Hraba & Grant (1969 data) Whites
1. (Play with)				
White doll..................................	67% (169)	30% (27)	36.2%**	83% (59)
Black doll..................................	32 (83)	70 (62)		16 (11)
Don't know or no response.........				1 (1)
2. (Nice doll)				
White doll..................................	59 (150)	46 (41)	5.7*	70 (50)
Black doll..................................	38 (97)	54 (48)		30 (21)
3. (Looks bad)				
White doll..................................	17 (42)	61 (54)	43.5**	34 (24)
Black doll..................................	59 (149)	36 (32)		63 (45)
Don't know or no response.........		3 (3)		3 (2)
4. (Nice color)				
White doll..................................	60 (151)	31 (28)	23.1**	48 (34)
Black doll..................................	38 (96)	69 (61)		49 (35)
Don't know or no response.........				3 (2)

Note: Data in percentage. Ns in parentheses. Individuals failing to make either choice not included, hence some percentages add to less than 100.
*$p \leq .02$
**$p \leq .001$
Source: Joseph Hraba and Geoffrey Grant, "Black Is Beautiful: A Reexamination of Racial Preference and Identification." Journal of Personality and Social Psychology 16 (November): 398-402. Copyright 1970 by the American Psychological Association. Reprinted by permission.

made by the authors is between the twenty-five subjects' assessed personality states and some ideal of personality structure.

Handlin (1957) noted that the comparative mental health of old and new immigrant groups was studied earlier in the century by comparing only their committals to public institutions. The newer immigrants, being overrepresented among the poor, would certainly be overrepresented among the committals to public institutions, even if their mental health was identical to that of the older immigrant groups. In this case, as is so often in the case of black Americans, assessments of the supposed pathology of minority groups lack systematic and unbiased comparisons between minority and majority groups.

Moynihan's (1972:199) statement that "at the center of the tangle of pathology is the weakness of the family structure," written in 1965, is his controversial conclusion on the role of the black family in the pathology of the black community as a whole. One year later, Rainwater (1966:200) expressed the same sentiment:

The impact of the system of victimization is transmitted through the family; the child cannot be expected to have the sophistication an outside observer has for seeing exactly where the villains are. From the child's point of view, if he is hungry it is his parents' fault: if he experiences frustrations in the streets or in the school it is his parents' fault; if that world seems incomprehensible to him it is his parents' fault; if people are aggressive or destructive toward each other it is his parents' fault, not that of a system of race relations.

While the problems of the low-income black families might begin in the system of ethnic stratification, those problems are perpetuated through the weaknesses of these families. This is the essence of Rainwater's position: There is a cycle which for each maturing generation begins with early pregnancy and proceeds through illegitimate births, the economic instability of adult males, female-headed households, the trap of public dependency, and inability to keep the next generation off the streets. Thus the cycle ends with entrapment of the next generation. Rainwater (1966:205–206) is specific about the impact of this cycle for each generation of black children:

In sum, we are suggesting that Negro slum children as they grow up in their families and in their neighborhoods are exposed to a set of experiences—and a rhetoric which conceptualizes them—that brings home to the child an understanding of his essence as a weak and debased person who can expect only partial gratification of his needs, and who must seek even this level of gratification by less than straightforward means.

This is the pathological view on the minority family. By no means do all students of American ethnicity agree with this view. Billingsley (1968:21) found a wide variety of family structures in every Negro neighborhood of any size in the country:

This range and variety does not suggest, as some commentaries hold, that the Negro family is falling apart, but rather that these families are fully capable of surviving by adapting to the historical and contemporary social and economic conditions facing the Negro people. How does a people survive in the face of oppression and sharply restricted economic and social support? . . . One way is to adapt the most basic of its institutions, the family, to meet the often conflicting demands placed on it. In this context, then, the Negro family has proved to be an amazingly resilient institution.

Hill (1972), in an essay on the strengths of the black family, wrote that many of the beliefs which underlie the pathological conception of the black family have been uncritically accepted as true but actually are false. This applies to the widespread belief about black matriarchy. Matriarchy in black families is not so prevalent as supposed, according to Hill (1972:281), who reported findings that "most black families, whether low-income or not, are characterized by an 'equalitarian' pattern in which neither spouse dominates, but [they] share decision making and the performance of expected tasks." Another traditional image of the black family is that of the black male who is weak, often irresponsible, and unable to measure up to the mainstream model of husband and father. This is clearly the image projected in Liebow's (1967) study of street-corner men. Contrary to this image, Hill (1972:281) noted that "in 85 percent of the black families with incomes under $3,000, the husband's earnings surpassed the wife's." Moreover, the desertion of the family by the male hardly characterizes the majority of AFDC families; "only one-fifth of the black families receiving AFDC in 1969 were so described" (Hill, 1972:282). Nor are all women who do head black families on welfare, contrary to the traditional view; rather "two-thirds of the women heading black families work—most of them full-time" (Hill, 1972:281).

It is the contention of Robert Hill that the black family has several strengths, most of which have been overlooked in the collective works of the social pathologists. As to what he means by family strength, Hill (1972:264) wrote that "we . . . define as family strengths those traits which facilitate the ability of the family to meet the needs of its members and the demands made upon it by systems outside the family unit." Hill indicated three major sources of strength in black families: strong kinship bonds, strong work orientation, and the adaptability of family roles. The strength of kinship bonds in black families is evidenced in their practice of taking in the children of other family members, the historical existence of black extended families, and the informal adoption of babies born out of wedlock. The practice of the informal adoption of dependent children is positively functional for the black community as a whole, for it "helps to minimize the number of new black families headed by a single woman" (Hill, 1972:266).

As evidence for the existence of a strong work orientation among black Americans Hill cites the fact that the black poor are more likely to work than the white poor. Moreover, black women are more likely to work than are white women, to help keep their families above the poverty line. This certainly appears to be a positive adaptation to social and economic reality, as black people experience it, and in no way does it seem to further disable people from being included into the larger society. Furthermore, the finding that black families are equalitarian at home appears to follow from the fact that both partners are typically in the work force outside of the home. Thus, the adaptability of family roles seems to be a functional adaptation for most black families and should not be mistaken for some sort of pathology which hinders the progress of the race.

Shimkin, Louie, and Frate (1973) found that a fundamental strength of the black community in Holmes County, Mississippi, has been the extended black family. Familial bonds among extended kin have been stable and durable, reinforced by patterns of residential propinquity and common church affiliation. The network of extended kin sanctions the obligations of family members toward one another, especially the responsibility of adults for children. These networks originating in Holmes County have acted as mechanisms for the migration of some family members to other areas of the country, mostly to the cities of the South and Midwest. Family members already located in urban areas have been important sources of job information for later migrants, have provided for an initial place for them to stay in the city, and generally have helped their own kin in the transition from rural to urban life, from an agrarian peasantry to a class of industrial workers. Shimkin et al. in no way overlook the economic marginality of most black families in Holmes County, particularly the absence of land proprietorship, but still conclude that the black family has been resilient and typically self-sufficient.

In his classical study of the black family, Frazier (1939) sounded the hopeful note that with economic progress the weakness he saw in the black family would be overcome. John Scanzoni (1971) initiated on that note a study of the overlooked majority (67 percent) of urban black families in which both husband and wife are present and which are above the poverty level. The sample consisted of 400 black households with both partners present in Indianapolis, Indiana, in 1968. Both spouses had to be black and married for at least five years to be in the sampling frame. Data collected on these families were compared with those on other families, black and white.

The major finding of the work is that most of the families in this sample had broken the cycle of economic deprivation and marital dissolution. Urban residence was important while not vital to this economic and social evolution, as were the resources passed to these people by their parents. Religious involvement was found to reinforce mainstream occupational and conjugal values and practices. Both husbands and wives in this sample of the "broad middle class of blacks" reported that their parents had been active in their preparation for participation in the larger society by providing certain class resources and stressing the values of that society. Even though middle-class blacks remain deprived relative to their white counterparts, Scanzoni observed that as blacks enter the larger society economically, they enter it conjugally as well. In other words, the evolutionary divergence evident in minority group family patterns, whatever their degree, is due to intergroup exclusion and discrimination. As the inclusion of a minority group proceeds, and as discrimination lessens, family patterns begin to converge with those of their class counterparts in the larger society.

ETHNIC COMMUNALISM AND CONSCIOUSNESS

The evidence contrary to the postulation of minority pathology has always suggested a second conceptualization of the American minority community. This view, ethnic communalism and consciousness, posits that the minority group can and does maintain its community in the course of its exclusion from the larger society, and its members find psychological succor among their own kind and in their own community. There is no necessary psychological deterioration in the course of evolutionary divergence, since minority group members can blame society rather than themselves for their circumstances. Instead, a minority group always has the potential of engaging in communal action, or action "which is oriented to the feelings of the actors that they belong together" (Weber, 1966:22). There is a consciousness of kind and of societal position. This position stands in sharp contrast to the contention that exclusion engenders only pathology. From the perspective of minority communalism, any deviation from mainstream standards is due to the persistence of the folk community in the course of evolutionary divergence, not to its disintegration and the pathology of its members. There is no necessary loss of the folk community in the modernization of society, for either the majority or minority group. Intergroup competition and conflict continuously make current ethnic boundaries and consciousness of kind, while the persistence of ethnic stratification keeps alive a minority group's sense of its societal position.

Communalism

Most immigrant groups to this country initially settled near where they worked, either in urban ghettos or in ethnic clusters in the countryside. At the time of their initial settlement, nearly all of these groups were minority groups, at the bottom of the labor hierarchy. The ethnic enclave of the immigrants represented their economic adaptation to the New World. They adapted as a class to the economy and ecology of their locale, which was all too often in the low-rent districts alongside factories, foundries, mines, and stockyards. Of course, the initial concentrations of immigrants was due to other reasons, including language barriers, the need to seek help from one's own kind, and the industrial ecology of the era. George Homans (1950) termed this process of adapting to an environment the *external system* of a group, those relations among group members that are initially conditioned by their need to adapt to a particular environment. Out of this external system a new set of relationships will emerge, however, which are not conditioned by economic adaptation and represent an elaboration on economic necessity. This is the *internal system*.

In her excellent survey of the writings on the American minority community, Judith Kramer (1970:52-53) turned primarily to Robin Williams, Jr. (1964) for an account of the emergence of the internal system, the communalization of the minority ghetto:

Due to the historical circumstance, there is initial categorization of those considered to have some important characteristic in common. Identifying symbols with social visibility are used as the basis for categorical definition. This is, of course, the source of the minority situation, and the ability to impose such categories on others is part of the dominant group's power to subordinate . . . . As a result, members of a category acquire a sense of common identity, which tends to increase interaction among themselves and to reduce contacts with others. Such social closure makes it even more likely that others will treat them as a unit; this treatment further enhances the new collectivity's cultural distinctiveness and social separation. It is not a completely closed social system since it is economically and politically dependent on the larger society. As a subordinate group, it must not only maintain relationships with others, it must accept the dominant rules of the game.

Ethnic communities represent economic and ecological adaptations, to be certain, but members of ethnic groups quickly elaborate on what is minimally required of them to adjust to their environment. For example, the description by Wirth (1928/1956:193) of the Chicago Jewish ghetto cited in Chapter 2 pointed out that:

In its initial stages the Jewish community is scarcely distinguishable from the rest of the city. As the numbers increase, however, the typical communal organization of the European ghetto gradually emerges. The addition of diverse elements to the population results in diversification and differentiation . . . .

In this passage Wirth describes in abstract terms the emergence of an internal system of one ethnic community, a process that includes both the elaboration of the external system into an internal community and the differentiation of that community. Elaboration itself is a complex process, including the formation of a network of ethnic formal associations, such as lodges, hospitals, even civil rights groups, and of informal networks of family and friends. Wirth provided some detail as to the elaboration of the Jewish ghetto in Chicago: By 1900 there were 50 congregations, 39 charities, 60 lodges, 11 social clubs, four Zionist organizations, and hospitals, cafes, and theaters in the Jewish community.

As the Jewish community was elaborated, it became more diversified as well, differentiated into various trades, functions, and activities, of course, but more importantly, it became differentiated into nationality and locality groups. Chinatowns were internally differentiated into clans, *Hui Kuans*, tongs, and trade guilds, and the Japanese were internally divided into *Kenjinkai*. Nearly all groups have become differentiated into ethclasses and have often become geographically dispersed as well. This is as true for minority groups as for majority groups. Communalism does not imply a static group, stuck in time and preserved by custom. The ethnic community is an evolving entity, undergoing the dual phenomena of elaboration and differentiation. Communalism as an internal system simply means that a group maintains enough of its organizational integrity to give structure and meaning to its members' lives.

Hannerz (1969) offered an example of the differentiation of a minority community. He observed that residents of a black ghetto tended to dichotomize each other into respectables and undesirables. The respectables saw themselves as the "good people," "model citizens," and the "middle class." They described their opposites, the undesirables, as "no good," "the rowdy bunch," and "trash." The self-named respectables characterize the undesirables collectively as exhibiting "drinking and drunkenness in public, spontaneous brawls, unwillingness to work, sexual license, and occasional trouble with police" (Hannerz, 1969:35).

Hannerz believed that the actual picture of differentiation within this ghetto was not nearly so neat. Instead of two status groups in the area, he discerned four: mainstreamers, swingers, street families, and the street-corner men described in Liebow's *Talley's Corner* (1967). The mainstreamers are the respectables by another name; they are steadily employed, often own their homes, and have stable family lives: "It is usually not very hard to detect from the outside which houses . . . are the homes of mainstreamers. The new metal screen doors, the venetian blinds, and the flower pots in the windows are usually absent from other people's houses" (Hannerz, 1969:39). Inside these homes, Hannerz reported finding paneled walls, stylish furniture, new TV and stereo sets, and wedding and graduation pictures of the family hanging on the walls. Outside, in the yards, Hannerz found aluminum garden chairs and a barbecue grill or two. Any middle-class American would immediately recognize such a home and feel comfortable in it.

The swingers are the young socialites of the neighborhood, from their late teens to their thirties. Their interest is in a good time. They buy clothing and stylish means of transportation, in a narcissistic celebration of self. These young men and women are usually where the action is, typically keep night hours, and are always cool. While mainstreamers and swingers are obviously different, there is little antagonism between them, and as they grow older swingers usually become mainstreamers.

However, antagonism between mainstreamers and street families and street-corner men does exist: "It is often the members of street families who are conspicuously engaging in affairs with the other sex outside marriage, whose children are born out of wedlock and engage in juvenile delinquency as they grow up, and who drink and fight in public" (Hannerz, 1969:46). This prompts the mainstreamers to regard street families as "trash." Street families, not mainstreamers and swingers, are characterized by the pathologies discussed earlier, including early pregnancy, conflict-ridden relationships between the sexes, the segregation of male and female social lives, flexible household composition, delinquency of the kids, and all the rest. Mainstreamers try to avoid contact with members of street families. A social distance is maintained between members of these two different status groups within the ghetto.

We see evidence of both ghetto pathology and ethnic communalism in this outline of the differentiation of a black ghetto. Drunkenness and abstinence, crime and concern for law and order, shacks and well-kept homes—all of these contrasts can be seen in a single black neighborhood, and they seem to vary by ethclass. This suggests that communalism characterizes the American minority community as much as does social pathology, and the center of gravity for ethnic communalism is the ethclass.

Communalism serves a variety of psychological and social functions for members of a minority group. The ethnic community is often an agency of socialization; its members come to share a common set of values and traditions, a subculture through which the larger national ethos is translated (Gordon, 1964). In the process, subcultural standards for self-worth are passed from generation to generation. Often minority group members are socialized into a shared definition of their minority situation, a sense of their societal position. This definition, more often than not, attributes minority poverty and deprivation to dominant group oppression, not to the shortcomings of minority group members. There is no necessary weakening of the self-image, since the system rather than the self is blamed. All of this protects the minority group members from the prejudice in the larger society, acting as a counter ideology to that prejudice. The subcultural values of a minority group serve as standards against which members of the minority group compare the competence of one another, and any "failures" to conform to mainstream standards can be easily attributed to discrimination. In effect, "it is the minority community that offers its members criteria for self-validation that are independent of the categorical criteria of the dominant group" (Kramer, 1970:66).

In their own communities, members of minority groups can see themselves as whole people, competent or incompetent, good or bad, in accord with their own criteria. Communalism of this sort can be a basis for social improvement "when there is a strong family at the core of the community" (Kramer, 1970:66). Communalism may hinder inclusion into the larger society, however, as the isolation of members of a minority group from outsiders may reinforce the existing pattern of social distance between themselves and others. Psychological relief from prejudice and oppression found within the confines of their own community may also cool out minority discontent about their circumstances. The "circle of lament" among members of a minority group about prejudice and discrimination "neither discharges the onus nor distracts from it" (Kramer, 1970:71).

Other functions of ethnic communalism include sustaining and giving structure to the lives of group members and maintaining the boundary exchange of the group with the outside world. With respect to the first function, Gordon (1964:34) wrote:

Within the ethnic group there develops a network of organizations and informal social relationships which permits and encourages the members of the ethnic group to remain within the confines of the group for all of their primary relationships and some of their secondary relationships throughout all the stages of the life-cycle.

Kramer (1970:56), on the other hand, looked to the boundary maintenance of the minority group:

It permits the self-sufficiency and the segregation that the family alone is unable to provide. The minority community formed by the ethnic group practices self-exclusion as a protection against the social exclusion of the dominant group. Its institutions and ideologies provide a way of life that is independent of the categorical status of its members. Their social honor is thereby secured against dominant derogation.

The degree to which minority communities can maintain their boundaries and thus regulate their exchange with the larger society varies from group to group, however, and the degree to which any given group can do this is a matter of debate. No ethnic subsociety can be an entirely closed system, having boundaries impermeable to all the pressures from the outside. Minority communities are from the start open systems, permeable to pressures from the outside, a fact to which their subordination attests. No minority group can protect its members fully from the effects of prejudice and discrimination, encasing them economically, politically, and socially, as if in quarantine. Williams (1964:18) offered these criteria for a fully developed communal group:

A fully developed collectivity . . . is *a people,* and is characterized by (1) a distinctive culture, (2) tests or criteria of membership, (3) a set of constitutive norms regulating social relations both within the collectivity and with outsiders, (4) an awareness of a distinct identity by both members and nonmembers, (5) obligations of solidarity, such as enforced requirements to help members in need and to resist derogation by outsiders, and (6) a high capacity for continued action on behalf of its members or of itself as a unit. In its most comprehensive development such a collectivity may become a potentially self-sufficient society, able to meet all internal needs from its own resources and to perpetuate itself as a functioning system from generation to generation.

Consciousness of Kind and Societal Position

It is within the minority community that minority group children experience their early and most important socializing influences, according to the perspective of ethnic communalism. The communal group is a socialization agency, in other words, and through its internal network of communication, members, young and old, are socialized into a consciousness of their ethnic identity and an awareness about their position in the larger society. This is one of the more important functions of the ethnic community. Consciousness of kind is the realization that one belongs with others by birthright to some particular group in a larger society and thus shares with them a common past, present, and future. Consciousness of kind means "a sense of us" among members of an ethnic group, and it enhances the solidarity of the group. While consciousness of kind is not fully dependent on ghetto experience—that is, on subordination, segregation, and occupational concentration—it is nevertheless rooted in human action, as that occurs day in and day out, and when people see each other through the reflections of having the same jobs, living in the same neighborhoods, sharing this and that experience, engaging in similar customs and rituals, excluded from the larger society, their consciousness of kind is more apparent and likely to be more prevalent.

Consciousness of societal position is the other side of the same coin. Consciouness of kind is self-reflexive, as members of a minority group see themselves reflected in the group's history and in their current "place" in society. Consciousness of societal position is the awareness of that "place" in society, which for a minority group usually means the realization that they face discrimination and have an inferior position in the system of ethnic stratification. You will recall from Chapter Five that Blumer (1958) located the prejudice of the majority group in their sense of social position, their superior status in the system of ethnic stratification. Minority groups are just as aware of their social position in the larger society. A minority group's sense of societal position is transmitted through the channels of communication in the minority community, as is its consciousness of kind, and it serves as a counter ideology to the prejudice of others (Hraba and Siegman, 1974). The more developed and comprehensive is this network, the more control the minority community can exercise over its participants.

EVOLUTIONARY DIVERGENCE: SOCIAL PATHOLOGY OR ETHNIC COMMUNALISM?

All minority groups by definition share the experience of having been excluded at one time or another from the larger American society. Many ethnic groups in American history have been excluded by their more powerful competitors from land, capital, and from the better positions in the labor market. That is, systems of ethnic stratification have been established around intergroup exchange, and these systems have been persistent phenomena, running through all three evolutionary phases of American society. Illustrations of ethnic stratification abound in American history; only some of these historical instances have been presented in this book (Chapters 7 through 9).

More often than not, a minority group follows a course of evolutionary divergence, one that is somewhere on the continuum between the extremes of social pathology and ethnic communalism. A minority group may evolve either toward a state of social pathology, becoming as it does less able to work toward its inclusion into the larger society, or it can evolve as a communal group in the face of prejudice and discrimination, maintaining its folk solidarity. In the one case the folk community disintegrates in the course of evolutionary divergence, while in the other it is conserved. It cannot be said that the history of any one minority group exemplifies either extreme, for the evolutionary course of most minority groups fall somewhere in the middle, between these two extremes. Minority groups generally show a mixture of pathology and communalism in the course of their evolutionary divergence. Some minority groups, however, have shown more signs of pathology than have others, and by the same token, some groups more than others appear to have conserved their communalism in the face of prejudice and discrimination.

What explains these different courses of evolutionary divergence? Why have some groups when excluded from the larger society evolved toward a state of pathology, meaning the loss of their folk community, while other minority groups have evolved as communal groups, preserving their folk community? The answer we propose lies in the degree to which a minority group is oppressed, and by the same token, its ability to control its own boundaries, to internally regulate to some degree its boundary exchange with the larger society, and thus to shelter its members to some extent from the debilitating effects of prejudice and discrimination. Boundary maintenance is rooted in the capacity of a minority group to provide to its members within their own community alternatives to the prejudice and discrimination in the larger society. Such an alternative can be provided by an ethnic subeconomy or its functional equivalents.

The Ethnic Subeconomy

Historically, the ethnic subeconomy has offered opportunity to members of a minority group unavailable in the larger American society, protecting participants from extreme hardships, preserving group boundaries, and conserving in-group cohesion and consciousness. This is a major role for capital accumulation on the part of minority groups; it can, by building a subeconomy, help buffer members of such groups from the full impact of prejudice and discrimination.

If fully functioning, a subeconomy can offer opportunity to members of a minority group that is not restricted by the caste barriers and ethnocentrism in the wider society. If the ethnic subeconomy as an opportunity structure is at all broad, then members of a minority group can truly circumvent the discrimination imposed on them by others. Perhaps no ethnic subeconomy has ever been so complete and without disadvantages, but Jews in Europe and Asians in America have made real, practical gains against discrimination in this way. Although it falls short of a subeconomy in providing alternatives to prejudice and discrimination, a viable social system and subculture can help minority group members, who face restricted opportunities without realistic alternatives, cope with the effects of such a life. It soothes the soul from the wear and tear of racism. It does not, however, preclude racism or the effects of it. Such a system can only maintain folks in the face of racism.

Members of a minority group without a subeconomy have no alternative but to seek opportunity on the outside, in the larger society, however limited those opportunities may be. Because of the power of their competitors, they face persistent discrimination and material deprivation, exclusion and evolutionary divergence. It also means that members of the minority group must face, day in and day out, the prejudice of others and the stigma that their ethnicity has in the larger society. Hope often contracts under such circumstances, serious ambitions sound absurd, and aspirations are scaled downward. This is the crucible for pathology.

A minority group without an opportunity structure of its own is, to phrase it abstractly, an open subsystem within a wider society. Its boundaries are so permeable to the forces of prejudice and discrimination in that wider society, its domination by others so complete, that little in the way of internal communalism is possible. Virtually nothing buffers members of such a minority group from the hardships of their exclusion, from prejudice, discrimination, and poverty, and the ghetto provides little more than a "circle of lament" over circumstances no one can change. There is no internal opportunity so that members of the group can practice their skills, workmanship, professional expertise, and so on on their own terms, in their own communities, away from the degrading and impeding ethnocentrism of others. Instead, they must face that degradation on a daily basis. Communalism and thus the sheltering of minority group members from prejudice and discrimination are severely limited when the life chances of minority group members are solely at the discretion of dominant outsiders, that is, when there is no ethnic subeconomy or internal opportunity structure of some kind. Pathology is an expected outcome in this minority situation. Rainwater (1966:200) expressed it this way:

　. . . if a subculture could exist which provided comfort and security within its limited world and the individual experienced frustration only when he moved out into the larger society, the family might not be thought so much to blame. The effect of the caste system, however, is to bring home through a chain of cause and effect all of the victimization processes, and to bring them home in such a way that it is often difficult even for adults in the system to see the connection between the pain they feel at the moment and the structured patterns of the caste system.

We would argue that a subeconomy is more important in this regard than is a subculture.

An ethnic subeconomy can provide internal opportunity and can prevent in large measure the social and psychological disorganization often associated with minority status in America. Some minority groups have overcome through communal effort the barriers to their mobility, and have built subeconomies in which their own kind have worked unencumbered by prejudice and discrimination. The Asian American case illustrates this course of action, as both Chinese and Japanese Americans became middleman minorities. The role of the internal formation of capital through rotating credit associations and communal associations in the Asian communities were vital in the establishment of Asian subeconomies. The ties of *Kenjinkai* between Japanese labor bosses and their crews were also important in the mobility of Japanese immigrants out of field labor and into a class of independent farmers and land owners. This movement was executed despite systematic attempts to exclude Japanese from land proprietorship. The infusion of blood and regional loyalties into the economic activity of urban Asian immigrants also resulted in the practice of businessmen financing their apprentices into businesses of their own. Asian labor and capital were integrated into a common ethnic community, which was a mutually reinforcing social entity and subeconomy, and both classes were thereby sheltered in a significant way from racism in the larger society. Asian labor benefited from a much better alternative to their categorical discrimination in the larger society, and Asian capital benefited from reduced labor costs. In the entire process, the Asian communal groups maintained their boundaries and buffered their members from the full impact of prejudice and discrimination.

A minority group with an opportunity structure of its own is a somewhat closed subsystem within a larger society. Its boundaries are to some extent impermeable to many of the pathological consequences of minority status in a society, since internal opportunities act as an alternative to poverty, prejudice, and discrimination on the outside. Group members do not necessarily have to exchange land, labor, and capital with outsiders when it is to their disadvantage. Away from the ethnocentrism of others, members of the group can practice their skills and workmanship, and can be whole people on their own terms and among their own kind. They are sheltered from the self-debilitating effects of their exclusion from opportunity in the larger society by having, within their own community, opportunities of their own. Hope does not contract under these circumstances, serious ambition need not sound absurd, and aspirations do not have to be scaled downward. On the contrary, advancement is possible and likely. This is the crucible of communalism and consciousness, the conservation of the sense and substance of the folk community in the face of prejudice and discrimination.

The cornerstone to an ethnic subeconomy is the communal solidarity of a minority group. Communal solidarity is a cause as well as an effect of the ethnic subeconomy. For instance, the Chinese and Japanese had cohesive immigrant communities, because of their Old World regional loyalties and their homogeneity with respect to age, gender, and generation. Many were sojourners, with little incentive for permanent residence in the United States, and they tended to settle in the same part of the country. Thus they stuck together in the face of prejudice and discrimination and established their own opportunity structure. By contrast, other immigrant groups were heterogeneous, reflecting the full regional, social, and economic diversity of their homelands. They also dispersed themselves across the entire country and more quickly conformed to the Anglo-American culture, due in part to their intention of permanent settlement. As the homogeneity and sojourning motives of the Asian immigrants engendered their communal solidarity and ethnic subeconomy, the heterogeneity and motives for permanent settlement of others precluded to some degree the same type of adjustment to prejudice and discrimination. Once established, the Asian subeconomy reinforced the broader Asian communalism.

It is equally important to note that Asian Americans were allowed to transplant their immigrant brotherhoods in this country while they were being excluded from the larger society. By contrast, blacks were unable, under slavery, to conserve their tribal communalism in the South. A critical mass of a single West African tribe was seldom reached on the small plantations in this country, and black slaves were systematically denied the right of assembly without the presence of a white. Both these factors hindered the transplantation of West African tribal communalism. Nor could slaves develop any semblance of a subeconomy of their own, since virtually all entrepreneurial acitivity in the Old South was dominated by whites. Another instance is the case of American Indians. The communalism of many Indian tribes disintegrated in the conquest, particularly as the ecological and economic base of Indian life was destroyed with the expropriation of their land. The deterioration of Indian communalism continued in the course of the several governmental programs that kept Indians in a state of economic and political dependence, all of which had the effect of undermining traditions within the tribes. The boundaries of many Indian tribes thus became porous to pressures that make for social pathology. All of this suggests that we might modify our definition of a minority group in line with that of Barth (1969): a group that faces both prejudice and discrimination in the larger society and is unable to provide its members an internal system sufficient for their access to desired ends.

While the ethnic subeconomy is here emphasized as one means to prevent minority pathology, it perhaps was possible in only a limited period of American history. The ethnic subeconomy is not as realistic an undertaking as it once was, now that the scale of business in this country has grown so great. Giant corporations, such as supermarket chains and fast-food franchises, have since taken over much of the economic niche once filled by small-scale ethnic enterprises (Bonacich, 1973). Programs for black capitalism, for instance, cannot duplicate today the ethnic subeconomy of the past.

An Eye to Politics

There are other ways a minority group can protect itself, however, and the political mobilization of minority groups appears to be increasingly important in this regard. Politics has always been important in a way; the destruction of the Japanese subeconomy and immigration restrictions were political acts. Political mobilization can protect minority group members to some extent from prejudice and discrimination and thus some of the pathological consequences of minority status. An ideology counter to racism often emerges in the course of ethnic political movements, providing its participants with an alternative to self-prejudice and other forms of pathology. Activism of this kind can pull a group together and restore its communalism. The symbolism of ethnic consciousness and communalism has certainly been coupled with the recent rise of minority protest in this country. If real political gains accompany mobilization, then discrimination against a minority might also be reduced. Black Americans have become an important voting bloc and political interest group in recent years and have consequently made some progress against prejudice and discrimination in American society. In addition, the historical relationship between American Indians and the federal government seems to be finally turning toward the benefit of the former. It would appear that an eye to politics is critical in forecasting the future of ethnicity in this country.

REFERENCES

Armstrong, C. P., and A. J. Gregor.
1964 "Integrated Schools and Negro Character Development." Psychiatry 27:69–72.

Asher, S. R., and V. L. Allen
  1969 "Racial Preference and Social Comparison Processes." Journal of Social Issues 25·157–165.
Ball, Richard A.
  1968 "A Poverty Case: The Analgesic Subculture of the Southern Appalachians." American Sociological Review 33 (December):885–895.
Barth, Fredrik (ed.)
  1969 Ethnic Groups and Boundaries: The Social Organization of Culture Difference. Boston: Little, Brown and Company.
Billingsley, Andrew
  1968 Black Families in White America. Englewood Cliffs, New Jersey: Prentice-Hall, Inc.
Blumer, Herbert
  1958 "Race Prejudice as a Sense of Group Position." Pacific Sociological Review 1(Spring):3–7.
Bonacich, Edna
  1973 "A Theory of Middleman Minorities." American Sociological Review 38(October):583–594.
Brown, W. O.
  1931 "The Nature of Race Consciousness." Social Forces 10(October):90–97.
Carmichael, Stokely, and Charles V. Hamilton
  1967 Black Power: The Politics of Liberation in America. New York: Random House, Inc.
Clark, K. B., and M. K. Clark
  1947 Racial Identification and Preference in Negro Children. In T. Newcomb and E. Hartley (eds.), Readings in Social Psychology. New York: Holt.
Coleman, James S., Ernest Q. Campbell, Carol J. Hobson, James McPartland, Alexander Mood, Frederic D. Weinfeld, and Robert L. York
  1966 Equality of Educational Opportunity. Washington, D.C.: Government Printing Office.
Dozier, Edward P.
  1966 "Problem Drinking among American Indians—the Role of Sociocultural Deprivation." Quarterly Journal Studies on Alcohol 27(March):72–78.
Etzioni, Amitai
  1959 "The Ghetto—A Re-Evaluation." Social Forces 37(March):255–262.
Fanon, Frantz
  1963 The Wretched of the Earth. New York: Grove Press, Inc.
Frazier, E. Franklin
  1939 The Negro Family in the United States. Chicago: University of Chicago Press.
  1957 Black Bourgeoisie. Glencoe, Illinois: Free Press.
Frenkel-Brunswik, E.
  1948 "A Study of Prejudice in Children." Human Relations 1:295–306.
Goodman, M. E.
  1946 "Evidence Concerning the Genesis of Interracial Attitudes." American Anthropologist 48(October–December):624–630.
  1952 Racial Awareness in Young Children. Reading, Massachusetts: Addison-Wesley Publishing Company.
Gordon, Milton M.
  1964 Assimilation in American Life. New York: Oxford University Press.
Greenwald, Herbert J. and Don P. Oppenheim
  1968 "Reported Magnitude of Self-Misidentification among Negro Children—Artifact?" Journal of Personality and Social Psychology 8(January):49–52.
Gregor, A. J.
  1963 "Science and Social Change: A Review of K. B. Clark's 'Prejudice and Your Child.'" Mankind Quarterly 3:229–237.
Gregor, A. J., and D. A. McPherson
  1966 "Racial Attitudes among White and Negro Children in a Deep South Standard Metropolitan Area." Journal of Social Psychology 68:95–106.

Handlin, Oscar
1957 Race and Nationality in American Life. Boston: Little, Brown and Company.
Hannerz, Ulf
1969 Soulside. New York: Columbia University Press.
Heiss, Jerold, and Susan Owens
1972 "Self-Evaluations of Blacks and Whites." American Journal of Sociology 78(September):360–370.
Hess, Robert D., and Virginia C. Shipman
1965 "Early Experiences and the Socialization of Cognitive Modes in Children." Child Development 36(December):869–886.
Hill, Robert B.
1972 "The Strengths of Black Families." Pp. 262–290 in David G. Bromley and Charles F. Longino, Jr. (eds.), White Racism and Black Americans. Cambridge, Massachusetts: Schenkman Publishing Company, Inc.
Homans, George C.
1950 The Human Group. New York: Harcourt, Brace.
Hraba, Joseph
1972 "The Doll Technique: A Measure of Racial Ethnocentrism?" Social Forces 50(June):522–527.
Hraba, Joseph, and Geoffrey Grant
1970 "Black Is Beautiful: A Reexamination of Racial Preference and Identification." Journal of Personality and Social Psychology 16(November):398–402.
Hraba, Joseph, and Jack Siegman
1974 "Black Consciousness." Youth and Society 6(September):63–90.
Kardiner, Abram, and Lionel Ovesey
1951 The Mark of Oppression: Explorations in the Personality of the American Negro. New York: Norton.
Kramer, Judith R.
1970 The American Minority Community. New York: Thomas Y. Crowell Company.
Landreth, C., and B. C. Johnson
1953 "Young Children's Responses to a Picture and Inset Test Designed to Reveal Reactions to Persons of Different Skin Color." Child Development 24:63–80.
Levy, Jerrold E., and Stephen J. Kunitz
1974 Indian Drinking: Navajo Practices and Anglo-American Theories. New York: John Wiley and Sons, Inc.
Lewis, Oscar
1961 The Children of Sanchez. New York: Random House.
Liebow, Elliot
1967 Talley's Corner. Boston: Little, Brown, and Company.
Lopez, David E.
1976 "The Social Consequences of Chicano Home/School Bilingualism." Social Problems 24(December):234–246.
Maccoby, Eleanor E., Theodore M. Newcomb, and Eugene L. Hartley (eds.)
1958 Readings in Social Psychology. Third Edition. New York: Henry Holt and Co.
Malcolm X with the assistance of Alex Haley
1964 The Autobiography of Malcolm X. New York, Grove Press, Inc.
McCarthy, John D., and William L. Yancey
1971 "Uncle Tom and Mr. Charlie: Metaphysical Pathos in the Study of Racism and Personal Disorganization." American Journal of Sociology 76(January):648–671.
McWilliams, Carey
1968 North from Mexico. New York: Greenwood Press, Inc.
Merton, Robert K.
1957 Social Theory and Social Structure. Glencoe, Illinois: Free Press.
Morland, K. J.
1958 "Racial Recognition by Nursery School Children in Lynchburg, Virginia." Social Forces 37:132–137.

1963 "The Development of Racial Bias in Young Children." Theory into Practice 2(June):120–127.

1966 "A Comparison of Race Awareness in Northern and Southern Children." American Journal of Orthopsychiatry 36:22–31.

1969 "Racial Awareness among American and Hong Kong Chinese Children." American Journal of Scoiology 75(November):360–375.

Moynihan, Daniel P.
1965 The Negro Family: The Case for National Action. Washington, D.C.: Office of Policy Planning and Research, United States Department of Labor.

1972 "The Tangle of Pathology." Pp. 197–218 in David G. Bromley and Charles F. Longino (eds.), White Racism and Black Americans. Cambridge, Mass.: Schenkman Publishing Company, Inc.

Pitts, J. P.
1974 "The Study of Race Consciousness: Comments on New Directions." American Journal of Sociology 80(November):665-687.

Radke, M. J., H. Trager, and H. Davis
1949 "Social Perception and Attitudes of Children." Genetic Psychology Monographs 19:327–447.

Rainwater, Lee
1966 "Crucible of Identity: The Negro Lower-Class Family." Daedalus 95(Winter):172–216.

1970 Behind Ghetto Walls. Chicago: Aldine-Atherton.

Roach, Jack L., and Orville R. Gursslin
1967 "An Evaluation of the Concept 'Culture of Poverty.'" Social Forces 45 (March):383–392.

Rodman, Hyman
1968 "The Lower-Class Value Stretch." Pp. 296–310 in Raymond W. Mack (ed.), Race, Class, and Power. New York: Van Nostrand Reinhold Company.

Rose, Arnold
1948 The Negro in America. New York: Harper and Row, Publishers.

Scanzoni, John H.
1971 The Black Family in Modern Society. Boston: Allyn and Bacon, Inc.

Schulz, David A.
1969 Coming up Black: Patterns of Ghetto Socialization. Englewood Cliffs, New Jersey: Prentice-Hall, Inc.

Shimkin, D., G. J. Louie, and D. Frate
1973 "The Black Extended Family: A Basic Rural Institution and a Mechanism of Urban Adaptation." Paper prepared for the Ninth International Congress of Anthropological and Ethnological Sciences.

Taviss, Irene
1969 "Changes in the Form of Alienation: The 1900s vs. the 1950s." American Sociological Review 32(February):46–57.

Trager, J., and M. Yarrow
1952 They Live What They Learn. New York: Harper and Row, Publishers.

Thomas, W. I.
1931 The Unadjusted Girl. Boston: Little, Brown and Company.

Valentine, Charles A.
1968 Culture and Poverty: Critique and Counter-Proposals. Chicago: University of Chicago Press.

Weber, Max
1966 "Class, Status and Party." Pp. 21–28 in Reinhard Bendix and Seymour Martin Lipset (eds.), Class, Status and Power. Second Edition. New York: Free Press.

Williams, Robin M., Jr.
1964 Strangers Next Door. Englewood Cliffs, New Jersey: Prentice-Hall, Inc.

Wirth, Louis
[1928] The Ghetto. Chicago: The University of Chicago Press.
1956

Index

THE BOOK MANUFACTURE

American Ethnicity was typeset, printed and bound at
Parthenon Press, Nashville, Tennessee. The interior
and cover designs were by John Goetz. Baskerville is
the type face. The text stock is 50# Supple Offset,
Smooth Finish. The cover material is Lexotone II.